Austrian Environmental History

Marc Landry and Patrick Kupper, eds.
Guest Editor Verena Winiwarter

CONTEMPORARY AUSTRIAN STUDIES | VOLUME 27

UNO PRESS   *innsbruck* university press

Printed in the United States of America

Book design by Allison Reu and Alex Dimeff

Published in the United States by
University of New Orleans Press
ISBN: 978-160801163-6

Published and distributed in Europe
by Innsbruck University Press
ISBN: 978-3-903187-24-5

UNO PRESS

iup

Publication of this volume has been made possible through a generous grant by the Federal Ministry of Science, Research and Economy through the Austrian Academic Exchange Service (ÖAAD). The Austrian Marshall Plan Anniversary Foundation in Vienna has been very generous in supporting Center Austria: The Austrian Marshall Plan Center for European Studies at the University of New Orleans and its publications series. The College of Liberal Arts at the University of New Orleans, as well as the Vice Rectorate for Research and the International Relations Office of the University of Innsbruck provided additional financial support.

Marshallplan-Jubiläumsstiftung
Austrian Marshall Plan Foundation

fulbrightaustria

Contemporary Austrian Studies

Sponsored by the University of New Orleans and University of Innsbruck

Table of Contents

II. NON-TOPICAL ESSAY

III. FORUM: AUSTRIANS AS VICTIMS? VICTIMHOOD DISCOURSES AND PRACTICES IN THE AGE OF WORLD WARS

IV. REVIEW ESSAY

V. BOOK REVIEWS

Austrian Environmental History

Introduction

Marc Landry
Patrick Kupper

The environment is a crucial component of contemporary Austria's identity as a state. Above all, Austria is associated with mountains. Austria is commonly referred to as the "*Alpenrepublik*" in both German and English. Since the reconstitution of the Austrian federal state in the immediate post-World War I period, the very first clause of its national anthem—"Land of mountains..."—has placed topography front and center. But mountains are not the only constitutive natural element of the country's image. Immediately after singing the praises of the mountains, the national anthem declares that Austria is also the "land on the river." The Danube River, one of Europe's longest, continues to occupy a critical space in Austrians' mental and material lives long after the disappearance of the "Danube Monarchy" that previously shaped outside and internal perceptions. More recently, an environmental politician in Austria have vaulted to the highest offices of the land. In 2016, Alexander van der Bellen became the first directly elected head of a European state from a green party.

Given these connections it is fitting that in the last few decades, Austria has emerged as a vibrant locale for the practice of a relatively new type of history that attempts to bring nature into the historical picture: environmental history. At its core, environmental history seeks to study the relationship between human societies and the natural environment in the past. In general, environmental historians have adopted three main avenues of inquiry into this relationship. Some concern themselves primarily with the human interaction with material environments, both how they have been altered and how they have influenced human affairs. Another strand of research, concerned primarily with intellectual and cultural aspects, has traced changes in ideas and representations of nature. The history of environmental politics makes up the final broad category of environmental history. In practice, the borders between these pursuits have always been porous, and the best environmental histories manage to incorporate attention to all three.[1]

---

1   The tripartite schema and some of what follows borrows from this good introduction to the field: J.R. McNeill, "Observations on the Nature and Culture of Environmental History," *History and Theory* 42 (December 2003): 5-43.

Of course the idea of considering the role of nature in history is not entirely new. Historians have been including attention to the material world in history at least since Thucydides wrote about the significance of the plague in Athens during the Peloponnesian War. The *Annales* school of historians also paid substantial attention to geographic factors in their histories. But it was not until the 1970s in the United States that historians consciously began identifying themselves as *environmental* historians. This initially small group gained formal institutional status with the founding of the American Society for Environmental History (ASEH) in 1977. At that time the Society's quarterly journal, now called *Environmental History*, also began appearing.

Not surprisingly, early practitioners were heavily inspired by the environmental movement of the 1960s, sparked by Rachel Carson's classic *Silent Spring* (1962). This background reflected in early scholarship, which tended to narrate modern environmental history in particular as a story of a humanity fallen from grace. Many early environmental historians focused their research on the American West, a region whose pristine-seeming natural landscapes tempted many to believe they were studying wilderness. In the intervening decades, many environmental historians have adopted a more nuanced understanding of environmental change, and focus has expanded to all corners of the globe. What has continued to distinguish environmental historians above all is their conception of nature. In the place of a static, passive backdrop to history, environmental historians posit a dynamic, at times even active one. Some go so far as to suggest that nature might be a historical agent in its own right.

Environmental history is now one of the fastest growing historical disciplines worldwide. For the United States, this fact was confirmed in a survey by the American Historical Association from December 2015. Analyzing the listings of faculty specializations in the AHA's *Directory of History Departments, Historical Organizations, and Historians* from 1975-2015, the survey determined that of those topical historical subfields that grew over the past forty years, environmental history posted the largest proportional expansion. Faculty specializing in environmental history rose from .2 percent of listings to 2.7 percent. Though those numbers seem small, it actually represents a 13 and ½ time increase. The percentage of history departments with an environmental historian also increased from 4.3 percent in 1975 to 43 percent in 2015. A final interesting finding was that specialists in environmental history were among the youngest practitioners (along with historians of sexuality). Almost seventy percent of historians in those fields earned their PhDs since 1994—compared to 47 percent of the total.[2] These figures, of course, do not explain anything about why these changes have been happening, or how they have actually affected the discipline. Nor do they predict the future. But they do suggest that at least over the last few decades, there has been increasing interest among historians in trying to understand the dynamic connections between the human and the natural in the past.

In Europe, institutionalized environmental history took off somewhat later. The European Society for Environmental History (ESEH) was founded in 1999, a little over twenty years after the establishment of the ASEH. ESEH also produces its own quarterly journal *Environment and History*. Since 2001 the ESEH has convened conferences on a biannual basis attracting ever more scholars from all over Europe and beyond. In 2003, Austrian environmental history researchers formed one of the earliest European scholarly networks for the discipline called "The Centre for Environmental History" (*Zentrum für Umweltgeschichte*, ZUG). Recently, ZUG has been joined in Austria by an inter-university research cluster for environmental history.[3] With the opening of the Rachel Carson Center for Environment and Society in Munich in 2009, Europe became the site of one of the most vibrant environmental history research centers worldwide.

Surely the recent inroads made by environmental history into the historical profession stem at least in part from its success in providing important new windows on the past. The field's greatest impact, perhaps, has been in revealing the environmental contexts of European overseas imperialism after 1500. To name only the best-known example, with the rise of environmental history the concept that European imperial interactions in the New World also took place at the biological level—the "Columbian Exchange"—has become widespread.[4] Perhaps more significant is the belief in the discipline's importance for the future. Despite valid criticisms of some of the problems associated with environmental history—for example its occasional brushes with environmental determinism—the discipline seems well-suited to shed light on the historical contexts of our current global environmental predicaments.

---

2   Robert B. Townsend, "The Rise and Decline of History Specializations over the Past 40 Years," https://www.historians.org/publications-and-directories/perspectives-on-history/december-2015/the-rise-and-decline-of-history-specializations-over-the-past-40-years (accessed May 4, 2018). Townsend offered that the survey could offer a "window on the specializations of historians—albeit primarily at four-year colleges and universities—for four decades."

3   The Environmental History Cluster Austria, http://ehca.at .

4   Alfred W. Crosby Jr., *The Columbian Exchange: Biological and Cultural Consequences of 1492* (Westwood, CT: Greenwood, 1972).

Concern for the environmental future helps explain the emergence of the field of environmental history in Austria at the beginning of the 1990s. As the opening chapter to this volume clarifies in greater detail, self-conscious environmental history in Austria was in many ways a product of the ecological movement and its alarm about environmental problems, starting in the early 1980s. In this manner, Austria proved quite similar to other western European countries whose promotion of environmental history has made the region a global hotspot for the field. Yet from the start, Austrian environmental history has possessed a pronounced orientation toward investigating material environments in the past. Austrian environmental historians have been particularly pioneering in advancing "long term socio-ecological research." This innovative methodology reconstructs the ecological bases of past societies and attempts to establish their "social metabolism": the inputs required and outputs created in order for societies to function. So far, research in this regard has focused on the pre-1918 period. In general, the environmental history of post-Habsburg Austria still remains to be written.

This volume takes a step in this direction. It offers an overview of and a showcase for contemporary Austrian environmental history. In addition to highlighting some innovative methodological approaches, the essays also show how significant the environment has been to some of the most crucial aspects of the recent Austrian past. Since the collapse of the Habsburg Monarchy, nature has continually been integral to the nation-building process within the new state. The economic mobilization of the National Socialist period was closely bound to reshaping landscapes and the changes endure to this day. Economic reconstruction in the postwar period also left its mark upon the country. Not only did the Marshall Plan provide crucial impetus to exploit natural resources on a previously impossible scale. The tourist industry, which has become so central for the Austrian economy in the postwar period, also transformed the socio-natural world. In the past few decades, Austria's heavy reliance on tapping into the energy of its swift flowing waterways has rearranged riverine ecosystems and led to political and social conflicts.

In the opening essay, Verena Winiwarter et al provide an overview of the "state of the field." As the authors note, the Austrian landscape alone suggests the logic of adopting environmental history approaches to contemporary history. In addition, Austria's peculiar path to industrialization is a potentially fruitful area of research. The essay highlights some of the excellent work that has already been done, particularly on the themes of agriculture and forestry, energy, water and hydropower, and tourism. At the same time, the authors note that the bulk of scholarship has focused on the long term, and that environmental history has not yet made huge inroads into contemporary history. Part of this, they argue, is attributable to the discipline's still weak institutional basis.

In their essay, Gerhard Siegl and Irene Pallua make the case for how environmental historians might expand their repertoire to make use of previously untapped sources. They refer above all to scholarship produced in the early twentieth century in a diverse array of fields: regional studies, folklore studies, forest history, agricultural history, landscape history, economic history, and historical demography among others. These secondary sources not only compiled social, geographic, and demographic data that can be useful for historians, they also offer models for potential approaches to current topics such as the history of energy and landscape utilization. Still, they recognize the necessity of reading such sources with a critical eye; in particular the political contexts for their creation require careful consideration. Though their reflections pertain specifically to western Austria, their conclusions are of value for the remainder of Austria and beyond.

Ortrun Veichtlbauer relates the story of efforts to remake the Danube in the nineteenth and twentieth centuries by constructing ports to promote commerce and trade. Veichtlbauer positions these alterations of the riverine environment within a longer history of the effects of war on transnational infrastructure, and in so doing contributes to the growing literature on the environmental history of war. In contrast to the mainstream, Veichtlbauer emphasizes the continuities created by European war-making. Indeed she finds important similarities between plans for harbor construction from the Habsburgs in the mid-nineteenth century through the National Socialist period and into the early Cold War.

Martin Knoll and Robert Gross focus on the environmental history of two tourist destinations in the western Austrian province of Vorarlberg. Knoll and Gross conceptualize these areas as "socio-natural sites" in order to trace how the unprecedented global environmental changes of the postwar period—the so-called "Great Acceleration"—manifested themselves in Austrian ski areas. Their essay shows how tourism in these ski towns fostered a demand for all kinds of mobility. Most important for its long-term impacts, however, was the road construction that provided tourist access to these previously remote locations. The piece highlights the paradox that the more planners used technology and infrastructure to save time for tourists, the more hurried visitors became. It also shows the complex ways in which technology and environment interacted in the ski industry.

Sofie Mittas fills a double gap in the historiography on the Marshall Plan in Austria in her contribution. First her essay focuses on an understudied industrial beneficiary of the European Recovery Program—namely the forestry and paper industry. More importantly for the purpose of this volume, Mittas adopts an environmental history approach to the history of the Marshall Plan. Exploring the environmental history of a program that nominally lasted for four years is a challenge for environmental historians, who often deal with natural processes that unfold on a geologic time scale. Mittas nevertheless demonstrates that Marshall funds had significant impacts on the wood-paper commodity chain in Austria and left important marks on the landscape.

In his essay, Christian Rohr employs a qualitative and quantitative analysis of Austrian stamps to explore "official" perceptions of the Austrian landscape since 1945. Rohr seeks to mine stamps—the "official business card of a country"—for what they reveal about the state promotion of certain landscapes and how they changed over time. Rohr finds that Alpine motives have been the dominant ones in regular issue stamps during this period. Through a comparison with neighboring Switzerland, Rohr determines that Austria has been unique in the large number of stamps it has devoted to celebrating high-Alpine hydropower dams. Nevertheless, the appearance of Alpine-themed stamps has fluctuated greatly over the years. At least from the official viewpoint, Austria's status as a "land of the mountains" has ebbed and flowed over the past seventy years.

Finally Christina Pichler-Koban recounts the history of hydropower development in twentieth-century Austria as an enduring confrontation between conflicting societal sectors and their values. In particular, hydroelectric development in the country has unfolded as a conflict between energy boosters and nature conservationists. Pichler-Koban's essay classifies several archetypical conflicts that occurred between power promoters and environmentalists in Austria. Her example highlights the dilemmas and ambiguities that exist in the dynamic relationship between economic development and environmental protection. These findings are relevant for regions of the world where hydroelectricity expansion is currently being considered such as the Caucasus, the Himalayas, the Andes, and East Africa.

This volume of CAS is also fortunate to include two fascinating, non-topical contributions. For the first time in English, Dieter Stiefel presents the results of his research on the Swarovski family and the renowned crystal-producing business they built. His essay focuses in particular on the actions of the family and the business during the National Socialist period. Though contemporary perceptions in Austria presume a close connection between the family and the National Socialist regime in Austria after 1938, Stiefel concludes that there were varying attitudes within the family toward

National Socialism, and many questions left to be answered. In joining the National Socialist party as a family in 1938 and later minimizing their affinity for the regime, the Swarovskis acted similarly to many Austrians. Conspicuously, however, the Swarovskis did not express guilt or remorse but painted their actions as arising out of necessity.

The second non-topical section is a Forum on Austrians' self-perception as perennial victims ever since the founding of the First Republic after World War I. Be it Freud dealing with the state of mind of "victims" of World War I fighting, or the politics of providing welfare for the many "*Kriegsopfer*", discourses on Austrian victimhood were front, line and center of interwar politics. After World War II Austrians again fashioned themselves as Hitler's "first victim." This served the country well to block Allied reparations and Jewish restitution demands. The many Austrian perpetrators of Hitlerite war crimes eagerly incorporated themselves in this vast postwar Austrian victims collective. Finally, the "victims" of the "Allied bombing terror" during World War II and the long (post-)memory among Austrians about the hardships of surviving the allied "bombing holocaust" provides another angle on Austrian victimhood, lasting to this day. The Forum does raise the question whether these perennial lachrymose victimhood discourses may have become part of Austrian identity construction.

*   *   *

Numerous people and organizations have been critical in enabling completion of this volume, and it is our pleasure to get to thank them here. We conceptualized this volume while Marc Landry was Fulbright-Botstiber Visiting Professor of Austrian-American Studies in the Department of History and European Ethnology at the University of Innsbruck in the fall of 2016. Thanks goes to the Botstiber Foundation, the Austrian-American Educational Commission, and former History Department Head Margret Friedrich for making the stay possible. We are sincerely thankful to our guest editor Verena Winiwarter for accepting responsibility for the opening article. Of course a special thanks goes to all of the contributing authors for their essays, and for their understanding as new members of the production team learned the ropes. Bela Teleky, the 2017/2018 Austrian Ministry of Economics, Science, and Research Dissertation Fellow at UNO and PhD student at Andrassy University in Budapest, has corrected and aligned the footnotes with our style sheet.

Katie Pfalzgraff at UNO Press was a pleasure to work with on the copyediting of the individual typescripts. Alex Dimeff ably typeset the final text and humored us in designing several iterations of the cover. G.K. Darby and Abram Himelstein, the leadership team at UNO Press, have been unfailingly helpful in shepherding the volume to publication. At Center Austria: The Austrian Marshall Plan Center for European Studies, Günter Bischof kindly provided advice and wisdom on the publication process gained during his co-editorship of the previous twenty-six volumes. Bischof also commissioned and managed Stiefel's essay and the editing of the Forum included in this volume. Gertraud Griessner managed the Center Austria's day-to-day business with her usual aplomb, freeing up the coeditor to focus on CAS. In the absence of all of these peoples' contributions, CAS would not exist. Birgit Holzner and her team at *innsbruck university press* were instrumental in producing the volume for the European market.

We continue to be grateful for our sponsors and supporters who make an enterprise like this possible in the first place. Thanks go to a number of dedicated patrons on both sides of the Atlantic. At the University of Innsbruck we recognize the support of Matthias Schennach, Barbara Tasser, Christina Antenhofer, Gerhard Rampl, and Janine Köppen. At the University of New Orleans, Dean Kim Long of the College of Liberal Arts, Education and Human Development, and Robert Dupont, chair of the Department of History and Philosophy, have been accommodating as always. We appreciate the support of *Rektor* Tilmann Märk and President John Nicklow for the UNO-University of Innsbruck partnership program. Thanks to Ambassador Wolfgang Waldner, the Austrian ambassador to the United States and his staff member Hannes Richter, for their continued backing. In the Federal Ministry of Science and Research and its student exchange office *Österreichischer Auslandsdienst* (ÖAD), we would like to thank Barbara Weitgruber, Christoph Ramoser, Felix Wilcek, Josef Leidenfrost, and Florian Gerhardus. Markus Schweiger, the executive secretary, Ambassador Wolfgang Petritsch, the chairman of the board, as well as the board members of the Austrian Marshall Plan Foundation continue to be our greatest champions. It is an honor to work with them and to acknowledge their ceaseless backing of Center Austria: The Austrian Marshall Plan Center of European Studies at UNO and its activities and publications.

New Orleans/Innsbruck, May 2018

Topical Essays

Environmental Histories of Contemporary Austria: An Introduction

*Verena Winiwarter, Michael Bürkner, Simone Gingrich, Robert Groß,
Gertrud Haidvogl, Severin Hohensinner, Martin Schmid, and Fridolin
Krausmann[1]*

The first stanza of Austria's National anthem reads like a summary of interesting topics of Austria's environmental history:

Land of mountains, land by the river,
Land of fields, land of cathedrals,
Land of hammers, with a promising future!
Home to great daughters and sons,
A nation highly blessed with beauty,
Much-praised Austria,
Much-praised Austria![2]

Indeed, mountains and rivers, cultivated land and cultural heritage, as well as the iron industry, have featured prominently among topics studied in Austria's environmental history. Given the diversity of climates, soils, landforms, and economic activities, and given the long and well-documented deep history and even pre-history, Austria's environmental history is well worth studying. The country's geographical situation, on the main south-north transit routes, often results in at times quite fierce environmental conflict with transit traffic along the Inn River Valley, a fact that also makes Austria's environment a unique area of study.

While the country shares Alpine characteristics (and borders) with Slovenia, Switzerland, Italy, and southern Germany, it shares steppe-like continental conditions, including a shallow lake surrounded by reeds, with Hungary. The Danube, one of the main European rivers—and the only one flowing from west to southeast and eventually draining into the Black

1   The authors thank Julia Lackner for preparations enabling the analysis of the Environmental History Database Austria. We would also like to acknowledge the many years of work that Ortrun Veichtlbauer put into compiling the database, and Anna Wögerbauer for maintaining it.
2   Translation from Wikipedia, https://en.wikipedia.org/wiki/Land_der_Berge,_Land_am_Strome.

Sea—has shaped and continues to influence economic activities and ecological processes alike. Invasive species have travelled with traders, leading
to long-lived environmental legacies. The Danube's flood-prone but fertile,
flat basins have been major areas of settlement.

The Alps are more than just an obstacle to transport. The rich mines in
Alpine valleys have spurred early settlement and been the centers of much
early industry. Among mined ores, iron, zinc, copper, and gold stand out; salt
(common table salt) is the most important mined good, and the only one
that continues to be mined in large quantities. In Styria, iron for specialized
steel is still produced from a local mine, because of the specific quality of
the ore, but all other mining has long ceased. Only some metal processing
industries at the fringes of the Alps remain as legacies of the historic activities. In referring to another topic resulting from its Alpine characteristics,
Austrian foresters will gladly point to the early attempts at conservation of
steep slopes for protection from erosion and the resulting mudslides. Alpine
societies were among the first to promote tourism and later among the first to
engage in efforts to protect fragile mountain ecosystems. Studying Austrian
glaciers has provided long-term data to climate scientists.

But much, indeed most of the existing historical research on these
issues does take a long-term perspective. Contemporary Austrian environmental history, despite its potential, currently remains understudied. This
might be due to the weak institutional basis of the field, with only one
university chair designated exclusively to environmental history, which is,
to further complicate things, not situated where most students of history
are. A lot of work has been and continues to be done either in research
projects financed via the Austrian Science Foundation (FWF) or smaller,
often regional funds; publications arise from exhibitions in catalogues,[3] and
qualification work is an important pillar.

Fifteen years ago, scholars congregated for the first environmental history network in the country, the Centre for Environmental History, "*Zentrum
für Umweltgeschichte*" (ZUG), and initiated a bibliographic "Environmental
History Database Austria," which is, despite its rather outdated technical
standard, a good resource to gain an overview about what has been done
and which subjects have garnered the most attention. When the initiative

---

3   Verena Winiwarter, Martin Schmid, *Umwelt Donau: Eine andere Geschichte. Katalog
zur Ausstellung des NÖ Landesarchivs "Donau - Fluch & Segen" in Ardagger Markt, 5. Mai –
7. Nov.2010* (St. Pölten: Niederösterreichisches Landesarchiv, 2010); Oberösterreichische
Umweltakademie ed., *Wo i leb ...: Kulturlandschaften in Österreich - Ausstellung vom 16. Mai
bis 14. September 1997 – ein Projekt im Rahmen des Forschungsschwerpunktes "Kulturlandschaft"*
(Linz: Stadtmuseum Linz-Nordico, 1997); Karl Brunner, Verena Winiwarter, *BAUERN:
Aufbruch in die Zukunft der Landwirtschaft* (Vienna, Cologne, Weimar: Böhlau, 1992).

was started, forty-one "thematic areas" were identified as potentially useful keywords to categorize the literature, and all literature published after 1945 was included. Almost 4,000 items are meanwhile searchable via a map, timeline, or by theme; full-text search is also possible. A large part of this material are studies that do not consider themselves "environmental history," but offer data and interpretations useful for environmental historians.

The bibliographic entries allow for investigating the penetration of environmental history into teaching by using the subset of qualification works for a more detailed analysis. Such an analysis is not easily possible via the interface; it has been done with the dataset as such. Of the more than 500 master theses included in the database, many deal with topics such as the history of the match or the telephone, with local conservation efforts or conflict; in general, the spread of topics is broad. 196 dissertations pertaining to subjects of the twentieth century are included, with the Universities of Vienna, Innsbruck, and Salzburg contributing most of those. They stem from fields as diverse as theology, German studies, law, policy sciences, cultural anthropology, ecology, and spatial planning. The main fields are, as expected, economic history, human geography and history as such. The earliest identified works originate from the late 1940s, dealing with topics ranging from the geography of a Tirolean Valley[4] to changes in Danube shipping since World War I,[5] or the development of agriculture between 1918 and 1938.[6] The study by Zimmermann is typical of an entire cluster of human geographies of Tirolean regions published from the late 1940s onwards, and into the 1970s at the University of Innsbruck.[7] Such studies are important sources for the environmental history of these regions nowadays (see for example the chapter by Siegel and Pallua in this volume). Later, a wide array of topics of interest to environmental historians were explored, among them urban histories, (of the rise of electricity and gas in Linz,[8]

---

4   Egon Zimmermann, "Bevölkerungsgeographische Untersuchungen über das Navis-Tal" (PhD diss., University of Innsbruck, 1949).
5   Neiko Peikoff, "Die Wandlungen in der Donauschiffahrt seit dem ersten Weltkrieg 1914" (PhD diss., University of Vienna, 1948).
6   Hans Kremaier, "Die Entwicklung der österreichischen Landwirtschaft vom Jahre 1918–1938 unter besonderer Berücksichtigung der Frage wieso es trotz schlechter Lage der Landwirtschaft zur Produktionssteigerung gekommen ist" (PhD diss., University of Vienna, 1949).
7   Ursula Kübler, "Bevölkerungsgeographische Untersuchungen über die Seefelder Senke" (PhD diss., University of Innsbruck, 1953); Inge Rohn, "Bevölkerungs- und agrargeographische Untersuchungen in Kitzbühel" (PhD diss., University of Innsbruck, 1967); Gerlinde Keuschnig, "Bevölkerungsgeographische Untersuchung über Karres und Karrösten" (PhD diss., University of Innsbruck, 1973).
8   Werner Györgyfalvay, "Geschichte der Gas- und Elektrizitätsversorgung der Stadt Linz" (PhD diss., University of Linz, 1979).

for example), how tobacco production shaped a small town in Styria,[9] and the development of waste management in Vienna[10] merit mention. From a mainly economic history viewpoint, studies were done on several mining topics, such as salt mining in the twentieth century,[11] iron and coal mining during Austria's years under National Socialist rule,[12] or the development of the Austrian mineral oil sector.[13] Histories of important Austrian industries such as wood, paper and pulp,[14] or sugar[15] have—not unexpectedly—been studied as economic histories, with the potential for an environmental historical perspective still untapped. The international sugar conventions, beginning in 1902, were treated in one of the few works from jurists.[16] While this brief glimpse cannot be a full overview, it becomes clearly visible that academic qualification work with potential for environmental history is not without precedent in Austria.

The rise of environmental consciousness that Austria witnessed from the mid-1970s onwards, culminating in the plebiscite of 1978 against the opening of the nuclear power plant Zwentendorf that had already been built, or in the demonstrations taking place in the alluvial forests of

9   Elisabeth Ernst, "Sie war der Lebensnerv der Stadt: Die Geschichte der Tabakverarbeitung in Fürstenfeld von den Anfängen bis zur Gegenwart" (PhD diss., University of Graz, 1991).

10   Thomas Friedrich, "Abfallwirtschaft in Wien: Analyse ihrer Entwicklung unter besonderer Berücksichtigung des wirtschaftlichen politischen und technischen Wandels sowie der Stadtentwicklung seit dem 19. Jahrhundert" (PhD diss., University of Vienna, 2006).

11   Christian Terink, "Die österreichische Salzindustrie im 20. Jahrhundert: Eine wirtschaftshistorische Studie" (PhD diss., University of Linz, 2001).

12   Hans Werner Pohl, "Die österreichische Industrie in den Jahren 1938 bis 1945: Unter besonderer Berücksichtigung des Erz- und Kohlenbergbaues" (PhD diss., University of Vienna, 2002).

13   Josef H. Reisel, "Die österreichische Mineralölpolitik seit April 1945" (PhD diss., University of Vienna, 1947); Herbert Rambousek, "Die 'ÖMV-Aktiengesellschaft:' Entstehung und Entwicklung eines nationalen Unternehmens der Mineralölindustrie" (PhD diss., University of Vienna, 1977).

14   Josef Ortner, "Die Entwicklung der österreichischen Holzfinalindustrie seit 1920 und ihre Versorgung aus den heimischen Forsten" (PhD diss., Vienna, 1953); Ulrike Pfiel, "Die Geschichte der niederösterreichischen Sägebranche: Von der Sägemühle zur Sägeindustrie" (PhD diss., University of Vienna, 1999).

15   Hedwig Pfeiffer, "Die Entwicklung des Zuckerrübenbaues in Österreich" (PhD diss., University of Vienna, 1948); Kurt Foltin, "Die Stellung der österreichischen Zuckerindustrie im Strukturwandel der österreichischen Volkswirtschaft" (PhD diss., University of Innsbruck, 1954); Richard Skene, "Zuckerindustrie und Zuckerrübenwirtschaft in Österreich seit der Gründung der ersten Republik" (PhD diss., University of Vienna, 1961); Mario Girardoni, "Die Entwicklung der Rohr- und Rübenzuckerindustrie seit dem Zweiten Weltkrieg: Mit besonderer Berücksichtigung der weltweiten Zuckerverknappung seit 1971" (PhD diss., University of Vienna, 1976).

16   Ladislaus Kratky, "Die internationalen Zuckerkonventionen seit 1902" (PhD diss., University of Innsbruck, 1952).

Hainburg in the winter of 1984 against a run-of-the-river power plant on the Danube downstream of Vienna, is not strongly reflected in the data, despite their important influence on the course of Austrian environmental policy. Dissertation numbers did not rise disproportionally.

When Marina Fischer-Kowalski published her landmark assessment of the environmental situation in Austria, "Ökobilanz Österreich," in 1988, a historical view was not the main focus.[17] In later years, the Faculty for Interdisciplinary Studies at the University of Klagenfurt, and specifically its Institute for Social Ecology, founded by Fischer-Kowalski, was instrumental in fostering environmental history in Austria. International guest professors were invited, among them Christian Pfister, Peter Sieferle, Mart Stewart, and Carole Crumley, to name but a few; the investigation of social metabolism and colonizing interventions into natural systems over the long-term became a main topic of the institute. This is reflected in part in the chapters on agriculture and energy below, but also visible in several contributions to volumes edited by the institute.[18] The Centre for Environmental History considers itself as promoting environmental history as an interdisciplinary undertaking, with PhD students coming from a variety of backgrounds, from (biological) anthropology,[19] human ecology,[20] to history,[21] as well as much more technical studies, such as Natural Resources Management

17   Marina Fischer-Kowalski, ed., Öko-Bilanz Österreich: Zustand, Entwicklungen, Strategien (Vienna: Falter-Verlag, 1988).

18   Verena Winiwarter et al., "Why Legacies Matter: Merits of a Long-Term Perspective," in *Social Ecology. Society-Nature Relations across Time and Space*, ed. Helmut Haberl et al. (Cham: Springer, 2016), 149–168; Fridolin Krausmann, Helga Weisz, and Nina Eisenmenger, "Transitions in sociometabolic regimes throughout human history," in *Social Ecology: Society-Nature Relations across Time and Space*, ed. Helmut Haberl et al. (Cham: Springer, 2016), 63–92; Marina Fischer-Kowalski et al., "Boserup's theory on technological change as a point of departure for the theory of sociometabolic regime transitions," in *Ester Boserup's Legacy on Sustainability*, ed. Marina Fischer-Kowalski et al. (Dordrecht: Springer, 2014), 23–42; Simron J. Singh et al., eds., *Long term socio-ecological research: Studies in society-nature interactions across spatial and temporal scales* (Dordrecht: Springer Science & Business Media, 2013); Verena Winiwarter, "Gesellschaftlicher Arbeitsaufwand für die Kolonisierung von Natur," in *Gesellschaftlicher Stoffwechsel und Kolonisierung von Natur: Ein Versuch in Sozialer Ökologie*, ed. Marina Fischer-Kowalski et al. (Amsterdam: G+B Verlag Fakultas, 1997), 161–175.

19   Ortrun Veichtlbauer, "Natur als Politikum - Beiträge zu einer österreichischen Umweltgeschichte" (PhD diss., University of Klagenfurt, 2014).

20   Robert Groß, "Die Beschleunigung der Berge. Eine Umweltgeschichte des Wintertourismus in Vorarlberg/Österreich 1920–2010" (PhD diss., University of Klagenfurt, 2017).

21   Dino Leon Güldner, "Zur Umweltgeschichte der Schießpulverproduktion in der Habsburgermonarchie" (MA thesis, University of Vienna, 2013); Dino Güldner, Fridolin Krausmann, and Verena Winiwarter, "From farm to gun and no way back: Habsburg gunpowder production in the eighteenth century and its impact on agriculture and soil fertility," *Regional Environmental Change* 16, no. 1 (2016): 151–162.

and Ecological Engineering.[22] The research focus is clearly on what J.R. McNeill has termed "material EH" in his overview.[23]

Environmental histories do reflect social, economic, cultural, and political changes, as all these changes are co-evolutionary with changes in human relationships to nature (or, if you will, the environment).[24] Therefore, several themes that stand for the most pertinent changes in Austria in the twentieth century can be identified, which, if studied, would pertain to central issues of contemporary Austrian environmental history. Industrialization is one of them: Austria's path to becoming an industrialized country was quite specific, not least due to its history as the remainder of a large empire and of its very particular natural endowment. The heavy industry left its mark on the entire Upper Styrian landscape, the Mur valley being a heavily industrialized zone, complete with iron mining in open pit mining. The steel works in Linz, where the famous process of Basic Oxygen Steelmaking, also known as "Linz-Donawitz steelmaking," or the "oxygen converter process", was developed into an industrially viable process in the 1950s, and the massive pollution the city suffered from coking plant, chemical factory, and blast furnaces await their environmental historian. Such a history would also be one of the rise of civil society: small children particularly suffered from the polluted air, and their mothers formed protest groups early on that would go on to protest against nuclear power. The tourism industry has a large bearing on perceptions of the country's natural environment, loading it with aesthetic appreciation for "wild, alpine" nature as well as with images of the steel and concrete that make up winter tourism infrastructure. This topic, as it is of particular relevance, has been treated in one of the three more detailed studies included in this essay.

Austria's energy history is also very specific in many ways. Hydropower plays an important role, both run-of-the-river and large Alpine storage plants are an important pillar of Austria's electricity supply. This topic, together with the larger issue of water in a land of complex hydrologies, draining into Black Sea and North Sea alike, is covered below. Austria's particular way of governance, with labor unions and trade unions and industrialists forming a "social partnership" to negotiate wages and benefits, together with a large sector of state-owned industries, has influenced the treatment of the environment in important ways, most visibly in the very strong role labor unions

---

22 Angelika Schoder, "Der Bau des Speicherkraftwerks Wienerbruck – die Transformation einer Landschaft aus der Sicht der Ingenieure," in *Alpen und industrielles Erbe: Kultur und Erinnerung, 19.–20. Jahrhundert*, ed. Luigi Lorenzetti and Nelly Valsangiacomo (Mendrisio: Academy Press, 2016), 99–124 and see below, Footnote 58.

23 John R. McNeill, "Observations on the nature and culture of environmental history," *History and Theory* 42, no. 4 (2003): 5–43.

24 Maurice Godelier, *Natur, Arbeit, Geschichte: Zu einer universalgeschichtlichen Theorie der Wirtschaftsformen* (Hamburg: Junius, 1990), 13.

took in promoting the further development of water power on the Danube, which led to one of the fiercest protests in the country's history, the now-famous fight for the water meadows and riparian forests of Hainburg.[25] Two Austrian chancellors from the Social Democratic Party were involved in major environmental conflicts: Bruno Kreisky lost a referendum to open the nuclear power plant at Zwentendorf, and Fred Sinowatz had to stop building the power plant at Hainburg. Additionally, the designation of national parks has led to prolonged conflicts between conservationists and developers.[26] In a recent book, Christina Pichler-Koban has compiled the first comprehensive history of such parks and their history.[27] The nuclear issue gives rise to yet another important insight into the ways Austria's environmental history is specific: all countries sharing borders with Austria operate nuclear power plants; some are of questionable technical standard and have given rise to concern time and again. Austria's environmental NGOs could not confine themselves to a domestic view, as pollution and environmentally dangerous emissions know no borders, and a small country can easily be threatened from surrounding danger. Ortrun Veichtlbauer, together with Martin Schmid, has written a short overview of Austria's environmental history[28] that also touches on this topic, and in a collection to celebrate one of the many anniversaries in Austria, Marina Fischer-Kowalski and Harald Payer (1995) have covered some of the history of conservation.[29] But a lot remains open to scrutiny; neither the war economies, nor the National Socialist period (1938–45), nor the decade of foreign occupation and the huge investment push of the Marshall Plan have as yet been covered in full-length studies. Ortrun Veichtlbauer's work on the Danube during National Socialism remains one of the few studies undertaken to date.[30]

25 Verena Winiwarter, and Sophia Rut, "Österreich ergrünt: Die Besetzung der Hainburger Au," in *100 Jahre Republik: Meilensteine und Wendepunkte 1918–2018*, ed. Heinz Fischer, Andreas Huber, and Stephan Neuhäuser (Vienna: Czernin Verlag, 2018), 203–216.
26 Patrick Kupper, and Anna-Katharina Wöbse, *Geschichte des Nationalparks Hohe Tauern* (Innsbruck: Tyrolia, 2013).
27 Christina Dominique Pichler-Koban, "Naturschutz Werte Wandel: Sozio-historische Analyse von Schutzgebietskonzeptionen am Beispiel von ausgewählten Schutzgebieten in Deutschland, Österreich und der Schweiz" (PhD diss., University of Klagenfurt, 2015).
28 Martin Schmid, and Ortrun Veichtlbauer, *Vom Naturschutz zur Ökologiebewegung: Umweltgeschichte Österreichs in der Zweiten Republik* (Innsbruck: Studien-Verlag, 2006).
29 Marina Fischer-Kowalski, and Harald Payer, "Fünfzig Jahre Umgang mit Natur," in *Österreich 1945–1995: Gesellschaft, Politik, Kultur*, ed. Reinhard Sieder, Heinz Steinert, and Emmerich Tálos (Vienna: Verlag für Gesellschaftskritik, 1995), 552–566.
30 Ortrun Veichtlbauer, "Braune Donau: Transportweg nationalsozialistischer Biopolitik," in *Graue Donau, Schwarzes Meer*, ed. Christian Reder, Erich Klein (Vienna: Springer, 2008), 226–245. An exemption is: Volkmar Lauber, "*Geschichte der Politik zur Umwelt in der Zweiten Republik: Vom Nachzügler zum Vorreiter - und zurück?*," in *Umwelt- Geschichte*, ed. Sylvia Hahn, Reinhold Reith (Vienna, Munich: Oldenbourg, 2001). 181–203.

The series of specialized chapters commences with a chapter on agriculture and forestry, not just because these remain very important for the country, but also because the Austrian contribution to environmental history has been most specific in this topical area, with methods developed and approaches pioneered over the past twenty years.

Agriculture and Forestry[31]

Working the land, harvesting crops, felling trees, and pasturing livestock are human activities directly and purposefully altering terrestrial ecosystems for human use; at the same time, environmental conditions and their dynamics strongly affect the human use of land. Agriculture and forestry are probably the most pervasive human-environment interactions and, therefore, a key theme in environmental history. This also holds true for Austria, where some of the first interdisciplinary environmental history studies were concerned with agriculture, land use, and the history of cultural landscapes.[32] Most of the genuine environmental history research on agriculture and land use in Austria, however, focuses on periods prior to the twentieth century; comparatively little has been done for the twentieth century. Agricultural history has a much longer tradition, and landmark publications similar to the two-volume history of Austrian agriculture in the twentieth century—volume one focused on "politics, society, economy"[33] and volume two on "regions, farms, people"[34]—are not available from an environmental historical perspective. Ernst Langthaler provides a comprehensive review of the achievements of twentieth century agricultural history in Austria and points out that this research has a strong focus on social and economic history.[35] Examples

31 Authored by Simone Gingrich and Fridolin Krausmann
32 Projektgruppe Umweltgeschichte, *Kulturlandschaftsforschung: Historische Entwicklung von Wechselwirkungen zwischen Gesellschaft und Natur* (Vienna: Bundesministerium für Wissenschaft und Verkehr, 1999), CD-ROM; Verena Winiwarter et al., *Der soziale Metabolismus der vorindustriellen Landwirtschaft in Europa*, (Stuttgart: Breuninger Stiftung, 2001); Rolf Peter Sieferle et al., *Das Ende der Fläche: Zum gesellschaftlichen Stoffwechsel der Industrialisierung* (Cologne: Böhlau, 2006).
33 Ernst Bruckmüller et al., eds., *Geschichte der österreichischen Land- und Forstwirtschaft im 20. Jahrhundert. Politik Gesellschaft Wirtschaft* (Vienna: Verlag Carl Ueberreuter, 2002).
34 Ernst Bruckmüller et al. ed., *Geschichte der österreichischen Land- und Forstwirtschaft im 20. Jahrhundert. Regionen Betriebe Menschen* (Vienna: Verlag Carl Ueberreuter, 2003).
35 Ernst Langthaler, "Gerahmte Landbilder. Agrargeschichtsschreibung in Österreich in der zweiten Hälfte des 20. Jahrhunderts," in *Agrargeschichte schreiben. Traditionen und Innovationen im internationalen Vergleich*, ed. Ernst Bruckmüller, Ernst Langthaler, and Josef Redl (Vienna: Studienverlag, 2004), 30–62.

include several regional agricultural histories,[36] a recent pioneering study on agriculture during the National Socialist reign,[37] and research on the emergence of farming styles.[38] Nature is typically not in the focus and not fully appreciated in its dynamics or as an "agent" shaping human practices. In one way or another, however, most contributions from agricultural history are also concerned with the physical environment and can provide important information for environmental history on the use of land, production statistics, fertilization, and pest management, as well as weather and climate. There are close links between the two fields and many possibilities for cross-fertilization, as V. Winiwarter has argued.[39] Also, forest history has a long tradition in Austria and is even more concerned with the physical environment and the management of natural resources as, for example, an overview chapter on the history of Austrian forestry in the twentieth century shows.[40] Austrian forest history often includes a strong material component, which makes it notable for environmental history. Contributions in forest history from the 1970s provide long-term histories of forestry in specific Austrian provinces or regions.[41] Recent forest history in Austria has dealt in more detail with specific parts of the twentieth century.[42] In particular, the work of forest historian Elisabeth Johann, who has extensively investigated the role of forest management practices in the evolution of cultural landscapes and the links between

---

36   e.g. Dinklage, Karl, et al., *Geschichte der Kärntner Landwirtschaft* (Klagenfurt: Heyn, 1966); Alfred Hoffmann, *Bauernland Oberösterreich: Entwicklungsgeschichte seiner Land- und Forstwirtschaft* (Linz: Trauner Verlag, 1974).
37   Ernst Langthaler, *Schlachtfelder: Alltägliches Wirtschaften in der nationalsozialistischen Agrargesellschaft 1938–1945* (Vienna: Böhlau, 2016).
38   Rita Garstenauer, Ulrich Schwarz, and Sophie Tod, "Alles unter einen Hut bringen," *Historische Anthropologie* 20, no. 3 (2012): 383–426.
39   Verena Winiwarter, "Landwirtschaft, Natur und ländliche Gesellschaft im Umbruch: Eine umwelthistorische Perspektive zur Agrarmodernisierung," in *Agrarmodernisierung und ökologische Folgen: Westfalen vom 18. bis zum 20. Jahrhundert,* ed. Karl Ditt, Rita Gudermann, and Norwich Rüße (Paderborn: Schöningh, 2001), 733–767; Verena Winiwarter, "Agrargeschichte als Umweltgeschichte?" in *Reguliertes Land: Agrarpolitik in Deutschland, Österreich und der Schweiz 1930–1960,* ed. Ernst Langthaler and Josef Redl (Innsbruck: Studien Verlag, 2005), 204–212.
40   Norbert Weigl, "Die österreichische Forstwirtschaft im 20. Jahrhundert – Von der Holzproduktion zum Ökosystemmanagement," in *Geschichte der österreichischen Land- und Forstwirtschaft im 20. Jahrhundert: Politik, Gesellschaft, Wirtschaft,* ed. Ernst Bruckmüller, Ernst Hanisch, and Roman Sandgruber (Vienna: Ueberreuter, 2002), 593–740.
41   Engelbert Koller, *Forstgeschichte des Landes Salzburg* (Salzburg: Verlag der Salzburger Druckerei, 1975); Franz Hafner, *Steiermarks Wald in Geschichte und Gegenwart: eine forstliche Monographie* (Vienna: Österreichischer Agrarverlag, 1979).
42   Norbert Weigl, *Österreichs Forstwirtschaft in der Zwischenkriegszeit 1918–1938* (Vienna: Österreichischer Kunst- und Kulturverlag, 1997).

forestry and nature conservation in Austria, provides close links to environmental history.[43]

An important research strand in material environmental history is that of long-term socio-ecological research (LTSER). Here, the biophysical aspects of agriculture and forestry are in the focus, meaning the role of land use in society's metabolism and links between human activity and ecosystem processes.[44] In Austria, this research has focused on the agrarian-industrial transition from the eighteenth century onwards, also touching on twentieth century issues.[45] Agriculture is conceived of as a coupled socio-ecological system, and the focus is on the evolution of physical interactions. Studies have investigated patterns of land use and changing stocks and flows of biomass in the twentieth century on different spatial scales.[46] A particular focus of this research is on the link between energy and agriculture[47]—that is, the human investment of energy in agriculture and its impact on ecosystems and land management, using novel approaches like the energy return on investment (EROI) or human appropriation of net primary production (HANPP).[48] The major argument based on socio-metabolic analyses in

43   Elisabeth Johann, *Wald und Mensch: die Nationalparkregion Hohe Tauern (Kärnten)* (Klagenfurt: Verlag des Kärntner Landesarchivs, 2004); Elisabeth Johann, "Traditional forest management under the influence of science and industry: the story of the alpine cultural landscapes," *Forest Ecology and Management* 249, no.1–2 (2007): 54–62; Elisabeth Johann, "The history of utilization and management of commons and consequences of current social change in the Alpine Region of Austria," in *Cultural Severance and the Environment*, ed. Ian D. Rotherham (Dordrecht: Springer, 2013), 133–146.

44   Simron J. Singh et al., eds., *Long term socio-ecological research: Studies in society-nature interactions across spatial and temporal scales* (Dordrecht: Springer Science & Business Media, 2013); Manuel González de Molina, and Víctor M. Toledo, *The Social Metabolism. A Socio-Ecological Theory of Historical Change* (New York: Springer, 2014).

45   Fridolin Krausmann, "Die Agrarmodernisierung als sozioökologischer Transformationsprozess: Fallbeispiel Österreich," in *Jahrbuch für die Geschichte des Ländlichen Raumes 3*, ed. Andreas Dix, and Ernst Langthaler (Innsbruck: Studien-Verlag, 2006), 17–45; Fridolin Krausmann, "Forest Transition in Österreich: Eine sozialökologische Annäherung," *Mitteilungen der Österreichischen Geographischen Gesellschaft* 148 (2006): 75–91.

46   Fridolin Krausmann, "Land use and industrial modernization: an empirical analysis of human influence on the functioning of ecosystems in Austria 1830–1995," *Land Use Policy* 18 (2001):17–26; Fridolin Krausmann et al., "Land-use change and socio-economic metabolism in Austria. Part I: driving forces of land-use change: 1950–1995," *Land Use Policy* 20 (2003):1–20; Simone Gingrich et al., "Long-term dynamics of terrestrial carbon stocks in Austria: a comprehensive assessment of the time period from 1830 to 2000," *Regional Environmental Change* 7, no. 1 (2007): 37–47; Maria Niedertscheider et al., "Influence of Land-Use Intensification on Vegetation C-Stocks in an Alpine Valley from 1865 to 2003," *Ecosystems* 20, no. 8 (2017): 1391–1406.

47   Fridolin Krausmann, "From Energy Source to Sink: Transformations of Austrian Agriculture," in *Social Ecology: Society-Nature Relations across Time and Space*, ed. Helmut Haberl et al. (Cham: Springer, 2016), 433–445.

48   Simone Gingrich, et al., "Regional specialization and market integration: Agroecosystem energy transitions in Upper Austria," *Regional Environmental Change* (2017): 1–14.

Austria is that agricultural modernization in twentieth century was intimately linked to the increasing availability of fossil fuels for socio-economic use with pervasive consequences for the intensity and spatial patterns of land use.[49] While this line of research has been criticized for concealing the important role of actors by adopting a "systems" perspective,[50] it has made important contributions to debates on sustainable development.[51] Interdisciplinary research dealing with the environmental history of agriculture and forestry is also performed by (historical) ecologists studying long-term processes and legacy effects of past land uses. Contributions deal with long-term change in land use and land cover ecosystem services provision[52] or changes in forest disturbance regimes.[53]

Energy[54]

After World War I, Austria had lost access to (previously domestic) coal deposits in Bohemia and Silesia. The most appropriate source for domestic energy supply in the subsequent decades was hydropower. Starting from the western provinces, hydropower generation gained increasing importance in the early and mid-twentieth century and continued to be the most important provider of electricity in Austria throughout the twentieth century.[55]

---

49   Helmut Haberl, and Fridolin Krausmann, "The local base of the historical agrarian-industrial transition, and the interaction between scales," in *Socio-ecological transitions and global change: Trajectories of social metabolism and land use,* ed. Marina Fischer-Kowalski and Helmut Haberl (Cheltenham: Edward Elgar Publishing, 2007), 116–138; Fridolin Krausmann, Heinz Schandl, and Rolf Peter Sieferle, "Socio-ecological regime transitions in Austria and the United Kingdom," *Ecological Economics* 65, no. 1 (2008): 187–201; Karl-Heinz Erb et al., "Industrialization, fossil fuels, and the transformation of land use," *Journal of Industrial Ecology* 12, no. 5-6 (2008): 686–703.
50   Ernst Langthaler, "Agrarsysteme ohne Akteure?" *Jahrbuch Geschichte des ländlichen Raumes 3,* ed. Andreas Dix, and Ernst Langthaler (Innsbruck: Studien-Verlag, 2006), 216–238.
51   Karl-Heinz Erb et al., "Bias in the attribution of forest carbon sinks," *Nature Climate Change* 3, no. 10 (2013): 854–856.
52   Uta Schirpke et al., "Multiple ecosystem services of a changing Alpine landscape: past, present and future," *International Journal of Biodiversity Science, Ecosystem Services & Management* 9, no. 2 (2013): 123–135; Lukas Egarter Vigl et al., "Linking long-term landscape dynamics to the multiple interactions among ecosystem services in the European Alps," *Landscape ecology* 31, no. 9 (2016): 1903–1918.
53   Peter Bebi et al., "Changes of forest cover and disturbance regimes in the mountain forests of the Alps," *Forest ecology and management* 388 (2017): 43–56.
54   Authored by Simone Gingrich and Fridolin Krausmann
55   Oliver Rathkolb et al., *Wasserkraft. Elektrizität. Gesellschaft. Kraftwerksprojekte ab 1880 im Spannungsfeld* (Vienna: Kremayr & Scheriau, 2012). Beatrice Wagner et al., "A review of hydropower in Austria: past, present and future development," *Renewable and Sustainable Energy Reviews* 50 (2015): 304–314.

Following the tradition set in place by the study of the history of technology, environmental issues started to be addressed in historical analyses of hydropower installation in the 1990s.[56] Since then, environmental history has addressed the topos of "white gold" (or "white coal") in the Austrian Alps, partly overlapping with the strong recent focus on the environmental history of Austrian rivers. Environmental history research has dealt with large-scale pumped-storage plants,[57] small-scale rural river plants,[58] the development of border rivers,[59] and of the Danube's main stream.[60] The interest shifted from the initial technical focus toward a more interdisciplinary approach, combining, for example, histories of knowledge and expertise with ecological issues such as hydrology or sediment transport. The exploitation of crude oil in Austria during the early and mid-twentieth century has also been touched upon by environmental history research. [61]

The fight against the construction of power plants was a major constituting factor for Austrian environmental movements in the 1970s and 1980s. The two largest projects, which were abandoned after mass protests from a broad civic society movement, were the nuclear power plant in Zwentendorf,[62] voted down by a national referendum in 1978, and the hydropower plant Hainburg, averted in 1984.[63] Such environmental con-

---

56   Peter Staudacher, "Das weiße Gold der Alpen: Vom physikalischen Phänomen zum Mythos," in *Katalog zur Ausstellung: Aus Dorfenger Welt ins Weltweite Dorf: Netzwerk,* ed. Rudolf G. Ardelt (Steyr: Verein Museum Arbeitswelt, 1995), 33–48; Georg Rigele, "Das Tauernkraftwerk Glockner-Kaprun: Neue Forschungsergebnisse und offene Fragen," *Blätter für Technikgeschichte* 59 (1997): 55–94.
57   Marc Landry, "Catalyst for Transition: The Anschluss, Kaprun, and a Dual Energy Transition, 1938–1955," *RCC Perspectives* 5 (2014): 43–52; Marc Landry, "Environmental Consequences of the Peace: The Great War, Dammed Lakes, and Hydraulic History in the Eastern Alps," *Environmental History* 20, no. 3 (July 2015): 422–448.
58   Angelika Schoder, "A History of Pebbles and Silt–Fluvial Sediment Transport, Hydropower and Technical Expertise at the Austrian Danube and its Tributaries," *Transylvanian Review of Systematical and Ecological Research* 18, no. 2 (2016): 1-18.
59   Ute Hasenöhrl, "'Weiße Kohle' oder 'Ausbeutung der Natur?' Konflikte um die Nutzung der Wasserkraft im (Vor-) Alpenraum am Beispiel bayerisch-österreichischer Grenzflüsse," *Bohemia-Zeitschrift für Geschichte und Kultur der böhmischen Länder* 54, no. 1 (2014): 119–141.
60   Ortrun Veichtlbauer, "Donau-Strom. Über die Herrschaft der Ingenieure," in *Graue Donau - Schwarzes Meer,* ed. Christian Reder, Erich Klein (Vienna: Springer, 2008), 170–195.
61   Jakob Calice, "Öldorado Zistersdorf. Skizzen zur Umweltgeschichte des niederösterreichischen Erdölabbaus," in *Niederösterreich im 20. Jahrhundert. Band 2: Wirtschaft,* ed. Peter Melichar, Ernst Langthaler und Stefan Eminger (Vienna: Böhlau, 2008), 449–456.
62   Peter Weish, "Zwentendorf aus der Sicht eines Zeitzeugen," in *Umwelt Stadt: Geschichte des Natur- und Lebensraumes Wien,* ed. Karl Brunner, and Petra Schneider (Vienna: Böhlau Verlag, 2005), 384–385.
63   Gernot Neuwirth, "Hainburg aus der Sicht eines Zeitzeugen," in *Umwelt Stadt: Geschichte des Natur- und Lebensraumes Wien,* ed. Karl Brunner, and Petra Schneider (Vienna: Böhlau Verlag, 2005), 390–391.

flicts were relevant in democratic terms, resulting in, for example, the formation of the Austrian Green Party, as well as in nature protection: not only in Hainburg,[64] but also in the alpine region Kalkalpen, did the fight against hydropower plants contribute to the later establishment of a national park. However, the political relevance of environmental movements fighting large energy infrastructures remains underexplored in Austrian environmental history.[65]

It is not only the generation of energy that has been addressed in environmental history, but also the changing uses of energy: cultural and economic history have contributed to understanding the effects of electrification and changes in energy supply.[66] A larger body of work in material environmental history emerged from social metabolism research. Several quantitative studies explored the changing use of energy in the course of the twentieth century or the "energy transition" from biomass to fossil fuels and how this changed the environment. Transitions in the provision and use of energy during twentieth-century industrialization have been extensively studied at the national scale and for the city of Vienna,[67] and also the impact on CO_2 emissions.[68]

64 Verena Winiwarter, and Sophia Rut, "Österreich ergrünt: Die Besetzung der Hainburger Au," in *100 Jahre Republik. Meilensteine und Wendepunkte 1918–2018*, ed. Heinz Fischer, Andreas Huber, and Stephan Neuhäuser (Vienna: Czernin Verlag, 2018) 203–216.
65 Martin Schmid, and Ortrun Veichtlbauer, *Vom Naturschutz zur Ökologiebewegung: Umweltgeschichte Österreichs in der Zweiten Republik* (Innsbruck: Studien-Verlag, 2006).
66 Roman Sandgruber, "Das elektrische Jahrhundert: Die Wirtschafts-und Sozialgeschichte der Elektrizitätsausnutzung in Österreich," in *Licht und Schatten: Dimensionen von Technik, Energie und Politik*, ed. Evelyn Gröbl-Steinbach (Vienna: Böhlau, 1990), 33–48; Christian Stadelmann, "Überall Strom: Elektrifizierung und Technisierung in Niederösterreichs Landgemeinden," in *Niederösterreich im 20. Jahrhundert: Band 2: Wirtschaft*, ed. Peter Melichar, Ernst Langthaler und Stefan Eminger (Vienna: Böhlau, 2008), 375–403.
67 Fridolin Krausmann, and Helmut Haberl. "The process of industrialization from the perspective of energetic metabolism: Socioeconomic energy flows in Austria 1830–1995," *Ecological Economics* 41, no. 2 (2002): 177–201; Fridolin Krausmann, "Sonnenfinsternis? Das Energiesystem von Wien im 19. und 20. Jahrhundert," *Umwelt Stadt. Geschichte des Natur- und Lebensraumes Wien*, ed. Karl Brunner, and Petra Schneider (Vienna: Böhlau Verlag, 2005), 140–150; Fridolin Krausmann, "A city and its hinterland: Vienna's energy metabolism 1800–2006," in *Long term socio-ecological research: Studies in society-nature interactions across spatial and temporal scales*, ed. Simron J. Singh et al. (Dordrecht: Springer Science & Business Media, 2013), 247–268.
68 Simone Gingrich, Petra Kušková, and Julia K. Steinberger, "Long-term changes in CO_2 emissions in Austria and Czechoslovakia—Identifying the drivers of environmental pressures," *Energy Policy* 39, no.2 (2011): 535–543.

Water[69]

Rivers have been a research focus of recent Austrian environmental history studies, although the twentieth century figured less prominently, as most projects focused on the eighteenth and nineteenth centuries. For the Danube, detailed investigations of the Machland section at the border of Upper and Lower Austria and the Viennese Danube represent urban and rural stretches of this main Austrian river.[70] The link between flood protection, floodplain colonization, urbanization, and urban planning was investigated for the Traisen, a right-hand tributary of the Danube in Lower Austria.[71]

Another—rather small—strand of historical research on water is related to water supply in the twentieth century. Studies of Vienna figure most prominently due to the importance of the city and due to its proverbial high quality of water, which stems from the alpine sources of the two major water pipelines.[72] For smaller cities, the history of water in the twentieth century was not investigated as deeply.[73] Also, research on water pollution in the twentieth century did not play a big role in historiography despite the huge problems that many lakes and rivers faced in this period due to untreated wastewater release.

Most of the historical research on Austrian bodies of water and fluvial landscapes is rooted in scholarly fields other than environmental history or history at large. Experts from fields such as water engineering or hydrobiology highlighted specific technical, biological, or socio-economic aspects

---

69   Authored by Severin Hohensinner and Gertrud Haidvogl.

70   for integrative summaries see Verena Winiwarter, Martin Schmid, *Umwelt Donau: Eine andere Geschichte. Katalog zur Ausstellung des NÖ Landesarchivs "Donau - Fluch & Segen" in Ardagger Markt, 5. Mai - 7. Nov. 2010* (St. Pölten: Niederösterreichisches Landesarchiv, 2010); Severin Hohensinner et al., "Changes in water and land: the reconstructed Viennese riverscape from 1500 to the present," *Water History* 5, no. 2 (2013): 145–172; Verena Winiwarter, Martin Schmid, and Gert Dressel, "Looking at half a millennium of co-existence: the Danube in Vienna as a socio-natural site," *Water History* 5, no.2 (2013): 101–119; Verena Winiwarter et al., "The long-term evolution of urban waters and their nineteenth century transformation in European cities – A comparative environmental history," *Water History* 8 (2016): 209–233; Gertrud Haidvogl et al., "The nature of urban waters and the long-term development of Vienna between 1683 and 1910," *Environmental History* (forthcoming).

71   Gertrud Haidvogl et al., "Historische Landnutzung und Siedlungsentwicklung in Flussauen und Hochwasserschutz: Das Beispiel der Traisen und St. Pöltens 1870–2000," Österreichische Wasser- *und Abfallwirtschaft* (2018): 1–11.

72   Ruth Koblizek, and Nicole Süssenbek, "Die Trinkwasserversorgung der Stadt Wien – von ihren Anfängen bis zur Gegenwart" (PhD diss., University of Vienna University, 2000).

73   but see e.g. Rabl Erich, *Wasser für Horn: Die Wasserversorgung der Stadt Horn in den letzten 100 Jahren: Eine Festschrift der Stadtgemeinde Horn* (Horn: Stadtgemeinde Horn, 1983).

and functions of the diverse aquatic environment. Prior to World War I, as a consequence of the rising importance of stream navigation, tremendous efforts were made to regulate and channelize most of Austria's running water systems. No wonder that, in the following decades, several studies were published in order to emphasize the achievements that had been made in the human transformation of the river courses.[74] Between the two world wars, when the Danube still functioned as an important trading route, several publications reviewed historical river training projects and suggested further hydraulic improvements for better navigability.[75] At the same time, several projects for the production of hydroelectric power, and, consequently, the further transformation of Austria's larger rivers, were proposed, and the (at the time) short history of planned and implemented projects was reviewed.[76] Besides river channelization for navigation and flow regulation for hydroelectric power, the large-scale drainage of marsh lands for the acquisition of arable land in the large alpine valleys also became a prominent topos, particularly when the new lands were compared to the nine provinces of Austria with a slogan that referred to them as a "tenth province" ("*zehntes Bundesland*").[77] The role of hydraulic and construction engineers in the transformation process of Austria's bodies of water and river landscapes has been highlighted from an environmental historical perspective by Veichtlbauer (2008, 2010).[78]

---

74 Georg Strele, "50 Jahre Erfahrungen bei der Wildbachverbauung in Österreich," *Wasserkraft und Wasserwirtschaft* 31 (1936): 61–77; Franz Baumann, *Vom älteren Flussbau in Österreich* (Vienna: Springer, 1951).

75 Rudolf Halter, *Wien und die Donau: Denkschrift des österreichischen Ingenieur- und Architekten-Vereines* (Vienna: Österreichischer Ingenieur- und Architekten-Verein, 1917); Brandl, L. "Die Regulierung der Donau als Schiffahrtsstraße." *Die Wasserwirtschaft* 4–6 (1920): 36; OÖ. Staatsbaudienst, *Die Regelung der Donau in Oberösterreich: Denkschrift anläßlich der Ausstellung für Wasserstraßen und Energiewirtschaft in München* (Linz: Verlag des oberösterreichischen Staatsbaudienstes, 1921).

76 WEWA – Wasserkraft- und Elektrizitätswirtschaftsamt, *Die Entwicklung des Großwasserkraftausbaus und die Gewinnung elektrischer Energie in Österreich seit dem Jahre 1918*, Elektrotechnik und Maschinenbau 41 (Vienna: Selbstverlag des Elektrotechnischen Vereins, 1930); Oskar Vas, *Grundlagen und Entwicklung der Energiewirtschaft Österreichs: Offizieller Bericht des Österreichischen Nationalkomitees der Weltkraftkonferenz. Ergänzungsband 1930–1933* (Berlin: Springer, 1933).

77 Bernhard Ramsauer, *Die österreichische Nährflächenreserve – das zehnte Bundesland* (Vienna: Springer, 1948); Franz Baumann, Vorgeschichtliches zum ostalpinen Flußbau (Vienna: Springer, 1960); Ernst Güntschl, *Festschrift 100 Jahre Ennsregulierung* (Vienna: Verlag Natur und Technik, 1960).

78 Ortrun Veichtlbauer, "Donau-Strom: Über die Herrschaft der Ingenieure," in *Graue Donau - Schwarzes Meer*, ed. Christian Reder, Erich Klein (Vienna: Springer, 2008), 170–195; Ortrun Veichtlbauer, "Von der Strombaukunst zur Staukette: Die Regulierung der Donau," ed. Verena Winiwarter, Martin Schmid, *Umwelt Donau: Eine andere Geschichte. Katalog zur Ausstellung des NÖ Landesarchivs "Donau - Fluch & Segen" in Ardagger Markt, 5. Mai - 7. Nov. 2010* (St. Pölten: Niederösterreichisches Landesarchiv, 2010), 56–73.

After the majority of Austria's larger fluvial systems had been regulated, the thorough transformation became a topic of research by historical geographers, cartographers, and civil engineers.[79] Among the latter, Karl Gerabek, who published several studies on rivers and streams in Austrian provinces, deserves mentioning.[80] Because of its alpine topography and the historical dependence on water power, many Austrian settlement areas are situated in larger valley floors in the vicinity of rivers. Accordingly, the threats of recurrent floods have been addressed by several authors over the last decades.[81] Public discussions and planning of several river restoration projects triggered a new type of historical study, on running water systems, in the recent decades. Such studies focus on the natural as well as human-caused modifications of river systems in the past primarily from the nature conservancy, river morphological, and ecological point of view.[82] In recent years, comprehensive publications on the history of certain large rivers have gained increasing public interest.[83]

The close links between a group of forestry and torrent management experts yielded investigations of the history of torrent control since the late nineteenth century parallel to forestry history studies. An Austrian

---

79   Friedrich Slezak, "Historische Veränderungen der Donaustromlandschaft im Tullner und Wiener Becken" (PhD diss., University of Vienna, 1948); Friedrich Slezak, "Wien und die frühe Donaukartographie: Stadtgeschichtsforschung und Kartenvergleich," *Mitteilungen der Österreichischen Geographischen Gesellschaft* 122 (1980): 256–275; Peter Mohilla, and Franz Michlmayr, *Donauatlas Wien: Geschichte der Donauregulierung auf Karten und Plänen aus vier Jahrhunderten* (Vienna: Österreichischer Kunst- u. Kulturverlag, 1996).
80   Karl Gerabek, *Gewässer und Wasserwirtschaft Niederösterreichs* (St. Pölten: Verein für Landeskunde von Niederösterreich, 1964); Karl Gerabek, "Die Gewässer im Stadtbereich von Salzburg," *Mitteilungen der Gesellschaft für Salzburger Landeskunde* 110/111, no.1 (1971): 381–396.
81   Kresser, Werner, *Die Hochwässer der Donau* (Vienna: Springer, 1957); Internationale Rheinregulierung ed., *Der Alpenrhein und seine Regulierung: Internationale Rheinregulierung 1892–1992* (Rorschach: BuchsDruck, 1993); Christian Rohr, "Zur Wahrnehmung, Deutung und Bewältigung von extremen Hochwasserereignissen in Österreich von der Antike bis heute: Das Beispiel Wels," *Historische Sozialkunde: Geschichte, Fachdidaktik, politische Bildung* 38, no. 2 (2008): 14–20; Severin Hohensinner and Martin Schmid, "The more dikes the higher the floods: Vienna and its Danube Floods," *Historical Geography* 3 (2015): 211–227.
82   Werner Konold, *Historische Wasserwirtschaft im Alpenraum und an der Donau* (Stuttgart: Wittwer, 1994); Severin Hohensinner et al., "Changes in water and land: the reconstructed Viennese riverscape from 1500 to the present," *Water History* 5, no. 2 (2013): 145–172; Severin Hohensinner, "Reconstruction of original habitat conditions of the Danube river/floodplain biocoenosis based on the morphological development from 1715–1991, Machland, Upper/Lower Austria" (PhD diss., University of Vienna, 2008); Mathias Jungwirth et al., Österreichs Donau. *Landschaft – Fisch – Geschichte* (Vienna: Institute of Hydrobiology and Aquatic Ecosystem Management, 2014).
83   Heinz Wiesbauer, and Heinz Dopsch, *Salzach macht Geschichte* (Salzburg: Verein Freunde der Salzburger Geschichte, 2007); Heinz Wiesbauer, *Die Ybbs – Ein Fluss macht Geschichte* (St. Pölten: Amt der NÖ Landesregierung, Abt. Wasserbau, 2015).

overview of the period, 1884 to 1984, focuses on the technical interventions and achievements.[84] Later studies cover shorter periods or focus on specific regions.[85]

For fish and fisheries, historians focused on periods before the twentieth century. However, as a consequence of major changes due to hydropower dams and systematic river channelization, fish biologists and fishery managers addressed the decline of fish stocks and effects on fisheries in publications from circa 1930 to 1950.[86] Since the 1950s, several ethnological studies on traditional fish species and their uses and fishery management on Austrian rivers were published. For example, Wagner described the situation in rivers of Carinthia,[87] Raab focused on traditional fisheries in Lower Austrian rivers,[88] Schneeweis investigated fisheries management on the Inn River,[89] and Liesenfeld concentrated on Danube fishery in the section between Vienna and Hainburg.[90] In recent years, Jungwirth wrote about a fishery association of the Upper Austrian Danube (Basin of Eferding).[91] Exceptionally, historians focused on fish and fisheries, but usually they were not established in scholarly circles, and developments in the twentieth century were not in the foreground of such studies; of those studies, at least some came from non-academic historians.[92]

---

84   Herbert Aulitzky, and Julian Stritzl, *100 Jahre Wildbachverbauung in Österreich: 1884–1984* (Vienna: Bundesministerium für Land- u. Forstwirtschaft, 1984).
85   Hubert Flachberger, "Wildbach- und Lawinenverbauung," in *Der Wald unser Leben - unsere Zukunft: Festschrift zum 150-jährigen Jubiläum des Forstvereins für Oberösterreich und Salzburg*, ed. Norbert Weigl (Linz: Forstverein für Oberösterreich und Salzburg, 2005), 180–187.
86   Hans Margreiter, *Gebirgsbach-Verbauung und Fischerei* (Innsbruck: Tiroler Landes-Fischereiverein, 1928); Hans Freudlsperger, "Kurze Fischereigeschichte des Erzstiftes Salzburg," *Mitteilungen der Gesellschaft für Salzburger Landeskunde* 76 (1936): 81–128; Adolf Cerny, *Die Fischereiwirtschaft in Österreich* (Vienna: Österreichischer Agrarverlag, 1947).
87   Hans, Wagner, "Zur Geschichte der Fischerei und der Jagd in Kärnten," *Carinthia I/ Geschichtliche und volkskundliche Beiträge zur Heimatkunde Kärntens* (1955): 622–647.
88   Alfred Raab, "Die traditionelle Fischerei in Niederösterreich, mit besonderer Berücksichtigung der Ybbs, Erlauf, Pielach und Traisen" (PhD diss., University of Vienna, 1978).
89   Felix Schneeweis, "Innfischerei: die traditionelle Fischerei im oberösterreichisch-bayerischen Inngebiet und ihre Wandlungen vom Ende des neunzehnten Jahrhunderts bis zur Gegenwart in volkskundlicher Sicht" (PhD diss., University of Vienna, 1979).
90   Gertraud Liesenfeld, "Zur Daubelfischerei zwischen Wien und Hainburg," in *Sammeln und Sichten: Beiträge zur Sachvolkskunde* (Vienna: Verband der Wissenschaftlichen Gesellschaften Österreichs, 1979), 333–348.
91   Regine Jungwirth, "Erwerbsfischerei an Donau und Nebenflüssen im Raum Eferding," *Jahrbuch des Oberösterreichischen Musealvereines* 146 (2001): 567–599; Regine Jungwirth, "Fischwassergrenzsteine am Beispiel einiger Objekte aus dem Eferdinger Becken in Oberösterreich," *Acta Ethnographica Hungarica* 53 (2008): 1–8.
92   Hermann Diem, "Beiträge zur Fischerei Nordtirols," *Veröffentlichungen des Museums Ferdinandeum* 43 (1964): 5–132.

Tourism and the Environment[93]

The environmental history of tourism has not been the focus of European environmental history from its beginnings. Only recently has tourism been recognized by international scholarship as being a subject worthy of study in the field.[94] This may be the effect of the dominant perception of tourism as a "smokeless industry."[95] Another reason for the absence of tourism from the study of environmental history might be found in the general development of tourism history and studies. Since the 1990s, this community was heavily influenced by the work of the sociologist John Urry. He claimed a "primacy of seeing" as the central activity in tourism. Referring to the work of Michel Foucault, specifically "The Birth of the Clinic: An Archaeology of Medical Perception,"[96] Urry holds that the "tourist gaze" serves as a power-producing knowledge machine, which disciplines the spatial behavior of tourists.[97] Verena Winiwarter picked up this approach when she studied how picture postcards instilled a desire in tourists to visit the depicted places and how these visual strategies created a need—fulfilled by the tourism industry—to transform cultural landscapes according to the expectations of tourists.[98] Ethnologist Bernhard Tschofen also emphasized the primacy of seeing, when he studied alpine tourism throughout the twentieth century. Tschofen addresses several topics that can be regarded as relevant for an environmental history of tourism, for example in his groundbreaking work on the modernization of alpinism through cable cars, alpine huts, and skiing culture.[99] In

93 Authored by Robert Groß and Michael Bürkner
94 Verena Winiwarter et al., "Environmental history in Europe from 1994 to 2004: enthusiasm and consolidation," *Environment and History* 10, no. 4 (2004): 501–530; Scott Moranda, "The emergence of an environmental history of tourism," *Journal of Tourism History* 7, no. 3 (2015): 268–289.
95 Andrew Holden, *Tourism studies and the social sciences* (London: Routledge, 2004), 163.
96 Michel Foucault, *The Birth of the Clinic*, trans. A. Sheridan (London: Tavistock, 1973).
97 John Urry, *Tourist Gaze: Leisure and Travel in Contemporary Societies* (London: Sage, 1990).
98 Verena Winiwarter, "Landschaft auf Vierfarbkarton: Betrachtungen zur kulturellen Konstruktion des Blickens," *ZOLLtexte* 35, no. 4 (2000): 48–53; Verena Winiwarter, "Buying a dream come true," *Rethinking History* 5, no. 3 (2001): 451–454; Verena Winiwarter, "Wahrnehmung von Landschaft – Zur Bedeutung von Vielfalt und Stereotypen der Landschaftswahrnehmung in der interdisziplinären Umweltforschung," *Die Bodenkultur* 53 (2002): 65–73; Verena Winiwarter, "Nationalized Nature on Picture Postcards: Subtexts of Tourism from an Environmental Perspecitve," *Global Environment* 1, no. 1 (2008): 191–215.
99 Bernhard Tschofen, "Die Seilbahnfahrt: Gebirgswahrnehmung zwischen klassischer Alpenbesteisterung und moderner Ästhetik," in *Tourimus und Regionalkultur*, ed. Burkhard Pöttler (Vienna: IFV, 1994), 107–128; Bernhard Tschofen, *Berg, Kultur, Moderne: Volkskundliches aus den Alpen* (Vienna: Sonderzahl, 1999); Bernhard Tschofen, "Tourismus als Alpenkultur? Zum Marktwert von Kultur(kritik) im Fremdenverkehr," in *Der Alpentourismus: Entwicklungspotenziale im Spannungsfeld von Kultur, Ökonomie und Ökologie*, ed. Kurt Luger and Franz Rest (Innsbruck: Studienverlag, 2002), 87–104; Bernhard Tschofen, "Ein Wintermärchen? Die Erfindung der österreichischen Moderne im Geiste des Schilaufs," in *Schnee von gestern: Winterplakate der österreichischen Nationalbibliothek*, ed. Christian Maryska (Vienna: Holzhausen, 2004), 63–73; Bernhard Tschofen, "Schnee-Kulturen: Vorüberlegungen zu einer Anthropologie des Schnees in populären Bilderwelten," in *Schnee: Rohstoff der Kunst*, ed. Tobias G. Natter (Bregenz: Vorarlberger Landesmuseum, 2009), 30–43.

a similar vein, a group of historians at Salzburg University addressed tourism history in the late 1990s and early 2000s.[100] These studies reveal how tourism advertising, the accommodation sector, and sociocultural developments as a whole contribute to the construction of cultural landscapes (of tourism).

An important research strand in tourism studies is that of geography and, more particularly, of human and economic geography. These studies focus on landscape changes caused by the increasing importance of the tertiary sector, the service economy, within agricultural settings. An influential pioneer in this field is Werner Bätzing, who has studied such changes from the micro scale of single villages to the macro scale of the entire Alps.[101] The dominant narrative in geographical studies is that of changes in socio-economic structures that alter settlement structures, transport, and mobility infrastructures and, with those, landscapes. Such studies are available for nearly all Austrian tourism regions, as they are a frequent topic of academic qualification works.[102] For environmental historians, these works provide an excellent starting point to better understand the impact of tourism on regional structures.

---

100   Kurt Luger, and Franz Rest, "Mobile Privatisierung: Kultur und Tourismus in der Zweiten Republik," in Österreich 1945–1995: Gesellschaft, Politik, Kultur, ed. Reinhard Sieder, Heinz Steinert and Emmerich Tálos (Vienna: Verlag für Gesellschaftskritik, 1995), 655–670; Kurt Luger, and Franz Rest, "Der Alpentourismus. Konturen einer kulturell konstruierten Sehnsuchtslandschaft," in Der Alpentourismus: Entwicklungspotenziale im Spannungsfeld von Kultur, Ökonomie und Ökologie, ed. Kurt Luger and Franz Rest (Innsbruck: Studienverlag, 2002), 11–47.
101   Werner Bätzing, Bad Hofgastein: Gemeindeentwicklung zwischen Ökologie und Tourismus; Perspektiven für eine Gemeinde im Brennpunkt des alpinen Fremdenverkehrs (Berlin: ISR, 1985); Werner Bätzing, "Der Stellenwert des Tourismus in den Alpen und seine Bedeutung für eine nachhaltige Entwicklung des Alpenraumes," in Der Alpentourismus: Entwicklungspotenziale im Spannungsfeld von Kultur, Ökonomie und Ökologie, ed. Kurt Luger and Franz Rest (Innsbruck: Studienverlag, 2002), 176–196; Werner Bätzing, Die Alpen: Geschichte und Zukunft einer europäpischen Kulturlandschaft (Munich: Beck, 2005).
102   Egon Lendl, "Der Fremdenverkehr als Gestalter der Salzburger Kulturlandschaft," Mitteilungen der Gesellschaft für Salzburger Landeskunde 100 (1960): 673–691; Peter Laimer, "Der Tourismus in der Region Kaprun-Zell am See im Wandel der Zeit: Eine fremdenverkehrsgeographische Analyse unter Berücksichtigung der Auswirkungen auf den Natur- bzw. Kulturraum der Region" (MA thesis, University of Vienna, 1992); Bernd Kreuzer, "Straßen für den Fremdenverkehr: Das Salzkammergut in der Zwischenkriegszeit," Oberösterreichische Heimatblätter 3, no. 4 (1999): 195–211; Anna Leithner, "Landschaftswandel in Gosau: Über die historische Entwicklung der Landschaft und den tourismusbedingten Landschaftswandel in der heutigen Dachsteinregion West insbesondere der Gemeinde Gosau" (MA thesis, University of Vienna 1999); Robert Wlattnig, Diex: Sonnendorf auf der Saualape: Von der mittelalterlichen Kirchenburg zur modernen Tourismusgemeinde (Klagenfurt: Heyn, 1996); Friedrich Koller, "Vom ersten Gast zum Massentourismus: Der Einfluß des Fremdenverkehrs auf die Veränderung der Menschen des Ortsbildes und der Ökologie in einer Gemeinde am Beispiel Millstatts" (MA thesis, University of Klagenfurt, 2005).

A particularly important precondition for many Austrian tourism destinations is the development of mobility and transport infrastructure from paths to railroads, cable cars, automobile roads, and ski lifts. As Ben Anderson and Katharina Scharf demonstrate, the establishment of infrastructure networks was contested from their very beginning in the mid-nineteenth century and led to the reformulation of land property rights.[103] Within tourism studies, road and railroad infrastructure was most prominently analyzed by using cultural history approaches, as in Wolfgang Kos's pioneering study on the construction of a cultural landscape by building a railroad crossing the Semmering mountain pass between Lower Austria and Styria.[104] Other scholars focused on building roads that were both national icons and, at the times of their construction, tourist attractions themselves, such as the high alpine road at the Großglockner.[105] Studies are also available on how road projects originally built to foster economic activity later turned into a curse for local populations.[106] Martin Knoll provides a somewhat different perspective, analyzing how different kinds of mobility (roads and ski lifts) were synchronized by constant interventions into particular nodes of the mobility network.[107]

Georg Rigele undertook the first attempt to study Alpine tourism in Austria from an environmental history perspective. He emphasized the infrastructures of tourism by focusing on how high alpine roads, ski lifts, and cable cars provided significantly increasing transport capacity for

103 Ben Anderson, "Alpine agency: locals, mountaineers and tourism in the eastern Alps, c. 1860–1914," *Rural History: Economy, Society, Culture* 27, no. 1 (2016): 61–78; Katharina Scharf, "Wem gehören die Alpen? Alpine Wege und Hütten in Salzburg," in Mitteilungen der Gesellschaft für Salzburger Landeskunde (forthcoming); Bernd Kreuzer, "Straßen für den Fremdenverkehr: Das Salzkammergut in der Zwischenkriegszeit." *Oberösterreichische Heimatblätter* 53, no. 3/4 (1999) 195–211.
104 Wolfgang Kos, "Imagereservoir Landschaft. Landschaftsmoden und ideologische Gemütslagen seit 1945," in: Österreich 1945–1995: *Gesellschaft, Politik, Kultur*, ed. Reinhard Sieder, Heinz Steinert and Emmerich Tálos, (Vienna: Verlag für Gesellschaftskritik, 1995), 599–580.
105   Georg Rigele, *Die Großglockner-Hochalpenstrasse: zur Geschichte eines österreichischen Monuments* (Vienna: WUV, 1998); Manuela Obersamer, "Die Großglockner Hochalpenstraße: Ihr Bedeutungswandel durch politische und gesellschaftliche Rahmenbedingungen" (MA thesis, University of Salzburg, 2002); Cord Pagenstecher, "Die Automobilisierung des Blicks auf die Berge: Die Grossglocknerstrasse in Bildwerbung und Urlaubsalben," *Histoire des Alpes = Storia delle Alpi = Geschichte der Alpen* 9 (2004): 245–264; Georg Zwanowetz, "Alpenstrassen und Alpenbahnen in Vergangenheit und Gegenwart," *Tiroler Heimat Jahrbuch für Geschichte und Volkskunde* 38 (1975), 175–206.
106 Magdalena Pernold, *Traumstraße oder Transithölle? Eine Diskursgeschichte der Brennerautobahn in Tirol und Südtirol (1950–1980)* (Bielefeld: transcript, 2016).
107 Martin Knoll, "Touristische Mobilitäten und ihre Schnittstellen," *Ferrum* 88 (2016): 84–91.

tourism destinations.[108] The study of winter tourism infrastructure is particularly well-suited for environmental history studies, as their emergence precipitated considerable protest, starting in the 1970s. Such conflicts involve different parties (farmers, ski lift entrepreneurs, regional politicians, and members of nature conservation NGOs, for example) and lead to rich sources for historical study. An important research strand focuses on conflicts in national parks.[109] At the Vienna Centre for Environmental History (ZUG), two studies on the conflict-ridden relationship between tourism entrepreneurs and nature conservationist responses were produced; both focus on protected areas.[110] Some of the nature conservation responses created a legacy of larger research projects that addressed the impact of ski lift infrastructure on agro-ecosystems.[111] Another area of interest was the historical interplay of tourism and agriculture.[112] Unlike studies in geography, which primarily take stock of statistical information on the socioeconomic change in their studied regions, environmental historians emphasize not

---

108   Georg Rigele, "Sommeralpen – Winteralpen: Veränderungen im Alpinen durch Bergstraßen, Seilbahnen und Schilifte in Österreich," in *Umweltgeschichte: Zum historischen Verhältnis von Gesellschaft und Natur*, ed. Ernst Bruckmüller, and Verena Winiwarter (Vienna: ÖBV & Hpt., 2000), 121–150.

109   Christina Pichler-Koban, and Michael Jungmeier, "Alpine parks between yesterday and tomorrow – a conceptual history of Alpine national parks via tourism in charismatic parks in Austria Germany and Switzerland," *eco.mont* 9, Special Issue (2017): 17–28; Edeltraud Gschoderer, "Nationalparks im Spannungsfeld von Tourismus und Naturschutz am Beispiel des Nationalpark Gesäuse," (MA thesis, Salzburg, 2008); Christoph Stadel, Heinz Slupetzky and Harald Kremser, "Nature conservation traditional living space or tourist attraction? The Hohe Tauern National Park Austria," *Mountain Research and Development* 16, no. 1 (1996): 1–16.

110   Stefan Lamprechter, "Das Aufeinandertreffen von Bildern: Auf einem Gletscher blühen keine Blumen" (MA thesis, University of Vienna, 2006); Ronald Würflinger, "Kultur statt verwilderte Natur: Nationalparkentwicklung in Österreich: Der Konflikt um die Errichtung des Nationalparks Gesäuse, 1996–2002. Eine historische Diskursanalyse zur Naturschutzgeschichte Österreichs" (MA thesis, University of Vienna, 2007).

111   Alexander Cernusca, "Zur Hydrologie von Wintersporterschließungen," in *Umwelt und Tourismus*, ed. Erich Gnaiger, and Johannes Kautzky (Vienna: Thaur, 1992), 157–168; Alexander Cernusca et al., "Auswirkungen von Schneekanonen auf alpine Ökosysteme: Ergebnisse eines internationalen Forschungsprojektes," in *Umwelt und Tourismus*, ed. Erich Gnaiger, and Johannes Kautzky (Vienna: Thaur, 1992), 177–199; Romain Molitor, Eva Burian and Robert Thaler, *Environmental balance of transport: Austria 1950–1996* (Vienna: Federal Ministry for the Environment Youth and Family Affairs, 1997).

112   Wolfgang Meixner and Gerhard Siegl, "Bergbauern im Tourismusland: Agrargeschichte Tirols im 20. Jahrhundert," in *Geschichte der österreichischen Land- und Forstwirtschaft im 20. Jahrhundert; Regionen, Betriebe, Menschen*, ed. Ernst Bruckmüller, Ernst Hanisch and Roman Sandgruber (Vienna: Ueberreuter, 2003), 73–187; Hugo Penz, "Bewirtschaftungsveränderungen in den Alpen und deren Auswirkungen auf den Tourismus," in *Naturforum Weissensee: Zusammenfassung und Ergebnisse des 8. Naturforums Weissensee*, ed. Brigitte Garz (Weissensee: Naturforum, 1999), 8–13.

only the transformation but also the conflicts that arose due to tourism industry-induced change of both landscape and societies.[113]

Alpine winter tourism has received growing attention in environmental history studies the last few years, both in Austria and internationally. Andrew Denning's and Tait Keller's books offer fresh insights into the cultural history of sports in the Alps, with particular reference to both the environment and Austria.[114] While these studies do a very good job of contextualizing Alpine sports within broader modernist developments from the turn of the century until the present, they are rather limited when it comes to covering the actual transformation of particular regions. These topics were dealt with in depth by Robert Groß in studies carried out between 2012 and 2017. In these projects, winter sport destinations were conceptualized as "socio-natural sites" transformed by ski lift technology into industrialized landscapes.[115] It could be shown that the process of industrialization increased the financial debt burden but also the vulnerability of ski resorts, leading to a spiral of further technical interventions.[116] By approaching studies of winter tourism in this way, the first steps toward the integration of tourism topics into the broader field of environmental history were undertaken.

Closing Remarks

As is true for much European environmental history, and as has been shown using the examples of agriculture, forestry, energy, water, and tourism as themes for which the richest research is available, environmental historians have only recently emerged as a self-conscious group in Austria, and a great deal of good research has been done by scholars from other fields. The institutional basis of the field is still weak, with only three permanent

---

113 Robert Groß, *Wie das 1950er Syndrom in die Täler kam: Umwelthistorische Überlegungen zur Konstruktion von Wintersportlandschaften am Beispiel Damüls in Vorarlberg* (Regensburg: Roderer, 2012).

114 Andrew Denning, *Skiing into modernity: A cultural and environmental history* (Oakland: University of California Press, 2015); Tait Keller, *Apostles of the Alps: Mountaineering and Nation Building in Germany and Austria* (Chapel Hill: The University of North Carolina Press, 2016).

115 Robert Groß, *Wie das 1950er Syndrom in die Täler kam: Umwelthistorische Überlegungen zur Konstruktion von Wintersportlandschaften am Beispiel Damüls in Vorarlberg* (Regensburg: Roderer, 2012); Robert Groß, "Die Beschleunigung der Berge: Eine Umweltgeschichte des Wintertourismus in Vorarlberg/Österreich, 1920–2010" (PhD diss., University of Klagenfurt, 2017); Robert Groß, "Uphill and Downhill Histories: How Winter Tourism Transformed Alpine Regions in Vorarlberg/Austria – 1930 to 1970," *Zeitschrift für Tourismuswissenschaft* 9, no. 1 (2017): 115–139.

116 Robert Groß and Verena Winiwarter, "Commodifying snow, taming the waters: Socio-ecological niche construction in an Alpine village," *Water history* 7, no. 4 (2015): 489–509.

appointments on the full professor level in the entire country, of which two are not just environmental history, but combined chair, and none of them at Austria's largest university, the University of Vienna. While many historians are interested in environmental perspectives nowadays, contemporary historians have not picked up the topic much. It is to be hoped that a growing interest by international scholars studying Austria might also increase interest by the Austrian research community.

What makes this a worthwhile national and international interest? The interdisciplinary approach of many Austrian environmental historians allows them to contribute to environmental debates. The sustainability discourse, the discussions on conservation of nature, but also the debate about future options for energy provision can profit from including historical insights. In addition, such history offers opportunities for the (self-) reflection of environmental scholars by historical contextualization.

Environmental history can, on the other hand, help to rethink or reconceptualize familiar topics in Austrian history of interest to contemporary historians. Austria's contemporary political history is characterized by caesuras, among them World War I and the breakup of the Habsburg Empire, the "corporate state" (*Ständestaat*) of the 1930s and the loss of its independence during National Socialist rule and during the allied occupation after World War II, and not least the integration into the European Union. Approaches based on investigating cultural landscapes (in the broadest sense) relativize the narrative of the twentieth century as one of fundamental changes, because they focus on long-term processes. The main caesura in the interaction between humans and the environment is the energy transformation, the fossilization of the country. While such a view is certainly inspired by the notion of *long dureé* coined by Fernand Braudel, environmental histories concede that nature's agency can also be deployed over very short times and still have a long-term effect, as in avalanches, mudslides, and forest pathogens, to name but a few.

In the beginning of this essay, we pointed to the diversity of landscapes in contemporary Austria, from its Alpine characteristics in the western provinces to the steppe-like conditions of the Hungarian plain in Burgenland, the southeastern province. Austria shares the Alps and the plains with its neighbors and countries farther afield. Its environmental history is also a shared one. Any national environmental history of the twentieth century has to include, although this often remains implicit, a transnational perspective. Neither the post-World-War-II economic miracle made possible by the European Recovery Program, nor the rise of environmentalism since the 1960s, neither the fight against nuclear energy nor the challenges of climate change are national phenomena. They are international, often transnational, but each comes in many guises, in as many national versions as there are nations, their study needing national depth and international context alike. Therefore, Austrian environmental history might not only interest historians of Austria.

Rediscovering Abandoned Quarries:
The Value of Twentieth Century Historical Literature for the Writing of Modern Environmental History in Western Austria[1]

Irene Pallua
Gerhard Siegl

Introduction

Environmental history focuses on the reconstruction of interrelations between societies and their respective natural environments and on the changing perceptions of these interrelations. These topics have been addressed in regional studies (*Landesgeschichte*), folklore studies (*Volkskunde*), forest history, agricultural history, landscape history, economic history, historical demography, and other modes of study throughout the twentieth century.[2]

The aim of this essay is to examine and evaluate the existing historical literature on Western Austria and discuss whether and how the application of an environmental history perspective offers a way to write shared histories of society and their respective environments tying together otherwise disparate literature. We want to illustrate this by highlighting the interrelated histories of energy and landscape utilization. Both are classical topics of environmental history with present relevance in sustainable development strategies.

By doing so, it should not only be possible to shed light on the state of research, at least for some aspects of energy and landscape history, but also to reveal starting points for further research in Western Austrian environmental history.

1   We thank the Tyrolean Science Foundation (Project TELg, UNI-0404-2137) for financial support and Marina Lucy Hilber (http://www.diehistoriker.at/en/die-historikerinnen/das-team/lebenslauf-hilber/) for translation. For constructive comments on an earlier version of this essay we are indebted to the anonymous reviewer.
2   The Environmental History Database Austria lists over 400 publications focusing on Tyrol (324) and Vorarlberg (90) from a variety of disciplines, such as history, sociology, geography, spatial planning, and climatology, including only works published after 1945 (Center for Environmental History, "EHDA, Environmental History Database Austria," accessed Sept. 12, 2017, http://www.umweltgeschichte.aau.at/index,3183.html?value=en).

Landscape History:
Landscape in the Western Austrian Scholarly Landscape

Contemporary landscape discourses in the Alpine area center around three prominent topoi. First of all, *loss* connected to the disappearance of distinctive landscape features such as glaciers, agricultural buildings (hay barns, mills, baking ovens, etc.), natural sights, traditional irrigation systems (*Waale*), and old crop varieties (flax, poppy, cereal, etc.).[3] The feeling of loss has prompted heritage councils and other societies to preserve fences, dry frames for grain, shepherd's cottages, hay barns, irrigation channels, and other relics of earlier times, thus leading to a (touristic) renaissance of such aged landscape features.[4] Secondly, landscape is often connected with the image of *protection*, in two senses of the word, not only implying the protection of landscape from human intervention in an environmental sense, but also the prevention of harm to human life and infrastructure inflicted upon society by natural disaster. On the one hand, the traditional appearance of the landscape should be preserved in order to further profit from ecosystem services;[5] on the other hand, intensive research activities are carried out in order to control or avert alpine dangers such as rockfall, mudslides, or avalanches occurring in the wake of increasingly common weather extremes (adaptation to climate change, risk management). This discourse is technical and scientific in character.[6] The third major theme is that of *change*. Due to the extreme socioeconomic restructuring throughout the twentieth century, the agricultural landscape has turned into a "post-industrial" landscape. The intensity of those changes in scenery can be made visible through the comparison of photographs.[7] The continuous and rapid change is of public interest, as it is connected to the development of future strategies for the utilization of landscape for energy production, tourism, and other reasons.[8]

---

3   See for example Christoph Hölz, and Walter Hauser, *Weiterbauen am Land: Verlust und Erhalt der bäuerlichen Kulturlandschaft in den Alpen* (Innsbruck: StudienVerlag, 2011).

4   As an example, see Montafoner Museen, *Jahresbericht 2016* (Schruns: 2017), here 106–116, on the preservation of irrigation channels see Tiroler Heimatpflege, "Waal-Erhebungen in Tirol," accessed Dec. 6, 2017, http://www.heimatschutzverein.at/restaurierungen_waal-erhebung-nord-tirol%20.php.

5   The concept of landscape services was introduced to ecologically oriented landscape research in the last decade (see i.e. Olaf Bastian et al., "Landscape services: the concept and its practical relevance," *Landscape Ecology*, 29 (2014): 1436–1479).

6   See e.g. the activities of alpS, accessed Dec. 6, 2017, http://www.alp-s.at/cms/en.

7   See the illustrated book with photo-comparisons by Thomas Defner and Susanne Gurschler, *Zeitblende Tirol: Defner-Fotografien 1925 bis heute* (Innsbruck: Tyrolia, 2017).

8   See for instance the discussions on the state energy provider TIWAG's future strategies and on the expansion of storage power plants in the local media Peter Nindler, "Kaunertal: Tiwag will Verfahren fortsetzen," *Tiroler Tageszeitung* (Dec. 16, 2017), accessed Dec. 17, 2017, http://www.tt.com/politik/landespolitik/13791779-91/kaunertal-tiwag-will-verfahren-fortsetzen.csp.

While the social sciences, ecology, and economic disciplines have (re) addressed landscape issues from various starting points in recent years, the historical sciences—with only very few exceptions[9] regarding Western Austria—clearly lag behind. The role landscape has played in historical research can be pointedly illustrated by the following example: Michael Forcher's book *Tirols Geschichte in Wort und Bild* ("an illustrated history of Tyrol") was first published in 1984.[10] The comprehensive volume dealt with Tyrolean history, from prehistory to the twentieth century, and five revised editions were published through 1999. The book was widely recognized and found broad distribution as the Tyrolean state government recommended the book as an official communal present for all adolescents upon attaining their majority. The sixth edition in 2000 showed a striking novelty as the Innsbruck geographer Franz Fliri (1918–2008) contributed seventy pages on "our landscape history." He presented historical cartographic works and depicted "Tyrolean natural and cultural landscapes" by means of a literary and pictorial "hike through the country and its regions." The historicity of landscapes was brought to public attention eventually, however, via the bypass of geography. This first history of the Tyrolean landscape was therefore dominated by scientific and human geographical influences: besides information on geology, climate, vegetation, landscape use, and natural disasters, cultural-historical issues like human/nature relationships were only marginally considered (apart from a double page on environmental protection), as were relations between landscape and tourism or landscape and the power industry. As a result, Fliri's account cannot be counted among modern environment and landscape histories, which usually tend to place human-environment relations at their core.

Fliri was the leading figure in establishing the discipline of "population geography" at the Innsbruck Institute of Geography. From the late 1960s up until the 1990s, his students wrote many theses on the socio-economic restructuring of rural space in the nineteenth and twentieth centuries and its impact on landscape. This tradition was continued by Fliri's successor

9   As for the more recent professional publications on Western Austrian landscape history see i.e. Michael Kasper, "Kulturlandschaftsentwicklung und gesellschaftlicher Wandel im südlichen Vorarlberg vom 19. bis zum 21. Jahrhundert," Österreich in Geschichte und Literatur 54, no. 4 (2010): 339–356; Erich Tasser et al., eds., *Wir LandschaftMacher: Vom Sein und Werden der Kulturlandschaft in Nord-, Ost- und Südtirol* (Bozen: Athesia, 2012). The first and currently the only environmental history of the Tyrolean capital town Innsbruck was published by Elisabeth Dietrich, see Elisabeth Dietrich, ed., *Stadt im Gebirge: Leben und Umwelt in Innsbruck im 19. Jahrhundert* (Innsbruck: Studienverlag, 1996).
10   Michael Forcher, *Tirols Geschichte in Wort und Bild*, 6th ed. (Innsbruck: Haymon, 2000).

until the mid-2000s.[11] Due to their orientation toward settlement and agriculture history, and the efficacy of parameters such as agriculture and settlement, those geographic-historical studies can profitably be used for a history of landscape.

It is remarkable, however, that in the year 2000 Fliri revived the "hiking" image that had previously been popularized in Tyrol by Hermann Wopfner (1876–1963). During the 1920s and 1930s, the folklorist and historian hiked through vast parts of Tyrol, thus acquiring a certain extent of fame. He documented the landscape, buildings, tools, and the local people in his excellent photographs. They illustrate his ethnological-historical studies, i.e. the well-known *Bergbauernbuch* ("book on Alpine farmers").[12] His documentations—alongside numerous historical picture postcards and the works of other photographers[13]—are a valuable treasure for the study of landscape history. Their existence enables the visualization of changes in landscape through a comparative approach.[14] The method of image comparison has not only proven to be a public attraction, and is therefore widely used in knowledge transfer, but provides manifold starting points for landscape historians.[15]

---

11   Representative for many others: Innsbrucker Geographische Gesellschaft, ed., *Alpine Kulturlandschaft im Wandel. Hugo Penz zum 65. Geburtstag* (Innsbruck: Innsbrucker Geographische Gesellschaft, 2007); Georg Jäger, "Kontinuität und Diskontinuität in der alpinen Kulturlandschaft: Das Problem der Persistenz im ländlichen Raum Tirols anhand ausgewählter Fallbeispiele" (Habilitation thesis, University of Innsbruck, 2003), 643; Maria Schmeiß-Kubat, *Das äussere Silltal: Landschaft, Siedlung, Bevölkerung und Wirtschaft der Gemeinden Igls, Vill, Patsch, Natters, Mutters und Kreith* (Tiroler Wirtschaftsstudien 28) (Innsbruck: Universitätsverlag Wagner 1973). These studies continued the tradition of human-geographical research on Tyrolean valleys since the late 1940s (Egon Zimmermann, "Bevölkerungsgeographische Untersuchungen über das Navis-Tal" (PhD diss., University of Innsbruck, 1949).
12   During his lifetime, Wopfner was only able to publish a fraction of his opus magnum; the major part was published posthumously, see Hermann Wopfner, *Bergbauernbuch, vol. 1: Siedlungs- und Bevölkerungsgeschichte,* (ed. by Nikolaus Grass); idem, *Bäuerliche Kultur und Gemeinwesen, aus dem Nachlass* (ed. by Nikolaus Grass, and Dietrich Thaler); idem, *Wirtschaftliches Leben* (ed. by Nikolaus Grass, and Dietrich Thaler), Schlern-Schriften 296–298; Tiroler Wirtschaftsstudien 47–49 (Innsbruck: Universitätsverlag Wagner, 1995–1997).
13   Among the crowd of professional photographers, Erika and Irmtraud Hubatschek, as well as the Defner family especially stand out. With their cross-generational landscape photographs, they have produced impressive picture comparisons. For regional photograph research see among others the Tirol Archiv Photographie (TAP), accessed Dec. 12, 2017, http://www.tiroler-photoarchiv.eu/index.php/en/.
14   Itinerant photographers have in fact documented every spot on the map; see for example, the collection of postcards in the Tiroler Landesmuseum Ferdinandeum (Innsbruck) or in Marienberg monastery (Burgeis, Südtirol).
15   Tasser et al., eds., *Wir LandschaftMacher:* 26–43.

Landscape and Politics

In the bibliographies of twentieth century Tyrolean historians, several eye-catching titles, hinting at a relevance to landscape history, stand out. In 1922, Hermann Wopfner, for instance, wrote about *Das landschaftliche Bild des Brennerpasses in der Vergangenheit* ("The scenic view of the Brenner Pass in former times").[16] Besides a topographic-historical depiction of the landscape north and south of the Brenner, it becomes quite clear what Wopfner really intended. His paper was less based on a genuine landscape-historical interest, but was rather a studied reaction to the most recent execution of the separation of Tyrol as a political consequence of World War I.

According to Wopfner, the quality of the Brenner Pass as "the natural border between Germany[17] and Italy" had "only been discovered by nineteenth century Italian imperialism, while in fact the Brenner had never functioned as a border between provinces, let alone as a border between states."[18] He further stated that the Brenner region had been "fully Germanized" by the thirteenth century. The fact that Woodrow Wilson's (1856–1924) Fourteen Points (particularly those regarding self-determination) were not applied to Tyrol south of the Brenner led Wopfner to call the American president "the hypocritical Holy Joe of humanity."[19] This view turns Wopfner's landscape-historical survey explaining topographical, agricultural, traffic, and settlement changes in the Brenner region into a testimony for the vindication of German culture in present-day South Tyrol. His viewpoint was supported by a vast majority of scholars at Innsbruck University[20] and remained the prevailing attitude until well into the twentieth century. A historical-geography article on the Brenner published by registrar and historian Otto Stolz (1881–1957) in 1931 took the same line: the Brenner was described as never having been a terminal point historically, but rather the focal point of political space creation; the Brenner border

---

16   Hermann Wopfner, "Das landschaftliche Bild des Brennerpasses in der Vergangenheit," Österreichische Touristen-Zeitung 42, no. 6 (1922): 61–63.
17   The fact that Wopfner used "Germany" instead of "Austria" has to be attributed to his greater-German mentality and the prevalent "unification mood" especially popular in Tyrol and Salzburg at the time. Only because of the Allied protest, Austria was not able to form a union with Germany after World War I. The national referendum in Tyrol on 24 April 1921 showed results of 98.7% in favor of the annexation.
18   Wopfner, "Das landschaftliche Bild des Brennerpasses."
19   Ibid. In German: *"Der scheinheilige Erzpfaffe der Humanität."*
20   In 1918 the academic senate of Innsbruck University published a commemorative study on "The Unity of German-Tyrol" in a relatively high circulation of 2.000 German and both 3.000 English and French editions.

was the goal of an imperialistic Italian state concept.[21] This core statement was embedded in elaborations in studies of landscape, settlement, and traffic history. Stolz's multivolume work on *Die Ausbreitung des Deutschtums in Südtirol im Lichte der Urkunden* ("The expansion of German culture in South Tyrol in the light of its deeds"), published in the early 1930s, adhered to the same political reasoning for revising the history of the Brenner border. Again, the politically motivated study also provides many references to the history of the Tyrolean landscape.

This political landscape discourse was only invented after the division of Tyrol in 1918. Conspicuously, these articles were often published in media provided by the tourism industry. The Tyrolean state tourist office, for example, engaged prominent writers and photographers for "services of cultural advertising."[22] The portrayal and (historical) depiction of the Tyrolean landscape was seen as having a central role in attracting "many new visitors and admirers." It becomes quite clear, however, that whatever contributions these depictions made to landscape history are based on an aged understanding of the German term *Landschaft* ("landscape"). In its original meaning, the term described the political representatives of a territory. In Tyrol, those representatives constituted the territorial assembly that had existed since 1363. In the course of time, the term gained further relevance, describing territories with uniform legal and social standards.[23] Therefore, if the "Tyrolean landscape" was addressed, both actual people and assemblies or spaces of uniform law and governance could be meant. This changed as artists tried to visualize such political landscapes. The semantic content of "landscape" thus shifted from political spaces to the naturalistic presentation methods of the fine arts (landscape painting) and even further to a physical segment of the earth's surface. The conceptual pair—natural versus cultural landscape—was established in the nineteenth century, and around 1900 the historicity of this cultural landscape found recognition. Yet Otto Stolz's 1927 "History of the Landscape" was—besides being a testimony of the "German character" of South Tyrol, as mentioned above—limited to a survey of settlement, legal and political history, as well as selected aspects of economic history.[24]

---

21   Otto Stolz, "Der Brenner: Eine historisch-geographische Betrachtung," in *Tirol: Natur, Kunst, Volk, Leben,* vol. 2, ed. Landesverkehrsamt für Tirol (Innsbruck: Landesverkehrsamt für Tirol, 1931), 35–41.
22   Landesverkehrsamt für Tirol, ed., *Tirol: Natur, Kunst, Volk, Leben,* preface of vol. 2.
23   Exemplary for the older meaning of landscape: Franz von Zimmeter-Treuherz, *Die Fonde, Anstalten und Geschäfte der Tiroler Landschaft, geschichtlich und sachgemäß dargestellt* (Innsbruck: Verlag der Tiroler Landschaft, 1894).
24   Otto Stolz, "Ausserfern: Ein Blick auf die Geschichte der Landschaft," in *Tirol: Natur, Kunst, Volk, Leben,* vol 1. ed. Landesverkehrsamt für Tirol (Innsbruck: Landesverkehrsamt für Tirol 1927), 198–201.

While efforts to establish a "connection between landscape and the people" had already been made in the nineteenth century, being successfully used in the conservative/nationalistic sense,[25] the (re)interpretation of landscape in the time of National Socialism was further intensified. In the ideological formula of blood and soil, blood stood for human beings and soil for the landscape the people inhabited. After the annexation of Austria by the German Reich in March 1938, the "soil" terminology was also adapted to Alpine conditions, constructing a novel relation between Alpine farmers and their surrounding environment. The Nazis went so far as to create the naïve analogy of the Alpine landscape being "big and hard" and "as hard as the nature is the work of the Alpine farmers."[26] It was further deduced that the mountain farmer was "a good, tough soldier." In an economic respect, the Alpine farmers, living on the verge of the permanent settlement threshold, had to earn their poor livelihoods through "boundlessly hard work." The increased demands would create an elite, forming "a source of the best blood for the entire people."[27] Thus the Alpine landscape became a racial selection criterion; it was said to evoke or enforce certain characteristics corresponding to the National Socialist ideals: abundance of children, morale, modesty, tenacity, and militancy. It is not surprising that, after the end of National Socialist rule, attempts to extrapolate certain human characteristics from landscape features were avoided for a long time.

After having been widely discredited through the National Socialist spatial and folkloristic studies, the spatial turn helped to put geographical space back on the conceptual map for the humanities. Two remarkable anthologies on Tyrol have been published recently. Both bear similar subtitles: one dealt with "components of Tyrolean identity," while the other focused on "Tyrol as both a landscape and identity."[28] In the first volume, historical characters, buildings, language, music, and food were identified as especially relevant to Tyrolean identity. Amazingly enough, the landscape or mountains were only assigned a minor role. The second volume, however, chose a different approach, pursuing the question of how landscape as a socially induced spatial category[29] can affect the individual

---

25   See Olaf Kühne, *Distinktion – Macht – Landschaft: Zur sozialen Definition von Landschaft* (Wiesbaden: Springer VS, 2008), 21.

26   Josef Wenter and Simon Moser, "*Das Land in den Bergen: Vom Wehrbauer – zum Gebirgsjäger*" (Innsbruck: Deutscher Alpenverlag, 1942).

27   Institut für Wirtschafts- und Konjunkturforschung, *Monatsberichte des Wiener Institutes für Wirtschafts- und Konjunkturforschung* 13, no. 7 (1939): 204.

28   Thomas Ertl, ed., *Der Ötzi pflückt das Edelweiss: Bausteine Tiroler Identität* (Innsbruck: Tyrolia, 2011); Ulrich Leitner, ed., *Berg & Leute: Tirol als Landschaft und Identität: Schriften zur Politischen Ästhetik I* (Innsbruck: Innsbruck University Press, 2014).

29   Ulrich Leitner, "Einleitung," in *Berg & Leute*, ed. Ulrich Leitner, 20–39, here 20.

and vice versa. The idea of physical space as a social and cultural "product" returned to the humanities, though it was no longer used to explain socioeconomic processes, but rather appreciated as a social construct.[30] Yet another anthology from the viewpoint of cultural studies intensified the new spatial approach in 2017. The authors not only discussed recent landscape theories, but also artistic and literary approaches to the concept of landscape.[31]

In summary, public interest in landscape themes can be observed at present. Numerous illustrated books, comparing old photographs with their contemporary counterparts, meet this public interest in landscape from a historical standpoint. Older historical studies of landscape focused more or less on two aspects: first, the vindication of the country's unity after the division of Tyrol in 1918, and second, the Tyrolean folklore studies of the interwar era in general, and National Socialist folkdom and spatial research in particular.[32] Since then, historians have shown a certain neglect of landscape-related topics, while geographers and later ecologists, sociologists, and economists turned their attention to the Western Austrian Alpine landscape.

Contemporary landscape history on the one hand has to take the existing research literature into account, but, on the other hand, can hardly draw on it. In fact, modern landscape history has to integrate relevant studies from neighboring disciplines and requires thorough bibliographic and archival research in regional libraries and archival holdings. In addition, the application of innovative theoretic and methodical approaches (e.g. transnational history, digital history) seems promising.

Energy History

Energy in the Tyrolean Scholarly Landscape

Issues of energy history have so far been widely neglected in Tyrolean regional historical research. If energy was at all addressed, it was solely

---

30   Ernst Langthaler, "Orte in Beziehung. Mikrogeschichte nach dem Spatial Turn," *Geschichte und Region / Storia e regione* 21 no. 1-2 (2012): 27–42 (here 29).
31   Markus Ender et al., eds., *Landschaftslektüren: Lesarten des Raums von Tirol bis in die Po-Ebene* (Bielefeld: Transcript, 2017).
32   See especially Michael Fahlbusch, Ingo Haar, and Alexander Pinwinkler, eds., *Handbuch der völkischen Wissenschaften: Akteure, Netzwerke, Forschungsprogramme,* 2 vol. (Berlin-Boston: De Gruyter, 2017).

mentioned in connection with other historically relevant topics, such as economic development, traffic, and tourism.[33] Although the standard works of Tyrolean history shed only a little light on the topic, they nevertheless enable us to recognize the outlines of a Tyrolean energy history.

Regional economic and social historical research certainly provide the most fruitful disciplines for energy history. Here, energy plays a more important role than in general Tyrolean historiography and is primarily regarded as a product of technical pioneer work and as an engine of economic growth and progress.[34] Historical studies problematizing energy supply have increasingly been published since the 1980s; only three sample studies will be mentioned here. The economic and social historian Helmut Alexander produced fundamental contributions, especially regarding his critical and highly insightful analysis of the electricity industry development between 1924 and 1994.[35] Josef Nußbaumer's social and economic history of post-war Tyrol also included a detailed study of the precarious situation of energy supply in the first post-war years.[36] Regional electricity production and consumption were the topics of Gabriela Prinoth's doctoral thesis, where again aspects of power shortage were addressed.[37] In addition, company histories and anniversary publications commissioned by individual electric utilities or the present state provider *Tiroler Wasserkraftwerke AG* (TIWAG, Tyrolean Hydro-energy Corporation)

---

33   See for instance: Josef Riedmann, *Das Bundesland Tirol* (1918–1970) (Bozen: Athesia, 1988), 931–936, 1347–1360. In the chapter "Tirol als Bestandteil des nationalsozialistischen deutschen Reiches 1938–1945" two pages are dedicated to the expansion of hydroelectric power (1160–1162). In contrast to this, the energy topic is widely neglected in another Tyrolean standard work, namely Forcher, *Tirols Geschichte in Wort und Bild*.

34   Exemplary, Otto Csikos, "Die Wirtschaftsentwicklung Tirols," in *Geographie und Wirtschaftsentwicklung: Teil I Beispiele aus Österreich*, ed. Leopold Scheidl (Vienna: Ferdinand Hirt Verlag, 1970), 83–116 (here 99–103); Karl Innerebner, "Dr. Ing. h.c. Josef Riehl: Ein Pionier auf dem Gebiete der Verkehrswege und der Energiewirtschaft Tirols (mit einer Tafel)," in *Tiroler Wirtschaft in Vergangenheit und Gegenwart: Festgabe zur 100 - Jahrfeier der Tiroler Handelskammer, vol. I: Beiträge zur Wirtschafts- und Sozialgeschichte Tirols*, eds. Hermann Gerhardinger, and Franz Huter (Innsbruck: Universitätsverlag Wagner, 1951), 353–392.

35   Helmut Alexander, *70 Jahre Tiroler Wasserkraftwerke Aktiengesellschaft* (Innsbruck, 1994).

36   Josef Nussbaumer, *Sozial- und Wirtschaftsgeschichte Tirols 1945–1985: Ausgewählte Aspekte (Tiroler Wirtschaftsstudien 42)* (Innsbruck: Universitätsverlag Wagner, 1992).

37 Gabriela Prinoth, "Die Elektrizitätswirtschaft in Nord- und Osttirol von den Anfängen bis zum Jahre 1938" (PhD diss., University of Innsbruck 1983), 401.

contribute to a Tyrolean energy history.[38] One has to be aware, however, that the construction of hydroelectric plants is positively appraised in these pieces of commissioned work, whereas negative effects are hardly ever broached. We therefore strongly recommend the use of contextualizing sources such as contemporary media reports or the consultation of archival sources. Publications dealing with the Austrian energy industry[39] or the energy history of the Alpine area[40] will enable a detailed evaluation of Tyrolean energy history in a trans-regional context as well as comparisons with other regions.

The almost exclusive concentration on hydroelectricity is characteristic of the existing literature on Tyrolean energy history. Since 2014, with the appointment of Patrick Kupper as professor of social and economic history at Innsbruck University, this topic gained notable popularity

---

38   See for example Paul Attlmayr, *60 Jahre Elektrizitätswerk Innsbruck 1889–1949* (Innsbruck: Universitätsverlag Wagner, 1949); Richard Lipp, *100 Jahre Elektrizitätswerke Reutte 1901–2001: Festschrift* (Reutte: EWR, 2001); Gustav Markt, "Die Wasserkräfte des Ötztals," Österreichische Zeitschrift für Elektrizitätswirtschaft, 3, no. 10 (1950): 313–324; Ludwig Mühlhofer and Carl Reindl, *Das Achensee- Kraftwerk der Tiroler Wasserkraftwerke A.G., Sonderdruck aus Wasserkraft und Wasserwirtschaft, 19/1928* (Munich: Pflaum, 1928); Wolfgang Pircher, *75 Jahre im Dienst der Tiroler Energieversorgung: Die Baugeschichte der TIWAG- Kraftwerke* (Innsbruck: Heimatwerbung Tirol, 1999); Heinz Reisinger, Johannes Wurnitsch, and Hans Neudecker, *50 Jahre TIWAG in Osttirol (1948–1998)* (Innsbruck: TIWAG, 1998); Tiroler Wasserkraftwerke AG, *Die Kraftwerke und Leitungsanlagen der Tiroler Wasserkraftwerke Aktiengesellschaft* (Innsbruck: TIWAG, 1935); idem, *25 Jahre Tiroler Wasserkraftwerke A.G.* (Innsbruck: TIWAG, 1949); idem, *Innkraftwerk Prutz-Imst* (Innsbruck: TIWAG 1954); idem, *Innkraftwerk Imst* (Innsbruck: TIWAG, 1960); Fridolin Zanon, and Tiroler Wasserkraftwerke AG, *Strom für Tirol. Kraftwerksgruppe Sellrain Silz* (Innsbruck: TIWAG, 1982).

39   See for example Oliver Rathkolb et al., eds., *Wasserkraft. Elektrizität. Gesellschaft. Kraftwerksprojekte ab 1880 im Spannungsfeld (Schriftenreihe Forschung in der Verbund AG 104)* (Vienna: Kremayr und Scheriau 2012); Roman Sandgruber, *Strom der Zeit: Das Jahrhundert der Elektrizität* (Linz: Veritas, 1992); Angelika Schoder, Martin Schmid, "Where Technology and Environmentalism Meet: The Remaking of the Austrian Danube for Hydropower," in *Environmentalism in Central and South Eastern Europe: Historical Perspectives,* ed. Hrvoje Petrić, Ivana Žebec Šilj (Lanham: Lexington Books 2017), 3–20; We would also like to refer to contemporary studies, such as Oskar Vas, *Wasserkraft- und Elektrizitätswirtschaft in der Zweiten Republik* (Vienna: Springer, 1956).

40   Marc Landry, "Europe's Battery: The Making of the Alpine Energy Landscape, 1870–1955" (PhD diss., Georgetown University, 2013), 244; idem, "Environmental Consequences of the Peace: The Great War, Dammed Lakes, and Hydraulic History in the Eastern Alps," *Environmental History* 20 (2015): 422–448; Marc Gigase et al., eds., "Energie: Erzeugung, Verbreitung und Nutzung im 19. und 20. Jahrhundert," *Traverse* 3 (2013); Angelika Schoder, "Der Bau des Speicherkraftwerks Wienerbruck: Die Transformation einer Landschaft aus der Sicht der Ingenieure," in *Alpen und industrielles Erbe. Kultur und Erinnerung, 19.–20. Jahrhundert,* ed. Luigi Lorenzetti, Nelly Valsangiacomo (Mendrisio: Academy Press, 2016), 99–124.

among students which resulted in a number of diploma theses.[41] In addition, questions of wood utilization are addressed in studies, primarily dealing with the late nineteenth century. However, both the history of fossil-based energy use as well as the development of mineral oil infrastructures, such as the erection of the Trans-Alpine Oil Line (TAL) running through Eastern Tyrol since 1967,[42] remains largely unaccounted for in the humanities and social sciences.[43] The history of renewable energy

---

41   Recently completed diploma theses include Simon Hämmerle, "Die TIWAG und unsere Illwerke. Ein Vergleich des öffentlichen Diskurses bei Kraftwerksprojekten in Tirol und Vorarlberg im Zeitraum 1954–1969 sowie eine schulische Umsetzung im Rahmen einer Bildung für nachhaltige Entwicklung" (Diploma Thesis, University of Innsbruck, 2017), Stefan Premstaller, "Die lange Geschichte der Wasserkraft im Sarntal bis 1960 mit didaktischer Aufbereitung für den Geschichtsunterricht" (Diploma Thesis, University of Innsbruck, 2017), Florian Mayr, "Die frühe Elektrifizierung und der Ausbau der Wasserkraft in Innsbruck und Tirol zwischen den Jahren 1854 bis 1914: Zeitgenössische Beiträge in den Innsbrucker Nachrichten als Schriftquellen für den Unterricht" (Diploma Thesis, University of Innsbruck, 2018), Lorenz Schuler, "Das Lech-Plansee Projekt von 1927. Ein Beitrag zur Elektrizitätswirtschaft in Tirol samt didaktischer Aufbereitung" (Diploma Thesis, University of Innsbruck, 2018), Christina Wechselberger, Die VERBUND-Kraftwerke im Zillertal. Unter besonderer Berücksichtigung der Talverträge, die zwischen dem Land Tirol und der Tauernkraftwerke AG/ Verbund AHP geschlossen wurden, sowie einer schulischen Umsetzung im Rahmen der Elektrizitätswirtschaft in Tirol im Nationalsozialismus" (Diploma Thesis, University of Innsbruck, 2018). For other projects on energy history in the department see "Research," accessed May 16 2018, https://www.uibk.ac.at/geschichte-ethnologie/institut/wirtschaft-sozial/forschung.html.
42   "Die Transalpine Ölleitung," in *Osttiroler Heimatblätter* 35 no. 11 (1967), 1–8.
43   In Tyrol, fossil-based energy sources like the sparsely occurring charcoal and oil shale were only subject to natural scientific studies. On charcoal: Oskar Schmidegg, "Der geologische Bau der Steinadler Decke mit dem Anthrazitkohlenflöz am Nößlachjoch (Brenner-Gebiet)," *Veröffentlichungen des Tiroler Landesmuseums Ferdinandeum* 26 (1949): 1–19; Oskar Schulz, and Herbert Fuchs, "Kohle in Tirol: Eine historische, kohlenpetrologische und lagerstättliche Betrachtung," *Archiv für Lagerstättenforschung* 13 (1991): 123–213; Fritz Vogt, *Die Nößlacher Kohle: Untersuchungen über den chemischen Charakter des Kohlevorkommens am Nößlacher Joch (Tirol)* (PhD diss., University of Innsbruck 1947), 34. Those studies only marginally address public utilization of charcoal. They all stress that charcoal supplies were of poor quality and bore only minimal economic potential; however, local supplies were nevertheless used in times of energy shortage throughout the twentieth century. On oil shale: Georg Fischer, "Seefeld/Tirol und seine Ölschiefer," *Jahrbuch des Vereins zum Schutze der Alpenpflanzen und –Tiere*, 36 (1971): 143–153; Guido Hradil, "Die Ölschiefer Tirols," *Veröffentlichungen des Tiroler Landesmuseums Ferdinandeum* 26–29 (1946–1949): 25–32; Oil shale is primarily used for medical purposes and is nowadays known as "*Tiroler Steinöl*" ("Tyrolean rock oil") or "*Ichthyol.*" The authors of this essay would like to draw attention to trials made during the 1920s and later during World War II, aiming at producing petrol from oil shale. From a historical perspective, Josef Nussbaumer has discussed local fossil-based energy sources. In his economic and social historical study on post-war Tyrol, the supply of fossil-based energy formed a focal point. (Nussbaumer, *Sozial- und Wirtschaftsgeschichte Tirols*, see especially 62–68, 85.) In addition, contemporary reports on the Tyrolean industry and economy provide several useful references to fossil-based energy utilization, e.g. Anton Roilo, "Energiequellen und Rohstoffe in Tirol," in *Festschrift zur 70-Jahr-Feier der Bundeshandelsakademie Innsbruck*, ed. Bundeshandelsakademie Innsbruck (Innsbruck: 1949), 19–36; Kurt Walde, *Industrie in Tirol* (Innsbruck: Kaufmännische Berufsschule Innsbruck, 1957).

sources like solar energy, ambient heat, and wind power have also not been investigated for Tyrol so far.[44]

The strong emphasis of research on hydroelectricity has to be seen in connection with the specific landscape characteristics of the country. In this regard, the region's glacier-fed, high-gradient watercourses are virtually predestined for hydroelectric exploitation. As suggested by the existing literature, electricity has outweighed fossil-based energy as a focal point on the economic and political agenda ever since the early twentieth century. Therefore, Tyrol turned from a region with varying electrification density, where shortages were likely to occur,[45] to a center for electricity production and transshipment,[46] leaving characteristic marks on landscape and environment. In the following paragraphs, these historical developments will be presented as a history of side effects, visualizing the close relationship between energy and landscape history. A first approach concentrates on the perception of landscape modification and its assessment in the years of the rapid expansion of hydroelectricity exploitation in the inter-war period. A second approach reveals the downsides: on the one hand, the destruction of landscape as an effect of storage power plant construction during the 1930s and 1940s is addressed; on the other hand, issues of forced labor deployed on the construction sites during the National Socialist era are mentioned.

---

44   Renewable energy sources are addressed from a present perspective in Hans Neudecker, and Stephan Oblasser, "Tirol – ein Land voll zukunftsreicher Energien," in *Tirol: Ein Bundesland im Überblick*, ed. Egon Pinzer (Innsbruck: Studienverlag, 2005), 382–391 and in Regula Imhof, "Energiewende Tirol – wir sind alle Akteure," in *Reinmichls Volkskalender für das Jahr 2017*, ed. Hans Augustin (Innsbruck: Tyrolia, 2017), 138–147, also including a critical evaluation of the commercial exploitation of hydroelectric energy.

45   The scarcity is not only attributed to natural circumstances, like the number of streams and lakes available or the seasonal fluctuation of drainage regimes in the alpine area, or the temporary lack of capital, but also to the specific development of the Tyrolean electricity industry Prinoth, "Die Elektrizitätswirtschaft in Nord- und Osttirol," 200–204, 218.

46   In 2104, the TIWAG produced around 6,500 GWh of electric energy, imported around 6,800 GWh and exported 7,100 GWh. The electricity consumption in Tyrol amounted to 5,257 GWh. (Amt der Tiroler Landesregierung – Büro für Energieangelegenheiten, *Tiroler Energiemonitoring 2015. Statusbericht zur Umsetzung der Tiroler Energiestrategie* (Innsbruck, 2016), 107–112.

Electricity Production in a "Picturesque Landscape": Lake Achen (*Achensee*)

In the wake of power shortages during World War I and the following years, many storage power plants were erected.[47] They were regarded a suitable measure to ensure power supply and have become a Tyrolean characteristic since the end of the 1920s. Discussions on the major impacts on landscape and environment accompanying the construction work were controversial. These contested issues shall be depicted on the basis of the history of the planning and construction of the first Tyrolean storage power plant on Lake Achen. The first project plans were published in 1900.[48] The lake, previously used for fishing, shipping, and for tourism purposes, should facilitate the country's energy supply. The pronounced opposition of the lake's owner, the Benedictine monastery Fiecht (*Benediktinerstift Fiecht*), impeded the plans for several years.[49] But the Tyrolean media also did not approve of the destruction of the natural reservoir and painted a bleak picture of heavy losses in tourism, fishing, timber rafting, and shipping. In addition, media outlets denounced the destruction of the "picturesque" landscape and water supply shortages in the surrounding villages,[50] as well as an increased threat of floods.[51] The situation changed in favor of hydroelectric utilization as Lake Achen was finally sold to the City of Innsbruck.[52]

47 The reasons can be found in the irregular, uncontrolled growth of electrification and the rapid expansion of consumer groups (Prinoth, "Die Elektrizitätswirtschaft in Nord- und Osttirol," 116, 137–140).

48 Especially local building contractors, private persons, and the industry, but also interested parties from the public sphere, like the k.k. Railway Division (Bettina Schlorhaufer, "Das Achenseekraftwerk im Spiegel seiner wechselvollen Baugeschichte," in *Siegfried Mazagg: Interpret Der Frühen Moderne in Tirol (Schriftenreihe des Archivs für Baukunst im Adambräu vol. 6)* ed. Bettina Schlorhaufer and Joachim Moroder (Vienna: Springer, 2013), 63–101 (here 63–65)).

49 Mühlhofer and Reindl, *Das Achensee- Kraftwerk*, 1, more detailed in Alexander, *70 Jahre Tiroler Wasserkraftwerke*, 7–8.

50 Due to sealing off of the drainage toward Bavaria and the rerouting of the *Ampelbach* into the lake, water shortage occurred on the Bavarian side. The TIWAG recompensed the affected for their losses in fishing and rafting (Mühlhofer, and Reindl, *Das Achensee- Kraftwerk*, 4–5).

51 Alexander, *70 Jahre Tiroler Wasserkraftwerke Aktiengesellschaft*, 6; Prinoth, "Die Elektrizitätswirtschaft in Nord- und Osttirol," 265.

52 The Tyrolean state government was originally also interested in purchasing Lake Achen, however, they foundered on a majority in the state parliament. At the same time, the state parliament passed a law that should make private waters available for public usage—if necessary, even by forced land alienation. The Fiecht monastery had no choice but to sell the lake to the City of Innsbruck for a small sum of money (Alexander, *70 Jahre Tiroler Wasserkraftwerke Aktiengesellschaft*, 9–10). See also Richard Hufschmied, "'Weißes Gold' in (Deutsch-) Österreich - Kontinuität und Wandel mit dem Epochenjahr 1918," in *Wasserkraft. Elektrizität. Gesellschaft*, eds. Oliver Rathkolb et al., 84–158 (here 117–122).

With the extensive natural reservoir, the new owners wanted to expand their precarious electricity supply.[53] However, the realization of the power plant project was thwarted by a massive shortage of capital. Only after the *Tiroler Wasserkraft AG* (TIWAG) had been founded as a finance company in 1924, could the construction work be started.[54] In 1927, the power plant went into operation, and in 1929 the full-scale expansion was completed.[55] The bulk of electricity was exported to Southern Germany. Therefore, the launch of the Lake Achen power plant can be seen as the starting point of Tyrolean export-oriented power industry.[56] The preservation of landscape beauty, closely interlinked with the lake's touristic exploitation, was considered a crucial factor throughout the planning process. The following measures aimed at protecting the pristine scenery: contrary to the plants at Lake Walchen (*Walchensee*) or Cardano near Bolzano, the pressure pipes between the surge tank and the powerhouse were subsurface and therefore invisible to the eye.[57] During the peak tourist season, between 1 July and 15 September, Lake Achen would regain its former appearance. The water level was to be neither significantly raised nor lowered, in order to preserve the original shoreline.

Otto Stolz, one of the most prolific and versatile Tyrolean historians, who gave history to various aspects of the natural environment, also contributed to energy history, connecting the topic of energy production with landscape-related study. In his depiction of Tyrolean waters, published in 1936,[58] he pointed to the scenic quality of Lake Achen. As a symbol for the Alpine beauty, it inspired numerous poems and novellas. According to Stolz, the construction of the Lake Achen plant profoundly affected the landscape, despite all the preservation measures taken.[59] In winter, the lake was completely drained to facilitate electricity production. Whenever the

---

53   Attlmayr, *60 Jahre Elektrizitätswerk Innsbruck*, 22.
54   Mühlhofer, and Reindl, *Das Achensee- Kraftwerk*, 2.
55   Tiroler Wasserkraftwerke AG, *Die Kraftwerke und Leitungsanlagen*, 2.
56   Alexander, *70 Jahre Tiroler Wasserkraftwerke Aktiengesellschaft*, 19. Prinoth, "Die Elektrizitätswirtschaft in Nord- und Osttirol," 312–313, "Streiflichter zur Elektrizitätswirtschaft (nach versch. Veröffentlichungen des Wasserkraft- und Elektrizitätswirtschaftsamtes W.E.W.A." in *Die Elektrifizierung Österreichs - Austria Electrified: Zweite Auflage der unter Mitwirkung des Österreichischen Wasserkraft- und Elektrizitätswirtschaftsamtes im Jahre 1925 veröffentlichten Broschüre zur Zweiten Weltkraftkonferenz* (Vienna: Wirtschaftszeitungs-Verlag, 1930) 5–8 (here 6).
57   Schlorhaufer, *Das Achenseekraftwerk im Spiegel seiner wechselvollen Baugeschichte*, 66.
58   Otto Stolz, *Geschichtskunde der Gewässer Tirols (Schlern-Schriften 32)* (Innsbruck: Wagner, 1936).
59   Ibid., 186–192. See also Siegfried Huber, "Die Elektrizitätswerke Nordtirols und Vorarlbergs, ihre Entwicklung, gegenwärtige Lage und Zukunftsmöglichkeiten" (PhD diss., University of Innsbruck, 1948), 34.

snow-melting period would be delayed, it would take a long time for the lake to reach its normal water level. The picture presented to the beholder was far from attractive.[60] Tyrolean newspapers reported extensively on the "landscape damage" and the harm inflicted upon fish stocks. Benefits to tourism, however, were unmentioned. Due to the storage, the water temperature had risen from thirteen degrees Celsius to between eighteen and twenty degrees during the summer months, increasing its popularity as a bathing lake.[61] The lake's utilization for electricity generation modified not only the scenery but also the natural water system in the catchment area.[62]

It is characteristic for the inter-war period that landscape preservation was addressed for purely economic reasons. The tourism branch, actively promoting the distinctive Tyrolean landscape, was a driving factor in this respect. Especially in the years of economic hardship after World War I, unused waters were indeed seen as "a waste of money" as their maintenance, melioration, and the construction of flood protection facilities was expensive. Through their utilization for energy generation, the waters eventually brought "a stream of gold to the country." In addition, the [electrified, A/N] "rail-, tram- and ropeways would even turn the few places remaining unexploited in the country into something valuable." Electricity could help to industrialize Tyrol "without losing its charm due to smoking chimneys."[63]

The utilization of landscape for electricity production, then, should contribute to the economic development of the country without hampering tourism, which had been a vital source of income since the turn of the century. The impact of electrification on the landscape and ecosystems was accepted as long as money could be made. Apart from a few exceptions,[64] the ecological impact of hydroelectric power and the establishment of

---

60 Alexander, *70 Jahre Tiroler Wasserkraftwerke Aktiengesellschaft*, 19.
61 Stolz, *Geschichtskunde der Gewässer Tirols*, 192.
62 Originally, the lake drained towards the north, into the Ache (river) and into the river Isar. Those drainages were artificially blocked and rerouted to the south towards the river Inn. In order to utilize the natural alpine reservoir for electricity production, the water was led down into the valley via pipes. (Mühlhofer, and Reindl, *Das Achensee- Kraftwerk*, 2–4).
63 Karl Polaczek, *Keine Illusionen! Betrachtungen über die Zukunft der Wasserkraft Tirols* (Innsbruck: Kinderfreund Anstalt, 1919), 4. According to Polaczek, this was the prevailing public attitude. He spoke out against the expansion of hydroelectric plants from a clearly technical perspective. He even called for an efficiency audit for newly erected plants, as he thought that Tyrol would not have enough demand for all the electricity produced (ibid., 10–11).
64 We would like to mention the lawyer, biologist, and geographer, botanist, and ornithologist enthusiast Kurt Walde as exemplary, working as a teacher at a higher school. At the end of the 1960s, he published an inventory of Tyrolean industry also including a critical perspective on the ecological effects of the hydroelectric plant in Kirchbichl (Walde, *Industrie in Tirol*, 88–90).

environmental protection criteria were not discussed before the 1980s.[65] Since then, however, also publications originating from the power industry have attended to the issue. While the conflict potential between preservation and environmental protection on the one hand, and the electricity industry on the other, has been thoroughly investigated for the border rivers between Austria and Bavaria,[66] the topic has been widely neglected for Tyrol.

The Dark Sides of Electricity Production: Forced Labor, Loss of Landscape and Home

When the German Reich finally annexed Austria in 1938, it had already been interested in the Western Austrian electricity industry for some time. The *Alpen Elektrowerke AG* (AEW,Alpine Electricity Plant Corporation), a subsidiary company of the *Vereinigte Industrieunternehmung Aktiengesellschaft* (VIAG, Corporation of United Industries) took responsibility for the erection of power plants in the Gau Tyrol-Vorarlberg as well as the construction of power transmission lines for electricity export to Germany.[67] Forced labor contributed to the construction and expansion of many power plants in the Ostmark during the National Socialist era.[68] In Tyrol, for instance, the Inn power plant near Kirchbichl, including flood protection facilities, the Gerlos power plant and the Stillup-Bösdornau plant in the Ziller Valley, were all built with forced labor. Although forced labor within the electricity industry was first addressed by contemporary history during the 1990s, the topic has still not

---

65   Herbert Gstöhl, *Umweltbelastungen durch Wasserkraftwerke in Österreich* (Innsbruck, 1984); Reisinger, Wurnitsch, and Neudecker, *50 Jahre TIWAG in Osttirol*; Zanon, and Tiroler Wasserkraftwerke AG *Strom für Tirol.*
66   Ute Hasenöhrl, "'Weiße Kohle' oder 'Ausbeutung der Natur?' Konflikte um die Nutzung der Wasserkräfte im (Vor-) Alpenraum am Beispiel bayerisch-österreichischer Grenzflüsse," *Bohemia* 54 (2014): 119–141.
67   Prinoth, "Die Elektrizitätswirtschaft in Nord- und Osttirol," 324. The tradition of energy exports started in the 1920s and was increased in those times. In this respect, the National Socialist era does not constitute discontinuity for the Tyrolean electricity industry, but a further consolidation of established structures Horst Schreiber, *Wirtschafts- und Sozialgeschichte der Nazizeit in Tirol* (Innsbruck: Studienverlag, 1994), 67–71.
68   On Vorarlberg: Harald Walser, *Bombengeschäfte: Vorarlbergs Wirtschaft in der NS-Zeit* (Bregenz: Vorarlberger Autoren-Gesellschaft, 1989), 76–93; on Austria: Oliver Rathkolb and Florian Freund, eds., *NS-Zwangsarbeit in der Elektrizitätswirtschaft der "Ostmark" 1938–1945*, 2 ed. (Vienna: Böhlau, 2014).

been extensively investigated.[69] In 2017, the Tyrolean government installed a historical commission aiming at an analysis of the joint history of the electricity industry and forced labor during the National Socialist era, based on the archival holdings of the TIWAG.[70]

Resettlement campaigns, especially in connection with the erection of large reservoirs, constitute another downside of electricity production. This is also true for Tyrol. Plans for the expansion of hydropower on the Inn and its right-hand side tributaries from the Swiss border to the city of Innsbruck existed since the 1920s.[71] A series of run-of-river as well as storage plants ensured, ideally, a year-round, even electricity production and especially facilitate export to the German consumption areas. Besides the creation of jobs in power plant construction, the export revenues were also thought to promote the Austrian national economy. The projected expansion also raised hopes for improved flood protection. According to a geological examination dedicated to identifying possible locations of storage and run-of-river plants, the rivers and streams in the Ötztal Alps with their "monumental ice reservoirs" held an extremely high potential for electricity generation. However, the Ötztal lacked a natural reservoir comparable to the facilities at Lake Achen. Therefore, an artificial reservoir was to be constructed on

69 Alexander, *70 Jahre Tiroler Wasserkraftwerke Aktiengesellschaft*, 27; Schreiber, *Wirtschafts- und Sozialgeschichte der Nazizeit*, 80; The TIWAG ignored this inconvenient part of its history for a long time. The 1949 jubilee book, published on the twenty-fifth anniversary of its founding, focused on a presentation of achievements in plant and pipeline construction and dedicated a special chapter to their employees. They showed how they cared for their well-being, either through the provision of housing, the obligatory commitment to pension payments to long-term employees or through a collective occupational accident insurance, financial support in times of need, and, last but not least, cheap energy fares. Forced laborers, who were only temporarily used during the construction phase and had to live under miserable circumstances, were not mentioned at all. (Tiroler Wasserkraftwerke AG, *25 Jahre Tiroler Wasserkraftwerke A.G.*, 38–40). In later company publications forced labor, which had laid the foundation for the success of the later state holding TIWAG was also never mentioned

70 ORF, "Experten erforschen NS-Zwangsarbeit in Haiming," (July, 31 2017), accessed Dec. 11, 2017, http://tirol.orf.at/news/stories/2857880/. The reason was the sale of a property to a Tyrolean bacon producer that had once been purchased by the TIWAG's predecessor company under dubious circumstances. Thus, the property went to the Tyrolean State Provider after World War II. On the property was a camp for forced laborers who contributed to the construction of power plants. The descendants of former agricultural owners demanded the restitution of the properties (ORF, "Bauern fordern von TIWAG Grundstücke zurück," (March 14, 2017), accessed Dec. 11, 2017, http://tirol.orf.at/news/stories/2830949/).

71 Markt, "Die Wasserkräfte des Ötztals," 1; Prinoth, "Die Elektrizitätswirtschaft in Nord- und Osttirol," 344.

suitable valley floors. One possible location was the Längenfeld basin;[72] however, plans to resettle around 2,000 people led to widespread public protest in 1940.[73] Even before the area had been subjected to thorough geological surveys, the "west Tyrolean power plant corporation" had already purchased swappable plots of land at the entrance to the Ötztal valley and in the Tyrolean Lower Inn Valley (*Unterinntal*).[74] One of the experts involved was the prominent Tyrolean geologist Raimund von Klebelsberg (1886–1967). He clearly objected to the suitability of the Längenfeld basin, as the danger of leakage was high in his opinion. According to Klebelsberg, the resettlement of the local population and the irreversible loss of cultivated area was by no means justifiable.[75]

However, forced resettlement in connection with electricity production was regarded as an appropriate means by authoritarian regimes. Even after the end of World War II, the population of a village near Lake Achen was almost forced to give way to an artificial storage, planned as an expansion of the Lake Achen plant. In this case, public protest against resettlement and for compensation with property elsewhere was successful.[76] The situation was more dramatic in South Tyrol, however; the area had been assigned to Italy in 1918 and had been under fascist rule since 1925. Especially since the 1930s, several large power stations were erected, producing the electricity supply for the northern Italian industrial centers.[77] One event, though not from fascist times, has left a special imprint on South Tyrolean collective memory: the flooding of Curon Venosta, a village in the tri-junction between Italy, Switzerland, and Austria. The local population had to

---

72   Friedrich Leitlich, "Die Vereinigte Westtiroler Kraftwerke," in *Die Elektrifizierung Österreichs – Austria Electrified*, 112–116 (here 116); Max Pernt, "Die Westtiroler Kraftwerke," in *Die Elektrifizierung Österreichs – Austria Electrified*, 107–111 (here 107).

73   Alexander, *70 Jahre Tiroler Wasserkraftwerke Aktiengesellschaft*, 26; Prinoth, "Die Elektrizitätswirtschaft in Nord- und Osttirol," 344–346.

74   Besides the *Alpenelektrowerke* (AEW) and the RWE the Gau Tyrol-Vorarlberg also held shares in the Westtiroler Kraftwerke AG (Alexander, *70 Jahre Tiroler Wasserkraftwerke Aktiengesellschaft*, 26).

75   Raimund von Klebelsberg, "Das Becken von Längenfeld im Ötztal: Ein Beispiel für Geologie und Kraftwerkplanung (mit einer Kartenskizze und einem Profil)," in *Tiroler Wirtschaft in Vergangenheit und Gegenwart* eds. Gerhardinger and Huter, 399–422.

76   Alexander, *70 Jahre Tiroler Wasserkraftwerke Aktiengesellschaft*, 33–34.

77   Helmut Alexander, "Schwarzer Rauch und weißes Gold: Importindustrie und Wasserkraft," in *Faschistenbeil und Hakenkreuz. 1920–1939 (Das 20. Jahrhundert in Südtirol, vol. 2)* ed. Helmut Alexander, and Gottfried Solderer (Bozen: Raetia, 2000); Vittfrida Mitterer, ed., *Zeitzeichen der Technik. Technische Kulturgüter Südtirols* (Bozen: Raetia, 1993); Vittfrida Mitterer, ed., *Megawatt & Widerstand: Die Ära der Groß-Kraftwerke in Südtirol; die Technik-Kathedrale von Kardaun, das Eisack-Kraftwerk im Spannungsfeld von Zeitgeschichte und Technikkultur; historische Fotodokumente (1925–1965) der Fotografenfamilie Pedrotti* (Bozen: Athesia, 2005).

give way to a storage lake developed through the merging of two natural lakes in 1950 on behalf of the Italian company Montecatini. One hundred and twenty agricultural families lost their means of existence as well as their identity, which had been closely related to the rural community of their native village. The compensation payments were exceptionally low, thus additionally hampering the process of rebuilding secure existences.[78] Montecatini had made a deal with the Swiss electricity industry to provide cheap electricity for a decade in exchange for the funding of certain parts of the reservoir.[79] The Swiss Heritage Society was concerned about the negative effects those forced resettlement measures could have on the "good reputation of Switzerland" and requested that the Swiss electricity industry exert its influence as investors to compensate the dispossessed following the Swiss standards of practice. The Swiss should not share responsibility for the "electricity produced from the Reschen waters, which were certainly accursed by the dislodged farmers."[80] Yet, the objections proved unsuccessful, and the area was finally flooded. Today, mass tourism has come to the region, especially renowned for its scenic beauty around the lake. This also includes the romantic church tower protruding above the water level, a remnant of submerged village life.[81] Pictures of the former buildings and their inhabitants are presented in the *Alt-Graun Museum*, showing interested visitors what the area once looked like.[82]

Conclusion

Questions of how to write a joint history of landscape and energy using an environmental history perspective dominated this essay.[83] How, and to

---

78   Brigitte Maria Pircher, "Der Reschen-Stausee von seinen Anfängen bis heute" (MA thesis, University of Innsbruck, 2003), 155.

79   The reason for this arrangement was the rejection of resettlement by the inhabitants of Splügen and Medels (Canton Graubünden) due to the planned construction of the Rheinwald plant. Switzerland had to substitute missing winter electricity, what could be reached through electricity import from the Italian Reschen area. (Ernst Laur, "Eine Bergbauerntragödie jenseits der Landesgrenze," *Heimatschutz* 44, no. 4 (1949): 101–118)

80   Ernst Laur, "Eine Bergbauerntragödie jenseits der Landesgrenze,"114.

81   Associazione turistica Passo Resia, "The curch tower in the lake," accessed Oct. 16, 2017, https://www.vinschgau.net/en/resia-pass/culture-arts/places-of-interest/tower-in-the-lake.html.

82   Associazione turistica Passo Resia, The Museum of Old Curon, accessed Oct. 16, 2017 https://www.vinschgau.net/en/resia-pass/culture-arts/places-of-interest/the-museum-of-old-curon.html.

83   The ongoing project from which this essay originates, aims at investigating the joint history of energy and landscape (TELg: Towards a history of energy and landscape in Tyrol, UNI-0404-2137).

what extent, can the contributions available for Tyrol be tied together using such an approach? What both energy and landscape have in common is the relationship between (local) communities and their natural environment. The characteristic Tyrolean Alpine landscape forms the basis for the production of hydroelectricity, but it is also subject to change—however, these changes are often related to problems of sustainability. In order for a historical assessment to succeed, a broad perspective has to be applied. Within the historical disciplines, several links can be found: between agricultural history, climate history, tourism history, history of technology, traffic history, economic and business history, but also links to contemporary historical research are evident. Topics like the agricultural history of National Socialism or the history of power plant projects seem highly compatible.[84] Besides, ethnological, ecological, sociological, and management approaches also have to be considered in order to accomplish a comprehensive history of energy and landscape in the twentieth century. Although the existing literature provides several references, further work with archival sources is imperative.

Due to the manifold characteristics and functions of landscape, an interdisciplinary approach seems fruitful. Proof of a successful cooperation between disciplines and their respective methods can be given on the basis of a sample project,[85] located at the intersection of energy and landscape history, sociology and ecology. It scrutinizes forest use as a central resource up until the mid-twentieth century. Forests not only supplied societies with firewood and timber for various purposes (building, cooking, heating), but their floors were also used for pasture or hunting purposes. Forests provided bedding material as well as berries and mushrooms. In addition, forest property formed a sort of "penny bank" for farmers in times of need. Ever since the beginning of the mining boom in the fifteenth century, wood use in

---

84 During the National Socialist era, environmental and landscape protection were ideologically elevated, manifesting itself in the planning of power plants. Harald Walser stated: "While prisoners of war and foreign laborers at the Ill plant construction had to endure severe conditions, wounds inflicted upon nature were "treated" in the middle the war." The Innsbruck University professor Helmut Gams generated "ideas for the greening of the Vermunt-Silvretta-plant" in September 1942. (Walser, *Bombengeschäfte*, 93) See also Helmut Maier, "'Unter Wasser und unter die Erde.' Die süddeutschen und alpinen Wasserkraftprojekte des Rheinisch-Westfälischen Elektrizitätswerks (RWE) und der Natur- und Landschaftschutz während des 'Dritten Reiches'" in *Die Veränderung der Kulturlandschaft, Nutzungen-Sichtweisen-Planungen*, eds. Günther Bayer and Thorsten Meyer (Münster: Waxmann, 2003), 139–157.
85 Project KuLaWi (Kultur.Land.(Wirt)schaft), accessed May 16, 2018, http://kulawi. eurac.edu/index_de.html.

Tyrol had always been discursively characterized by shortages.[86] This lasted until the second half of the twentieth century, when firewood was largely replaced by other sources of energy. After World War II, the Tyrolean firewood demand had still amounted to sixty-four percent of the total loggings; however, these rates were quickly and dramatically reduced, beginning in the 1950s.[87] While its relevance as a source of energy decreased, other forms of utilization gained importance, and forests remained a dominant landscape factor. Recreational as well as protective functions have now taken the lead. The metamorphosis from a rare commodity to a surplus product in combination with modern, sustainable forestry methods facilitated the commercial utilization of wood.

Due to its vital importance as a resource in former times, literature on forest history is quite dense and gives a comprehensive view of the administrative, statistical, and legal issues prior to 1900.[88] Along with the decreasing everyday relevance of forests, historical interest is also minimized. Not a single study dedicated to a specific history of Tyrolean or Vorarlberg forests exists for the twentieth century.[89] Yet Norbert Weigl published a survey on twentieth century Austrian forest history;[90] besides traditional economic historical and forestry related topics, Weigl also took innovative approaches like ecosystem services or rural conservation into account.

Nevertheless, important questions remain unanswered, as the following example illustrates: since the early nineteenth century, the forested area has increased in Austria. Although forest expansion rates in Western Austria lie significantly below the Austrian average, due to the central Alpine

---

86   See Klaus Brandstätter and Gerhard Siegl, "Waldnutzungskonflikte und nachhaltige Waldbewirtschaftung in Tirol vom Mittelalter bis ins 21. Jahrhundert," *Histoire des Alpes – Storia delle Alpi – Geschichte der Alpen,* 19 (2014): 145–162.
87   Franz Aubele, *Wirtschaftskunde Nord- und Osttirols (Tiroler Wirtschaftsstudien 5)* (Innsbruck: Wagner, 1957), 45.
88   For example Heinrich Oberrauch, *Tirols Wald und Waidwerk: Ein Beitrag zur Forst- und Jagdgeschichte (Schlern-Schriften 88)* (Innsbruck: Wagner, 1952) or *Tiroler Waldwirtschaft. Festschrift zum 100-jährigen Bestehen des Reichsforstgesetzes in Tirol (Schlern-Schriften 125)* (Innsbruck: Wagner, 1954).
89   Wolfgang Meixner, and Gerhard Siegl touched upon forest history in their agricultural-historical work on the twentieth century, see Wolfgang Meixner, and Gerhard Siegl, "Bergbauern im Tourismusland: Agrargeschichte Tirols im 20. Jahrhundert," in *Geschichte der österreichischen Land- und Forstwirtschaft im 20. Jahrhundert, vol. 2: Regionen-Betriebe-Menschen,* ed. Ernst Bruckmüller, Ernst Hanisch, and Roman Sandgruber (Vienna: Ueberreuter, 2003), 73–187 (here 99–105).
90   Norbert Weigl, "Die österreichische Forstwirtschaft im 20. Jahrhundert – Von der Holzproduktion über die Mehrzweckforstwirtschaft zum Ökosystemmanagement," in *Geschichte der österreichischen Land- und Forstwirtschaft im 20. Jahrhundert, vol 1: Politik-Gesellschaft-Wirtschaft,* ed. Ernst Bruckmüller et al. (Vienna: Ueberreuter, 2002), 593–740.

topography,[91] an increase in tree biomass has nonetheless been recorded. What began as a moderate growth during the nineteenth century has rapidly increased since the 1950s.[92] These scientific findings call for scrutiny and contextualization of the data by (environmental) historians. How can forest areas and biomass grow in times of increased population growth and before the replacement of wood by other energy sources? While the corresponding increase can be easily comprehended after 1950, it is hard to find explanations for the phenomenon before this time. According to the present state of research, the contrary seems to be more likely: historical sources indicate that forests were subject to heavy exploitation and even over-exploitation,[93] due to logging and agricultural usage up until the post-war era. It is hard to imagine and seems even paradoxical that forest areas and tree biomass should measurably increase in this time. A profound critique of historical sources often used by natural scientists without reservations could probably bring light to the case: what data was used for the calculation? How and for what purpose was it gathered by contemporaries? Is the data based on measures, estimations, projections, full-scale, or only sample collections? What method was applied for the evaluation of data? What do the parameters "forest area" and "tree biomass" in fact reveal about the real existence of wood as a resource? What local differences were taken into account? Such heuristic, methodical, and content-related questions could probably be answered in an interdisciplinary approach. However, until cooperation is realized, the open contradiction between the increase in forest area and tree biomass versus a growing demand for firewood and timber caused by population growth remains unanswered. This question, together with the research gaps mentioned above, remain desiderata for an environmental history of Western Austria.

These gaps can only be closed by intensive archival research, methodical diversity, and a critical approach to twentieth century literary output, thus returning to the starting point of our essay. Besides historical studies, we encourage the integration of other disciplines and want to stress the

---

91   Fridolin Krausmann, "Forest Transition in Österreich: Eine sozialökologische Annäherung," *Mitteilungen der Österreichischen Geographischen Gesellschaft* 148 (2006), 75–91 (here 79, 87).
92   Monika Patek, "Waldentwicklung und Biomassenveränderung in Neustift im Stubaital in Tirol seit 1834" (MA thesis, University of Vienna, 2013), 48.
93   Klaus Brandstätter, Georg Neuhauser, and Bettina Anzinger, "Waldnutzung und Waldentwicklung in der Grafschaft Tirol im Spätmittelalter und der Frühen Neuzeit," in *Bergauf Bergab. 10.000 Jahre Bergbau in den Ostalpen*, eds. Thomas Stöllner and Klaus Öggl (Bochum: VML Verlag Marie Leidorf, 2015), 547–552; Klaus Brandstätter, and Gerhard Siegl, "Waldnutzungskonflikte und nachhaltige Waldbewirtschaftung in Tirol vom Mittelalter bis ins 21. Jahrhundert," 145–162.

importance of gray literature (i.e. business reports), commemorative or anniversary books, and journalistic contributions in newspapers and magazines. Of special interest are also source-rich studies (often, but not always, authored by historians) on other topics, which can be real data repositories for environmental historical approaches. Those content-rich "quarries," such as Otto Stolz's book on the Tyrolean waters, have so far not been used for environmental historical studies in Western Austria. The accumulation of knowledge on conflicting historical utilization interests, concerning, for instance, agriculture, tourism, or energy production, could finally provide present or future stakeholders with suitable conflict prevention strategies.

Port of Vienna:
Infrastructures and War on the Danube River in Vienna, 1850–1950

Ortrun Veichtlbauer

The world is obviously a place where there is a logic to the spatial distribution of things as well as their interactions. Infrastructures, being one element of the spatial order, are influenced by physical space and political power as well as having an influence on them. Infrastructure conditions are a main ingredient in any economic, technological, and social development. As can be seen in history, infrastructure systems integrated markets, allowed greater division of labor, accelerated information flows, and facilitated the enforcement of political power. It is therefore no coincidence that the Western "industrial revolution" was accompanied by an "infrastructure revolution."

Although standard narratives of European history between 1850 and 1950 focus on the topic of war and rupture, the cross-border linking, and in some cases the disruption of, transnational infrastructures in connection with wars is still rarely discussed, despite their long-lasting environmental impact.[1] In terms of lastingness and path dependence, war-driven material infrastructures not only enabled their own survival across multiple regimes, but also, in certain aspects, the survival of the different power regimes they served. Material representations not only speak to material developments and concerns of an industrializing age, when state engineering became a model of planned efficiency throughout the (Western) world. The tension around humanity's power to control rivers as water infrastructures within the limits asserted by their complex "naturalness" has always been a key feature of the so-called Anthropocene.[2] Especially during "high modernism," as defined by James Scott,[3] characterized by an overwhelming pace

---

1 Influential work done on this topic by: Dirk van Laak, "Technological Infrastructure: Concepts and Consequences," *ICON Journal of the International Committee for the History of Technology* no. 10 (2004): 53–64; Per Högselius, Arne Kaijser and Erik Van der Vleuten, *Europe's Infrastructure Transition: Economy, War, Nature* (New York: Palgrave Macmillan, 2016).

2 Stephanie C. Kane, "Engineering an Island City-State: A 3D Ethnographic Comparison of the Singapore River and Orchard Road," in *Rivers of the Anthropocene*, ed. Jason M. Kelly et al. (University of California Berkeley Press, 2017), 135–149 (here 138).

3 James Scott, *Seeing like a State: How Certain Schemes to Improve the Human Condition Have Failed* (New Haven: Yale University Press, 1999).

of life and "an awful moment of transition" (Alfred Lord Tennyson),[4] the taming of a river into a lifeline was a project for the ages. Nevertheless, rivers—waterways—transformed infrastructurally are a "natural" monopoly in the true sense of the word: the majority of waterways are formed by river courses, and their primary function not only depends on their complex dynamics as hybrid systems, but also, for example, on aspects of seasonality, in which the "indomitable element" usually mocks human power.[5]

War along the banks of the river Danube has defaced European history from medieval times into our own. These wars have been imperial, dynastic, national, and global; they were followed by the Cold War, and finally an ethnic war in the 1990s. Only after Austria's defeat by Prussia at Königgrätz-Sadowa in 1866 and the failure of her plans for hegemony in the west, Austria oriented herself toward the southeast and the Danube. The valley of the Danube became the common center of government, communication, and trade. The whole Danube mission was in some measure a "makeshift ideology," arising from policy failures in Germany.[6] The Habsburg Empire was the first Danubian power to realize the economic potential of the flowing river as a means of imperial communication.[7] The Danube waterway, with its ports—centrally planned "transport nodes"— became the infrastructure lifeline system of the Habsburg Empire for centuries and indeed almost performed the function of a lifeline toward the end of their reign.[8] Canalizing "Europe's messenger" by deepening its channels, by embanking its shores, and by reducing or suppressing altogether its seasonal rise, fall, and overflow was usually justified in terms of improvement, convenience, and progress—three of the main forces of the transforming nineteenth century. The connection between the civil *conquest of nature* and any culturally imperialistic connotation was not as explicit as it was in the later National Socialist war period, when waterways, characterized as nauseating, were associated with inferior race—but it is not to be doubted that some sort of baseline continuity existed among the Habsburg

---

4   Hallam Tennyson, *Alfred Lord Tennyson: A Memoir*, 2 vols. (London: Macmillan, 1897), II: 337.
5   When Napoleon massed his army on the Lobau at the time of the battle of Aspern-Essling in May 1809, he affected to ascribe his defeat to the great swelling of the river, which he styled "*général* Danube."
6   Claudio Magris, *Danube* (London: Collins Harvill, 1989), 30.
7   Neal Ascherson, "Danube: Europe's Messenger," in *Danube: River of Life*, ed. Neal Ascherson, Sarah Hobson (Athens: Religion, Science and the Environment 2002), 1–9 (here 2).
8   Heinrich Montzka, "Die Donau: Ihr Stromlauf als dominierende Wasserader und Völkerstraße der Monarchie," in *Mein Österreich, mein Heimatland: Illustrierte Volks- und Vaterlandskunde des Österreichischen Kaiserstaates*, 2 vols. ed. Siegmund Schneider, Benno Immendörffer (Vienna: Verlag für Vaterländische Literatur, 1915), I, 97–105.

Monarchy's technocratic and cultural missions in southeast Europe and later imperialistic expansions.[9]

How the changing physical, technological, and social landscape of Europe would affect any future war was an issue that had concerned intellectuals, politicians, and legal experts across the continent in the decades before the beginning of the First World War, especially after the Franco-Prussian War of 1870–1871 and the starting of new methods of warfare.[10] After this war and in the following twentieth century, the rather pragmatic and technical infrastructure objectives established in the nineteenth century for the River Danube area were not replaced by radically new ones, but adapted to the changed landscape and power relations. During "high modernism," the Danube was the focus of repeated battles between developers and conservationists, the latter steadily losing ground.

The transformation of the Viennese river wetlands may be seen also as a consequence of warfare in the last two centuries. Particularly military usage, types of warfare, and above all, relationships between the manner of warfare and the availability of infrastructure and material resources for the combatant states played a significant role in terms of this spatial transformation. A comprehensive re-naturalization of war not only corresponded to the modern war's spirit of far-reaching territorial and economic ambitions; it also found its reflection in the form and degree to which wars penetrated the physical realms of a landscape.

Vienna, the Danube, and its Ports in the Long-Transforming Nineteenth Century

Before the monumental European project of the "Great Viennese Danube Regulation" took place, the river at this section, characterized by a dynamic hydrology and high gravel transport, split after passing through the *Wiener Pforte*[11] into countless smaller and larger branches to create riverine islands and alluvial zones, among these the Lobau island. A bird's-eye view from the height of the forested hills of the Vienna woods on the city's fringe would have revealed an ever-changing flux of tangled rivers and abandoned channels, "gliding across the plain across which the eye gazes, almost

---

9   See for example, Ortrun Veichtlbauer, *Zwischen Kolonie und Provinz: Herrschaft und Planung in der Kameralprovinz Temeswarer Banat im 18. Jahrhundert* (Vienna: Social Ecology Working Paper 167, 2016).

10 Modris Eksteins, *Rites of Spring: The Great War and the Birth of the Modern Age* (Boston: Houghton Mifflin, 1989), 157.

11 *Wiener Pforte* = a gap between the Bisamberg and the Leopoldsberg, the last foothills of the Alpine chain.

unable to find a single point of reference."[12] Large areas were perennially or temporally inundated, and the riverscape area lying north and southeast of the city was changed by every flood, even by the snow-melt in spring. Islands and sandbars disappeared, and new ones continually formed where none were before. In some considerable risings, the Danube dug new beds, caused by the deposit of fresh accumulations of stones and gravel, bringing with them flooding and destruction to miles of fertile country in Vienna's immediate "hinterland" and "breadbasket"—the Marchfeld. Nonetheless, the remarkable wealth of plant and animal life of this island labyrinth in the Viennese Danube floodplains—where it was difficult to discern a main channel—was not the reason for its "European renown"[13] at the beginning of this century; rather, the wooded Lobau was first and foremost a "natural military training ground" during the Napoleonic wars.[14]

The Danube's very course has been continually remapped, stretched, and compressed according to economic, political, and sociocultural pressures. Like all large rivers in Europe, the ecology of the Danube has been considerably affected, especially by land use; by changes in the catchment that influences runoff, sediment transport, and pollution levels; and, most importantly, by hydraulic engineering.

The importance of Vienna as a transshipment center and as a port, and the consequent necessity to improve the city's infrastructure installations, have given rise to schemes for development on considerable scale through centuries. Most of the schemes discussed since the 1850s were embedded in multifunctional transitional pathways across diverse contexts to ensure the industrial transition of Vienna's whole riverscape. Schemes were to serve at the same time as a protection against floods, as an improvement of the waterway for large vessels, and as a basis for the development of spacious ports. Essential parts of the programs of the nineteenth century were dedicated to the prevention of floods in the area on the left bank of the Danube in Vienna and the construction of a navigable channel near the city, adapted for large boats and for unloading purposes, with riverside sites to be transformed into prosperous transshipment stations.

The frequent changes of the great water highway made the construction of permanent quays and wharves and the erection of warehouses a near

---

12 Friedrich Emanuel von Hurter, *Ausflug nach Wien und Pressburg im Sommer 1839*, 2 vols. (Schaffhausen: Kurter'sche Buchhandlung, 1840), I, 254.

13 *Oesterreichische National-Encyclopädie, oder alphabetische Darlegung der wissenswürdigsten Eigenthümlichkeiten des österreichischen Kaiserthumes*, ed. Franz Gräffer and Johann Jakob Czikann, 6 vols., (Vienna: Friedrich Beck, 1835), I, 739.

14 *Der Rheinische Bund: Eine Zeitschrift historisch-politisch-statistisch-geographischen Inhalts*, ed. Peter Adolph Winkopp (Frankfurt am Main: J.C.B. Mohr, 1809), vol. 13, issues 37–39, 311.

impossibility. The city had to be content with wooden bridges, exposed every winter to destruction particularly due to ice jams. The flood of February 1862, with devastating consequences to both life and property, brought about the implementation of a major river regulation scheme (the "Great Danube Regulation"), commenced in 1869/70, constraining the floodplain considerably and radically transforming the whole river landscape in this stretch. Before this permanent transformation between stream kilometer mark 1935 through 1919, starting in the year 1870, Vienna's industrial expansion had been oriented toward the southern suburbs, instead of spreading along the unstable river.

With the rise of steamboats in the 1850s, the main technological approach in making the Viennese Danube a more useful and controlled pathway was to construct a single, straightened channel with uniform width, stabilized by substantial embankments with heavy stone rip-raps and cargo concentrated at a few riverside sites. Former sidearms were cut off, and large levees separated parts of the former floodplains from erosive, scouring flood flow. The regulation heavily impacted urban land use and has been a permanent intervention in Vienna's urban planning. Although new construction areas suitable for settlement expansion could be acquired due to the filling up of old river channels with material from the excavation of a new bed, other areas had to be "sacrificed" for the ideal river line. The regulation scheme not only moved the river into suburbia, but it also lowered the water table and increased the speed of the current. This lowering created disadvantages for large-scale shipping and unintended consequences for the environment, critically observed by early Austrian conservationists, who, under the influence of Hugo Conwentz, a German pioneer of nature protection visiting Vienna for propaganda reasons in 1903, eagerly collected every information on natural monuments deserving to be inventoried and protected.[15]

Regulation of the Danube and the construction of the Nordbahn and Nordwestbahn railroads, which connected Vienna to northern coal deposits in the 1850s, were both part of Vienna's modernization and industrialization project. Although railways and rivers are competing infrastructure systems in a metropolitan area, their regulation was originally coupled: for example, in the case of bridges over a navigable stream, railway construction depended on stable, regulated banks.

---

15 "The best example of a bad solution with bad consequences [...] the Danube regulation near Vienna," in Günther Schlesinger, *Mensch und Natur*, = Österr. Flugschriftenreihe Dürerbund 2 (Munich: Georg D. W. Callwey, 1926), 17. Under Schlesinger's leadership, the society Österreichischer *Verein Naturschutzpark* was founded in 1912 and the first Austrian law dealing with the preservation of nature was passed in 1924.

Drawing migrants from other parts of the Habsburg empire from the 1850s onward, Vienna was compelled to seek its extension, expanding in 1857, 1890/92, and 1904/05 to incorporate surrounding suburbs across the Danube and along the Vienna woods (*Stadterweiterungen*). In order to make provisions for the future growth and to regulate the expansion of the suburbs, a great effort was made in 1905 to acquire a broad green belt of land—highly acclaimed by the early conservationists inside the city—known as the *Wald- und Wiesengürtel*. At a cost of about 50 million Kronen, the forested hills of the *Wienerwald*, the fields of Simmering to the east, the Danube wetlands, and the fields to the north were incorporated into the city as a permanent nature preserve, with areas reserved for mass recreation.[16] This planning policy was thought capable of transforming Vienna into "one huge garden city, within well-defined boundaries and with ample means of communication," or so predicted by the leading British city architect H. Inigo Triggs.[17]

Nevertheless, until the late nineteenth century—when Vienna underwent rapid growth; the building of port infrastructure outside the main current of the Danube in Vienna was deemed worthless and inappropriate.[18] Flat banks as natural landing points along the river's right bank (called *Donauländen*, derived from landing) and an 1875-built wharf (*Praterkai*) with an industrial track (*Donau-Uferbahn*) were considered sufficient for the loading and unloading of freight barges. The unenclosed wharf occupied a twelve kilometer stretch of the right Danube riverbank. Shipping companies from riparian states all had their own docks to moor their ships, as well as their own freight sheds and depots.

But at the close of the nineteenth century, when steamers with cargo and passengers began to appear in ever greater numbers, a harbor that offered winter berths came to be indispensable—all the more relevant in view of the fact that navigation in this river section was possible only for about 300 days per year. In particular, when thirty vessels had been crushed by an ice jam in 1881,[19] the need for a secure winter harbor became a critical issue. The so-called Danube Canal at Vienna, an arm of the river Danube

---

16 Robert Rotenberg, *Landscape and Power in Vienna* (Baltimore: The John Hopkins University Press, 1995), 152.

17 Henry Inigo Triggs, *Town Planning Past, Present and Possible*, 2nd ed. (London: Methuen & Co., 1911), 190–191.

18 By, for instance, James Abernethy and Georg Sexauer, both members of the Danube Regulation Commission who were appointed to consider upon an all-embracing regulation project for the riverscape at Vienna.

19 Anton Becker: "Die Donau und Wien," *Monatsblatt des Vereines für Landeskunde von Niederösterreich*, Neue Folge, no. 1 (1928): 125–129, 147–162 (here 159).

some sixteen kilometers in length, had been canalized by a number of movable dams and locks, thus protecting against floods by gates at Nussdorf on the model of the "*barrage de Poses*" in the lower Seine valley.[20] When the river flooded or froze, existing landing facilities did not offer sufficient protection. The "commission for the Vienna transport systems" (*Commission für Wiener Verkehrsanlagen*) therefore decided in 1892 to develop the Danube Canal into a freight and passenger harbor that could be used in winter.[21] The Danube Canal should become part of a comprehensive infrastructure plan. Following the "law for the Vienna transport systems," adopted by the Reichsrat on 18 July 1892 (R.G.Bl. No. 109),[22] the bed of the canal was excavated; quays and retaining walls were built. The Nussdorf shut-off, the wharves, and the barrage *Kaiserbad* were completed. Thus, the set amount of public funding was exhausted before the project could be finished, and a supplementary credit had to be granted to complete the work. But before the beginning of World War I, key decision makers had lost interest entirely. The transformation of the Danube canal remained a torso, an unrealized infrastructure utopia.[23] During World War I and shortly afterwards, the Danube canal merely functioned—as in former times—as a trading port for "local provisioning."[24]

The legislative creation of the "law for the Vienna transport systems" was followed by the "law for the accomplishment and completion of the Danube regulation in Lower Austria" (G. 4/1 1899 L. 2), which granted, among other things, funding for the construction of a winter harbor at Freudenau and of a harbor basin at Kuchelau in the northwest of the town for use as an outer port, especially for rafts and rowing ships. The construction of the Freudenau port (kilometer mark 1920, right bank) began in 1899, integrating previous engineering interventions at this location. Completed in 1902, the construction was actually intended to function solely as a harbor of refuge and wintering port to shelter more than 400

20 Léonce-Abel Mazoyer, *La navigation intérieure: rivières et canaux* (Paris: E. Bernard et Cie., 1902), 113.

21 Donau Canal projects discussed in Rudolf Halter, "Die Ausgestaltung des Wiener Donaukanals zum Hafen: Ein Projekt Ing. Paul Klunzingers," *Zeitschrift des Österr. Ingenieur- und Architektenvereins* 12 (1919): 109–110.

22 Following Karl Lueger's appointment as mayor in 1897, the city's transport system was then taken into public ownership, in some ways pioneering the municipal socialism expanded later during the 1920's.

23 For details, see Bertrand Michael Buchmann, Rupert Schickl, Harald Sterk, *Der Donaukanal: Geschichte, Planung, Ausführung* (= Beiträge zur Stadtforschung, Stadtentwicklung und Stadtgestaltung vol. 14) (Vienna: Magistrat der Stadt Wien, 1984).

24 *Wien und die Donau: Denkschrift des österreichischen Ingenieur- und Architekten-Vereines* (Vienna: Selbstverlag des Vereines, 1917), 54.

barges of 500–700 tonnes cargo capacity.[25] The first winter season the harbor was open, about 160 vessels docked there.[26] Prior to this, ships berthed in the winter harbor at the entrance to the river Fischa at Fischamend or at the Korneuburg shipyard harbor.[27] Until the First World War, the new port of Freudenau was used in the first place for the purposes for which it had been constructed. It had an area of 43.5 ha, a total length of 6,200 m, and was dredged out to a depth of five meters below the mean water level. The new infrastructure was integrated into the city's transport system by new railways and roads, with an extensive infrastructure system of power stations and electric light installations; it also had a water main, bringing water from the Alps and was connected directly by lines of railway to the Danube riverside railway (*Donau-Uferbahn*).[28] Since the whole Upper Danube stretch is characterized as a mountain river with high gravel transport, which historically created large alluvial deposits, about 15,000 cu.m. (= 20,000 cubic yards) of dredging had to be carried out annually at the entrance of the port (see Fig.1).[29]

In 1853, a trade association, "Vienna fruit and flour exchange" (*Wiener Frucht- und Mehlbörse*), was formed under direct control of the city of Vienna; it remained in municipal possession until 1869. At this time, Vienna had no grain warehouses or grain stocks for wholesale, and export trade was not analogous to the lumber yards on the river Danube's banks;[30] the Municipal Council decided to set up large cereal storehouses from municipal funds. Nevertheless, this decision was not carried out,[31] because the unstable nature of the riverbanks of the Danube precluded the building of granaries. It was only after completion of the Great Regulation and the construction of a double-track railway on the right bank for a length of 18.6 miles, and following the first Austrian Warehouse Law (Ministerial

25 See also: Anton Schromm, "Schiffahrt," in *Wien am Anfang des XX. Jahrhunderts: Ein Führer in technischer und künstlerischer Richtung*, ed. Paul Kortz, vol. 1 (Vienna: Gerlach & Wiedling 1905), 141–145 (here 145).
26 Eugen Guglia, *Wien: ein Führer durch Stadt und Umgebung* (Vienna: Gerlach & Wiedling, 1908), 202.
27 Donau-Regulierungs-Commission ed., *Der Freudenauer Hafen in Wien: Denkschrift zur Eröffnung des Freudenauer Hafens am 28. Oktober 1902* (Vienna: k.k. Hof- und Staatsdruckerei, 1902); Rudolf Halter, "Der Schutz und Winterhafen in der Freudenau," *Oesterr Wochenschrift f. den oeffentl. Baudienst* 12, no. 19 (1906): 281.
28 League of Nations, *General Transport Situation in 1921: Statements submitted by the States which took part in the First General Conference on Communications and Transit, held in March–April 1921* (Geneva: League of Nations, 1922), vol. 1, 30.
29 Jack Allen, *Scale models in hydraulic engineering* (London: Longmans, Green 1952), 139.
30 Anonymous, *Die Theuerung des Getreides und Brennholzes im Verkehrsgebiete von Wien; deren Ursache und Hilfsmittel dagegen* (Vienna: Braumüller, 1857), 87.
31 Karl Victor Heller, *Der Getreidehandel und seine Technik in Wien* (Tübingen: J.C.B. Mohr, 1904), 18.

Order of 19 June 1866, R.-G.-Bl. No. 86), the Vienna City Council decided on the construction of the first municipal warehouse (*Lagerhaus der Stadt
Wien*) in 1876, which started in a vacant machinery hall left over from the
world exhibition 1873.

Fig. 1: Bucket-chain dredger "*Fafner*" dredging the Freudenau Port Basin, ca.
1910. Picture Archive Austrian National Library Sign. ÖNB PCH 6467 C

Besides Vienna's ambitions to become the trading center for grain
transports from east to west, the necessity for the establishment of public
entrepots, after the French model, resulted from the strong increase in railway and ship traffic,[32] but also from progressive enlargement of the urbanized area in the late nineteenth century. The growing city's provisioning, the
infrastructure services it offered, the goods, food, and energy it produced or

---

32 The first through train of the Southern Railway from Vienna to Trieste ran on 12 July
1857.

imported, the so-called *Approvisionierung*, became an urgent issue on the urban agenda.[33] Warehouses in general were primarily built for the purpose of grain trading; furthermore, they were the "modern" surrogates of the old fairs and markets, a postulate of traffic transformed by rail activity and steam navigation.

Two grain storehouses (*Magazin* VIII and IX) with elevators were built on Danube landing grounds in 1877 and a third, large one (*Magazin* X) in 1883.[34] Before the First World War, the Danube Steamship Co. (*Erste Donau-Dampfschiffahrts-Gesellschaft*, DDSG) maintained regular express services for goods traffic on the whole of the Danube as far as Sulina. A new chief granary of the city was erected at the Handelskai during the years 1911–13, when the total figures for goods transport arriving at and dispatched from DDSG offices (ports, stations, agencies, landing quays) on the Danube peaked with about 2.5 million tonnes.[35] The eleven-story high grain silo of reinforced concrete (transformed into a luxury hotel in the 1980s) was of "modern design," with a capacity of 3,000 truckloads or 30,000 tonnes of grain, 140 m long, 23 m wide, and 46 m high.[36] The massive concrete terminal elevator made Vienna more than ever a port city, with this monumental waterfront landmark made of concrete as the symbol of the modern age (see Fig. 2).

A junction canal between the Rhine and the Danube was discussed as becoming an increasingly urgent project, not only for the Dual Monarchy, but also for France.[37] As the city had never been self-sufficient in bread grains, vessels arrived in Vienna, the geographical center of the Middle Danube, filled with grain and flour from the blacksoil breadbaskets of the Habsburg Empire. The "backland" of the Marchfeld, on the other hand, was thought to be largely protected from flood damage, while a dam stretched from Vienna straight through the wetlands to the provincial border. Largely in isolation from both the river and its flooding and formative influences, a rich supply of nutrients through the depositing of suspended sediment,

---

33 See Julius Hartmann, "Die Tätigkeit der Gemeinde Wien auf dem Gebiete der Approvisionierung," *Ztschr. für Volkswirtschaft, Sozialpolitik und Verwaltung* 18 (1909): 616–655.
34 "Die Lagerhäuser der Stadt Wien," in *Wien im Aufbau: Markt und Käufer* (Vienna: Magistrat der Stadt Wien, 1937), 37– 47 (here 37).
35 Robert Kinnl, "In the hulls of ships: Goods transportation," in *blue: Inventing the River Danube*, ed. Vienna Technical Museum (Salzburg: Fotohof edition, 2005), 86–88 (here 88).
36 *Der neue Speicher im Lagerhause der Stadt Wien am Handelskai* (Vienna: Gerlach & Wiedling, 1913), 3; Erwin Hammer, "Die Städtischen Lagerhäuser," in *Das neue Wien. Städtewerk*, vol. 4 (Vienna: Magistrat der Stadt Wien, 1927), 170–174 (here 170).
37 "Vienna as a Seaport," *The Technical Review: A Weekly Summary of Development and Progress of Engineering and Technology Throughout the World* 8–9, May 24 (1921): 113.

commonly known as *Letten*, was absent and the groundwater, moisture, and fertility levels of surrounding soils all declined. Though there were many gains in terms of agricultural land, the natural rejuvenation of the softwood floodplains, with their light-loving alders, poplars, and willows, was rarely possible, and the transformation of the region into hardwood floodplain became inevitable. Thus formed, the Lobau created an arcadian impression through its often-changing landscape of broad meadows, bushes, and impressive groves of silver poplars and field elms—an impression strengthened further by its acclaimed "magical" wealth of woodland and game stocks during the years leading up to the First World War.

Fig. 2 Municipal Warehouses, Main Building (Chief Granary) and Stores at *Handelskai*, 1920s. Picture Archive Austrian National Library Sign ÖNB/ Reiffenstein 105.362 D

Arcadian Warscape: the First World War on the Viennese Danube

The Danube played an important role in the Great War from the beginning. The imperial and royal monitor *Temes* fired the opening shots of the First World War on 29 July 1914, shelling the Serbian capital, Belgrade. As a bridgehead on both sides of the Danube, Vienna was to be fortified with a *noyau* (fortified core zone) north of the river.[38] As early as the end of August 1914, when the "Russian steamroller" had destroyed the imperial armies' defenses in the plains of Eastern Galicia, a ring of fortification works was erected around the Viennese bridgehead, built by some 28,000 laborers in accordance with wartime service regulations (*Kriegsleistungsgesetz*). Parts of the Danube floodplain on the left bank were dug up to create obstacles and trenches, which were occupied until the bridgehead command was disbanded in May 1916. Thereafter, Vienna was declared an open city. The blockade by the Allied forces meant that Austria-Hungary became an almost hermetically sealed economic area, within which agricultural production was too low to compensate for the loss of imported goods. Up until 1914, the capital city had secured its existence primarily from its hinterlands, the Sudetenland regions, Galicia, and Hungary. From the second half of the war onward, there was little available in the way of food other than what was governed by the "office for national nutrition" (*Amt für Volksernährung)*, established in 1916. Satisfying the nutritional and accommodation needs of the army required vast quantities of cereals and flour, hay and straw, pigs and cattle. Even during the first winter of the war, deficiencies in supply became apparent; these became ever more dramatic and eventually catastrophic over the course of the war until November 1918.

As early as the autumn of 1915, the Vienna municipal authorities had made public appeals to the city's inhabitants to become urban "wartime market gardeners" and make use of every available piece of land. Alongside this campaign for wartime food production, the city's authorities also encouraged the transformation of private gardens into allotments. In 1915, on the initiative of Vienna's mayor Richard Weiskirchner, an area of forty-three hectares was also cleared in the Lobau, before being built upon at the behest of the municipal authorities by the forest inspectorate.[39] The military administration declared itself willing to make 500 Russian prisoners of war available as laborers for the project, and the barracks accommodation (still known today as the "Russian camp" or *Russenlager* in the Lobau) was to be provided by the office of the "grand master of the hunt" (*Oberstjägermeisteramt*).[40]

In 1917, the Municipal Council of Vienna voted on an important resolution with regard to the general usage rights of Vienna's Danubian

---

38 Manfried Rauchensteiner, *The First World War and the End of the Habsburg Monarchy, 1914–1918* (Vienna: Böhlau, 2014), 221.

39 *Die Gemeindeverwaltung der Stadt Wien 1. Jänner 1914 bis 30. Juni 1919 unter den Bürgermeistern Dr. Richard Weiskirchner und Jakob Reumann* (Vienna: Magistrat der Stadt Wien, 1923), 430.

40 Hermann Prossinagg, Gottfried Haubenberger, eds., *Kaiserliche Jagdreviere in den Donau-Auen: Ein jagdgeschicht-licher Rückblick* (Vienna: Österreichischer Jagd- und Fischerei-Verlag, 2007), 82.

wetlands. The starting point for discussions was a bequest from 1745 made by Empress Maria Theresia, leaving the Castle and Estate of Ebersdorf to the "Vienna general welfare fund" (*Wiener Allgemeinen Versorgungsfond*, then known as the *Wiener Armenkasse*), in order that the castle might be turned into a government-administered workhouse; hunting rights were, however, excluded from the bequest. In an agreement signed in December 1917 in the Municipal Parliament between the imperial state authorities (*Hofärar*) and the Vienna municipal authorities, the Lobau region was divided; the portion located upstream (*Obere* Lobau) was exempted from hunting rights, and the local authority in the name of the *Allgemeinen Versorgungsfond* was accorded unrestricted ownership rights to this area; in contrast, the downstream portion of the Lobau region (*Untere* Lobau) remained in state ownership; both hunting rights and land ownership rights were accorded by the state authorities, with their right of easement. The local authorities commissioned the municipal authorities to carry out preliminary investigations into further agricultural utilization of suitable land within the Lobau and to prepare applications for redesigning the Lobau region as a nature conservation park with leisure area for use by the recreation-seeking public. At that time, a conflict of interests regarding land use was not foreseen.[41]

Supplies of coal and petroleum had also become scarce and were integrated in the wartime economy, not least because of increasing infrastructure problems and disorganized distribution. The monarchy, which in 1909 was still the third largest oil producer in the world, (behind the USA and Russia), thanks to the Galician oilfields near Boryslav,[42] slid into a fuel crisis as domestic production stopped due to the war. Although the army tried hard to find an extension of the geological trend in the central Vienna basin after oil discoveries in Slovakia (Gbely) in 1914, drilling campaigns during the war were without success.[43] Drillings in the Marchfeld near Hohenau and at Raggendorf also failed to find oil.[44]

In the wooded wetland areas, unregulated "wild" settlements developed, partially consisting of the most basic of homes excavated from the Danubian silt and huts constructed from wooden boards and boxes. Largely separated from the domestic colonization ideas that were flourishing at

41 *Gemeindeverwaltung der Stadt Wien 1. Jänner 1914 bis 30. Juni 1919*, 434.
42 See: Alison Fleig Frank, *Oil Empire. Visions of Prosperity in Austrian Galicia* (Cambridge: Harvard University Press, 2007).
43 See *detailed information in:* Karl Friedl, "Die Erdölfrage in Deutsch-Oesterreich," *ZS d. Internat. Ver. d. Bohring. u. Bohrtechn.* 32, no. 14 (1924): 105–110; no. 15 (1924): 113–120; Karl Friedl, "Ueber die jüngsten Erdölforschungen im Wiener Becken," *Petroleum* 23, no. 6 (1927): 189–241.
44 *Report II–IV of the Federal Oil Conservation Board to the President of the United States* (Washington: Office of the Board Interior Department Building, 1928), 92.

the time among those of all political persuasions, Vienna's settler movement developed during a time of great deprivation and an increasing power vacuum, when of 186,000 school-age children in Vienna, only 6,732 were not malnourished.[45] War gardens transformed into shantytowns and surrounded the city "like a ragged girdle,"[46] recalling shelters on the frontline.

Both the housing famine and food crisis in Vienna intensified in the third year of the war. The central war offices played an important role in the war economy. The first such office was the "war grain trade institute" (*Kriegs-Getreideverkehrsanstalt*) set up already in 1915—the year bread and flour were being rationed after Hungarian grain embargoes and poor local harvests. It was not until the food supply for men and animals of the Central Powers worsened dramatically that the Danube "lifeline" was brought to focus.

The following quote from Arthur Oelwein (1837–1917), who was involved in most of the public waterworks in Vienna, affords the dominant version of "seeing like an engineer" at that time, where the Danube was transformed into an "imperial waterway", governed by war administration and regulation—presenting also a trajectory over time to come:

In foreign countries, the word has been coined: 'The present war is a war of the railways!' [...] This great dependence on overseas traffic is not in our people's interest. We must, at all costs, ensure that there are inland connections with perfect security, which we can control at any time. These new ways are clearly marked out today; these are the connections through the Balkans and the Black Sea to Asia Minor, Mesopotamia, Persia, etc. If we have these areas for our economic supply and as a large new sales area, a later war with England can no longer be just as dangerous [...] The German Baghdad Railway will become increasingly important thereby. By this land route, inland waterway transport, especially by an entire navigable Danube integrated into a network of German waterways, gains a very important task, because this stream will become a world trade route. Then there can never be a shortage of boat space, as the fleet of ships of a huge hinterland will be available; All that is required is technical improvement of the slope of the river, of the yards and ports required, as indicated earlier, in order to make this glorious river carry the same quantity of freight as compared with the Rhine.[47]

45 Otto Bauer, *Die österreichische Revolution* (Vienna: Wiener Volksbuchhandlung, 1923), 121.

46 Solita Solano, "Vienna—A Capital without a Nation," *National Geographic* XLIII, no.1 (1923): 79–102 (here 79).

47 Arthur Oelwein, "Die Binnen- und Seeschiffahrt im Kriege," *Zeitschrift des österreich. Ingenieur- und Architektenvereines* 68, no. 12 (1916): 234–235 (here 234).

In the first half of 1916, more than eighty percent of Austrian grain supplies had come from Romania.[48] All that stopped when Romania declared war in spring 1916 and prohibited the export of grain. Nevertheless, in the same year, port Freudenau was equipped with an additional four public grain yards by the Danube Regulation Commission, with a total capacity of 960 trucks for direct transshipment.[49] In May 1916, the city assumed also an eight-story granary (*Zwischenbrücken*) on the Handelskai riverbank (a former warehouse of the Hungarian trading joint stock company S. & W. Hoffmann)[50] opened in 1903, with a total capacity of 1,000 trucks. A municipal cold-storage house (*Kühlhaus Engerthstrasse*) was constructed by the Danube Regulation Commission[51] after one mild winter when no ice formed on the Danube thick enough to cut and store, whereas ordinarily large quantities were obtained each year from this source. At the same time, the demand increased owing not only to food (especially meat) storage, but also to the large quantities required at the hospitals.[52]

But it was not until the late spring of 1917, following the Treaty of Bucharest, which materially affected conditions on the river, that supplies (grain, oil) started flowing upstream again. Ship traffic on the Danube rose rapidly, especially since the railways were reserved for troop transports.[53]

War economists searched for ways to use transnational infrastructure systems to create supply chains. From the end of nineteenth century, several initiatives had attempted to interconnect the Danube basin and Black Sea ports via a waterway network to both the North and Baltic Sea markets using a canal connection (Danube-Oder Canal). During the war, Viennese authorities were still thinking of implementing long-term plans of Minister-President (1900–04; 1916) Ernest v. Koerber's program for economic development, including a scheme for the construction of a canal infrastructure with a line that would have entered the Danube near Vienna. In June 1917, the City of Vienna organized an international symposium on "the building of waterways," which dealt extensively with the question of a canal network. In the end, after the imperial parliament had voted for

---

48 Lothar Höbelt, "The context of the Somme: The Pripet Marshes to the Federal Reserve," in *The Battle of the Somme,* ed. Matthias Strohn (Oxford: Osprey, 2016), 23– 40 (here 29).

49 "Lagerhäuser der Stadt Wien," *Wien im Aufbau,* 38.

50 Christian Ulrich, "Lagerhäuser," in *Wien am Anfang des XX. Jahrhunderts,* 376– 378 (here 378).

51 "Lagerhäuser der Stadt Wien," *Wien im Aufbau,* 39.

52 Scarcity mentioned in a short note in: *Ice and Refrigeration Illustrated* 50, no. 6 (1916): 384.

53 Kurt Bednar, *Der Papierkrieg zwischen Washington und Wien 1917/18* (Innsbruck: Studienverlag, 2017), 199.

the construction of new Alpine railways linking Salzburg with the harbor of Trieste, all the succeeding governments "dragged their feet with the implementation of the 1901 waterways act."[54] Once enacted by law as part of the envisioned Austrian imperial waterway network, the Danube-Oder canal was supposed to retain "its momentum" throughout the twentieth century.[55]

At the end of the war, in February 1918, the Viennese municipal authorities created a "municipal agricultural office" (*Städtisches Landwirtschaftsamt*), also tasked with responsibility for the agricultural use of the Lobau. Once again, prisoners of war were employed, planting the fields of the Lobau largely with potatoes and cabbage. After the war, Austria was rundown and on the verge of starvation. Vienna had become an impoverished city, in which the sale of valuable tapestries from Schönbrunn Palace to finance grain imports led to heated dispute both in politics and society at large.[56]

Danubian Interwar

With the redrawing of the political map of Europe after the war and the simultaneous collapse of the Dual Monarchy, Russia, and the Ottoman Empire, power relations along the Danube changed. By virtue of the Statute of 1921, for the first time a system of international administration was in effect on the whole navigable course of the river, in which riparians and non-riparians participated.

In 1918, the First Republic of Austria became an inland country whose performance was shaped by its initial resource-poor conditions—economically cut off by former provinces of the monarchy, the new nation suffered from scarcity of coal and food. The Danube fleet was considerably reduced by war losses, and the DDSG had to reconstruct its infrastructures and installations to resume normal shipping traffic again. Immediately after the war, the goods traffic on the Danube was almost entirely interrupted, whereas the passenger traffic increased in 1918 in comparison with the traffic of 1913, owing to the fact that the Austrian railway service was still extremely defective.[57] Outside Austria, sailings only took place in exceptional cases

---

54 Jacek Purchla, "Central location. The Port of Vienna," *Austria Today* 3 (1992): 19–20.

55 Jiří Janác, *European Coasts of Bohemia: Negotiating the Danube-Oder-Elbe Canal in a Troubled Twentieth Century* (Amsterdam: Amsterdam University Press, 2012), 24.

56 In a detailed essay on this controversy entitled "Bread and Lies" ("*Brot und Lüge*," 1919), Karl Kraus decisively supported the position of the first government of the new state in accepting an offer from an American company related to this.

57 League of Nations, *General Transport Situation in 1921*, Introduction, LVI.

and then only when a safe conduct was granted by the Inter-Allied Danube Commission. The regular goods traffic at this time was resumed as far as Baja (southern Hungary); in cooperation with the new riparian states, certain services were established for transport of important supplies in large quantities intended for Austria, especially wheat and oil.[58]

Since the dissolution of the Monarchy in 1918, the Vienna warehouses were struggling with major economic problems. Central business operations shifted to the wharfage on the main riverstream, the warehouses at the winter harbor were closed. Port Freudenau, which until then had been the property of the state, came into the possession of the City of Vienna, but the new owner, suffering from a shortage of funds for both investment and maintenance, was not able to invest heavily in the city's river infrastructure. The vast pre-war schemes—measures to improve the conditions of navigation and to render the banks of the river immune from floods once again—could not be realized. The territorial changes that were the consequence of the war had completely removed the possibility of the radically shrunken Austria having any influence on the construction or course of the intensely discussed Danube-Oder Canal.

Due to the economic crisis, the expansion of the thirteen kilometers- long, but unfortunately only sixty meters-wide port Freudenau, did not bring any increase in cargo handling, although the site accommodated numerous commercial branches, stations, and warehouses.[59] By the decision of 12 June 1922, the Danube Regulation Commission was allowed to construct a new transshipment area for mineral oil trading and storage (*Mineralöllände*), replacing the former public *Petroleumlände*.[60] The new wharf, about three kilometers long, was yet the furthest downstream, with about fifty tanks belonging to different oil companies and a storage capacity for petroleum and its products of about 60,000 t.[61] Although Austria was not important as a consumer in the 1920s (with annual consumption of about 25,000 tonnes of Kerosene and about 20,000 tonnes of gasoline), it handled an extensive intermediary and transit trade, particularly in Vienna. Romanian and Russian mineral oil was shipped on tank barges as far as Vienna, where it was either stored or immediately transferred into tank cars for further transportation by rail.[62]

58 League of Nations, *General Transport Situation in 1921*, 35.

59 Johann Hawlik, *Wien: Spuren in die Zukunft* (Vienna: Edition Atelier, 1997), 172.

60 *Die Gemeindeverwaltung der Bundeshauptstadt Wien in der Zeit vom 1. Juli 1919 bis 31. Dezember 1922 unter dem Bürgermeister Jakob Reumann* (Vienna: Magistrat der Stadt Wien, 1927), 512.

61 Richard Künstner, Wilhelm Jarosch, "Die Wiener Wasserbauten," in *Festschrift herausgegeben anlässlich der Hundertjahrfeier des Wiener Stadtbauamtes*, ed. Rudolf Tillmann (Vienna: Deutscher Verlag für Jugend und Volk, 1935), 126–136 (here 132).

62 Consul Carol II. Foster, "The Austrian Petroleum Trade," *Commerce Reports* 4, no. 46 (1924): 404.

In 1925, a mooring for floats and flying boats (*Wiener Wasserflughafen*) was completed,[63] which was later to be of military strategic importance during the Second World War.[64]

The Habsburg Law of 1919 provided for ownership of the former imperial property of the Lower Lobau to pass to the Foundation for the Victims of War (*Kriegsgeschädigtenfond*), while the few arable areas there were partly gifted to former employees or used for the cultivation of game feed. At that time, in the Upper Lobau, agricultural use was predominant—410 ha were intensively farmed by the "forest and agricultural office" (founded in 1919, *Forst- und Landwirtschaftliche Betriebsgesellschaft*).[65] Fighting illegal settlement, the municipal authorities granted leasehold plots to sixty-one unemployed industrial workers' families covering a total area of 104 ha, most of which was Danube wetland downstream from the Stadlau rail bridge.[66] But by the end of the 1920s, there were also increasing calls for a rehabilitation and restoration of the former arcadian landscape to its pre-war state. Even the German zoo director Lutz Heck, the later leader of the "Division of Nature Conservation of the Forestry Department" during the National Socialist regime, wrote a letter to Austria's foremost nature conservationist Günther Schlesinger in 1918, in which he had warned against opening the Lobau to public access. In calling for wilderness preservation of one of the most important natural landmarks with a unique colony of cormorants, he rejected the concept of a leisure area in the Lobau for the benefit of the Viennese people almost completely.[67] Others—like councilor for the Floridsdorf district Karl Kirschner, an active member of the allotment movement, and Günther Schlesinger before him, in his expert report on the Lobau—claimed for the agricultural lands to be returned to river meadows, as a "restoration of the former topographical effect (Fig. 3)."[68]

---

63 Peter Krause, *OeLAG: Oesterreichische Luftverkehrs Aktien Gesellschaft 1923–1938* (= Österreichs Luftfahrt in Einzeldarstellungen vol. 6) (Graz: Weishaupt, 1983), 29.
64 In 1944 in particular, aircraft had to clear the Danube of mines dropped by the RAF operating from bases around Foggia, curtailing the movement of river shipping.
65 Ferdinand Strauß, *Die Lobau* (Vienna: Deutscher Verlag für Jugend und Volk, 1935), 11. In comparison: today's agricultural land use is at about 120 ha.
66 Österreichisches Kuratorium für Wirtschaftlichkeit, Ernst Streeruwitz, *Der Aufbau des österreichischen Siedlungswerkes: Bericht des ÖKW-Arbeitsausschusses Innenkolonisation* (Vienna: Springer, 1933), 176.
67 Heck's letter was printed "Zur Lobaufrage," *Blätter für Naturkunde und Naturschutz* 2–3 (1918): 29–31.
68 Günther Schlesinger, "Gutachten über die Lobau und ihre Verwendung als Naturpark," in *Die Krongüter und ihre Zukunft: Lainzer Tiergarten, Lobau, Schönbrunn*, ed. Verein Für Denkmalpflege und Heimatschutz Nieder-österreich (Vienna: Gerlach & Wiedling, 1919); Prossinagg, *Jagdreviere*, 86.

Fig. 3: Lobau: the "green living room" for a large number of Vienna's inhabitants, 1920s. Postcard *Panozzalacke*, Publisher: *Land- und Forstwirtschaftliche Betriebsgesellschaft* Vienna. Private Archive

Grain and Oil—Total War on the Danube

A few years later, in 1938, the newly annexed former capital Vienna, although claiming its key position and historical role in the southeast, appeared a thoroughly backward place to economic experts from the Reich, who bemoaned an export trade that was "lacking in the necessary drive," a hopelessly antiquated Danube shipping fleet and a "fragmentation" of trade, commerce, industry, and banking.[69] Field Marshal Hermann Göring went to great trouble to propagate the notion that Austria was to be showered with blessings under the new rule. Much was made of his steamer trip down the Danube from Linz to Tulln on 25 March, during which he discussed Austria's new design and contributions to the Reich's Four Year Plan with selected German and Austrian economic experts, industrialists, and technicians. It was on this scenic trip on the Danube steamboat *Franz Schubert* where Austria's development program for economic integration and the projected exploitation of all the locally available raw materials was

---

69 "Wien, wie es exportiert und importiert," BArch, R 104-F/1–45 Reichskommissar für die Wiedervereinigung Österreichs mit dem Deutschen Reich, quoted in Götz Aly, Susanne Heim, eds., *Vordenker der Vernichtung: Auschwitz und die deutschen Pläne für eine neue europäische Ordnung* (Frankfurt am Main: Fischer, 1993), 35.

originally developed. By harnessing existing hydroelectric facilities as well as undeveloped hydropower resources, and mineral and oil resources, the Ostmark program aimed for Greater Germany's rearmament. The German Reichswerke's interest in the Austrian shipping companies (DDSG, Comos) as part of the transport infrastructure became plainly evident in the following years, with logistics and critical infrastructure (implanted and envisioned by German authorities and engineers) to transport natural resources and goods within a German-led greater economic sphere (*Großraumwirtschaft*).[70]

Germany's aim was to convert southeastern Europe into a kind of hinterland, to reactivate expansion plans of the late nineteenth century ("yearning for the East," *Drang nach Osten*), and to organize a large segment of this part of Europe as a single unit under her economic and political leadership.[71] The government's Four Year Plan, introduced in September 1934, was closely coordinated with the political program and integrated the commercial exchange control system and infrastructure policy with Germany's totalitarian armed economy. Planning and rationing of imports began, and only the most urgently needed goods were to be imported; mainly raw materials (minerals, ores, petroleum) and agricultural products (wood, grain, fodder, fats), formerly obtained from overseas. All reorganizations of trade and land use were based on aspects of the military demands of the coming war. The ultimate goal, however, goes beyond the mere maintenance of the German economic war machine. In the case of eastern Europe, especially after 1936, when the Four Year Plan became the main instrument for planning, the National Socialist system sought to create a German *cordon-économique* consisting of dependent satellite states.[72] As a result, the importance of trade relations between Germany and the agricultural countries of southeast Europe, whose staple exports were accessible by land or water-based infrastructure, greatly increased. As Minister of Economics (1934–37) Hjalmar Schacht said, it was possible between 1934 and 1937 to increase imports of petroleum by 116 percent, and that of grain by 102 percent.[73]

---

70 This term refers mainly to Werner Daitz, "Zum Umbau der Volks- und Weltwirtschaft," *Das freie Wort* 16, no. 15/16 (1916).

71 Göring was reported to have said that economic-political expansion in this part of Europe was indispensable for the success of the Four Year Plan, quoted in Antonin Basch, *The Danube Basin and the German Economic Sphere* (London: K. Paul, Trench, Trubner & Co., 1944), 206.

72 Hans-Joachim Braun, *The German Economy in the Twentieth Century: The German Reich and the Federal Republic* (London: Routledge, 2003), 64.

73 German Institute for Business-Cycle Research, *Weekly Report*, no. 47/48 (1938): 5–6.

With Austria's disappearance as an independent state in 1938, the German envelopment of the southeast assumed the character of a drive towards a self-sufficient "Continental Europe" under German tutelage, involving stringent economic regimentation (*Wirtschaftslenkung*).[74] Moreover, with Austria's Anschluss, Germany obtained economic supremacy in the Danube basin and an infrastructural springboard for further expansions with Vienna as a jumping-off point for Germany's interests in this region. Ever since the "Hamburg of the Southeast" idea had been launched as Vienna's new port mission, Germany tried to become a successor to the old Austrian policy in regarding the Danubian area.[75] The Gauleiter of Vienna, Baldur von Schirach—working on Metternich's writing desk— planned a spectacular harbor gate to span the Danube as a visual landmark and indication of the opening up of the Southeast.[76] Austria's last foreign minister, Guido Schmidt, wrote a memo about "opening a southeast trading post" using the semiannual Vienna trade fair as a southeast showcase, before leaving for key industrial jobs in the National Socialist system.[77] On 8 February 1940, the *Südosteuropagesellschaft* (Society for Southeast Europe, SOEG) was established in Vienna, producing confidential snap studies of the economic assets of the Balkans. German war scientists of *Südostforschung* (research on the southeast) explained that long-range programs would be carried out to transform the backward Danubian agricultural system, increasing its intensity and efficiency with German techniques, and to adapt, to whatever extent possible, associated biophysical (i.e. transport systems, irrigation) and socio-economic conditions. Ernst Wagemann, founder of the German Institute for Business Research, which provided the intellectual foundations for the organization of the war economy,[78] assumed that not only all the food and fodder that Germany had imported from global markets could be obtained from South-Eastern Europe, but also all agricultural raw materials.[79] Thus, in 1939, before the outbreak of war, central

---

74 "Continental European Cooperation," term in Walther Funk, *Das wirtschaftliche Gesicht des Neuen Europa*. Special print from Walther Funk et al., eds., *Europäische Wirtschaftsgemeinschaft* (Berlin: Paschke, 1942), 10.

75 See also Nicholas Dascovici, "Le problème du Danube après les derniers changements dans la politique européenne," *Affaires Danubiennes: Revue de l'Europe Centrale et du Sud-Est* 1, no. 1 (1938): 57–61.

76 Hawlik, *Wien*, 172.

77 AT-OeStA/Denkschrift über die Frage einer zu errichtenden Südosthandelsstelle, July 14, 1939, quoted without signture in Thomas Weyr, *The Setting of the Pearl: Vienna under Hitler* (Oxford University Press, 2005), 142.

78 J. Adam Tooze, *Statistics and the German State, 1900–1945: The Making of Modern Economic Knowledge* (Cambridge University Press, 2001), 105.

79 Ernst Wagemann, *Der Neue Balkan* (Hamburg: Hanseatische Verlagsanstalt, 1939), 77, 95.

and southeastern Europe was subject to German economic domination to a greater extent than before 1914.[80] Doubtlessly foreseeing the upcoming empire, a shrewd local expert described the situation in 1939 as follows:

If Hitler survives the present European war and endures until 1945, the Nazi Reich will have a great port at Vienna and a Rhine-Danube canal, all built at a cost of 300 million dollars. Then the Danube will be the Imperial Waterway, inexpensive and unassailable, carrying the German military flotilla into southeastern Europe and returning car-loads of supplies to the heart of Germany to feed her plump body. [81]

Since *Blitzkrieg*, military technology no longer concentrated on the barrage fire of artillery but rather "inverted air and earth into a vertical battlefield,"[82] and offensive fronts could push from the very first day deep within the hinterland using tanks, bombers, and paratroopers—the requirements in terms of fuel supplies were correspondingly far higher. Oil had become both one of the key resources for warfare and a war aim in itself. In World War I, wherein, as British War Cabinet member Lord Curzon, put it at the Inter-Allied Petroleum Conference in 1918, "the Allied cause had floated to victory upon a wave of oil," fuels had already been key to feeding the global war machines. Since then, petroleum has developed into the lifeblood of contemporary societies, and its steady flow has always been deeply influenced by power constellations.

Under National Socialist rule, oil-poor Germany got a "chemical empire" built on coal, air, and water.[83] Until the late 1930s, most of Germany's liquid fuels had been imported; only one third of all liquid fuel requirements in 1936 was German-produced.[84] The extremely costly (in every sense) synthetic oil programs were then started. Although conversion methods had already been developed after World War I, it was the National Socialist war economy that made synthetic oil a "native raw material."[85] More than ninety-two percent of Germany's aviation gasoline and half its

---

80 Basch, *The Danube Basin*, 222.
81 Stoyan Pribichevich, *World without End: The Saga of South-Eastern Europe* (New York: Reynal & Hitchcock, 1939), 365.
82 Franz Theodor Csokor, *Als Zivilist im polnischen Krieg* (Amsterdam: De Lange, 1940), 107.
83 United States Strategic Bombing Survey, *Oil division: Final Report*, 2nd ed. (Washington: U. S. Govt. print. off., 1947), 1.
84 Ibid.
85 The Association of German Engineers (Verein Deutscher Ingenieure VDI) committed itself to the "native," "indigenous" generation of industrial raw materials, "Deutsche Technik und Rohstoffwirtschaft," *Zeitschrift des Vereins Deutscher Ingenieure*, 78 (1934): 1285–1290.

total petroleum during the war years came from synthetic fuel plants. At its peak in early 1944, the German synfuels effort produced more than 124,000 barrels per day from twenty-five plants,[86] with high costs: fifteen times as much steel was needed for synthetic oil plants as for crude oil refineries, and the comparative amount of labor necessary was equally enormous.[87]

Before the annexation of Austria, German oil production was concentrated in the vicinity of Hannover. After 1938, the declining crude oil production in the "Old Reich" was offset by Austria's domestic production. German oil companies tried to secure licenses and oilfields, together with the control of the country's existing refineries.[88] The Reich's "drilling program" was expanded to include Austria, and a new Ostmark "Bitumen Law" rendered all existing natural resources the property of the state. The discovery of new oilfields in the Vienna basin enabled the production of crude oil at a rate of about 1.1 million tonnes a year in 1943.[89] The production for 1944 was put at about 1.5 million tonnes and was estimated at three times the country's normal pre-war requirements. German and Austrian production together, however, never exceeded 2 million tonnes in one year, and Germany needed four times that much.[90] The strategic importance of the Austrian oil production also lay in the fact that it was located close to Vienna and thus fairly close to existing oil refineries operating primarily on Romanian stock and the Danube.

Along with efforts to increase production, the regime began to stockpile petroleum at great expense. At the outbreak of the war, Germany's stockpiles of fuel consisted of a total of 15 million barrels.[91]

The "economic research company" (*Wirtschaftsforschungsgesellschaft*, WIFO), founded in 1934 in partnership with I.G. Farben, was established partly to buy and store reserves of fuel and lubricants, but was also in charge of testing, blending, storing, and distributing gasoline and oil to the air forces. Therefore Berlin-based WIFO built many storage depots, mostly underground and scattered throughout the Reich.[92]

---

86 U.S. Department of Energy, Office of Fossil Energy: Early Days of Coal Research, accessed Jan. 12, 2018, https://energy.gov/fe/early-days-coal-research.
87 United States Strategic Bombing Survey, *Oil division*, 15.
88 In the vicinity of Vienna: Floridsdorf, Kagran, Schwechat, Korneuburg, Vösendorf.
89 NARA M1934. Records created for Project Safehaven, 1942–1946, to restrict German financial networks and prevent the country from funding another war. WASH-SPDF-INT-1: Documents 1601–1650, 218.
90 United States Strategic Bombing Survey, *Oil division*, 14.
91 Peter W. Becker, "The role of Synthetic fuel in World War II Germany. Implications for today?," *Air University Review* 32, no. 5 (1981): 45–53 (here 46).
92 For details see Hans-Dieter Götz, *Geheime Reichssache WIFO* (Germering: Selbstverlag, 2009).

With the large increase of domestic oil production after 1939, the capacity of the existing Austrian refineries was expanded, their technical equipment modernized, and the erection of a sixth refinery begun. During the 1939 "phoney war," WIFO started the construction of a huge storage plant and oil refinery in the Lobau, Vienna's traditional recreation area, including a special harbor for unloading tank ships bringing crude oil from Romania, Hungary, and southern Poland.[93] Refined products were reloaded, to be shipped up the river to Germany by barges. Pumping installations and pipelines from the Austrian oil fields to the refinery were also built, together with forty underground oil storage tanks, each with a capacity to store about 120,000 tonnes of fuel.[94]

The actual harbor construction work in the Danube wetlands, which were requisitioned for this purpose, was largely assigned to companies from the so-called Altreich. Two Munich construction firms (Hoch- und Tiefbau München-Wien and Philipp Holzmann A.G.) were commissioned to undertake large-scale excavation activities.[95] From 1940, up to 500 prisoners held in a forced labor camp in the Lobau worked for these companies (see Fig. 4).[96]

Since the forty-five meter-wide entrance to the Lobau harbor was also planned to be the entry point for the revitalized (and as yet unfinished) project of a Donau-Oder Canal,[97] the harbor basin was (and still is) located 1.3 km further away. A docks light railway opened in 1941 to Stadlau station, and a harbor road was laid along the *Hubertusdamm*, the flood barrier on the left bank of the Danube. Loading pontoons and pumping stations enabled the transshipment of oil products from barges to the storage tanks built on specially constructed earthworks along the banks. Construction was continually interrupted by flooding, five times in 1941 alone. In August of the same year, the *Hubertusdamm* was broken through to allow the

---

93 NARA Report On Wirtschaftliche Forschunggesellschaft M.B.H. Economic Research Limited Liability Co. Berlin, Called WIFO From GEA Branch Prelim. Report, 30 Sept 47; 2.

94 Rudolf Tillmann, "Der Wiener Hafen – Rückblick und Ausblick," *Zeitschrift des Österreichischen Ingenieur- und Architekten-Vereines* 93, 1/2 (1948): 1–20 (here 4).

95 Alois Ammer, "Neue Hafenanlagen an der Donau in der Ostmark," *Der Deutsche Baumeister* 3 (1939): 18–21.

96 Manfred Pohl, *Philipp Holzmann Geschichte eines Bauunternehmens 1849–1999* (Munich: C.H.Beck, 1999), 265.

97 The new canal was to extend over 325 km in total, leading off from the "Adolf Hitler Canal" (today Gliwicki Canal) and dividing into two branches at Angern/March. One branch was planned to run across the Marchfeld to the Danube downstream from Vienna, while the other branch was to consist of the March river which entered the Danube at Theben. However, of the roughly forty-kilometer stretch of the planned waterway, no more than a few kilometers had been finished by 1943, and it is now used as recreation area.

Danube to flow into the new harbor basin. In the summer of 1941, while the first consignment of crude oil was being distilled, an above-ground air raid defense system was built, and from 1942 to 1943, what were known as slit trenches (i.e., uncovered trenches) were also constructed to protect the area against air raids. The first barge train transporting Romanian oil arrived at the Lobau port on 10 November 1942 and was unloaded at the WIFO plant.[98]

Fig. 4 Lobau, with the construction site of the WIFO oil depot in the background, and to the right, river bank excavation using an electric excavator, with a harbor pumping station in the foreground (March 1941). Private Archive

---

98 *Die Gemeindeverwaltung des Reichsgaues Wien vom 1. April 1940 bis 31. März 1945*, Verwaltungsbericht (Vienna: Magistrat der Stadt Wien, 1949), 449.

There were changes in the Lower Lobau too. After Austria's authoritarian *Ständestaat* government dissolved the "war victims fund" (*Kriegsgeschädigtenfond*) in 1937, the Lobau became the legal property of the Vienna Municipality on 19 January 1938. Renamed the "Reich hunting ground of Lobau," the Lower Lobau was made the property of the German Reich through an agreement between the City of Vienna and the German Reich, to be managed by the Reich's forestry department, enlarged by compulsory acquisition,[99] and to be used solely as feudal hunting area for the Nazi elites.

"Food is a weapon!" was the slogan of German agricultural policy during the food war.[100] Support for stockpiling food was proclaimed as a particular goal of the Four Year Plan as early as 1936, during the Reich Farmers' Day meeting in Goslar.[101] Since there was not enough state-owned storage space available for the Reich's planned grain reserves, the provision of storage space for food supplies was declared the duty of the entire German people, and particularly of private German businesses. As early as 1935, subsidies of up to thirty-five percent of building costs and tax benefits were made available to encourage the construction of grain silos. Hermann Göring, the commissioner for the Four Year Plan, regarded the construction "as belonging to military armament."[102] Following a record harvest in the summer of 1938, the *Reichsgetreidestelle* requisitioned 1.8 million tonnes for "emergency storage" and Herbert Backe, made "special commissioner for the construction of grain storage units" by Göring, developed a "program for the accelerated construction of grain storage depots." The new storage depots for use by the Reich were originally to have been constructed privately, so that the construction project would conform to the Reich's uniform standards and exist without the need for protracted authorization procedures; nonetheless, the types of silo construction permitted were already specified by the state.[103] Both the location and size of storage spaces were also to be determined by central authorities. In almost every case, the concrete construction was, ideally, to reflect "vernacular styles" in line with ruling

---

99 Peter Böhmer, Ronald Faber, eds., *Waidmannsheil! – der Fall Abensberg-Traun: Die österreichische Finanzverwaltung und die Restitution entzogener Vermögen 1945 bis 1960* (Vienna, 2003), 421.
100 Hanns Deetjen, "Nahrung ist Waffe! Agrarwirtschaftliche Aufklärung im Kriege," *Deutsche Agrarpolitik*, 1, (1942/43): 301–305.
101 *Reichsbauerntage in Goslar,* Tagungsberichte 1934/1938, (Berlin: Reichsnährstandsverlag, n.d.).
102 Quoted from: Götz Aly, *Hitlers Volksstaat–Raub, Rassenkrieg und nationaler Sozialismus* (Frankfurt am Main: Fischer, 2005), 195.
103 Kurt Seidel, "Bau und Einrichtung von Getreidespeichern zur Förderung unserer Vorratswirtschaft," *Der Vierjahresplan* 3, no. 11 (1939): 719–721.

aesthetic requirements. The overall authority for the important war project lay with the "Reich department of economic development" (*Reichsstelle für Wirtschaftsausbau*) in Berlin, with Fritz Todt, the general inspector of buildings, having responsibility for the implementation and monitoring of the Reich's large-scale silo construction projects.

Reich silos for grain were also constructed in Vienna, to store goods from the cereal producing regions of the Danubian lowlands. The construction of "Europe's largest inland port" was planned in Albern's wetlands downstream from the confluence of the Danube canal.[104] Albern, formerly a small fishing village on the Danube, had been incorporated within Greater Vienna in October 1938. The city authorities now were obliged to make land available for this purpose; the actual harbor construction was subject to the control of the "Reich transport ministry" in Berlin. The Albern harbor area extended over sixty hectares. The basin, roughly one kilometer long and ninety meters wide, had steel sheet piles to protect the banks. On both quaysides of the harbor, intended for the transshipment of grain supplies, five grain silos were erected. These had their own elevators and a total storage capacity of about 90,000 tonnes. Transshipment began in October 1941, when the first vessel carrying Romanian grain could be unloaded into the 500-tonne silo, belonging to the Friesacher company.[105]

Although loyal to the regime, nature conservation experts protested more or less cautiously ("paradise lost!") against the destruction of a nature reserve,[106] but were not able to address their concerns due to war effort priorities. Günther Schlesinger, "commissioner for nature conservation" (*Sonderbeauftragter des Naturschutzes für die Ostmark*), had not been integrated in any planning process. He suggested afterwards to hide the "native worthlessness" of the "desolated," already existing concrete silos with *Ampelopsis* or other climbing plants (see Fig. 5).[107]

Inevitably, what was thought to be an arterial road of German conquest soon became the regime's battleground after the air war over Vienna had become a serious menace on 10 September 1944, with the 15th U.S. Air Force attacking oil facilities in *Schwechat* and *Lobau*. On 5 November, an armada of 500 B-17s and B-24s was sent against Vienna, dropping 1,100

104 Kurt Sommer, *Das schöne Groß-Wien* (Vienna: Deutscher Verlag für Jugend und Volk, 1941), 39.
105 *Die Gemeindeverwaltung des Reichsgaues Wien vom 1. April 1940 bis 31. März 1945*, 448.
106 L. Schr. (= Leo Schreiner), "Ein verlorenes Paradies vor den Toren Wiens," *Blätter für Naturkunde und Naturschutz* 10 (1940): 103–105.
107 NÖLA RStH ND IId-3–Fachliche Angelegenheiten des Natur- und Denkmalschutzes, Geheime Akten, Höhere Naturschutzbehörde des Reichsgaus Wien, I-a-N, 1941, Carton 39.

tonnes of bombs (including fire bombs) on oil refinery targets. Half a dozen raids followed over the next weeks, with refineries in the Vienna area the major targets again. Results were impressive: production was down to about thirty percent of what it had been in the spring 1944.[108] A few weeks before the end of the war, a series of raids again did heavy damage to oil and infrastructure targets.[109] Hitler's "pearl" lay in ruins. All port facilities on the Danube were heavily damaged (see Fig. 6).

Fig. 5: Albern, view of grain silos and quay walls (sheet piling construction) on the southern bank of the harbor basin (Summer 1941). Private Archive

As erratic blocks, the concrete Albern storage facilities survived the war more or less undamaged. Approximately 12,000 bomb craters were recorded in the wooded areas of the Lobau. The environmental damage caused by oil spillages resulting from the bombings was enormous, and the cleanup of contamination was only concluded in 2014. But in 1957, the *Arbeiter-Zeitung* seemed optimistic that the Lobau port looked "as though it had been placed by chance within the glorious green landscape of the river wetlands." Despite the oil floating on the

---

108 Johann Ulrich, *Der Luftkrieg über Österreich 1939–1945* (Vienna: Österr. Bundesverlag, 1994), 18.
109 Ibid., 26–27.

water, and the gray, fume-emitting barges, "It is almost as though nature has not yet acknowledged the industrialization fashioned by war."[110]

After the war, the Cold War began. The Soviet Union was the "undisputed master of the Danube" from the Black Sea to Vienna.[111] Control of the river was again a strategic necessity for military control of southeastern Europe, but from the point of view of infrastructure and logistics, the Danube was still both an asset and a liability. While U.S. experts discussed the possibility of applying the methods and principles of the TVA (Tennessee Valley Authority) on the Danube,[112] the Iron Curtain had already descended "like a guillotine" across the continent.

Fig. 6: Bombing Of *Lobau* Island by Consolidated B-24 Liberators Of The 15th Air Force, 1 July 1944. NARA Black and White and Color Photographs of U.S. Air Force and Predecessor Agencies Activities, Facilities, and Personnel - World War II . Reference Number: 342-FH-3A04937-61951AC.

---

110 "Die Binnenstadt Wien ist eine Hafenstadt," *Arbeiter-Zeitung*, 10 May 1957, 3.
111 *Future Danube River Navigation and Control,* NARA Record Group 263: Records of the Central Intelligence Agency 1894–2002, Series Intelligence Publication Files 1946–50; File Unit ORE 34–48, 1.
112 George Kiss, TVA on the Danube? *The Geographical Review* 37, no. 2 (1947): 274–302.

Critical Hubs of the Great Acceleration: The Social Ecology of Alpine Tourism in Vorarlberg, Austria after World War II[1]

Robert Groß
Martin Knoll

Intersections of Environmental and Tourism History

"While historians of tourism have always concerned themselves with their subjects' quixotic quest for idealized and unblemished nature, environmental historians often dig deeper. They do not just consider how tourists imagined or protected nature, but also consider the ecological or material transformations associated with the tourism industry."[2] The Alpine landscapes of Austria, a country that hosted some 144 million overnight tourist stays in 2017, and more than a hundred million of them by visitors from abroad,[3] seem to be a rewarding study area to explore. The Alps, popularized and developed as the "Playground of Europe" (Leslie Stephen, 1871), primarily by well-to-do British tourists during the nineteenth century,[4] have since been transformed and modernized in many ways, albeit sometimes in the form of a "masked transformation", as Laurence Cole and Katharina Scharf suggest when analyzing the tourism history of the Austrian provinces Salzburg and Tyrol.[5] While recent social science approaches to modern tourism try to avoid spatial essentialism by

1 This paper is an output of the project "*Alpine Skiläufer und die Umgestaltung alpiner Täler*," funded by the "*Fonds zur Förderung der wissenschaftlichen Forschung*" (FWF) (Nr. P24728-G18). Special thanks goes to Univ. Prof. Ing. Dr. phil. Verena Winiwarter for supervising the project.
2 Scott Moranda, "The Emergence of an Environmental History of Tourism," *Journal of Tourism History* 7, no. 3 (2015), 268–289 (here 272).
3 N. N., "Tourism statistics," *austriatourism.com* (January 18, 2018), accessed Jan. 30, 2018, http://www.austriatourism.com/fileadmin/user_upload/Media_Library/Downloads/Tourismusforschung/2018G_Kalenderjahr_2017__Hochrechnung_ZusFassung.pdf.
4 Paul Bernard, *Rush to the Alps: The Evolution of Vacationing in Switzerland* (New York: Columbia University Press 1978); Susan Barton, *Healthy Living in the Alps: The Origins of Winter Tourism in Switzerland, 1860–1914* (Manchester: Manchester University Press 2008); Burkhart Lauterbach, "Als der Berg die Viktorianer rief.' Alpentourismus im 19. Jahrhundert als Handlungsfeld kulturellen Transfers," *Schweizerisches Archiv für Volkskunde* 101, no. 1 (2005), 49–66.
5 Laurence Cole and Katharina Scharf, "Alpine Tourism and 'Masked Transformation:' Salzburg and Tyrol before 1914," *Zeitschrift für Tourismuswissenschaft* 9, no. 1 (2017): 33–63.

advocating a constructivist concept of tourism destinations and adopting practice theory for their purposes,[6] environmental history perspectives have the potential to fully acknowledge the hybrid nature of tourism landscapes as being "both material and cultural: products of ecology, economic exploitation, and cultural preferences."[7] A more recent concept in the environmental history debate suggests that all human history appears in dynamic nexuses of social practices and the material realm.[8] Historians, accordingly, study these nexuses, also called "socio-natural sites" in their historical dynamic.[9] Research focusing on the environmental history of tourism can thus be understood as the attempt to analyze the development of socio-natural sites of tourism, the social and material precipitates of tourism-related practices.

Social practices of tourism are tightly connected to processes of spatial mobility by nature. Unsurprisingly, dealing with tourism history necessarily implies the investigation of mobility,[10] or, to put it more precisely, of different mobilities. This leads to the first of two assumptions guiding the perspective of this chapter: environmental history of tourism particularly benefits from the investigation of critical hubs, where different types of mobility merge.[11] Tourism destinations are interconnected within supra-regional networks of infrastructures that enable mobility. This connection is typically a precondition for development as a tourism

---

6   As the Finnish Geographer Jaarko Saarinen puts it: "Tourist destinations are not 'out there' waiting to be discovered, explored and consumed: like regions 'they are our and others' constructions' (see Allen et al., 1998: 2). Destinations can be understood as constantly changing products of a certain combination of social, political and economic relationships that are specific in space and time (see Getz, 1999). This process was conceptualized here through the discourse of region and discourse of development and the identity of tourist destination based on the socio-spatial manifestations of the previous discourses." Jaarko Saarinen, "Destinations in Change: The Transformation of Tourist Destinations," *Tourism Studies* 4, no. 2 (2005), 161–179 (here 172).

7   Moranda, "The Emergence of an Environmental History of Tourism," 281.

8   Theodore R. Schatzki. "Nature and technology in history," *History and Theory* 42, Theme Issue (2003): 82–93; Verena Winiwarter et al., "The Environmental History of the Danube River Basin as an Issue of Long-Term Socio-ecological Research," in *Longterm Socio-Ecological Research: Studies in Society-Nature Interactions Across Spatial and Temporal Scales*, ed. Simron Jit Singh et al. (Heidelberg: Springer, 2013), 103–122 (here 105).

9   Verena Winiwarter and Martin Schmid, "Umweltgeschichte als Untersuchung sozionaturaler Schauplätze? Ein Versuch Johannes Colers *Oeconomia* umwelthistorisch zu interpretieren," in: *Umweltverhalten in Geschichte und Gegenwart: Vergleichende Ansätze*, ed. Thomas Knopf (Tübingen: Attempto, 2008), 158–173 (here 162).

10   Shelley Baranowski, "Common ground. Linking transport and tourism history," *The Journal of Transport History* 28, no. 1 (2007): 120–124 (here 120); John K. Walton, "Transport, travel, tourism and mobility: A cultural turn?" *The Journal of Transport History* 27, no. 2 (2006): 129–134; John Urry, *Mobilities* (Cambridge: Polity Press, 2007), 3.

11   Martin Knoll, "Touristische Mobilitäten und ihre Schnittstellen," *Ferrum* 88 (2016), 8486.

destination. At the connection points to supra-regional networks, as well as on the local level, different types of mobility have to be synchronized, and the transitions between them have to be organized.[12] These different types of mobility include, for example, individual motorcar traffic, public transport, and vertical mobility provided by cable cars, but also individual somatic mobility such as hiking, skiing, or cycling. The extent to which actors in a tourism destination succeed in organizing the critical hubs of mobilities is decisive for the success of the site in tourism business. In his study on transport systems, tourism, and conservation in the Swiss Alps, historian Wolfgang König refers to a situation reported by a Swiss cable car company in the 1930s.[13] The reported constellation is a well-suited example to highlight the peculiarities of the addressed critical hubs: in Davos, the *Parsenn* cable car, which took on service in 1932, turned out to be a very popular new means of transportation. In 1933, the cable car transported some 99,000 passengers; in 1936, this number had increased to some 160,000. During the 1936/37 winter season, reservation tickets had to be issued in order to shorten the queue around the valley station. Waiting times of up to two hours provoked "*sichtliche Verstimmung des Publikums*"[14] ("obvious annoyance within the public").[15] The report portrayed the situation around the valley station as a chaotic one: autobuses and the passengers boarding and deboarding them, cars, sleighs, the queuing line of skiers, and pedestrians blocking each other. Contemporaries saw two options for dealing with the problem: first, an extension of the cable car's transport capacity; second, an improvement of the traffic around the station. What happened in Davos during the 1930s is but one example of similar problems all around the Alpine region, particularly after World War II, when mass car ownership began to revolutionize tourism mobility in Europe. This chapter focuses on two types of critical hubs created by winter tourism: roads and ski slopes.[16]

---

12 Ibid., 86.
13 Wolfgang König, *Bahnen und Berge: Verkehrstechnik, Tourismus und Naturschutz in den Schweizer Alpen 1870–1939* (Frankfurt a. M.: Campus, 2000): 153.
14 Ibid.
15 Passages translated by the authors unless otherwise indicated.
16 Robert Groß, *Wie das 1950er Syndrom in die Täler kam: Umwelthistorische Überlegungen zur Konstruktion von Wintersportlandschaften am Beispiel Damüls in Vorarlberg* (Regensburg: Roderer, 2012); Robert Groß, "Die Modernisierung der Vorarlberger Alpen durch Seilbahnen, Schlepp- und Sessellifte," *Montfort – Vierteljahresschrift für Geschichte und Gegenwart Vorarlbergs* 64, no. 2 (2012): 13–25; Robert Groß and Verena Winiwarter, "Commodifying snow, taming the waters: Socio-ecological niche construction in an Alpine village," *Water History* 7, no. 4 (2015): 489–509; Robert Groß, "Uphill and Downhill Histories: How Winter Tourism Transformed Alpine Regions in Vorarlberg/Austria – 1930 to 1970," *Zeitschrift für Tourismuswissenschaft* 9, no. 1 (2017): 115–139.

Furthermore, this chapter aims to specify notions of "The Great Acceleration."[17] Will Steffen and colleagues argued in 2004 that

The human enterprise switched gears after World War II. Although the imprint of human activity on the global environment was, by the mid-twentieth century, clearly discernible [from earlier periods] the rate at which that imprint was growing increased sharply at midcentury. The change was so dramatic that the 1945 to 2000+ period has been called the Great Acceleration. [...] What finally triggered the Great Acceleration after the end of World War II?

The war itself produced a cadre of scientists and technologists, as well as a spectrum of new technologies (most of which depended on the cheap energy provided by fossil fuels), that could then be turned towards the civil economy. [...] New international institutions [...] were formed to aid economic recovery and fuel renewed economic growth. Led by the USA, the world moved towards a system built around neo-liberal economic principles, characterized by more open trade and capital flows. [...] More and more public goods were converted into commodities and placed into the market economy, and the growth imperative rapidly became a core societal value that drove both the socio-economic and the political spheres. [...] The post-World War II economy integrated rapidly, with growth rates reaching their highest values ever in the 1950–1973 period.[18]

The chapter intends to anchor the dynamic of the Great Acceleration spatially and thematically by analyzing the development of winter-tourism infrastructure as a vehicle of transformation of alpine landscapes and economies. Andrew Denning's notion of "alpine modernism" was an important starting point. This transnational ideology formed in an early stage of the Great Acceleration in the late nineteenth century.[19] It shaped the macro-region, winter sports practices, and the relationship between

---

17 John R. McNeill and Peter Engelke, *The great acceleration: An environmental history of the anthropocene since 1945* (Cambridge: The Belknap Press of Harvard University Press, 2014); Kathleen D. Morrison, "Provincializing the Anthropocene," *SEMINAR* 673 (September 2015): 75–80.

18 Will Steffen et al., "The trajectory of the Anthropocene. The Great Acceleration," *The Anthropocene Review* 2, no. 1 (2015): 1–18.

19 Andrew Denning, *Skiing into Modernity: A Cultural and Environmental History* (Berkeley: University ofCalifornia Press, 2015).

humans and alpine nature. Growing networks of winter tourism infra-structure result, according to Denning, from a growing capitalization of the industry within a challenging environment.[20] In contrast to Denning's explanatory model, in which the acceleration of downhill practices is an important indicator of "alpine modernism," this study focuses on the technical uphill acceleration by ski lifts.[21] Technical acceleration, which is the "intentional acceleration of a purposeful process by means of a novel technique,"[22] challenges social groups. Its social acceptance depends on the ability to increase speed in corresponding structural and cultural interfaces. Technical acceleration of practices often impinges on friction surfaces, as the timing of social practices is beyond the interest spheres of individuals but predefined in collective temporal patterns of societies, requiring novel synchronization practice, as Hartmut Rosa argues.[23] If synchronization fails, sections will desynchronize, resulting in a dysfunc-tional slowing down, as in traffic jams.[24]

In this chapter, we will analyze how ski lift entrepreneurs techni-cally accelerated skiers' bodies on their ascent and in return downhill, resulting in a profound transformation of skiing practices. Other than the entanglement of ski lifts and human bodies, ski lift entrepreneurs had to synchronize colliding social and biological timescales:[25] seasonal snowfall periods, but also the vegetative succession of the grassland that served as ski slopes. The concern over vegetative succession is typical for land use practices such as dairy farming, tillage, and forestry. It points to the impact human activities have on agro-ecosystems through any kind of management practices: fertilizing, pest control, moving, and species selection; or, in the case of the winter tourism industry, building activities, revegetation, and grassland management. These practices aim to keep veg-etative succession in a desirable state as part of co-evolutionary dynamic of society, nature and technology.[26]

---

20 Ibid., 180.
21 Hartmut Rosa, *Beschleunigung: Die Veränderung der Zeitstrukturen in der Moderne* (Frankfurt a. Main: Suhrkamp, 2005), 32–33.
22 Ibid., 137.
23 Ibid., 44 and 33.
24 Ibid.
25 Stuart Elden, preface to Henry Lefebvre, *Rhythmanalysis: Space, time and everyday life* (London/New York: Continuum, 2004), vii–xv (here viii).
26 Schatzki, "Nature and technology in history," 82–93; Theodore Schatzki, "Materiality and Social Life," *Nature and Culture* 5, no. 2 (2010): 123–149.

Roads as "Critical Hubs" in Alpine Tourism: Damüls and Mittelberg

Vorarlberg, the region studied in this chapter, faced a great deal of change in the second half of the nineteenth century. Railway lines from Nuremberg/Germany and Switzerland were built to the Austrian border and eventually connected to a railway between Bludenz and Lochau (villages in the Rhine valley). The so-called Arlberg tunnel was opened, linking Vorarlberg with Innsbruck, Salzburg, Linz, Vienna, and the rest of the Austro-Hungarian monarchy. In the beginning of the twentieth century, the railroad networks were gradually enlarged and expanded into Alpine peripheries.[27] Time and space shrank as a result of these infrastructures, creating new kinds of spatial densifications, attracting tourists and tourism entrepreneurs alike. St. Anton am Arlberg, Kitzbühel, Innsbruck, and the Semmering were early winter sport destinations profiting from the building of the main railroads crossing the monarchy. Others, such as Schruns, Bezau, or Mariazell, became popular only when the fine-grained railroad network was further expanded in the early twentieth century. These infrastructures enabled "visitors to calculate an escape rationally from their no less rationalized working routines in the city, matching leisure and working time by making use of technologies such as chronographs, travel guides and train timetables."[28] The integration of high Alpine tourist sites, however, was beyond the reach of collective transport infrastructures, as extreme topographies provided insurmountable obstacles for the railway technology in the early twentieth century. When the proliferation of roads, combustion engines, and diesel fuel accelerated individual mobility from the 1920s onward, these peripheral sites experienced a considerable inflow of tourists during the winter. This required, however, considerable work efforts and monetary investments into road infrastructure building from authorities.[29]

---

27   Robert Groß, "Damüls im Strom der Modernisierung," in *Damüls: Beiträge zur Geschichte und Gegenwart,* ed. Michael Kasper and Andreas Rudigier (Damüls: Frei, 2013), 247–284 (here 258).

28   Bernhard Tschofen, *Berg – Kultur – Moderne: Volkskundliches aus den Alpen* (Vienna: Sonderzahl, 1999), 91.

29   Georg Rigele, "Sommeralpen – Winteralpen: Veränderungen im Alpinen durch Bergstraßen, Seilbahnen und Schilifte in Österreich," in *Umweltgeschichte: Zum historischen Verhältnis von Gesellschaft und Natur,* ed. Ernst Bruckmüller, Verena Winiwarter (Schriften des Institutes für Österreichkunde 63) (Vienna: Öbv & Hpt., 2000), 121–150.

Damüls

The village of Damüls provides an illuminating example of a road building effort in which engineers were confronted with a range of different obstacles when they aimed to accelerate mobility. The village's center was 1,400 meters above sea level on the valley head of the *Argental*. The next train station of the narrow-gauge railroad *Bregenzerwaldbahn* was 750 meters lower, at a distance of 11.5 kilometers in Bezau. A traveler from the regional capital, Bregenz, which was at the same time a transfer point to the Austrian Western Railway connecting Vorarlberg with Vienna, had to plan around four hours to Bezau and, depending on the weather conditions, another four to six hours either by foot, horse drawn carriage, or sledge to Damüls. In 1924, the village became popular among skiers. Winter after winter, groups of skiers, mostly organized by alpine associations, skiers' clubs, schools, or the military, visited Damüls. This first tourist boom encouraged locals and immigrants alike to build up hotels, guesthouses, huts, and ski schools, providing novel income possibilities for rather impoverished Alpine farmers. However, the road to Damüls proved to be completely insufficient, especially during the winter, when four to six meters of snow covered the land, hampering not only the influx of tourists but also the transformation of the village into a winter tourist destination. New ski lifts were planned as early as the late 1930s, but as long as Damüls lacked a suitable road connection to ensure economic viability, local entrepreneurs were unable to acquire necessary capital. The muddy, stony, steep path, combined with the strict austerity measures of road authorities because of the global economic crisis in the 1930s and the war economy between 1939 and 1945, narrowed the scope of action for entrepreneurs.[30] Thus, the road as a critical hub of tourism mobility remained a bottleneck in the transport network connecting Damüls with the points of origin of winter tourists in the valleys.

In 1945, the road was in such a poor condition that the road authorities decided to close it for motorized traffic, except for motorcycles, local drivers, and postbuses.[31] Due to the lack of conservation work between 1939 and 1945, landslides had moved road ditches, and the road surface as well as its gravel bed were washed away by water runoff. Only one guard, two laborers, and an unskilled young man maintained the road, which was completely inadequate given the length of the road, about ten kilometers. Those in charge suspected that the venture would be extremely costly

---

30 Groß, *Wie das 1950er Syndrom in die Täler kam*, 72–73.
31 Ibid.

and time-consuming, as the area has a very complex and unstable geology. Furthermore, the route of the road crossed countless smaller streams, plunging along the slopes and ravines in the depths. Wherever possible, the engineers tried to span the streams with bridges or tunneled them to keep the water away from the road. A network of drainage channels was planned to tame groundwater and stabilize the road. Initially, road construction was limited to rehabilitating enough so it was suitable for motorized vehicles. In 1956, only vehicles weighing three tons or less could use the road. From the point of view of tourism operators, this was untenable, as they planned to build up a ski lift network. In 1958, the provincial road authorities calculated that twenty-three million Austrian Schillings would be required to improve the situation. However, such costs by far exceeded the budget of the road authorities, given that the road was only of local importance; the authorities ranked the planned construction activities according to their importance.[32]

The first unintended side effects of the road works occurred in 1958, when mudflows and landslides destroyed the efforts of the road building authorities. Local inhabitants argued that road engineers planned generous road widths to accelerate the traffic but ignored local conditions, which were known for centuries to be unstable. The road was planned along a steep slope. Farmers used the land below the road for intense forestry. Thus, the road building caused considerable damage to landowners that made further expenses and building measures necessary to stabilize soil and road infrastructure. In 1962, further complications arose: this time, they affected not only farmers land but also hotels, houses, and restaurants. At an area further up the road, construction had been drenched over the years. Wherever the slopes were cut by infrastructure – houses, parking lots, roads, and paths – veritable streams flooded the grassland after heavy rainfall or during thaw. A drainage system that was built during the years of National Socialist rule had apparently been damaged in the course of the road construction, destabilizing an entire district of Damüls. In 1964, the regional government provided 400,000 Schillings from the federal budget to prevent further harm.[33] The money was used to renew the drainage system. It was only when the building of the drainage began that the engineers realized the actual spreading of the underground watercourses. The supporting measures increased the costs of the road building considerably. At the same time, the drainage finally lifted traffic bottlenecks, which in turn

---

32   Groß, "Damüls im Strom der Modernisierung," 271–277.
33   Robert Groß and Verena Winiwarter, "How Winter Tourism Transformed Agrarian Livelihoods in an Alpine Village: The Case of Damüls in Vorarlberg/Austria," *Ekonomska I Ekohistorija* 10, no. 11 (2015): 46–63 (here 54–57).

fostered a significant response among tourism entrepreneurs. As road engineers increased the road capacity, they transformed critical hubs of mobility, providing the necessary inflow of tourists, which resulted in a demand for mechanization uphill in the form of ski lifts.

Mittelberg Kleinwalsertal

Kleinwalsertal provides another example for the role road traffic plays within the mobility pattern in which cable cars, ski lifts, and skiing are integrated. After some very difficult years between 1945 to 1948, tourism in Kleinwalsertal had made a tremendous recovery. With 616,810 overnight stays in the winter of 1950/51, the valley hosted nearly forty-six percent of Vorarlberg's visitors.[34] In the valley, where a first ski lift had been built early on, in 1940, local authorities considered cable cars as important infrastructures for attracting more visitors.[35] Consequently, the valley was developed with this technology from the 1950s on. To name but some of the most important projects: the chairlifts of Hirschegg-Heuberg and Mittelberg-Zaferna, opened 1950 and 1952; the cable cars of Kanzelwand and Walmendingerhorn, opened in 1954 and 1966; and finally the ski arena at Mount Ifen, developed from 1972 on.[36] But this success in tourism had a downside: more and more cars jammed the only road leading into the valley. From the late 1940s on, complaints about growing road traffic and overburdened and damaged streets are topics regularly debated in the municipal council and the local press,[37] for good reason: on a Sunday, 2 March 1952, some 1,000 vehicles were counted entering the valley; thirty years later, in a count on Sunday, 21 February 1982, the number had risen to 3,117.[38]

---

34 Ulrich Nachbaur, *Vorarlberger Territorialfragen 1945 bis 1948: Ein Beitrag zur Geschichte der Vorarlberger Landesgrenzen seit 1805* (Konstanz: UVK Verlagsgesellschaft, 2007), 146–147.

35 "Niederschrift über die am 18. April 1953 – 13.30 Uhr – im Rathaus Riezlern stattgefundene Gemeindevertretungsversammlung" (Records of the Municipal Council of Mittelberg, April 18, 1953), agenda item no. I/6, *Der Walser* 34, no. 17, April 26, 1953, 1.

36 Walter Hämmerle et al., *Ausflugsverkehr und Fremdenverkehr am Beispiel Kleinwalsertal: Schlußbericht* (Innsbruck: Verlag d. Inst. für Verkehr u. Tourismus, 1984), 38.

37 For example: N. N., "Aus unserer Heimat," *Der Walser* 33, no. 26, July 8, 1951, 1; N. N., "Straßen-Sorgen im Kleinen Walsertal," *Der Walser* 42, no. 4, January 30, 1960, 2.

38 N. N., "Bedeutende Verkehrsleistungen im Kleinen Walsertal," *Der Walser* 33, no. 10, March 8, 1952, 2; Walter Hämmerle, *Ausflugsverkehr und Fremdenverkehr am Beispiel Kleinwalsertal: Schlußbericht*, 48.

Figure 1: Car traffic in Riezlern, Kleinwalsertal, Austria, January/February 1960.
Courtesy of Mittelberg Municipal Administration, Austria.

The picture in Figure 1 is part of a series of photographs taken by the communal authorities in winter 1960 to document the traffic situation, one other of these photographs also was published in the local newspaper.[39] What these photographs depicting traffic jams have in common is that they resemble clichéd pictures from urban metropolises rather than from a small Alpine village. To make things worse, the development of ski lifts and cable cars promoted a new and far less desirable type of mobility: visitors entering the valley by car on a daily basis without using lodging. A study commissioned by Vorarlberg's government and the municipality of Mittelberg made this problem visible in the 1970s. The capacity of cable cars and lifts in the valley (without t-bar lifts) had increased sixfold, from 361,000 passengers per meter per hour in winter 1971/72 to 2,178,800 passengers/meter/hour in winter 1981/82. Over the same period, the amount of overnight stays in winter did not even double, rising from 577,800 to 866,800.[40] Daily visitors, however, cause considerably more road traffic related to the time of their stays in the valley. At first, the extension of infrastructure such as roads and bridges was the dominant strategy promoted by the administrations

39   N. N., "Autoverkehr im Kleinwalsertal," *Der Walser* 42, no. 5, February 6, 1960, 1.
40   Walter Hämmerle et al., *Ausflugsverkehr und Fremdenverkehr am Beispiel Kleinwalsertal: Schlußbericht*, 38.

on federal, state, and municipal levels to deal with the traffic problem – a strategy with clear constraints within the topography of the narrow valley. From the early 1980s on, local authorities experimented with park-and-ride concepts based around an upgrade of public transport.[41]

Figure 2: Cover picture of the local newspaper "Der Walser" presenting the recommendations for a new traffic concept in 1992 and claiming, "less car, more Walser valley." Courtesy of Mittelberg Municipal Administration, Austria.

In the early 1990s, a traffic concept was commissioned, elaborated by Swiss experts, whose results were published in the local newspaper and led to ongoing discussions (Figure 2).[42] Finally, an efficient public bus system was implemented in the late 1990s. In 2010, the magistrate of Mittelberg commissioned a new traffic analysis for evaluating the measures taken; for several years, the public debate on the results of this analysis overlapped with debates about the further development of ski areas and about the planned building of a 2.5-kilometer-long horizontal cable car connecting the two ski areas of Walmendingerhorn and Ifen.[43] These discussions prominently featured questions of mobility and leisure. The proposed cable car project

41 Knoll, *Touristische Mobilitäten*, 90–91; N. N., "Weniger Auto - mehr Kleinwalsertal: Vorschläge für ein Verkehrskonzept für das Kleinwalsertal," *Der Walser* 66, no. 8, February 28, 1992, 2–20.
42 Ibid.
43 N. N., "Bekanntgabe der Beschlüsse der Gemeindevertretungssitzung vom 28. Februar 2011," *Der Walser* 85, no. 9, March 4, 2011, 2–6.

promised to improve Kleinwalsertal's attractiveness as a ski destination, not the least because skiers, as local politician Tom Egger put it, want to move from A to B on their skis, not by bus.[44] While the project of the cable car shuttle has been suspended by a referendum,[45] the integration of vertical mobility within complex mobility patterns of Alpine tourism and their enormous transformative power on the entire socio-natural site remain on the agenda of the valley's debates, as they do in many other Alpine destinations.

Early Mechanization of Skiing Practices

In the 1930s, engineers and skiers alike interpreted the ski lift as a victory over time and space. While an increasingly growing middle class praised time- and space-conscious novelties as amenities, factory workers suffered the downsides of the increased emphasis on efficiency and scientific management on assembly lines.[46] For skiers, in contrast, the accelerating ski lifts opened up new ways of perceiving their bodies and the Alpine landscapes.[47] Principles of scientific management were very common, not only in disciplining factory workers, but also for skiers. Time measurement and the standardization of physical motions was at the very core of this Taylorist ideology. Similar to Frank Bunker Gilbreth, who integrated photography as well as time and motion studies, skiing pioneers such as Mathis Zdarsky, Arnold Fanck, and Hannes Schneider utilized photo and film cameras to optimize the knowledge transfer from experts to greenhorns.[48] Skiing education combined a range of elements, among them the proper training of the body to master exhausting uphill treks, technical skills to manage speedy downhills in an erratic terrain, but also the adoption of environmental knowledge to interpret risks and pleasures of the landscapes. Time, and the formability of skiers' bodies, were key features of the acceleration of the ascent, but also of synchronizing up- and downhill with other practices, as a growing number of winter tourists were members of social groups with limited leisure time. Aristocrats, who could spend the entire so-called

---

44   Ibid., 6.

45   Andreas Roß, "Bürger lehnen Panoramabahn ab," *sueddeutsche.de* (October 21, 2012), accessed July 25, 2013, http://www.sueddeutsche.de/bayern/streit-im-kleinwalsertal-buerger-lehnen-panoramabahn-ab-1.1502362.

46   Robert Groß, "Die Beschleunigung der Berge: Eine Umweltgeschichte des Wintertourismus in Vorarlberg/Österreich, 1920–2010," (PhD. diss., University of Klagenfurt, 2017).

47   Denning, *Skiing into Modernity*, 93.

48   Michael Ponstingl, "Mathias Zdarskys 'Posen des Wissens.' Zu einer fotografischen Kodierung des Skifahrens," in: *Skilauf – Volkssport – Medienzirkus: Skisport als Kulturphänomen*, ed. Markwart Herzog (Stuttgart: Kohlhammer, 2005) 123–149 (here 125).

Winterfrische, lasting several weeks, in the Alps, became a minority in the 1930s. Bourgeois physicians, lawyers, architects, and journalists constituted the majority of winter tourists. They had to synchronize different temporal dynamics of their urbanized places of origin and Alpine holiday destinations. Local entrepreneurs met tourist demands through various forms of trade and commerce, thus importing not only urban culture into rural areas, but also synchronization services, which relieved tourists from time constraints.[49]

The ski lift technology, at its very core, contributed to an infrastructural manifestation of a zeitgeist of acceleration in alpine landscapes. Ernst Constam, its inventor, transferred Frederick Winslow Taylor's method of time studies to skiing. By studying the time use of the guests, he drew conclusions about the efficiency of ski education. It turned out that ski students spent the majority of a paid ski lesson climbing on skis uphill or standing around. Only six minutes of an hour were devoted to training downhill skiing, which was, from Constam's perspective, an irrational waste of time.[50] Finally, his wife encouraged him to design a machine that would relieve skiers from exhausting ascents. In 1934, Ernst Constam applied for a patent of a *Schlepporgan für Skiläufer-Schleppseilbahnen* ("drag lift"). He erected the first drag lift in Davos, Switzerland with a transport capacity of 150 persons/hour but doubled its capacity already in the next winter due to its tremendous success.[51] The drag lift would help to rationalize time use on skis, as Sepp Bildstein, a ski lift pioneer employed as a designer in the automobile manufacture Daimler in Lech, Austria, argues:

> There is no doubt that ski lifts gain importance, as it relieves skiers from exhausting ascent for small costs. Its advantage is obvious: Firstly, skiers save an enormous amount of time, if she/he invests three minutes instead of twelve to fifteen for one hundred meters uphill but secondly, also muscle power for the downhill. Experienced skiers and beginners benefit alike. Furthermore, low operating costs keep prices on an affordable level, which motivates users to a repeated use of the ski lift.[52]

In this quotation, Bildstein argues that the time- and energy-saving features of the ski lift introduce a novel feature of repetition into skiing practices. The following photographs (Figure 3) from the *Albona Grat* in Stuben/Austria demonstrate the effects of the ski lift.

---

49 Groß, *Beschleunigung der Berge*, 79–80.
50 Luzi Hitz, "Ernst Gustav Constam, Erfinder des erfolgreichsten Skiliftsystems," unpublished manuscript, 1–10 (here 2); quoted from: Groß, *Beschleunigung der Berge*, 79–80.
51 Ibid.
52 Sabine Dettling, Bernhard Tschofen and Gustav Schoder, *Spuren: Skikultur am Arlberg* (Bregenz: Bertolini, 2014), 230.

Figure 3: Skiing area at Madloch in Stuben am Arlberg/Austria before and after a ski lift was built. Source: Wolfgang Allgeuer, *Seilbahnen und Schlepplifte in Vorarlberg. Ihre Geschichte in Entwicklungsschritten* (Neugebauer: Graz, 1998), 61.

The photographs give a comparison of the situation before and after the ski lift was built in 1957. The ascent, which is depicted in the lefthand image, was promoted in guidebooks as a four-hour tour. As the many different tracks demonstrate, skiers went in groups, but, depending on snow conditions, they could adapt their route. Often, when the group of skiers reached the top, the skiers took a longer break to survey topography and discuss a suitable downhill run. The downhill itself took a few minutes; however, the depicted tour could fill an entire day for a winter tourist.[53] The ski lift considerably transformed skiing in this area, as the righthand photograph shows. It clearly defined space for skiers amidst top and valley station, forced them into a queue at the access to the ski lift, and turned the ascent into a market-related commodity. The most striking feature was, however, the feature of repetition, as Bildstein argues earlier. According to an advertising leaflet, the ski lift trip took twenty minutes.[54] An individual skier could replicate one up- and downhill cycle up to eight times more often than before, when the ascent was muscle-powered. By doing so, the ski lift became a tool that considerably sped up the

---

53 N. N., "Gott sei Dank oder leider?," *Alpenvereins-Mitteilungen der Sektion Vorarlberg* 4, no. 3 (March 1952): 18, quoted from: Groß, *Beschleunigung der Berge*, 100.
54 Dettling, Tschofen and Schoder, *Spuren: Skikultur am Arlberg*, 194.

down- and uphill cycles; at the same time, it displayed the characteristic side effects of technologies of acceleration – the "speed up" paradox – as Hartmut Rosa argues,[55] meaning that the more individuals aim to move in parallel, the lower the average speed gets, convincingly depicted in the right photograph of Figure 3. After the brief rush of departure, there followed the hangover in the queue, resulting from problems of synchronization of different temporalities. To put it simply, the ski lift, designed as a tool of acceleration led to disruptions of the flow of skiers due to the provoked replications of up and downhill cycles. Ski lifts initially bestowed time gains; however, they fizzled out in the longer run and created constraints for ski lift managers to increase transport capacity and extend networks.

Ski-lift-based acceleration of the ascent displayed favorable economic growth effects. However, the lifts' sharply limited transport capacity, combined with a growing demand, turned out to bottleneck the flow of skiers on their way uphill. Waiting lines in front of the valley stations, displayed by tourism advertisers, symbolized their popularity; at the same time, technical experts from the ski lift industry proclaimed that ski lift entrepreneurs should take recurring waiting lines seriously. They argued that "a modern skier will not be satisfied with one or two single lifts with low transport capacities, if a neighboring ski destination could offer an entire network of ski lifts. Experts warned that the abundance of skiers would be able to choose among many different options due to the use of cars. Thus, a ski lift operator was responsible for diversifying what he offered, otherwise he would not be able to compete anymore."[56]

When winter tourism destinations began to accelerate the ascent technically, they increased their attractiveness, as tourists perceived ski lifts as a high-end amenity. The new technology linked winter sports destinations to a rather novel industry sector and caused a veritable boom. Competition among winter sports destinations was fought out primarily by purchasing technical ski lift novelties, to the benefit of the industry. As a result, some manufacturers of mechanical devices in Alpine valleys began to specialize in ski lift construction and provided relevant consultation services.[57] In contrast to the drag lift, which was developed in Switzerland, the chair lift resulted from efforts based on knowledge brought to the U.S. by two students from who returned from their vacation in Davos, Switzerland; they brought the information to the U.S. companies American Steel and

---

55 Rosa, *Beschleunigung: Die Veränderung der Zeitstrukturen in der Moderne*, 137.
56 Th. Veiter, "Die Schleppliftbauart Doppelmayr," *Internationale Seilbahnrundschau* 1, no. 2 (1958): 66–68 (here 68).
57 Groß, "Die Beschleunigung der Berge: Eine Umweltgeschichte des Wintertourismus in Vorarlberg/Österreich, 1920–2010," 127.

Wire Company (AS&W) and the Union Pacific Railroad (UPR).[58] UPR was managed by Averell Harriman, who sought novel sales markets for transport technology by transforming snow-rich wilderness areas into winter sport destinations equipped with high efficiency ski lifts.[59] In winter 1937/38, the chair lift had its premiere in Sun Valley, Idaho.[60]

Drag and chair lifts were a real sensation in terms of comfort, although they were very limited in transport capacities. Ski lifts accelerated skiing practices and generated an emerging sector in transport facility industries in the post-World War II years, but they also caused a public sensation; their transport capacity had to be increased considerably. Engineers considered the interaction between moving chairs and stationary bodies in the valley station the critical factor that would make efficiency gains possible. The inventor of the double chair lift, Samuel Huntington, designed a special entrance area, aiming at ordering and accelerating skiers' bodies, as depicted on the photographs (Figure 4).

Figure 4: Regulated flows of skiers on the valley station of the chairlift on the Albona-Grat in Stuben am Arlberg. Risch-Lau 1956 (1956). Retrieved from <http://pid.volare.vorarlberg.at/o:4455>

58   Morten Lund, "An editorial postscript," *Skiing Heritage* (June 1999): 27–28 (here 27).
59   Dick Dorworth, "High times at the Harriman," *Skiing Heritage* 17, no. 1 (March 2005): 5–7.
60   Gordon H. Bannerman, M. James Curran and H. Glen Trout, "Aerial Ski Tramway, Patent No. US 2152235 A, issued by the U.S. Patent Office, March 19, 1938," *google.com/patents*, accessed Aug. 7, 2016, http://www.google.com/patents/US2152235?dq=aerial+ski+tramway&ei=tFhzVOXqGYLfPaXYgMAP.

Huntington's design forced skiers to organize themselves in pairs long before they reached the entrance area. Fences channeled the crowd in long rows and made individuals turn their bodies and focus their attention on the loading process of skiers ahead. Ideally, the terrain was sloping; this would improve the flow of skiers through the valley station. Once skiers reached the loading point of the ski lift, they were exposed to the mechanical force of moving chairs that stroke against their bodies. While the pain for the skiers intensified with the speed, boarding time decreased. To mediate between moving chairs and flows of skiers, Huntington designed ideal motion patterns to rationalize ski lift operation.[61]

Apart from chairlift improvements, engineers also focused on drag lifts. Similarly, boarding was considered a critical moment when engineers aimed to optimize existing drag lift models, as the U.S. engineer Charles van Evera argued in 1960: "One of the problems in operating a ski lift is that a time interval is required for skiers to maneuver from the waiting line into the loading station and prepare themselves for boarding the lift. This time period cannot be shortened without endangering the safety of the skiers [...]. The situation clearly limits the speed of the cable [...] and therefore the number of skiers which can be transported on the lift per unit of time."[62] Charles van Evera proposed a disciplining mechanism for the crowds, building on the ideas of Samuel Huntington. Figure 5 illustrates the mechanism.

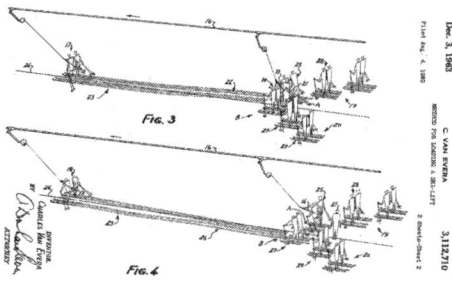

Figure 5: The choreography of efficiency as suggested by Charles van Evera in 1963.

61   Samuel Sterling Huntington, "Ski Lift Patent, Patent No. US 2582201, issued by the U.S. Patent Office, January 8, 1952," *worldwide.espacenet.com*, accessed Dec. 2, 2016, http://worldwide. espacenet.com/publicationDetails/biblio?CC=US&NR=2582201A&KC=A&FT=D#.
62   Charles van Evera, "Method for loading a ski-lift, Patent No. US 3.112.710, issued by the U.S. Patent Office, December 3, 1963," *worldwide.espacenet.com*, accessed Dec. 2, 2016, http://worldwide.espacenet.com/publicationDetails/ biblio?CC=US&NR=3112710A&KC=A&FT=D#.

The sketch demonstrates the zipper-like spatial ordering of skiers' bodies. Van Evera designed the transitional zone between waiting line and ski lift to allow alternating boarding from the left and right row. By doing so, each pair of skiers would have doubled time, which would open up the possibility to either double the speed of the lift or the number of t-bar sticks. Both modifications of the ski lift would double their transport capacity, thus synchronizing the timing of up- and downhill practices according to the needs of the ski lift entrepreneur.[63]

Ski lift engineers used these technologies to further increase the transport capacity and speed of the ski lifts. Triple and quadruple chairlifts, developed in the mid-1960s, built on optimized entrance areas and spatial control systems of the flow of skiers.[64] Conveyor belts aimed to accelerate pairs of skiers before they accessed the loading point, thereby reducing force, which was transmitted from moving chairs on the bodies of skiers. Their utilization enabled further transport capacity gains.[65] Consequently, fenced off waiting zones became equipped with information boards that taught skiers how to use their bodies efficiently. Turnstiles that were actually developed to support cattle herds in slaughterhouses were adapted and applied by ski lift engineers to prevent conflicts among waiting skiers eager to get on the slopes. Visual and acoustic systems around the gates were combined to direct the skiers' attention to the boarding.[66]

These innovations aimed to accelerate the flow of skiers uphill and reduce undesirable waiting time for skiers. Their effects on transport capacity was considerable, as Figure 6 demonstrates.

---

63   Ibid.
64   N. N., "Höhere Förderleistung bei Sesselbahnen," *Internationale Seilbahndrundschau* 15, no. 4 (1971): 221–224 (here 221).
65   Edward M. Thurston, "A Loading means for chair lift, Patent No. US 3548753, issued by the U.S. Patent Office, December 22, 1970," *worldwide.espacenet. com*, accessed Dec. 2, 2016, http://worldwide.espacenet.com/publicationDetails/ biblio?CC=US&NR=3548753A&KC=A&FT=D#; William R. Sneller, "Apparatus for loading passengers on a ski tow, Patent No. US 3339496, issued by the U.S. Patent Office, September 5, 1967," *worldwide.espacenet.com*, accessed Dec. 2, 2016, http://worldwide. espacenet.com/publicationDetails/biblio?CC=US&NR=3981248A&KC=A&FT=D#.
66   René Montagner, "Method and installation for loading passengers on a mobile suspender carrier, Patent No. US 4223609 A, issued by the U.S. Patent Office, September 23, 1980," *worldwide.espacenet.com*, accessed Dec. 2, 2016, http://worldwide.espacenet.com/ publicationDetails/biblio?CC=US&NR=4223609A&KC=A&FT=D#.

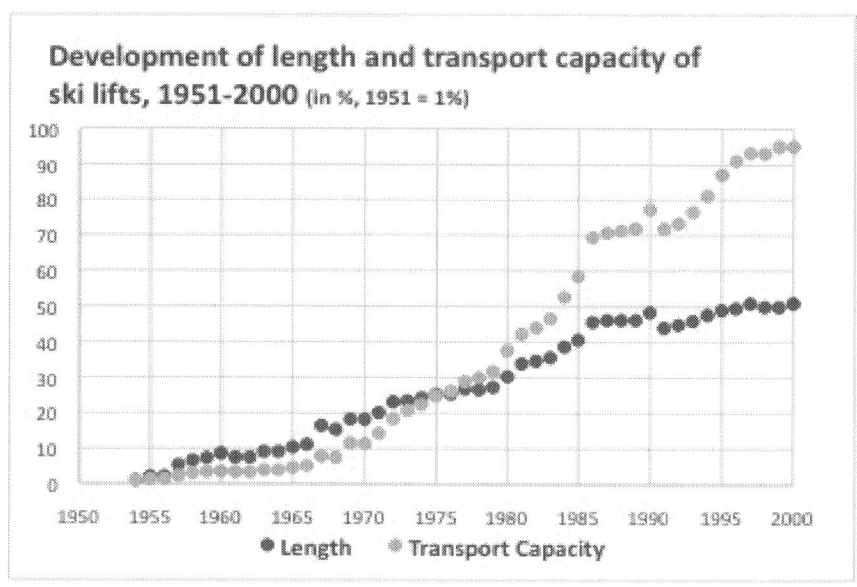

Figure 6: Comparison of transport capacity and length of ski lifts in the major winter sport destinations of Vorarlberg/Austria. Source: Groß, "Die Beschleunigung der Berge. Eine Umweltgeschichte des Wintertourismus in Vorarlberg/Österreich, 1920-2010," 181.

The discussed measures aimed to increase the transport capacity of ski lifts, to accelerate the flow of skiers through the infrastructure, and to reduce undesirable waiting time for skiers. Their effects were considerable. As depicted in Figure 6, the innovations had a prominent influence in the long run. While both the length and transport capacity of ski lift networks grew by about thirtyfold in the four largest ski destinations in Vorarlberg between 1951 and 1975, this trend was replaced by a new one: length of the ski lifts and their transport capacity gradually decoupled from each other. Between 1975 and 2000, transport capacities skyrocketed by seventy-fold, while the ski lifts' length only grew by about twentyfold. This points to enormous gains in productivity and capacity in the ski lift industry; the innovations turned out to be comparable to the automobile or aircraft industry. Furthermore, it sheds light on the scale of capital ski lift operators invested to transform Alpine landscapes according to the needs of both the skiers and the ski lift industry.

Snow: From Menace to White Gold

Before Ernst Constam invented the T-bar lift to disburden skiers from the exhausting ascent, they had to anticipate possible downhill routes while walking upwards to avoid subsequent exhausting maneuvers in snowy terrain. Sound environmental knowledge and flexibility in downhill techniques were essential skills for skiers to master the terrain. As early as the 1930s, ski producers began to equip skis with edges made of celluloid or steel. Their aim was to improve the grip of skis. Consequently, skiers could maneuver much easier by using less muscle power in different types of snow, which fostered pleasure—and speed—in the descent. In combination with an improved skiing technique, these edges accelerated the velocity of the descent significantly.[67] Soon after Constam invented the T-bar lift, the research and development units of the ski lift industry began to develop ever faster ski lifts with higher transport capacities. Within a couple of years, they increased transport capacities fivefold. A skier in the 1960s completed within one day as many kilometers on slopes as his/her grandfather did in a whole year, as a contemporary observer mentioned, after ski lifts were introduced.[68] This acceleration of up- and downhill cycles exposed wooden skis to unknown mechanical forces so that they wore out. In 1965, the German weekly magazine *Der Spiegel* reported that wooden skis would soon be completely replaced by synthetic materials, aluminum, and steel, as these materials were more durable than wood. New materials could help to save skiers lots of money. They supported the technical acceleration of up- and downhill cycles, as they considerably increased the endurance of skiers. Another side effect of the technical acceleration, however, was not solved by such a simple change, but was instead enhanced by a combination of ski lifts and faster, more durable skis.

In the mid-1960s, public health experts began to critique modern skiing practices. They addressed ski lift entrepreneurs, engineers, educators, and physicians as the number of injuries literally exploded. Public health experts spoke about a *Beinbruchbilanz* ("balance of leg fractures") to emphasize the most common type of injuries caused by skiing.[69] They counted about 100,000 injured persons in the Alpine region per year, resulting in estimated losses for national economies due to missed work and social insurance that

---

67   F. Zbil, "Fragen der Sicherheit, Kennzeichnung und Haftung auf Schipisten," *Internationale Seilbahnrundschau* 13, no. 1 (1970): 53–54 (here 53).

68   Bernhard Zehentmayer, *Der alpine Schisport in Österreich: Seine Entwicklung im 20. Und 21. Jahrhundert im Spannungsfeld von Schifahrtechnik, -material, Tourismus und Seilbahnen* (Saarbrücken: Dr. Müller, 2009), 111.

69   Ibid.; F. Zbil, "Fragen der Sicherheit, Kennzeichnung und Haftung auf Schipisten," 53.

cost up to 150,000 million Deutsche Marks. Such announcements forced ski area managers to increase safety measures on downhill routes.[70] They aimed to improve safety by removing trees, rocks, shrubs, or fences from areas used for the downhill. Such measures made skiing safer, provided that property owners issued permission. Given the abundance of downhill routes running across private property in Austria, however, not every property owner was interested in technologically accelerated descent skiing on his or her grassland.

Another measure to accelerate the downhill flow of skiers in a safe way was to diversify downhill routes according to skiers' skills. Skiers should be brought to decide on a downhill route appropriate to their experience and abilities, which, as it was believed, would reduce individual risks but also decrease stress on the snow cover. While this measure was promoted as early as the mid-1960s, it was standardized by experts from the *Fédération Internationale de Ski* (FIS), the International Ski Federation, based on the gradient of the downhills. Easy routes, with a gradient of less than twenty-five percent, were announced as blue slopes; medium-difficulty routes, with less than a forty percent gradient were marked in red. Black was reserved for those areas that had more than forty but less than sixty percent slope. If necessary, danger points caused by icing, little snow, rocks, stones, or intersection areas were to be signaled by easy-to-decipher information panels. However, these signposts were not meant be interpreted by skiers as compulsory. Appealingly designed communication tools should motivate them to opt for the most suitable downhill.[71] Skiers should learn to consider this as an amenity for paying customers. Ski resort planners and ski lift industry consultants, however, warned that a dense jungle of signs could discourage skiers, as it would hamper the "joy of quick gliding and lively movements."[72] Instead, they called for a fundamental paradigm shift in resort planning toward completely artificially designed landscapes of experience and safety: ski lift managers should model their downhills by using excavators and prepare highway-like, wide, and obstacle-free slopes. That way, skiers would behave in a more predictable way, but also the planned areas would accommodate masses of skiers with ease. Clumsy and disciplining signs would thus become unnecessary.[73]

---

70   K. Schleuniger, "Berichte aus der Schweiz: Sicherheit auf der Skipiste," *Internationale Seilbahnrundschau* 9, no. 3 (1966): 92–93 (here 92).
71   Roland Rudin, "Markierung von Schipisten," *Internationale Seilbahnrundschau* 14, "Sondernummer Alpine Skiweltmeisterschaften" (1971): 21.
72   Zbil, "Fragen der Sicherheit, Kennzeichnung und Haftung auf Schipisten," 54.
73   Ibid.

While ski lift managers and planners began to develop deeper interventions into the Alpine grassland, some property owners reacted with resistance. As ski lift managers did not compensate the seasonal utilization of the grassland, they faced a wave of legal actions. The *Landesregierung* ("provincial government") of Vorarlberg attempted a broad solution by enacting a law, the so-called *Landessportgesetz*, which contained a clause that forced property owners to remove all obstacles, such as fences, from their grassland in order to provide smooth skiing on flat slopes. To compensate landowners, mostly farmers, the law foresaw that municipalities should pay for their labor.[74] As one might expect, the *Landessportgesetz* caused strong resistance, too, as it repealed an older law, the *Feldschutzgesetz* ("law to protect fields"). This law had been enacted in 1875 to authorize farmers to fence their land and protect their harvest from thievery.[75] When this legal institution, crucial for a successful and secure agricultural sector, was abolished in favor of winter tourism, even lawyers from Austrian Ministry of Justice opposed. They argued that dairy farmers in Alpine regions needed fences to secure their cattle. Thus, they are economically dependent on the fences that the law sought to remove. The *Landessportgesetz* would discriminate against them, but also it would oblige municipalities to subsidize the workload of property owners for the benefit of ski destination managers. The intervention by the Ministry of Justice, however, was ineffective, and the *Landessportgesetz* was enacted in 1968.[76]

The weakening of traditional private property rights on grassland used for skiing was a tipping point in the development of ski slopes. Until then, skiers were only tolerated, but the *Landessportgesetz* authorized ski lift operators to seasonally utilize the grassland and to turn it into an economic resource without buying it or organizing necessary services like mowing, fertilizing, or grazing. Though the law clearly favored ski tourism over other forms of land use, it took only three years until property rights were even more restricted. Complaints by the mayor from Lech am Arlberg gave the impetus for a revision of the law. Seven landowners opposed the *Landessportgesetz* by banning the use of snow groomers on their property. Such selfish behavior could threaten the economic success of the diverse ski lift operators in Lech am Arlberg.[77] Thus, the *Landessportgesetz* was amended in 1972 to include the responsibility of mechanical snow grooming without making provisions for financial compensation to the

---

74   Amt der Vorarlberger Landesregierung (ed.), Vorarlberger Sportgesetz, LGBl. Nr. 9/1968.
75   Sportgesetz I. Teil 1, PrsG, 1968, 19/306/16/1966, Vorarlberger Landesarchiv.
76   Ibid.
77   Sportgesetz I. Teil, 2. Oktober 1970, PrsG 1972, 56/306/14, Vorarlberger Landesarchiv.

property owner. This had an enormous effect on the rights of property owners, but also affected the social ecology of grassland: "In practice, all land being used as ski slope dropped in value. The ski lift operators were legally entitled to extend their control over the natural dynamics on the land. On this legal basis, ski lift operators began to invest not only in ski lifts but also in ski slope buildings, refined snow management practices, changes in topography, and later the installation of artificial snow systems."[78]

Building Slopes, Transforming Agroecosystems, Fighting Climate Change

Lech am Arlberg not only set the starting point for the loosening of private property rights in ski destinations across Austria, it also pioneered snow grooming in Vorarlberg. As early as the late 1940s, ski lift managers organized troops of volunteers, such as school kids, ski educators, or family members, who stamped fresh-fallen snow into slopes that made skiing safer and more comfortable. Over time, practices of slope management were refined. Once the slopes were stamped, overnight frost was used to produce a solid surface. Snow crystals, already destroyed by mechanical forces, were transformed into ice granules due to nocturnal frost and became more resistant to thawing and the stress of steel-edged skis. This technique helped to increase the durability of the slope, a necessary precondition for a good economic return of the ski lift business, especially during peak season, when each day counted.[79]

Slope management became increasingly important in ski destinations, as many of the businesses were highly indebted and obliged to pay back loan installments and interests. As early as the late 1940s, ski lift managers praised this technique as tool to synchronize ecological cycles, such as precipitation, thaw, and frost episodes with economic cycles like loan agreements, opening times of a ski lift, and holiday periods. Enthusiasts even advertised such activities as a measure to liberate the ski lift operation's fate from the whims of winter.[80]

---

78 Groß, "Uphill and Downhill Histories. How Winter Tourism Transformed Alpine Regions in Vorarlberg/Austria – 1930 to 1970," 131.
79 CCE [Cable car entrepreneur, on request anonymized] to Robert Groß, 15 June 2014, Oral History Interview "Historischer Umgang mit Schnee aus der Sicht des Seilbahnbetreibers," recorded at Talstation Sessellift Schlegelkopf, 6763 Lech; digital record and transliteration in possession of the author.
80 W. Langenfelder, "Präparieren von Schiabfahrten," *Internationale Seilbahnrundschau* 7, no. 4 (1964): 164.

At the end of the 1950s, the muscle-powered slope management was drawn into crisis. Expanding ski lift networks and the considerable increase of transport capacities forced ski lift operators to utilize more and more grassland as ski slope. Both the growing demand of slope management and the declining willingness of volunteers provided opportunities for creative contemporaries to enter market with more effective technologies. The so-called *Schipistenwalze* ("roller to flatten ski slopes"), was, according to its inventor, developed at the Arlberg. Comparably designed to a harrow and maneuvered by two skiers, the roller rationalized slope management by the seven- to tenfold.[81] Despite its rationalization gains, the *Schipistenwalze* remained only a footnote in the history of winter tourism. The development of the technical preparation of ski slopes began in the U.S., in Sun Valley, Idaho. As early as the 1930s, a technician rebuilt a track vehicle originally developed for polar expeditions. This type of snow groomer was first introduced at the Winter Olympics in Squaw Valley, U.S.A. in 1960. European observers were enthusiastic about the efficiency of the technology. In 1962, the Swiss company Dr. K. Schleuniger and Co. developed the Ratrac, which could groom 30 to 35,000 square meters of slope per hour.[82] In comparison to the *Schipistenwalze*, the Ratrac promised a twenty-fold efficiency gain to ski destination managers. This was a strong argument. Within only a few years, 124 ski destinations in Austria, Switzerland, France, Italy, Germany, Turkey, Czechoslovakia, and Yugoslavia possessed Ratracs.[83] From then on, technical snow grooming, with all its economic benefits and environmental side effects, was the standard.

The transformation of snowy grassland into a profitable and safe ski slope that at least partly liberated ski lift managers from burdens of erratic winter weather, revealed its consequences as soon as the snow masses melted off in spring: when farmers brought cattle on their pastures, they noticed that the heavy vehicles had selectively wrecked the turf.[84] Mostly, damages were limited to small areas, especially on sharp terrain-edges or little hills. Untreated, the little damages could have big effects, when heavy rainfalls increased erosion. Over time, the soil became deeply eroded, causing the loss of more and more humus, and hay harvests declined at an increasing

---

81 Ibid.

82 N. N., "Entwicklungsgeschichte der mechanischen Pistenpräparierung," *Motor im Schnee,* Historische Ausgabe (1991): 60–72.

83 K. Schleuniger, "Berichte aus der Schweiz: Sicherheit auf der Skipiste," *Internationale Seilbahnrundschau* 9, no. 3 (1966), 92–93 (here 92).

84 Gustav Türtscher to Robert Groß, 12 May 2014, Oral History Interview "Arbeiten am Skilift und mit der Pistenraupe," recorded at Landhaus Trista, 6884 Damüls; digital record and transliteration in possession of the author.

rate.[85] Farmers counteracted these damages by bringing cattle dung out to prepare the soil for seeding hay flowers; their aim was to regenerate the turf. This practice was effective in short term, but once the snow groomers marched out following winter, the tracks caused damage again, which over time considerably increased the farmers' workload.[86] Hay flowers were a suitable seed insofar as they helped to reproduce the local biodiversity. However, the seed was available only in small amounts, and its capacity to germinate was dependent on cutting time and storage of the hay. If farmers cut meadows too early, the biodiversity was limited to a few species. A late cut due to short vegetation periods, however, was rather risky in the high Alps. To put it simply, the large-scale production of the requested amount of seed required botanical knowledge and sure instincts. Thus, hay flower availability was limited, especially when the demand sharply increased due to the introduction of snow groomers. Furthermore, the utilization of hay flowers remained a risky endeavor. Their quality was not proven, as was the case in commercial seeds, which led to cases when farmers or ski lift managers sowed them but only a very limited share of the seeds sprouted.[87] Professional seed, however, was only available for the lowlands. As the demand was still not big enough compared to lowland seeds, commercial seed producers were not able to provide seed mixtures containing herbs, woody plants, shrubs, and grasses adapted to the Alpine climate until the 1990s. Rather, ski lift managers utilized large quantities of lowland species, carrying out constant species transfers of highly productive grasses and leguminous plants.[88]

The regional government in Vorarlberg originally assumed that the use of snow groomers did not do any harm to the grassland. In the late 1970s, however, ecologists increasingly doubted that one could compare the impact of snow groomers on the biodiversity with downhill skiing with areas that were not technically groomed. Thus, they started to systematically study the effects by comparing groomed and ungroomed testing areas. The ecologists' initial hypothesis claimed that snow groomers would prolong the snow cover and that this, in combination with the weight of the machines, would reduce soil activity. Over the course of the investigation, it turned out that ground level snow layers were considerably warmer on ungroomed than on groomed areas. By grooming the slopes, the snow lost its function to safeguard the

---

85   Alexander Cernusca et al., "Auswirkungen von Schneekanonen auf alpine Ökosysteme. Ergebnisse eines internationalen Forschungsprojektes," *Umwelt und Tourismus*, ed. Erich Gnaiger and Johannes Kautzky (Vienna: Thaur, 1992), 177–199 (here 178).
86   Türtscher to Groß, Oral History Interview.
87   Leonhard Köck, "Veränderungen des Pflanzenbestandes rekultivierter Skiflächen in Abhängigkeit des Einsaatalters und des Standortes," unpublished transliteration of the workshop "4. Tagung der Hochlagenbegrünung" in Lech (October 6-7, 1984), 18–47 (here 46).
88   Ibid.

soil from frost. The freeze was considerably harder, and it damaged plant roots. Furthermore, machine-compacted snow was less permeable to air, leading to an undersupply of carbon dioxide in the early growth phase of plants. To put it briefly, the use of snow groomers altered ecologically selective forces on Alpine flora and fauna. Plants and animals that were adapted to certain environmental conditions were usurped. In the long run, this caused declining soil activity and reduced amount, density, and mass of soil organisms.[89] The ecologists claimed that this was not only a momentary effect; it could result in shrinking soil horizons over time.[90] The research results were a real breakthrough insofar as they led to a reformulation of the *Landessportgesetz* toward a clause that required ski lift managers to compensate any hay harvest losses financially.

The history of ski slopes is a classic tale of ski lift managers dealing with side effects of human interventions into landscapes, resulting from the anticipated need to adapt technical infrastructure to dynamic snow-fall and temperature patterns. These interventions were facilitated in order to process ever more skis, even if there was little snow. Excavators, Caterpillars, and explosive charges were utilized to model straightened inclined surfaces into the grassland. While in the early years of ski slope building, planners advised ski lift managers to plant them with conventional seeds to avoid erosion, their recommendations changed in the 1980s. Approaches involving counteracting erosion with commercial hydro seed, whereby seeds, fertilizer, and a glue were sprayed over straw covered soil, turned out to be the biggest mistake. Many ski lift mangers all over the Alps had to pay a high price for this service, only to find it pointless in the fight against erosion.[91] As a result of applied research undertaken by ski lift managers, the much older technique of grass sods was revitalized and reintroduced into ski destination planning. Though this technique is rather expensive in the beginning, its advantage becomes perceivable in the long run. Small excavators are used to remove smaller

---

89   Erwin Meyer, "Beeinflussung der Fauna alpiner Böden durch Sommer- und Wintertourismus in Westösterreich," *Revue Suisse de Zoologie* 100, no. 3 (September 1993): 519–527 (here 523).
90   Alexander Cernusca to Robert Groß, 18 May 2014, Oral History Interview "Umweltverträglichkeit von Beschneiungsanlagen," recorded at the Institut für Botanik, Universität Innsbruck, Innrain 52, 6020 Innsbruck; digital record and transliteration in possession of the author.
91   N. N., "Hydrogreen: Umweltfreundliche Spritztour in Grün!," *Internationale Seilbahnrundschau* 16, „Sonderheft Technik im Winter" (1973): 23; Winfried Lackner, "Maschineneinsatz bei der humuslosen Begrünung bzw. Re-kultivierung," unpublished transliteration of the workshop "4. Tagung der Hochlagenbegrünung" in Lech (October 6–7, 1984), 49–60 (here 53–54).

patches of turf from the soil. Then the patches of turf are stocked, while the terrain is modelled according to the concept of an ideal winter sport arena. Finally, turf-patches are put back, and the growing roots fix them in place. While hydro seed approaches were considerably cheaper in their initial application, they could cause decades-long and at time permanent issues for ski lift managers' investments. With the grass sod technique, however, both biodiversity and soil stability were considerably improved, which helped save many investments in the longer run.[92] Due to the potential of the technique to control the side effects of slope building, the cases where it was applied in Vorarlberg rapidly multiplied between 1980 and 2011.[93]

The technical acceleration of skiing through the use of ski lifts forced skiers and ski lift managers alike to evolve a novel relationship to snow and the landscape. The ski lift managers were primarily concerned with adapting to the needs of economy. As early as the 1960s, researchers estimated that a skier would consume up to one ton of snow a day by shoving it downward with skis. Snow groomers and ski slope buildings were originally developed to increase safety on the slopes. With time, however, it turned out that built slopes could reduce snow losses, and snow groomers could suitably redistribute snow cover on the slopes. The more popular a ski slope was, the higher the dependency was on both snow grooming and slope building, due to increased transport capacity. Snow scarcity in ski destinations was thus not only a weather-related problem but in the first instance caused by already high and constantly growing transport capacities. Technical aids or terrain design could only partly lighten the self-induced burden; they could not entirely solve this problem. Periodically, winters would come with little snowfall and/or high temperatures and put the already shaky balance into crisis. In combination with the limitations of ski slope management practices, such as snow grooming and slope building, outstanding weather conditions and the constant increase of ski lift transport capacities put severe pressure on ski lift managers in the late 1980s and early 1990s. As a result, ski lift managers began to build snow systems to compensate for missing snowfalls, using spray nozzles connected by widespread infrastructure to distribute snow. Both snow groomers and ski slope buildings were necessary preconditions for snow systems, as they enabled an efficient utilization of pricey artificial snow. The introduction of snow systems into winter sport destinations is,

---

92   Robert Groß, "Die Beschleunigung der Berge: Eine Umweltgeschichte des Wintertourismus in Vorarlberg/Österreich, 1920–2010," 211–216.
93   Naturschutzanwaltschaft Vorarlberg, Aufstellung der Bewilligungsansuchen.

while pointing to a major issue of future developments in times of global warming,[94] beyond the scope of this chapter.[95]

Conclusion

Tourism and mobility can be seen as playgrounds of the Great Acceleration. This article contributes to the broader discussion about tourism as a major driver of transformation in social ecology. Analyzing the development of destinations for winter sports in Vorarlberg, Austria's westernmost province, it becomes obvious that tourism history in general and post-World War II Alpine winter tourism in particular are well-suited to test the narrative of the Great Acceleration of western consumer societies in the second half of twentieth century. Tourism by its very nature is tightly connected to different types of mobility, which is necessarily defined by material infrastructure bound to manifold interventions into the geo- and hydrosphere but also into ecosystems and the living environments of the inhabitants. Automobility increased in general in the second half of the twentieth century. This boom became particularly visible in winter tourism destinations in Alpine peripheries, where everyday and leisure mobility overlapped seasonally. In this chapter, we addressed the problematic nature of these tourism-related effects by studying critical hubs, where different types of mobility are organized and synchronized as indicators for socio-ecological transformation. Our aim has been to demonstrate how such interventions are accompanied by side effects, whose handling provides a fruitful source for environmental historians on the one hand; on the other hand, the mostly technical responses to the side effects of intensifying use can be regarded as a driving force that acts as a positive feedback loop, which stabilizes adopted development paths. Time use seems to be of pivotal meaning. As our analysis showed, Hartmut Rosa's notion of the "time paradox" (the more time we save through technical means, the less we have) also displays effects in the material world, as the saved time and the technically accelerated ascent increases demand for more efficient, spectacular, and comfortable ski lifts. While ski lift infrastructure is theoretically limited only by the available capital of ski lift entrepreneurs, the situation of ski slopes is different. They connect the valley with the top station and

---

94   Robert Steiger and Bruno Abegg, "Klimawandel und Konkurrenzfähigkeit der Skigebiete in den Ostalpen," in *Tourimsus und mobile Freizeit: Lebensformen, Trends, Herausforderungen,* ed. Roman Egger and Kurt Luger (Norderstedt: Books on demand, 2015), 319–332.
95   Robert Groß, "Die Beschleunigung der Berge: Eine Umweltgeschichte des Wintertourismus in Vorarlberg/Österreich, 1920–2010," 216–218.

function as a generator of bodily sensations for skiers, but, at the same time, they are prone to natural influences such as erosion, lack of snow, and changing temperature patterns. From the perspective of a ski lift entrepreneur, they are central to winter tourism, thus their temporal momentum became, over time, manipulated and adapted to the economic requirements of the tourism industry. However, full control remained beyond the sphere of influence of the managers, adding another positive feedback loop on the material growth of ski tourism infrastructure and the biophysical transformation of landscapes into the central resource for winter tourism.

Reconstruction and Transformation of the Austrian Wood-Paper Commodity Chain, 1945–1955

Sofie Mittas

Introduction

The European Recovery Program (ERP) was an extensive aid program that facilitated financial as well as technology and knowledge transfer. Austria was among the sixteen countries that were included in this program. While many aspects of the ERP have already been researched, Günter Bischof, one of the most active ERP researchers in Austria, states in his 2017 book that forestry and the paper industries (from now on, the system of paper production will only be addressed as the paper industry for simplification) is still a desiderata of ERP research.[1]

In this article, I will show that restoring the paper industry to its prewar production levels had already been achieved before the start of the ERP. However, the measures financed and enabled by the ERP actively changed the wood-paper commodity chain on many levels. This comprised change in raw materials, technologies, energy supply, and other aspects that have implications for the environment, which merits an environmental history perspective.[2]

Related Work

ERP Research in Austria

According to Günter Bischof, Austrian ERP research proceeded in three phases. The first phase of research dealt mostly with the aid programs that preceded the ERP as well as the negotiations and the early phase of the ERP. The ERP was mostly viewed in a very positive light and was not critically challenged.[3]

---

1   Günter Bischof and Hans Petschar, *Der Marshallplan: die Rettung Europas & der Wiederaufbau Österreichs: das europäische Wiederaufbauprogramm, der ERP-Fonds, die Marshallplan-Jubiläumsstiftung*, 1. ed. (Vienna: Christian Brandstätter Verlag, 2017), 133.
2   I want to thank Mag. Patrick Mader from Austropapier for granting access to archival material from the Austrian paper industries. I also want to thank my colleagues for many fruitful discussions.
3   Bischof and Petschar, *Der Marshallplan*, 17.

A second phase, which Bischof calls the revisionist phase, represents the first critical analyses of the ERP. When archival material became available, a more critical view on the ERP was developing, and that view dominated ERP scholarship until the 1990s. In this phase, many scientists viewed the ERP as a tool of US imperialism.[4]

The third phase of the ERP research is the current, post-revisionist phase. In this phase, critical analyses of the impact and success of the ERP are being conducted in a different way. International ERP research was incorporated into Austrian ERP research. Starting with Alan S. Milward's *The Reconstruction of Western Europe, 1945–51*, this new research concluded that, considering the whole program, its impact on Europe was most likely less profound than previous research had assumed. Milward's study was also the first attempt to analyze the ERP quantitatively. He showed that the ERP was most likely not the turning point in European economic development, but rather that it boosted an existing trend. He argues that the ERP has helped to increase private investments and widen (material) bottlenecks;[5] similarly, Long and Eichengreen[6] dub the ERP a "large highly successful structural adjustment program."[7]

Very often, Austria is seen as a special case, since it was one of the best-funded countries within the ERP. Austria was also in a special situation because of the ministration of its Soviet occupation zone, with companies in this zone nevertheless receiving ERP-funds.[8] This was also acknowledged in Milward's studies.[9]

Environmental History Research

If natural circumstances are to be taken into account, but a culture/nature dichotomy is to be avoided to give due credit to hybridity, (for example, a forest planted by humans), the concept of socio-natural sites is particularly helpful. Socio-natural sites are nexuses of co-evolutionary interaction of practices and biophysical arrangements via four modes: perception,

---

4   Ibid.; Gene R. Sensenig, *Österreichisch–amerikanische Gewerkschaftsbeziehungen 1945 bis 1950* (Cologne: Pahl-Rugenstein, 1987).

5   Alan S. Milward, *The Reconstruction of Western Europe 1945–51* (London: Methuen, 1984), 96–98, 107.

6   J. Bradford De Long and Barry Eichengreen, "The Marshall Plan: History's Most Successful Structural Adjustment Program," in http://www.nber.org, November 1991, <http://www.nber.org/papers/w3899> (11 Dec. 2017).

7   Ibid., 3–5.

8   Bischof and Petschar, *Der Marshallplan*, 108–109.

9   Milward, *The Reconstruction of Western Europe*, 92.

representation, programs, and work.[10] These modes can be identified in the ERP. On the political level, representations were negotiated (containment of communism through economic growth and a better standard of living, for example), and then experts and professionals translated these representations into programs (strengthening exporting industries like the paper industry). The applicants drafted programs that had to be approved by foreign experts and were often modified by these experts. These programs were translated into practices (application of new technology, resource extraction…) by companies and economic actors and interacted with material arrangements in many ways.[11]

Most ERP research has focused on two of the four modes: representations and programs. Only a few post-revisionist studies have gone beyond and looked at the material interactions involved in these programs through their practices and touched on the material aspect of the ERP. Since environmental history is dealing with the material implications, it can offer a constructive addition to the post-revisionist view on the ERP.

An Environmental History of the ERP

Environmental histories of the ERP in Austria are scarce. Robert Groß has accomplished an analysis of the ERP's impact on winter tourism in Vorarlberg, and Georg Rigele gives an account of the impact of the ERP on Austrian hydroelectricity focusing on the power plant Kaprun.[12]

Several environmental history studies that deal with forestry and the paper industry as well as research from other scientific fields can be used in developing an environmental history of the paper industry in Austria. These include economic studies of the reconstruction of the paper industry after the Second World War,[13] the forest history of Austria during the twentieth

---

10   Verena Winiwarter and Martin Schmid, "Umweltgeschichte als Untersuchung sozionaturaler Schauplätze: Ein Versuch, Johannes Colers „Oeconomia" umwelthistorisch zu interpretieren.," in *Umweltverhalten in Geschichte und Gegenwart*, ed. Thomas Knopf (Tübingen: Attempto Verlag, 2008), 158–173.

11   Wilfried Mähr, *Der Marshallplan in Österreich* (Graz: Verl. Styria, 1989), 208–209.

12   Georg Rigele, "The Marshall Plan and Austria's Hydroelectric Industry: Kaprun," in *The Marshall Plan in Austria: [Dedicated to the Memory of Joseph Logsdon; March 12, 1938 – June 2, 1999]*, eds. Günter Bischof and Joseph Logsdon (New Brunswick, NJ: Transaction, 2000); Robert Groß, "Die Beschleunigung der Berge: eine Umweltgeschichte des Wintertourismus in Vorarlberg/Österreich 1920–2010" (PhD diss., University of Klagenfurt, 2017).

13   Arnold Bubik, "Die Ausbaupolitik in der österreichischen Papierindustrie seit dem Jahre 1945" (PhD diss., Hochsch. für Welthandel, 1958); Franz Hromatka, "Strukturprobleme und Entwicklungstendenzen in der österreichischen Papierindustrie" (PhD diss., University of Vienna, 1971).

century,[14] and technical studies that deal with technology in forestry as well as in the paper industry.[15]

Although it deals with the paper industry in the United States, *The Slain Wood* by William Boyd gives a good example of aspects and dynamics to be considered when researching the paper industry. In his book, Boyd traces how the paper industry managed to thrive in the United States' South. He shows how technological inventions (the sulphate process that allowed the use of loblolly pine, for instance), in combination with a very specific economic situation (cheap land) and ecological conditions, (decline of cotton and introduction of forest management), on top of social conditions favoring the paper industry and discriminating against forest workers, created special incentives for the paper industry. He also shows how the "nature" of technologies plays an important role and describes the intrinsic problems that the sheer size of the machines creates for the paper industry. The machines of the paper industry are among the biggest in all industries and are quite often custom-made for the specific site. This causes a low mobility for factories and a huge part of the company capital fixed in the machines.[16]

The Wood-Based Paper Industry in Austria

Producing paper from wood was begun in the early nineteenth century. When the capacities for paper production grew with the invention of the paper machine in 1799, the collected amount of the original resource—textile fiber—could not keep up with the growing demand. The innovation of using wood for the production of paper offered a unique opportunity for the Austrian part of the Habsburg Empire. During the nineteenth century, a thriving paper industry developed.[17] The geography of Habsburg Austria (especially the region of today's Austrian republic) provided good

---

14   Norbert Weigl, "Die österreichische Forstwirtschaft im 20. Jahrhundert – Von der Holzproduktion über die Mehrzweckforstwirtschaft zum Ökosystemmanagement," in *Geschichte der österreichischen Land- und Forstwirtschaft im 20. Jahrhundert: [in zwei Bänden]. 1. Politik, Gesellschaft, Wirtschaft*, ed. Franz Ledermüller (Vienna: Ueberreuter, 2002), 593–740.

15   Wilfried Pröll, "Arbeiten Der FBVA-Forsttechnik in Vergangenheit, Gegenwart und Zukunft," in *Forsttechnik an der Schwelle zum 21. Jahrhundert*, 21–33, in http://bfw.ac.at <http://bfw.ac.at/040/pdf/1815.pdf > (16 Aug. 2017); Avi J. Cohen, "Technological Change as Historical Process: The Case of the U.S. Pulp and Paper Industry, 1915–1940," *The Journal of Economic History* 44, no. 3 (1984): 775–799.

16   William Boyd, *The Slain Wood: Papermaking and Its Environmental Consequences in the American South* (Baltimore: Johns Hopkins University Press, 2015), passim.

17   Hromatka, "Strukturprobleme und Entwicklungstendenzen in der österreichischen Papierindustrie," 7, 18.

conditions for the development of the wood-based paper industry because of its extensive forest areas as well as accessibility to rivers. The regional concentration became a problem when close to forty percent of the Austrian-Hungarian paper manufacturing companies remained within the new Austrian borders in 1918.[18] The separation from its customers after the First World War forced the Austrian paper industry to focus on exporting their products.[19]

It can be safely assumed that new technology (faster and wider paper machines or the burning of spent lye, for instance) and infrastructure (new forest roads, for example) introduced after the Second World War changed the energy supply, production capacities, and the raw materials that were used by the paper industry. This strengthened the wood-paper commodity chain and loosened its embeddedness in its environment.

While many aspects of the wood-paper commodity chain have changed during the twentieth century, the next paragraph will show its main features and its embeddedness in its environment.

The wood-paper commodity chain is dominated by water and energy. Water serves multiple functions in the paper production process. It is not only a raw material but also a means of (wood) transportation,[20] used in several stages of the paper production process, (in the process of grinding wood and the production of steam, for instance), and is used to flush effluents into rivers.[21] In the past, water was also used to generate energy for the production process. This made paper production dependent on the region's seasonal climate. The paper industry had to deal with changing amounts of water flow due to seasonal changes as well as with frozen water during the winter months.[22] Other energy sources throughout the production process were the human body as well as fossil fuels such as coal.[23]

---

18 Ulrike Felber, *Ökonomie der Arisierung: 2. Wirtschaftssektoren, Branchen, Falldarstellungen* (Vienna: Oldenbourg, 2004), 282.
19 Hromatka, "Strukturprobleme und Entwicklungstendenzen in der österreichischen Papierindustrie," 20–22.
20 Hans Peter Bobek and Österreichischer Forstverein, *Österreichs Wald: vom Urwald zur Waldwirtschaft*, 2., völlig überarb. u. erw. Aufl. (Vienna: Eigenverl. Autorengemeinschaft Österreichs Wald, 1994), 345.
21 Werner Baumann and Bettina Herberg-Liedtke, *Papierchemikalien: Daten und Fakten zum Umweltschutz* (Berlin: Springer, 1993), 25; Wilhelm Vogel, *Belastung von Fließgewässern durch die Zellstoff- und Papierindustrie in Österreich. 17, B. Ökologie und Immissionen* (Vienna, 1989), 1.
22 Erwin Heidl, "Die geographischen Grundlagen der österreichischen Papier-, Zellulose-, Holzstoff- und Papierindustrie und ihre Bedeutung für die österreichische Wirtschaft," (PhD diss., Hochsch. für Welthandel, 1948), 87.
23 Hromatka, "Strukturprobleme und Entwicklungstendenzen in der österreichischen Papierindustrie," 25.

When the paper industry based its production on wood, it became dependent on an economic sector with its own set of rules. Since wood is a slowly growing "crop" that needs decades to mature, the forest sector cannot easily react to short-term business cycles. To secure the long-term supply of wood, forests have to be managed sustainably and ecological factors have to be considered. This includes restricting harvests to secure usable timber for coming years as well as regular management to keep the forests healthy.[24] Short-term events like storms and forest pests interfered with long-term forest plans. Before the 1950s, the harvest cycle was strongly connected to the seasons, with harvest taking place in spring and the transportation of the wood in the following winter.[25] Because of the heavy mechanical work, originally without the aid of machines other than early chainsaws, the physical abilities of workers' bodies was a necessity.

The next link in the wood-paper commodity chain was the pulp producers, which can be divided into mechanical and chemical pulp producers. The mechanical pulping process uses mostly mechanical energy and water to make the wood fibers available for cardboard and low-quality paper production. The chemical pulping process additionally needs large amounts of heat as well as chemical energy to produce lignin-free pulp that is used for high quality paper.[26]

In the next step, the pulp was transformed into various forms of paper and cardboard on huge paper machines. In this process, more water, as well as chemical and thermal energy, were needed.[27] All these steps of the wood-paper commodity chain are connected through transport, also dependent on energy from human bodies, animal muscles, as well as fossil fuels.

The First Half of the Twentieth Century

The impact of the ERP must be evaluated in context. Many events had a bearing on the paper industry during the first half of the twentieth century. After the First World War, new borders and a much smaller country area forced the paper industry to focus on export;[28] the economic

24 Bobek and Österreichischer Forstverein, *Österreichs Wald*, 208.
25   Peter Handel-Mazzetti and Arnold Elsässer, *Moderne Holzernte: Bericht über eine Studienreise in die Vereinigten Staaten auf Einladung der ECA-Mission für Österreich vom 26. Oktober 1949 bis 6. Februar 1950* (Vienna: Österr. Produktivitäts-Zentrum, 1950), 21.
26 Baumann and Herberg-Liedtke, *Papierchemikalien*, 24–33.
27 Ibid., 55–57.
28 Felber, Ökonomie der Arisierung: *2. Wirtschaftssektoren, Branchen, Falldarstellungen*, 282.

depression was also the start of a concentration process that still continues today. Although short, Austria's integration into the German Reich had a profound impact on Austrian industry, and the paper industry was no exception.[29]

Although there were few investments in the paper industry between 1938 and 1945, the ongoing concentration accelerated. A 1951 study from WIFO (also known as the Austrian Institute of Economic Research) sees the reason for this concentration process not only in the excess capacities after the First World War but also in technological reasons. They found that many companies were too small and that mixed/integrated companies had an advantage. The biggest concentration happened in the cardboard and wood grinding sector; the sector shrunk to sixty-seven companies in 1949, down from 184 companies in 1925.[30]

Forestry and the Paper Industry after the Second World War

After the Second World War, both forestry and the paper industry faced a dire situation. Austrian forestry faced the overuse of easily accessible forest stands and a lack of management due to a shortage of workers.[31] In the paper industry, problems included the lack of raw materials as well as a lack of modernization and rationalization. After the war, paper industry officials believed that the Austrian companies were not able to compete on the world market.[32]

Changes Between 1945 and 1950

The paper industry joined the ERP as late as 1950; therefore, it is important to take a closer look at the preceding five-year period in order to get a better understanding of the impact of the ERP. Although further research is needed, some of the measures that were taken before 1950 can be documented using the yearly reports of the paper industry. The paper industry faced multiple problems: the newly enforced borders of the occupation zones cut them off from important administrative and trade connections, and the industry suffered from significant wood and energy shortages. Additionally, forestry workers were, like many other Austrians, suffering from

---

29   Ibid., 287, 466–68.
30   WIFO, *Die österreichische Papierindustrie* (Vienna, 1951), 4.
31   Weigl, "Die österreichische Forstwirtschaft im 20. Jahrhundert – Von der Holzproduktion über die Mehrzweckforstwirtschaft zum Ökosystemmanagement."
32   WIFO, *Die österreichische Papierindustrie*, 4.

undernutrition and a lack of basic equipment.[33] The dire nutrition situation after the war made physical human strength a "bottleneck" for paper production.[34] To deal with the interruption of formal structures, the paper industry quickly formed new administrative organizations (for instance, a local organization "*Gebietsverband*" for the British occupation zone).[35]

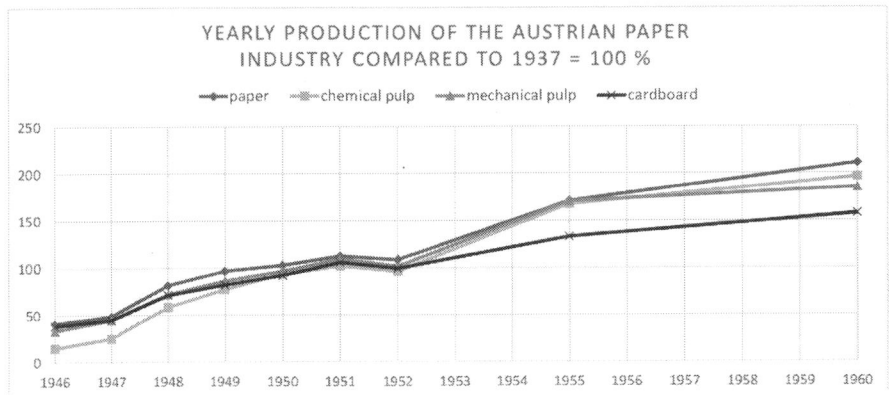

Figure 1: Yearly production of paper, chemical pulp, mechanical pulp, and cardboard. Production 1937: paper: 232,130 tonnes, chemical pulp: 268,000 tonnes, mechanical pulp: 96,760 tonnes, cardboard: 64,100 tonnes. Own illustration based on: Fachverband der Papier-, Zellulose-, Holzstoff- und Pappenindustrie Österreichs, "Jahresbericht 1952." (Vienna, n.d.), 5; Ulrike Felber et al., Ökonomie der Arisierung. 2. Wirtschaftssektoren, Branchen, Falldarstellungen. *Zwangsverkauf, Liquidierung, und Restitution von Unternehmen in Österreich 1938 bis 1960* (Vienna: Oldenbourg, 2004), 470.

The following examples show the active role of the paper industry in restoring and securing their resources. To improve the raw material supply, the paper industry devised the Pa-Ko[36] campaign to gain access to wood. One of the reasons for the wood shortages after the war was the reluctance of owners of small forests to sell their wood due to currency instabilities. This was important because of the structure of forest ownership in Austria. A large part of the forest area was made up of smaller forests, mostly owned

33   Othmar Pickl, *Geschichte der Papiererzeugung in der Steiermark*, Sonderdr. (Graz: Leykam, 1963), 63.

34   Fachverband der Papier-, Zellulose-, Holzstoff- und Pappenindustrie Oesterreichs, "Jahresbericht 1948" (Vienna, n.d.), 2.

35   Pickl, *Geschichte der Papiererzeugung in der Steiermark*, 62.

36   PaKo is short for Papier und Kohle (paper and coal).

by farmers.[37] To deal with this problem, the paper industry bought coal with foreign currency and offered this coal in exchange for wood (at an exchange rate of one tonne of coal to four cubic meters of wood).[38] In 1948, about one quarter[39] of the wood supply to the paper industry originated from the Pa-Ko campaign.[40]

Archival material shows the industry's efforts to improve the situation of forestry workers. Negotiators from the paper industry played an active role in providing forestry workers with more calories during the period of rationing after the war.[41] To provide forestry workers with shoes, the paper industry devised a scheme similar to the Pa-Ko campaign, using foreign currency from paper export to buy raw hides for the production of shoes. The paper industry also recruited forestry workers from Italy to supplement their workforce.[42]

The measures implemented by the paper industry show the important role of the human body in the wood-paper commodity chain. The well-being of the forestry workers was essential to maintain their productivity. The workers were undernourished, and, because of a shortage of raw hides, not enough shoes were available for the heavy work in the forests. Therefore, many of the forestry workers, who were often recruited from nearby farms, preferred to stay home.[43]

The production numbers show significant improvements between 1945 and 1950.[44] "Reconstruction" to pre-war values had been nearly achieved in all areas of production (see Figure 1).

The European Recovery Program

Between 1948 and 1953, the U.S. transported goods with a value of approximately one billion dollars to Austria, which were sold at domestic prices. The proceeds were put into a special account that was called the "*ERP-Sonderkonto*." From this *ERP-Sonderkonto*, low-interest loans were

---

37   Waldstandsaufnahme 1952/56: 40% private forest below 50 ha.
38   Fachverband der Papier-, Zellulose-, Holzstoff- und Pappenindustrie Oesterreichs, "Jahresbericht 1948," 1.
39   In 1948 1,337.034 m³ of the total of 351.719 m³ wood used by the paper industry were supplied by the Pa-Ko campaign.
40   Fachverband der Papier-, Zellulose-, Holzstoff- und Pappenindustrie Oesterreichs, "Jahresbericht 1948," 3.
41   KLA, Österr. Wirtschaftskomitee Box 1, Folder 4, May 26, 1946.
42   Fachverband der Papier-, Zellulose-, Holzstoff- und Pappenindustrie Oesterreichs, "Jahresbericht 1948," 1.
43   KLA, Österr. Wirtschaftskomitee Box 1, Folder 4, April 26, 1946.
44   Felber, Ökonomie der Arisierung: *2. Wirtschaftssektoren, Branchen, Falldarstellungen*, 470–471.

granted to Austrian businesses, which had to be repaid into the same account.[45] Applicants had to cover part of their investments with own capital. This account, now called the *ERP-Fonds*, still exists and is managed by the Austrian *Wirtschaftsservice*. It was handed over to Austria in 1962.[46]

While the aid programs launched immediately after the war offered mainly short-term relief, the ERP was inspired by the New Deal of the 1930s.[47] It aimed at short- and long-term transformation of the economies that were involved. Although the impact, motivations, and benefits of the ERP are still discussed, it can be said that the program aimed at stabilizing European markets through productivity, economic growth, and the stabilization of local currencies. On a European level, it encouraged free trade and political integration.[48]

While the Marshall Plan undoubtedly had political goals such as the containment of communism, its economic goals like closing the dollar gap and economic growth are of more immediate importance here, because they translate directly into resource questions. Charles S. Maier was the first to discuss the "American foreign productivity policy":[49] "Washington's effort [...] was to ensure the primacy of economics over politics, to de-ideologize issues of political economy into questions of output and efficiency."[50]

In Austria, the ERP evolved in three phases. In the first phase, 1948–1949, direct aid was delivered to the Austrian people in the form of food and raw materials. In the years 1950–1951, aid went into the reconstruction and modernization of "basic industries," including pulp and paper. During the third phase, 1952–1953, ERP measures targeted finished products as well as export goods. The restoration and enhancement of Austrian infrastructure such as railways, roads, agriculture, and forestry was a main target for investments.[51] To achieve economic stabilization, the

---

45 Franz Tinhof and Wien Österreichische Staatsdruckerei, *Zehn Jahre ERP in Österreich 1948–1958: Wirtschaftshilfe im Dienste der Völkerverständigung* (Vienna: Verlag der Österreichischen Staatsdruckerei, 1958), 54; Ferdinand Lacina, "The Marshall Plan-A Contribution to the Austrian Economy in Transition," in *The Marshall Plan in Austria: [Dedicated to the Memory of Joseph Logsdon; March 12, 1938 - June 2, 1999]*, ed. Günter Bischof and Joseph Logsdon (New Brunswick: Transaction Publ., 2000), 11–12.
46 "AWS - Historie," in *www.aws.at*, <https://www.aws.at/historie/> (1 Feb. 2018).
47 Bischof and Petschar, *Der Marshallplan*, 11, 55–59.
48 Ibid., 13.
49 Bent Boel, *The European Productivity Agency and Transatlantic Relations; 1953–1961*, Studies in 20th and 21st Century European History 4 (Copenhagen: Museum Tusculanum Press, 2003), 12.
50 Charles S. Maier, "The Politics of Productivity: Foundations of American International Economic Policy after World War II," *International Organization* 31, no. 4 (October 1977): 629.
51 Lacina, "The Marshall Plan-A Contribution to the Austrian Economy in Transition," 11–12.

ERP grants and the investments should help to generate foreign currency to close the "dollar gap" that was viewed as an important threat during this time.[52] This explains the generous grants that were awarded to the paper industries. The following, Figure 2, shows that the paper industry and the wood industries constituted an important part of the Austrian export value before and after the Second World War and especially after the effect of the ERP kicked in after 1950.

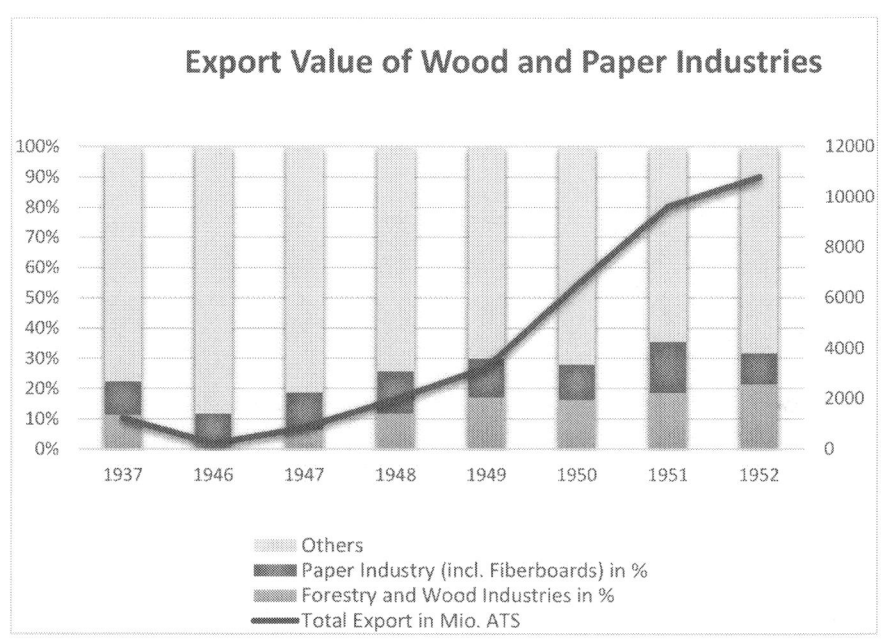

Figure 2: Export value of the wood and paper industries in % and value of total export in millions ATS. Own illustration based on: *Memorandum der österreichischen Forstwirtschaft für die Investitionen 1949/50 bis 1955* (Vienna: Österr. Staatsdr., 1953), 32.

To achieve an increase in productivity, several organizations and programs were founded.

The OEEC (Organization for European Economic Cooperation, the predecessor of the OECD) and the ECA (Economic Cooperation

---

52 Hans Seidel, *Österreichs Wirtschaft und Wirtschaftspolitik nach dem Zweiten Weltkrieg* (Vienna: Manz, 2005), 281–282.

Administration) oversaw the economic coordination of the ERP. The OEEC was founded in 1948 by the sixteen European countries that participated in the ERP (with the US and Canada acting as observers).[53] Its purpose was to distribute ERP aid and to "implement an economic recovery program for the western European countries."[54] It targeted industry, energy, agriculture, and technology. It also worked to improve trade liberalization and currency convertibility after the war.[55]

The U.S. Congress founded the ECA in 1948. Its purpose was to administer ERP aid. The ECA was important because it dealt with applications for investment programs and granted loans and aid. It employed experts to assess applications and suggest changes and modifications to the investment programs. These experts had a big influence on the development of the paper industry.[56]

The Foreign Assistance Act of 1948 installed the Technical Assistance Program (TAP) as one of the management tools of the ERP. The money invested in the TAP rose from two million dollars in 1948 to twenty million dollars in 1952. The TAP's mandate was to "transfer U.S. production and management techniques and know-how to Europe," but it was also about exporting the "American productivity spirit."[57] The TAP was maybe minor in financial terms, but it constitutes an important part of the ERP in terms of transforming business practices on all levels. Employees from all levels within the participating companies were encouraged to go on study trips (mostly to the United States and northern countries). There they saw and learned about new technologies and work organization. Back home, these people would act as multipliers, as several reports, written by participants, show.[58] These travel reports were published by the ÖPZ (Austrian Productivity Center), another organization that aimed at increasing productivity.[59]

---

53   Matthias Schmelzer, *The Hegemony of Growth: The OECD and the Making of the Economic Growth Paradigm*, First published (Cambridge: Cambridge University Press, 2016), 40.

54   Organization for Economic Co-operation and Development, *The European Reconstruction 1948–1961 Bibliography on the Marshall Plan and the Organisation for European Economic Co-Operation (OEEC)* (Paris: OECD, 1996), 11.

55   Ibid.

56   Statistics and Report Division, "MSA European Industrial Projects" (Mutual Security Agency, July 1953), 22–23, http://pdf.usaid.gov/pdf_docs/pdacq095.pdf; WIFO, *Die österreichische Papierindustrie.*

57   Boel, *The European Productivity Agency and Transatlantic Relations; 1953–1961*, 28.

58   James M. Silberman, Charles Weiss, and Mark Dutz, "Marshall Plan Productivity Assistance: A Unique Program of Mass Technology Transfer and a Precedent for the Former Soviet Union," *Technology in Society* 18 (1996): 444–445.

59   "Geschichte," in *www.opwz.com*, accessed Feb. 1, 2018, https://www.opwz.com/de/das-oepwz/geschichte.html.

The Investment Programs

To understand how the investment programs changed the wood-paper commodity chain, it is important to understand their goals, the processes that influenced the planners while drafting these programs, and the changes that were applied to them in the ECA application process. Although further research is needed to answer these questions fully, a short overview is possible.

The Investment Program for the Austrian Paper Industry

The Austrian paper industry joined the ERP late because industry officials were afraid to lose their independence when entering into such a large investment program. The investment proposals had to be written by Austrian entities but were reviewed by the ECA and their experts.[60] Thirty-one companies finally participated in the program. Major changes were applied to the investment proposals by the ECA experts. They were convinced that Austrian companies did not think big enough and so suggested larger proposals.[61]

As has been shown previously, the pre-war production levels were restored by 1950 (see Figure 1). In line with the goals of the ERP, the goals of the investment program for the paper industry were an increase in capacities and productivity as well as export. The investment program that was approved and implemented transformed the Austrian paper industry on many levels. These included changes in energy use, raw materials, efficiency, and technology. By June 1953, 771 million ATS in ERP loans had been released to the Austrian paper industry (which represents close to eight percent of all counterpart releases). Additionally, the industry was using 326 million ATS of their own capital by this time.[62]

Two options for increasing the capacity of the paper industry exist: increasing the speed of the machines and their width. Both changes needed expertise to avoid technical problems in conjunction with faster speeds and bigger—and therefore heavier—parts of the machinery.[63] Comparisons concerning the speed and width of Austrian paper machines with the paper

---

60 WIFO, *Die österreichische Papierindustrie*, 26; Hromatka, "Strukturprobleme und Entwicklungstendenzen in der österreichischen Papierindustrie," 32.
61 WIFO, *Die österreichische Papierindustrie*, 26.
62 "Das Investitionsprogramm der österreichischen Papier-, Zellulose-, Holzstoff- und Pappen-Industrie und die ERP-Hilfe," Bericht über den Zeitraum vom 1. Juli 1952 bis zum 30. Juni 1953 (Vienna: Vereinigung österreichischer Papier-, Zellulose-, Holzstoff- und Pappenindustrieller, 1953), 11–12; "Die wirtschaftliche Bedeutung des ERP-Counterpartfonds," *WIFO Monatsberichte*, no. 5 (1953): 160–166.
63 Cohen, "Technological Change as Historical Process," 780.

machines used in Canada and Sweden showed that Austria was not able to compete on the world market. While the largest paper machine in Austria had a width of 3.5 meters in 1950, the largest machine in Sweden reached six meters and the largest machine in Canada reached even seven meters.[64] The machines used in the paper production process were among the biggest machines in industry. They were often custom-built for specific sites and were therefore very expensive.[65] This may explain why Austrian company owners were at first cautious in their investment plans.

The paper industry depended on a raw material: wood. Using this raw material efficiently was important for both financial and ecological reasons. Several technological changes that affected the material efficiency were introduced during the investment program. New technologies for bark removal, both in the groundwood process as well as in the pulping process, had the potential to decrease wood losses by about ten percent. Further losses occurred when the wood was chipped for pulp production. American experts assessed the chipping machines and concluded that they lacked the proper maintenance. Edgeless blades caused too much sawdust, which could not be used in the process. Losses also occurred during cooking and bleaching in the pulping process; these factors could also be reduced with new machines. New technological solutions were also found and developed to use the waste and by-products of the ground wood and pulping process-es. These included burning of the spent lye, the production of spirit, and the production of glue.[66] Another measure to reduce the necessary amount of raw material was the building of thirty-three machines for fiber recovery.[67]

Another suggestion from the American experts was to increase sul-phate pulp production and the construction of new sulphate pulp factories. The sulphate process allowed higher pulp yields and offered the possibility of using a wider range of woods. It also allowed the use of pine, hard-wood, and waste wood from the sawmill industry (see Figure 3). Since there were few other uses for the waste products of the sawmill industry, this presented a significant advantage for these factories.[68] A new sulphate factory in Nettingsdorf was added to the existing sulphate pulp factory in Frantschach, Carinthia.[69] WIFO criticized the process in 1951, stating that technologies to produce new kinds of fibers were not considered in the investment program.

64   WIFO, *Die österreichische Papierindustrie*, 8.
65   Boyd, *The Slain Wood*, 117.
66   WIFO, *Die österreichische Papierindustrie*, 13–14.
67   Bubik, *Die Ausbaupolitik in der österreichischen Papierindustrie seit dem Jahre 1945*, 156.
68   WIFO, *Die österreichische Papierindustrie*, 14.
69   Bubik, *Die Ausbaupolitik in der österreichischen Papierindustrie seit dem Jahre 1945*, 154.

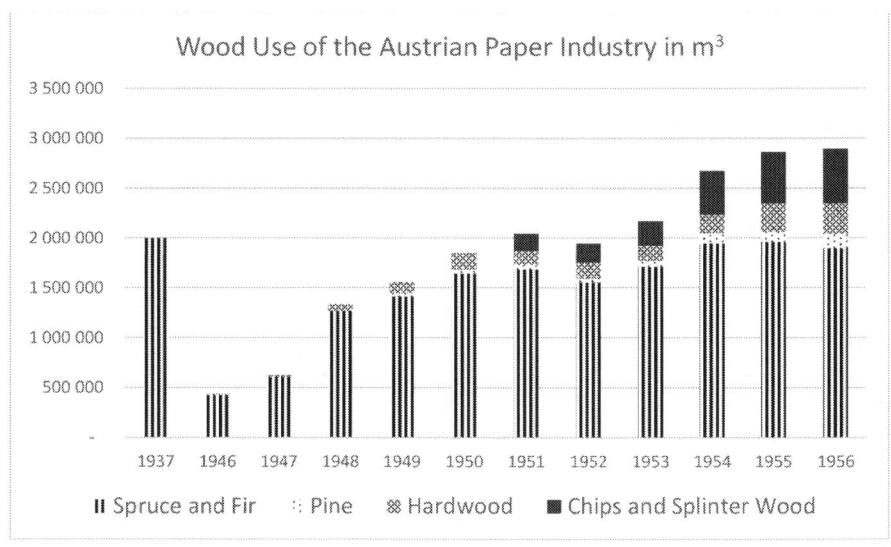

Figure 3: Wood used by the Austrian paper industry 1937, 1946–1956. Own illustration based on: Arnold Bubik, "Die Ausbaupolitik in der österreichischen Papierindustrie seit dem Jahre 1945" (Diss., Hochsch. für Welthandel, 1958), 201.

In the energy sector, there was also a large potential for improvement. The WIFO report states that, in most pulp factories, the spent lye was not burned for energy production because the new technology for using the chemical energy from the lye was not available in Austria. The method of reusing the spent lye was already common in countries like Sweden.[70] The investment program of the paper industry shows that new machines that allowed the reuse of spent lye were planned and installed. New boiler systems were installed that allowed to reuse the thermic energy that was saved in the spent lye. The energy basis of the paper industry was also changed through the installation of new water power (2,940 kW) and caloric power equipment (15,000 kW). This allowed the industry to save fuel as well as use different kinds of fuels like coal dust and oil. This enabled the Austrian paper industry to use mainly Austrian fuels by 1952.[71]

After 1952, production grew significantly (see Figure 1). Although the number of production sites continued to decline during the second half of the twentieth century, the production of paper rose throughout this time. Given the changes described above, it is likely that ERP investments laid the foundation for one of the strongest sectors of the economy today. In

---

70 WIFO, *Die österreichische Papierindustrie*, 17–18.
71 Bubik, *Die Ausbaupolitik in der österreichischen Papierindustrie seit dem Jahre 1945*, 154.

2015, twenty-one companies were producing approximately five million tonnes of paper products on twenty-four sites.[72]

Long-Term Investment Program for Forestry 1950–1952

Forestry and agricultural entities, in addition to industries, were allowed and encouraged to apply for ERP grants. As it was for industries, forestry officials also had to draft an investment program. The original program was designed by the Austrian Ministry for Agriculture and Forestry and submitted to the ECA late because of a lack of staff. The program included (sorted according to financial volume) logging, reforestation, and plant production; a forest survey, research and education, forest protection, thinning, and stock tending.[73] As with the investment program for the paper industry, the ECA also played an important role in the design of the investment program. A FAO forest mission reviewed and improved the program and facilitated coordination with the wood processing industries.[74] Financial priority was given to logging, reforestation, and a forest survey. Logging aid included the construction of forest roads, aimed at providing access to previously inaccessible forest stands, and the acquisition of new machines for harvesting and wood transport. This reflected the rising industrial demand for wood. Forestry officials were afraid of a wood shortage. In his very detailed overview on Austrian forestry in the twentieth century, Norbert Weigl shows that the ERP was important for Austrian forestry. He concludes that modernization, an increase in productivity, and mechanization only started after the beginning of the ERP.[75]

A report from 1953 shows the short-term effects of the investment program. Between 1950 and 1952 (see Figure 4), the amount of forest roads increased by 1,681 kilometers. Through the increase of forest roads, the amount of available wood increased by 697,000 cubic meters and the accessible forest area increased by 228,000 hectares.[76] At that time, the estimated sustainable harvest per year was around seven million cubic meters of wood.[77]

---

72 Austropapier, "Die Österreichische Papierindustrie: Branchenbericht 2015/16," 2016, 2.

73 Weigl, "Die österreichische Forstwirtschaft im 20. Jahrhundert – Von der Holzproduktion über die Mehrzweckforstwirtschaft zum Ökosystemmanagement," 648; *Memorandum der österreichischen Forstwirtschaft für die Investitionen 1949/50 bis 1955* (Vienna: Österr. Staatsdr., 1953), 11, 16.

74 Weigl, "Die österreichische Forstwirtschaft im 20. Jahrhundert – Von der Holzproduktion über die Mehrzweckforstwirtschaft zum Ökosystemmanagement," 648.

75 Ibid., 663.

76 *Memorandum der österreichischen Forstwirtschaft für die Investitionen 1949/50 bis 1955*, 51.

77 Weigl, "Die österreichische Forstwirtschaft im 20. Jahrhundert – Von der Holzproduktion über die Mehrzweckforstwirtschaft zum Ökosystemmanagement," 675.

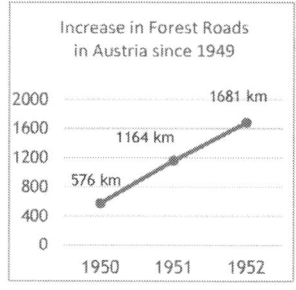 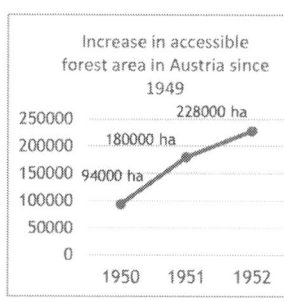 

Figure 4: Increase in forest roads, accessible forest area, and available wood in Austria through ERP measures. Own illustration based on *Memorandum der österreichischen Forstwirtschaft für die Investitionen 1949/50 bis 1955* (Vienna: Österr. Staatsdr., 1953), 51.

The TAP offered a study exchange to train forestry workers in the use of newly available machines such as power chainsaws. These trainings proved to be very effective.[78]

Afforestation was another important part of the program; the official reports, as well as the research by Norbert Weigl, show that experiments were conducted with new tree species, especially fast-growing trees like poplars.[79] This was also reflected in the TAP program, which included one study visit focusing on poplars.[80]

Although not funded as generously as logging and afforestation, the forest survey was an important part of the "long-term investment program for forestry": it allowed the assessment of acute needs for wood. Part of the anxiety among both forestry and industry officials resulted from not knowing how much wood was available and what condition the Austrian forests were in. The biggest insecurity concerned small, privately-owned forests. The last Austrian forest survey dated back to 1935; it had been based on records from large forest estates and did not include information on small forests.[81] The ERP-funded forest survey was conducted from 1952 until 1956. It introduced many new techniques and technologies. Personnel was especially trained and sent into the forests, aerial pictures were taken, and

---

78   Mark Dutz and James Silberman, *Building Capabilities: A Marshall Plan Type Productivity Enhancement Program for Eastern Europe and the Former Soviet Union* (Vienna: Inst. für Höhere Studien, 1994), 8.

79   Weigl, "Die österreichische Forstwirtschaft im 20. Jahrhundert – Von der Holzproduktion über die Mehrzweckforstwirtschaft zum Ökosystemmanagement," 654; *Memorandum der österreichischen Forstwirtschaft für die Investitionen 1949/50 bis 1955*, 27–28.

80   Wolfgang Wettstein, *Pappeln aus der Neuen Welt: Bericht über eine von der OEEC organisierte Technical-Assistance-Reise zum Studium der Pappelkulturen in den Vereinigten Staaten; (25. April bis 14. Juni 1950)* (Vienna: Österr. Produktivitäts-Zentrum, 1951).

81   *Memorandum der österreichischen Forstwirtschaft für die Investitionen 1949/50 bis 1955*, 24.

new machine-based technology was used to process the data.[82] The survey not only included wood reserves but also the condition of vegetation and soils.[83] It changed the view on the Austrian forests literally as well as figuratively. According to Norbert Weigl, the survey served as an important input in the debate on sustainability within the forestry community.[84]

How Did These Programs Change the Wood-Paper Commodity Chain?

In the following paragraphs, the programs' effects on the wood-paper commodity chain that have been identified, starting with the production of raw material in forestry, will be summarized. Through the construction of new forest roads, the commodity chain extended its access into Austrian forests. The new forest roads transformed the forests to meet the needs of motorized vehicles, which became more important after the war due to changes in rural structures, a lack of horses, and the quest for increased productivity.[85] This increased the available amount of wood by approximately ten percent according to contemporary estimates (see Figure 4). The mountainous Austrian terrain proved to be a challenge to this process and special vehicles, like the "*Motormuli*" had to be developed. These new infrastructure facilities and machines also offered the possibility of reducing forest work's dependency on the seasonal cycle.[86]

The reforestation experiments with trees that allowed shorter rotation, like poplars, shows that forest management tried to shorten the production cycles to increase productivity. The active involvement of the paper industry in poplar research and planting is an example of their engagement in securing resources.[87] The study of the challenges the poplar program faced, as well as its ecological and economical outcome, promises to be a rewarding research question for the future.

The second step of the wood-paper commodity chain is pulp production. While the Austrian paper industry before the late 1940s had used

---

82 *Österreichische Waldstandsaufnahme: 1952/56; Gesamtergebnis* (Vienna: Bundesmin. f. Land- u. Forstwirtschaft u. Forstl. Bundes-Versuchsanst. Mariabrunn in Schönbrunn, 1960).
83 Weigl, "Die österreichische Forstwirtschaft im 20. Jahrhundert – Von der Holzproduktion über die Mehrzweckforstwirtschaft zum Ökosystemmanagement," 649.
84 Ibid., 650.
85 Ibid., 652.
86 Handel-Mazzetti and Elsässer, *Moderne Holzernte*, 20–21; Weigl, "Die österreichische Forstwirtschaft im 20. Jahrhundert – Von der Holzproduktion über die Mehrzweckforstwirtschaft zum Ökosystemmanagement," 652.
87 Bubik, *Die Ausbaupolitik in der österreichischen Papierindustrie seit dem Jahre 1945*, 123–125.

mostly spruce, in the form of logs, the introduction of new technologies allowed the use of by-products of the sawmill industry. This development added sawmills as a new component to the wood-paper commodity chain. Another development was the rise in the use of the sulphate process to produce chemical pulp. This allowed the paper industry to use a wider variety of tree species. This had several implications: it widened the resource base and allowed the paper industry to use trees with less market competition.[88] As Figure 3 shows, the increased wood demand was mostly covered with this new source for raw material.

The pulping sector of the industry was also a key factor in using wood more efficiently. The debarking process was transferred from the wood to the factories.[89] New machines reduced losses in the debarking and grinding process and enabled a more efficient use of energy in the production of chemical pulp.[90]

The next step in the commodity chain is the cardboard and paper production factories. Here the capacities were increased through the installation of new machines and adaption of old machines to become wider and faster. This increased production capacities and therefore the demand for raw material and energy. The previous paragraphs showed that the technological improvements in other parts of the commodity chain made this increase of capacities possible.

We will go one step further to discuss the use of waste paper as a raw material. Especially in times of crisis, reusing material became an important source for raw materials. After the Second World War, the paper industry organized waste paper collections to supplement their needs. Coal from the Pa-Ko campaign was used as trading material (four kilograms of waste paper could be traded for one kilogram of coal).[91] The installation of new machines that improved the recycling process, and sometimes even the demand of one single machine (for example, a new cardboard machine at Mayr-Melnhof in 1951) was reflected in the amounts of recycled waste paper.[92]

Some aspects become obvious only when we look at the whole commodity chain. While the production of energy within the factories had been partly based on fossil fuels for a long time, forestry became increasingly

---

88 WIFO, *Die österreichische Papierindustrie*, 14.
89 Weigl, "Die österreichische Forstwirtschaft im 20. Jahrhundert – Von der Holzproduktion über die Mehrzweckforstwirtschaft zum Ökosystemmanagement," 667.
90 WIFO, *Die österreichische Papierindustrie*, 13.
91 Fachverband der Papier-, Zellulose-, Holzstoff- und Pappenindustrie Oesterreichs, "Jahresbericht 1948," 12.
92 Fachverband der Papier-, Zellulose-, Holzstoff- und Pappenindustrie Österreichs, "Jahresbericht 1955" (Vienna, n.d.), 27.

based on fossil fuels with the introduction of motorized vehicles for forest work and transportation and fossil-fuel-powered machines like the chain-saw.[93] The investment programs also literally changed insiders' views of the Austrian forests by providing the first attempt at a thorough assessment of the Austrian forests using aerial pictures.[94]

Continuing our journey to the paper factories, a look into the invest-ment program also shows that the production sites themselves had to adapt to the technological changes. In eight factories, rails for transport were built or adapted, and thirty-four new houses for employees of the factories were provided.[95]

On the consumer side, the demand for paper increased significantly, from fourteen kilograms per person in 1947 to thirty-three kilograms per person in 1955.[96]

Conclusion

This article presents the first results of research in progress. It aims at showing how a program that, in the cases of the paper industry and forestry, only lasted two to three years, changed basic structures of all parts of the wood-paper commodity chain. In 2015, the Austrian paper industry pro-duced close to five million tonnes of paper and around 1.8 million tonnes of chemical and mechanical pulp. In quantitative terms, the developments after the 1960s overshadow the developments that can be observed between 1945 and 1955, but many of the trends that were set and introduced at that time are still visible today. This includes the growing utilization rate of waste paper (close to fifty percent in 2015), the increasing amount of sawmill by-products (more than fifty percent of the wood that was used in 2015 belonged in this category), and the growing energy efficiency that today even allows some of the pulp factories to supply energy to the nation-al electricity grid.[97]

Effluents, however, are not mentioned in this article. In the sources used for this article, which mainly include reports and research conducted shortly after the implementation of these programs, this topic is mostly absent, and therefore the sources did not allow for a conclusive statement

---

93 Pröll, "Arbeiten Der FBVA-Forsttechnik in Vergangenheit, Gegenwart und Zukunft."
94 *Österreichische Waldstandsaufnahme*, 16.
95 "Investitionsprogramm Papierindustrie." Table 6.
96 Fachverband der Papier-, Zellstoff-, Holzstoff- und Pappenindustrie Österreichs, "Jahresbericht 1955," 6.
97 Austropapier, "Die Österreichische Papierindustrie: Branchenbericht 2015/16," 2, 33, 38.

on this issue. It can be said that effluent and its effects were not part of a broader discourse at the time, but hints in the sources show that stream pollution caused local conflicts between factories and their neighbors nearby and downstream.[98] The yearly report of the paper industry, as well as a dissertation from the late 1950s, also hints at the existence of a working group that dealt with questions of how to deal with the spent lye.[99]

Viewing the interface of nature and society in the paper industry provides a basis for future environmental history research. Such research will have to take a closer look at the specific links of the wood-paper commodity chain and the socio-natural sites created by the reconstruction between 1945 and 1950 and their development during the time of transformation from 1950 onward.

98   Karl Dinklage, *Vom Eisenwerk zur Kraftpapier-Fabrik: Geschichte des Industriewerkes Frantschach* (Frantschach: Selbstverl, 1954), 126.
99   Bubik, *Die Ausbaupolitik in der österreichischen Papierindustrie seit dem Jahre 1945,* 91 Fachverband der Papier-, Zellulose-, Holzstoff- und Pappenindustrie Oesterreichs, "Jahresbericht 1954" (Vienna, n.d.), 41.

The Austrian Environment en Miniature: "Official" Perceptions of the Austrian Landscape Reflected through Postal Stamps since 1945

Christian Rohr

Introduction

Austria is considered *the* "Alpine Republic," besides Switzerland, and has defined itself in this way for generations. According to the definition by the Alpine Convention of 1991, approximately two thirds of modern Austria belongs to Alpine landscapes.[1] Whereas the image of Switzerland has generally been perceived as an Alpine country at least since the eighteenth century, when mainly British tourists travelled through parts of Switzerland within their Grand Tour, this self-definition came later in Austria. Until the end of the Habsburg empire in 1918, the Alps accounted for a much smaller proportion of the total area, and the metropolises of Vienna, Budapest, and Prague lay apart from, or only in the foothills of, the Alps. Following the reduction of Austria to its present territory, however, the Alps became one of the dominating landforms.

The national identity was and is also shaped by transalpine transport routes, from the first Alpine railway line ever over the Semmering pass route to the Großglockner High Alpine Scenic Road and the *Europabrücke* ("Bridge of Europe") of the Brenner Motorway. High Alpine storage power plants, such as Kaprun in the Hohe Tauern, became symbols of autarky and reconstruction in turbulent times of global politics. Furthermore, the Alpine eagle, which is native to the Alps, became an Austrian heraldic animal. Since 2002, the Alpine flowers gentian, edelweiss, and Alpine primrose have graced the Austrian one-, two- and five-cent coins. "*Land der Berge*" ("Land of the mountains") are the first words of the Austrian national anthem.

---

1   The delimitation of which regions are attributed to the Alps therefore follows approximately the areas defined by the Alpine Convention. See http://www.alpconv.org/en/organization/parties/default.html (last accessed 20 April 2018). Austria accounts for 28.5 percent of the total Alpine area, the largest share of all Alpine countries. The Mühlviertel and Waldviertel are therefore not included in the consideration, despite their partly mountainous structure. However, exceptions are made to this rule when, for example, a landscape is depicted that shows extra-Alpine regions in the foreground, but the Alps are consciously staged in the background.

However, this definition of Austrian identity across the Alps is juxta-posed with the Alpine foothills and midlands, with its urban centers: the cultural metropolis of Vienna, the steel city of Linz, and the Mozart city of Salzburg. Finally, rivers and lakes not only characterize the country with-in the Alps, as in Wachau, a famous part of the Danube Valley in Lower Austria. *"Land am Strome"* ("Land along the stream") is therefore the second line of the Austrian national anthem, mentioned even before the fields and domes.

If one understands stamps as a kind of "official business card of a coun-try," one can ask to what extent this Alpine self-understanding of Austria is also reflected in the motifs of the stamp issues. Can developments in the perception of the environment be recognized in the long-term comparison? This essay investigates the period from 1945 to 2015; this results in a source corpus that can be tapped with both quantifying and serial iconographic approaches. The aim is to analyze the proportion of Alpine-related motifs in the definite stamps and special editions and how these motifs are dis-tributed over the decades. Such quantifying considerations on the choice of subject have hitherto scarcely been made in the context of stamps and can thus meaningfully supplement qualitative studies and analyses of single editions. The last section of this investigation will examine whether there are significant differences between Austria and Switzerland.[2]

According to Ulrike Pilarczyk and Ulrike Mietzner, the serial iconog-raphy originally used for large image corpora with similar motifs, such as for the bourgeois portrait photography of the nineteenth century, possesses significant variations that would not stand out in an individual analysis of specific icons. For the area chosen here, this means that, firstly, one can determine how often certain motifs return; secondly, it becomes clear how their representation changes over the decades and which constants can be observed; and, thirdly, how these findings can reflect general political and social developments.

In this article, emphasis is given to a quantifying analysis, which is supported by a qualitative one for a restricted number of examples. For the contextualization of the results for Austria, it will be essential to compare them with findings for Switzerland, the second major Alpine country, in the conclusion. Both the quantifying considerations and the qualitative analysis deliberately differentiate between definitive stamps and special

---

2   For details concerning this comparison, see, for the future Christian Rohr, "Land der Berge? Alpine Landschaften, Kultur und Infrastruktur im Spiegel österreichischer und Schweizer Briefmarkenemissionen nach 1945" in *Gezähnte Geschichte: Briefmarken als historische Quelle*, eds. Pierre Smolarski, René Smolarski, and Silke Vetter-Schultheiss (forthcoming 2018).

issues. The first group, by virtue of its ability to be printed and circulated in unlimited quantities, has the function of acting as an ambassador and advertiser on average domestic and foreign broadcasts, at least until the time when automatic postage stamps became normal. The second group is strongly oriented on current events and anniversaries. In addition, special stamp series reveal even more clearly the important trends of an era.

As far as the figures for the quantifying portion of the investigation are concerned, these are to be understood as approximations, since the assignment of individual stamps to the overall "Alps" theme is not always clear. For example, in the group "Flora, Fauna, and Minerals," some motifs are quite clearly "Alpine," as with edelweiss, marmot, or rock crystal because of their character as "icons of the Alps." Other motifs from this group were less clearly related to the Alpine area; they were only included if the entire series of special stamps was dubbed "Alpine flowers," or something similar. The same applies to the "Arts and Traditions" subject matter, which includes, among other things, regional costumes. Cities and villages in the Alps were only considered if the Alpine environment was at least hinted at. The representation of a building alone in a city in the Alps is therefore not sufficient. Similarly, an image depicting winter sports events or people who practice these sports where there was no or only a vague reference to the Alpine environment, such as only the snow as a base for a skier, was not sufficient. Finally, the exact number of stamps evaluated also depends on the numbering in the different stamp catalogues. Due to the high practicability, all quantities are based on the Austria Netto Katalog (ANK), but the identification of the stamps cited will be given both by the ANK and the German Michael-Katalog.[3]

Quantifying Considerations on Austrian Stamps, 1945–2015

The total body of the official Austrian stamps[4] comprises 2,612 issues according to the ANK, which corresponds to an average of 36.8 stamps per year. However, this average is misleading; until the changeover to the Euro in early 2002, the average was 26.9 stamps per year (1,537 total expenditure),

---

3   Consulted editions of the stamp catalogues cited: *Austria Netto Katalog (ANK) Briefmarken. Vierländerkatalog Österreich – Deutschland – Schweiz – Liechtenstein 2018*, 72nd ed. (Vienna: Austria Netto, 2017); *Michel Europa, vol. 1: Mitteleuropa 2017*, 102nd ed. (Munich: Schwaneberger, 2017).
4   Since the turn of the millennium, stamps for private purposes as well as corporate advertising can be designed in Austria individually. These are not taken into account for the analysis. Nor are the commemorative stamp books published by Österreichische Post AG for a number of years with motif stamps of all kinds, which are sold in the post shops.

while for the period between 2002 and 2015, it jumped to 63.5 (875 stamps in total). The vast majority of editions appeared in 2008, a total of eighty-nine stamps, forty of them for the European Football Championship 2008. In contrast, only seven stamps were issued in 1956. However, the number of issues per year also fluctuates strongly for the years before the turn of the millennium: in 1945, separate stamps for the western Allied and the Soviet occupation zone were first brought into circulation, and then editions for the whole of Austria were released. In the following years, the catch-up demand for stamps was very high, so that the number of stamps issued remained very high until 1949, but then declined significantly in the 1950s and only increased sharply toward the end of the decade.

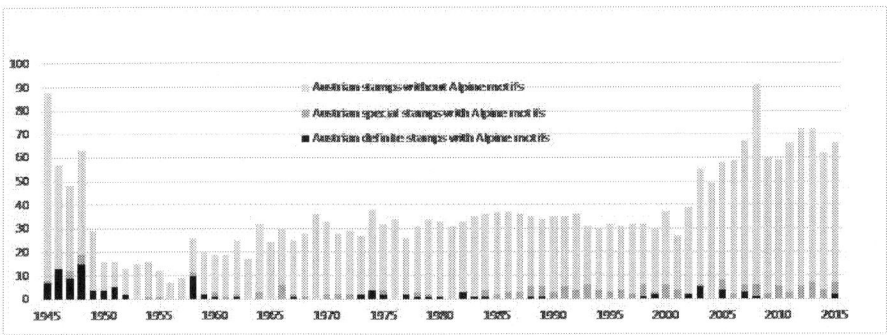

Fig. 1: Number of Austrian stamps issued per year, 1945–2015. Design by the author.

Figure 1 shows the total number of issues per year as well as the number of stamps with an Alpine reference. Around 264 stamps have a clear motivic reference to the Alps, i.e. just about 10.1 percent. Of these, 114 are definitive stamps, which, for a total of 398 definitive stamps, equates to around 28.6 percent of issues related to the Alps. By contrast, the 150 special stamps with Alpine themes account for only about 6.8 percent of all special editions (2,214 in total). This alone makes it clear that an Alpine self-image of Austria is for the most part represented in the definitive stamps and not in the special stamps. As will be clarified below, however, ups and downs can also be identified, i.e. periods in which Alpine motifs accounted for a significantly larger proportion of the total number of releases, and vice versa, phases when the Alpine environment was almost impossible to find on stamps.

Alpine Motifs on Definite Stamps

Following independence in 1945, the Austrian Postal Service (*Österreichische Post AG*)—having initially been under occupation—had a high demand for the issue of several definitive stamp series in the late 1940s. These stamps are strongly dominated by images of nature and homeland, by folklore and, at least at first sight, unpolitical topics. This is a trend that continues from the 1930s and is also recognizable in the area of Austrian tourism posters before 1938.[5] Naturally, Alpine space plays a central role, for example in the series "Landscapes" from 1945–1947, which was published again in uniform shades of orange and violet in 1947–1948. Thirty-six out of fifty-five editions and eighteen out of twenty-seven motifs clearly refer to the Alpine environment; so it is in Fig. 2a (Michel No. 845 = ANK No. 854), with a representation of the Silvretta massif in Vorarlberg.

One of the most used definitive stamp series was the edition of traditional costumes ("*Trachten*"), which first appeared on yellow paper 1948–1952 (and once again in 1958–1959 on white paper). It shaped the image of Austria as a deeply traditional, mountainous country and dominated the letters and postcards in and from Austria for more than a decade. Thirty-five of out of fifty-eight editions and twenty out of thirty-three motifs are related to Alpine regions, with almost exclusively female persons dressed in regional costumes, creating a rural-Alpine impression among the recipients (even if the edition also includes traditional urban and other non-Alpine costumes as well). The mountain landscape is usually indicated only in the background. The political statement of this stamp series is given not only by the emphasis on conservative homeland, but, on closer inspection, also by the choice of region of the costumes. The most frequently used value of one Schilling is adorned with a costume from the Tyrolean Pustertal Valley (Fig. 2b), a region that had belonged to Italy since 1918. After the Second World War, the Austrian government vigorously sought the return of at least this part of South Tyrol. The valley is on the one hand an important link between the remaining parts of Tyrolean Austria, North and East Tyrol, and was on the other hand inhabited by a predominantly German-speaking population even after the Fascist resettlement policy. Although the so-called Gruber-De Gasperi Agreement of 1947 ended this suggestion initially, in return it provided

---

5   See Wolfgang Kos: "Das Plakat als Leitmedium der Tourismusbewegung," in *Alpenreisen: Erlebnis, Raumtransformationen, Imagination*, eds. Kurt Luger and Franz Rest (Innsbruck: Studien Verlag, 2017), 533–552, in particular 544–545. Kos recognizes a "recourse to the rural-catholic" ("Rückgriff auf das Bäuerlich-Katholische") since the establishment of the so-called Ständestaat in 1933 (544).

for the elaboration of a comprehensive autonomous status for South Tyrol (which was, however, considered fulfilled only in the 1990s). The stamp with the Pustertal motif appeared in three different colors,[6] so one can assume that this implicit political message had been omnipresent.

With the definite stamp series "Buildings," most of which appeared in the period 1957–1963 (with additions up to 1970), Alpine motifs on definitive stamps took a backseat for the first time: only three of thirty-four editions and twenty-nine different motifs show an Alpine reference. Although some of the buildings are indeed situated in towns and villages within the Alps, the Alpine environment is not even referenced. Exceptions are a farmhouse in the Pinzgau district, *Bundesland* of Salzburg from 1962 (Michel No. 1115 = ANK No. 1096), the mint tower of Hall in Tyrol against the backdrop of the Tyrolean Nordkette mountains from 1960 (Fig. 2c, Michel no. 1048 = ANK No. 1101), and the Schattenburg castle in Feldkirch, Vorarlberg from 1967 (Michel number 1232 = ANK No. 1261). Overall, it can be observed that it was not only the basic motivic orientation that was responsible for this decline in Alpine reference, but that the Alpine environment of the buildings was obviously left out deliberately in most cases.

With the "Landscapes" series (1973–1983), the Alpine region moved back into focus: sixteen out of twenty-eight editions and fifteen out of twenty-seven motifs show a clear relationship to the Alpine environment. The representations are kept largely realistic, so that a recognition effect in terms of tourism advertising is given in any case. Fig. 2d from 1974, (Michel No. 1442 = ANK No. 1587), with the Bischofsmütze ("Bishop's cap") mountain in the Dachstein Massif (*Bundesland* of Salzburg) can serve as a good example of this. The stamp shows an idyllic alpine pasture with a hut that invites you to stop for a mountain hike, with the rugged, imposing mountain scenery in the background.

In the last two decades of the twentieth century, Alpine motifs on definitive stamps largely disappeared again, which—as will be shown below—is in contrast to the development of the special stamps. On the definitive stamp series "Monasteries I" (1984–1992), mountains appear in the background only in three out of eighteen motifs;[7] in the series "Monasteries II" (1993–1995), which was mostly limited to architectural details, there is no stamp with an Alpine reference. In the series "Legends from Austria" (1997–2000), three out of twelve motifs—that is to say, one third—have clear references to an Alpine environment.[8]

---

6   Blue edition of 1948 (Michel No. 910 = ANK No. 904), red edition of 1950 (Michel No. 911 = ANK No. 905), green edition of von 1951 (Michel No. 912 = ANK No. 906).
7   Michel No. 1791, 1915, and 1967 = ANK No. 1807, 1946, and 1994.
8   Michel No. 2257, 2290, and 2300 = ANK No. 2290, 2321, and 2330.

At the beginning of 2002, the Euro was introduced as the new currency in Austria. As a result, a new series of stamps came into circulation, once again displaying a large number of individual values and motifs. The series *Ferienland Österreich* ("Vacation country Austria"), which ran from 2002–2006 also emphasized the intention of advertising Austria as a leading tourist destination at home and abroad (Fig. 2e). Since both landscape and urban motifs were included in this series, the proportion of subjects with Alpine references no longer reaches the dimensions of the "Landscape" series in the late 1940s and 1970s, but with eleven out of twenty-eight editions and four out of thirteen motifs, it is still an above average showing.

The very traditional-looking motifs of snow-covered winter landscapes (Fig. 2e), pastures with cows or cellar lanes in wine-growing villages, however, led to some polemics and even an outcry from the Austrian art scene. An unnamed editor of the left-liberal daily *Der Standard* first presented the new definitive stamp series in April 2001. However, he was unstinting in his critique: Austria is ironically portrayed as a nation of homosexual xenophobes with a special affinity for kitsch and lies, which manifests itself once more in the stamps of the country. "The stranger should know what we stand for. And the locals cannot be reminded often enough. If at some point it should turn out to be a concession with the [currency] Union, then we have demonstrably never been Europeans. Our motifs are already proving that."[9] The author of the article commented on the largest illustration of the article, the stamp with a cow on an alpine pasture in the Tyrolean Alpbachtal:[10] "A picture of Austria goes around the world. In the inner Alpbachtal is the culmination of that which defines us: the commitment to modernity."[11]

On 9 May 2001, Gerald Bast, then rector of the University of Applied Arts in Vienna, wrote a letter to the editor. On the one hand, he complained about the aesthetics of the stamps. On the other hand, he pointed out that contemporary artists, including those at the university he led, had not been included: "Obviously, the Austrian Postal Service is trying to position Austria internationally as the land of alpine dwellers and wine drunkards with the new Euro stamps. The new stamps are not only designed in the aesthetics of the 1940s, but also with the chosen motifs (dim old town

9   "Ansichten keiner Republik," Der Standard, April 25, 2001, 13: "Der Fremde soll wissen, wofür wir stehen. Und der Einheimische kann nicht oft genug daran erinnert werden. Wenn sich das mit der Union irgendwann einmal als Vereinnahmung herausstellen sollte, dann waren wir eben nachweislich nie Europäer. Unsere Motive beweisen das schon jetzt."
10   Michel, No. 2366 = ANK, No. 2400.
11   "Ansichten keiner Republik," Der Standard, April 25, 2001, 13: "Ein Österreich-Bild geht um die Welt. Im inneren Alpbachtal kulminiert, was uns ausmacht: das Bekenntnis zur Moderne."

romance, wine cellar, cow on the pasture, snowy mountain village), Austria presents itself in a way that probably makes everyone shudder who considers Austria a modern country in which art, culture and science play an important role. Is this a manifestation of the infamous Austrian self-hatred or merely the thoughtlessness of a backward minded philatelist? Even if one should not overestimate the importance of stamps, the impression that Austria wants to create with these stamps in the world is devastating both artistically and in terms of the message. [...]"[12]

The reaction to the criticism is noteworthy: In 2005, a number of eight stamps of the series *Ferienland Österreich* was again issued with overprint, which was created in collaboration with the University of Applied Arts in Vienna and was justified in tariff adjustments.[13] Not only were new values printed on the definitive stamps of the years before, but also the motif was portrayed in a humorous manner. For example, ski jumpers fly over a wintry Alpine hut in the Steinerne Meer mountains, in the *Bundesland* of Salzburg (Michel No. 2514 = ANK No. 2544), or cows on an Alpine pasture in the Tyrolean Alpbachtal mutate into a "Cowbra" ("Kubra") (Fig. 2f, Michel No. 2515 = ANK No. 2543).

Also, in the new stamp series "Flowers," issued 2007–2008, typical Alpine plants are represented in only four out of thirteen motifs.[14] In the following years, however, there was obviously a drastic change in the choice of motif for definitive stamps. Naturally, with the series "Art museums," (2011–2012), which shows museum buildings in modern architecture in Austria and abroad, there is no reference to the Alps, even if singular buildings are definitely situated in the Alps. Since the presentation is concentrated only on the contours of the buildings, the environment around the building plays no role. For the first time ever, the Austrian Postal Service chose motifs for a permanent stamp series that are "modern," and sometimes even avant-garde. This trend is also reflected in the series "Austrian

---

12 "Gerald Bast: Verheerendes Bild, " *Der Standard*, May 9, 2001, 38: "Offensichtlich versucht die Österreichische Post mit den neuen Euro-Briefmarken Österreich als Land der Almbewohner und Weindippler international zu positionieren. Nicht nur, dass die neuen Briefmarken in der Ästhetik der 40er Jahre abgefasst sind, auch mit den gewählten Motiven (schummrige Altstadt-Romantik, Weinkeller, Kuh auf der Alm, verschneites Bergbauerndorf) stellt sich Österreich in einer Art dar, die wohl alle erschauern lassen muss, die Österreich als modernes Land sehen, in dem Kunst, Kultur und Wissenschaft eine wichtige Rolle spielen. Ist das die Manifestation des berüchtigten österreichischen Selbsthasses oder bloß die Gedankenlosigkeit eines in der Vergangenheit lebenden Philatelisten? Auch wenn man die Bedeutung von Briefmarken nicht überbewerten sollte, der Eindruck, den Österreich mit diesen Marken in der Welt erwecken will, ist jedenfalls sowohl künstlerisch als auch was die Botschaft betrifft, verheerend. [...]."
13 Michel No. 2509–2516 = ANK No. 2543–2550.
14 Michel No. 2631, 2679, 2681, and 2749 = ANK No. 2658, 2706, 2708, and 2788.

landmarks" (2013-2014), which shows buildings in the Austrian provincial capitals, but does not require any reference to the Alps due to its abstract and cubic representation of the sights, both historic and modern buildings. The harsh critique of alpine romance in the style of the 1940s, cited above, has evidently—consciously or unconsciously—led to a reorientation of the graphic design.

Particularly noteworthy is the decline of Alpine references in the last series "Impressions from Austria" (2015), analyzed here. In earlier decades, one might expect Alpine motifs to be represented in one or two thirds of the releases, but there are just two out of sixteen. They show the modern Bergisel ski jump in Innsbruck, a new building designed by star architect Zahra Hadid, towering high into the Alpine landscape (Michel No. 3197 = ANK No. 3222), and once more, as an Austrian "mountain icon," the Großglockner (Fig. 14d, Michel No. 3190 = ANK No. 3221).

However, there is a striking exception for this decade-old trend of moving away from the "land of mountains" cliché. In 2012, two postage franking machine stamps appeared, which show the two mountain massifs of Dachstein and Großglockner, emphasizing the reference to the "Land of the mountains" explicitly even by the inscription (Figs. 2g and 2h, Michel No. ATM s. n. = ANK No. PFK 1-2). Here again, the aspect of tourism advertising, (but also traditional self-understanding, as it also describes the first line of the Austrian national anthem), is clearly expressed. Stylistically, there is a departure from the engraved stamp image, which has shaped Austrian stamp issues for a long time and has probably contributed significantly to their high popularity as collectors' items. As with many special stamps, the presentation is now based on photos.

Fig. 2: Alpine motifs on Austrian definitive stamps: a) Silvretta mountains (1947, Michel No. 845 = ANK No. 854); b) Costume from the (South) Tyrolean Pustertal (1950, Michel No. 911 = ANK No. 905); c) Mint tower of Hall in Tirol from the "Buildings" series (1960, Michel No. 1048 = ANK No. 1101); d) Bischofsmütze mountain near Filzmoos (1974, Michel No. 1442 = ANK No. 1587); e) Winter landscape in the Kleinwalsertal valley from the "Vacation country Austria" series (Michel number 2454 = ANK No. 2488); f) "Cowbra" ("Kubra") in the Tyrolean Alpbachtal valley (2005, Michel No. 2515 = ANK No. 2543); g) Postage franking machine stamp showing the Dachstein mountain (2012, Michel No. ATM s. n. = ANK No. PFK 1, Type II); h) Postage franking machine stamp showing the Großglockner mountain (2012, Michel No. ATM s. n. = ANK No. PFK 2, Type II). All images: © Österreichische Post AG.

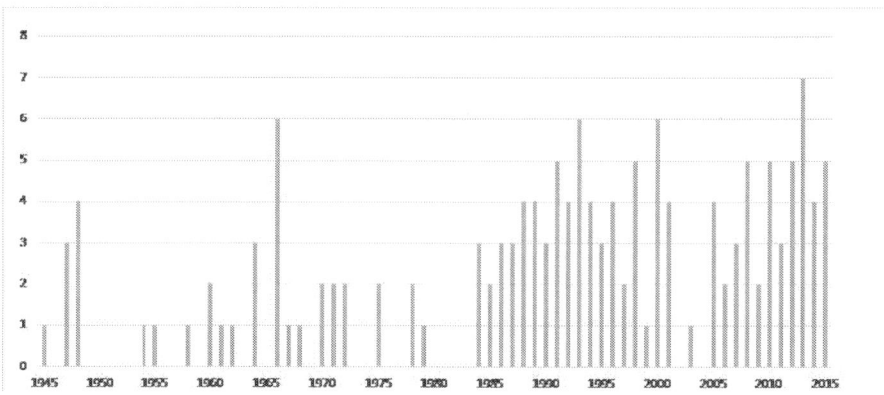

Fig. 3: Number of Austrian special stamps with Alpine topics and motifs per year, 1945–2015. Design by the author.

Alpine Motifs on Special Editions

Once again, we will begin our exploration of Alpine motifs and themes on Austrian special editions and commemorative stamps since 1945 with a quantitative analysis. Figure 3 shows the distribution of motifs over the investigation period. On the one hand, relatively few examples of special stamps with an Alpine reference can be found between the mid-1950s and 1983; an exception is the year 1966, in which a six-part special stamp series with Alpine flowers appeared.[15] On the other hand, there is a distinct trend toward (Alpine) nature, but also toward Alpine cultural heritage and customs for the last fifteen years of the twentieth century, a trend that continues even after the turn of the millennium. This development is also congruent with the general political and social environment, because around the mid-1980s, environmental issues became more relevant in politics than ever before, both at the Austrian level and in a global context. After the emergence of the Green Party in Austria, especially in the early 1990s, there was a greater shift toward environmental issues in politics, within the established major parties as well, leading even to actionist media appearances in front of breathtaking alpine scenery.

In absolute terms, the number of special stamps portraying the Alps remained at about the same level as it was between 1984 and 2001, even after the changeover to the Euro. However, in terms of the total number of special stamps, the proportion has decreased in recent years (see Figure 1 above). This is due to the fact that extensive block issues and individual

---

15 Michel No. 1209-1214 = ANK-No. 1239-1244.

stamps are more *en vogue* than ever before. The case of the forty stamps on the occasion of the European Football Championship 2008 has already been pointed out above.

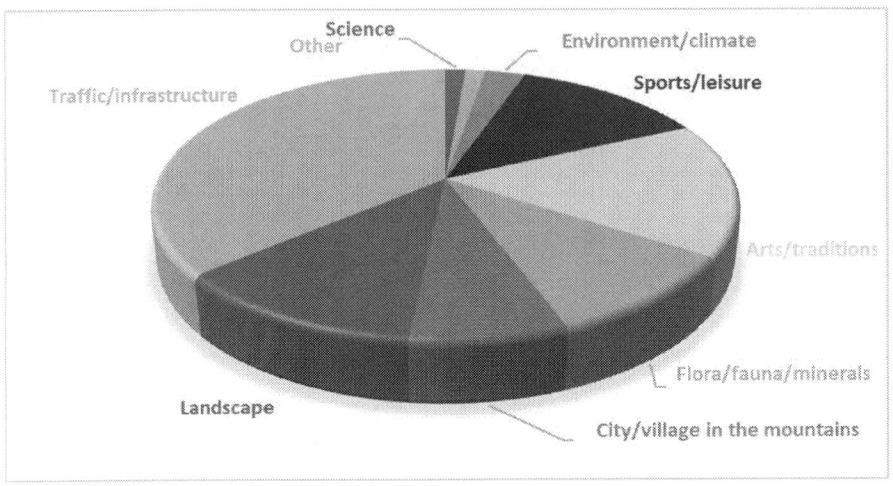

Fig. 4: Groups of Alpine motifs represented on Austrian special stamps, 1945–2015. Design by the author.

Within the special stamps related to Alpine themes, several important motifs can be recognized, whose proportional distribution is shown in Figure 4.[16] According to this, images of the infrastructure, (i.e., trans- and inner-alpine traffic routes (railways, highways) and alpine hydropower stations), account for the largest share with fifty-four stamps (thirty-six percent); around three-fifths (thirty-four stamps) are dedicated to anniversaries. The group "Alpine Arts and Traditions" (twenty-four stamps, sixteen percent) is constituted in particular from the special edition series "Popular customs" (*"Volksbrauchtum,"* 1991–2006); of the total of thirty-six motifs, fourteen are clearly attributable to the Alpine region, at least suggesting the Alpine environment. In the category of "Alpine Landscapes" (eighteen stamps, twelve percent) falls the special issue series "Sites of natural beauty in Austria" (1984–2001) with thirteen (out of twenty) motifs. Other groups are "Towns and Villages in the Mountains" in front of appropriate Alpine scenery (twelve stamps, eight percent); "Flora, Fauna, and Minerals" (fifteen

---

16   The allocation to a group is sometimes not clear, and some stamps could be assigned to several groups. The dominating element in the presentation was considered authoritative for the allocation on a case-by-case basis.

stamps, ten percent); and "Sports and Leisure" (nineteen stamps, thirteen percent); an image was only assigned to the last group when a reference to the surrounding landscape was clearly recognizable. If one included the numerous pictures of successful skiers that appeared after the turn of the millennium, this group would grow even more. Remarkably low—and that is significant, too—are the groups on the topics of "Environmental and Climate protection"[17] and of "Alpine Science,"[18] with only four and two stamps respectively.

In the following qualitative analysis of Austrian special stamps with reference to the Alps, naturally only a small selection will be discussed. Depending on the content, discussion takes place on individual pieces or groups of motifs. At the same time, continuities and changes in content and style will become clear and, in addition, "iconic" Alpine motifs will be explicated.

In 1945, the very first special release, following the Second World War and the regaining of sovereignty, carried a surcharge for the welfare work and appeared in favor of the repatriated prisoners of war (Fig. 5, Michel No. 720 = ANK No. 737): a gaunt man stands high above the "sea of fog" on a mountain peak and looks toward a high Alpine mountain range behind which the sun is just rising; a peace dove floats down from the sky, while the chains framing the picture remember captivity. The Alpine nature thus plays a central role in the presentation of the new beginning, referring both to the returnee and to the re-established state of Austria.

In January 1954, one of the heaviest avalanche winters ever recorded occurred in the western parts of Austria. In the village of Blons in the Große Walsertal valley, Vorarlberg, fifty-seven people were killed in two avalanches. Likewise, the Montafon valley, the Klostertal valley, and the Bregenzerwald were severely affected.[19] In support of the victims, the Austrian Postal Service brought out a charity stamp with a surcharge of twenty Groschen to the nominal value of one Schilling. The motif of the wintry village of St. Christoph am Arlberg from the "Landscapes" definitive

---

17 Fifth European year of nature conservation, 1970, with a depiction of the Krimml waterfalls (1970, Michel No. 1325 = ANK No. 1355); 100 years of torrent control (1984, Michel No. 1779 = ANK No. 1812); Protect the Alps! (Alpine Convention) (1992, Michel No. 2065 = ANK No. 2099, joint issue with Switzerland); Conservation of glaciers and polar regions, with a representation of the Venediger glacier (2009, Michel No. 2797 = ANK No. 2825).

18 Commemorative stamps on the Seventy-fifth (1961) and One-hundredth (1986) anniversary of the Sonnblick summit Observatory (Michel No. 1091, and 1857 = ANK No. 1133, and 1888).

19 On the avalanche disaster of 1954 in Vorarlberg see in detail Helga Nesensohn-Vallaster, *Der Lawinenwinter 1954: Der 11. Jänner 1954 aus der Sicht einer Betroffenen* (Schruns: Montafoner Museen, 2004).

stamp series of 1946 (Michel No. 768II = ANK No. 772) was re-used, with an additional imprint "*Lawinenopfer* 1954" ("Avalanche victims 1954") (Fig. 6, Michel No. 998 = ANK No. 1007). It is noteworthy that this stamp, with three million copies issued, had a higher circulation than any other special stamp from the first half of the 1950s, including the Christmas stamps or another charity stamp with a surcharge to help the Hungarian refugees in 1956 (Michel No. 1030 = ANK No. 1039).

Fig. 5: Charity stamp with a repatriated prisoner of war looking at a sunrise behind an Alpine mountain range (1945, Michel No. 720 = ANK No. 737). © Österreichische Post AG.

Fig. 6: Charity stamp with a surcharge to support the victims of the avalanche disaster of 1954 (Michel No. 998 = ANK No. 1007). © Österreichische Post AG.

Fig. 7: Special stamp celebrating the opening of the Brenner Pass motorway
(1971, Michel No. 1372 = ANK No. 1402). © Österreichische Post AG.

The area of transport infrastructure and means of transport of all kinds is a particularly popular motif on Austrian stamps and does not only reference the Alpine area. This is probably also due to the proximity between the post office and the railways, both of which have long been run as state-owned enterprises in Austria and whose structures were closely interlinked. In addition, it is obvious that a large group of philatelists have an interest in historical railways and similar motifs. However, railways were not the only infrastructure frequently portrayed; road construction was also a common image.[20] Analyzing the special stamp motifs with reference to the Alpine transport infrastructure, analogues to the mobility behavior of the economic boom ("*Wirtschaftswunder*") of the 1960s, and subsequently in the 1970s, become evident. In 1971, for example, a special stamp was issued celebrating the completion of the Brenner Pass motorway, which shows the *Europabrücke* ("Bridge of Europe"), then the highest bridge in Europe. In the background rise the Stubai Alps (Fig. 7, Michel No. 1372 = ANK No. 1402). The motorway and the high Alpine landscape form a harmonious unity. Transalpine road construction was seen as a major technical achievement at that time, whereas the negative consequences of the Alpine transit—the Brenner motorway is one of the busiest routes through the Alps—are hidden.

---

20   See also the commemorative stamp on the twenty-fifth anniversary of the opening of the Großglockner-High Alpine Scenic Road (Fig. 14a, 1960, Michel No. 1080 = ANK No. 1122).

The 1980s saw the beginning of a series of anniversary stamps commemorating the construction of railway lines, the commissioning of tourist shipping lines and mountain railways, and other anniversaries. This accumulation is due in particular to the fact that at the end of the nineteenth and the beginning of the twentieth century the development of the transport network took place against the background of the tourist boom of the Belle Époque. At the same time, however, tourism advertisement related to the present was associated with these motifs, as the stamp published in 1993 for the centenary of the cog railway on the Schafberg in the Upper Austrian Salzkammergut district shows (Fig. 8, Michel No. 2104 = ANK No. 2134). The presentation is similar in style to the advertising poster art of the time around 1900; the cog railway itself is emphasized as it bursts out of the oval image, while the view opens onto the Wolfgangsee lake and the mountains of the Salzkammergut district. The aspect of tourism advertising via commemorative stamp is thus obvious.

Fig. 8: Commemorative stamp on the centenary of the Schafberg cog railway
(1993, Michel No. 2104 = ANK No. 2134). © Österreichische Post AG.

Another clear reference to tourism advertising was published since 1984 in the series "Sites of natural beauty in Austria." One stamp, and in some years two stamps, came out every year showing beautiful landscapes from all over Austria. Two thirds of them are dedicated to Alpine motifs, from waterfalls (Fig. 9a) to mountain panoramas (Fig. 9b) to stalactite and ice caves. They serve as an invitation for a future visit by the recipients both from Austria and abroad. Occasionally, those special stamps were also an indication of the new national parks that had been created in the 1980s and 1990s, as shown in Fig. 9b (Hohe Tauern National Park).

Fig. 9: Special stamps series "Sites of natural beauty in Austria:" a) Tschaukofall waterfall and Tscheppaschlucht canyon, Carinthia (1986, Michel No. 1853 = ANK No. 1884); b) Eiskögele glacier landscape in Hohe Tauern National Park, Salzburg/East Tyrol/Carinthia (1996, Michel No. 2183 = ANK No. 2214). All images: © Österreichische Post AG.

The subject area "Sports and Leisure" has a tourism component as well. In the first place, a distinction is made between winter sports, which traditionally play a very important role in Austria, and alpinism or hiking tourism, focused in the summer. The latter will be presented in more detail based on three examples. In 1970, at a time when Alpine motifs were scarcely to be found, a stamp on the subject of "Hiking and mountaineering" was published (Fig. 10a, Michel No. 1341 = ANK No. 1371). The motivation for this choice of topic cannot be ascertained with certainty. It would be conceivable that this stamp should propagate the hiking tourism in the mountains, which at that time lost much ground in favor of individual and group holidays by the sea. Two hikers stand or sit, respectively, in the high Alpine terrain and look out over a mountain backdrop, in front of which there is a small lake. Two other stamps are dedicated to anniversaries of the two major Alpine hiking clubs: in 1995, a commemorative stamp on the centenary of the *"Naturfreunde"* ("Friends of nature"), a leisure organization of the working class (Fig. 10b, Michel No. 2154 = ANK 2186). The stamp shows the picture on the title page of the first issue of the club magazine *"Der Naturfreund"* ("Nature's friend"): similar to the returnee charity stamp of 1945 (Fig. 5), a hiker stands on a hill and looks out over a mountain landscape; behind a high mountain in the background, the sun is just rising. At the time of its creation (1895), this motif also had a high symbolic value, promising a better future for the working class. Finally, in 2012, a commemorative stamp was issued for the 150th anniversary of the Austrian Alpine Club (Fig. 10c, Michel No. 2974 = ANK No. 3003). Again, the depiction refers to the past, but in this case, a photo of an interwar climber hanging on a rope in a vertical wall is used. For both jubilee stamps, tourism advertising plays only a minor role, but the centerpiece is the history of alpinism.

Fig. 10: Hiking and mountaineering as topics of Austrian stamps: a) Special stamp "Hiking and mountaineering" (1970, Michel No. 1341 = ANK No. 1371); b) Commemorative stamp on the centenary of the "Naturfreunde" (1995, Michel No. 2154 = ANK No. 2186); c) Commemorative stamp on the 150th anniversary of the Austrian Alpine Club (2012, Michel-No. 2974 = ANK No. 3003). All images: © Österreichische Post AG.

As already mentioned, environmental protection and climate awareness occupy a negligible share of the Alps-related stamps. One of the exceptions is a stamp entitled "Protect the Alps" as a joint issue with Switzerland (1992, Fig. 11a, Michel No. 2065 = ANK No. 2099),[21] which appeared quite obviously in response to the Alpine Convention signed in 1991. Numerous national flags can be seen in front of an Alpine backdrop, with the two flags of Austria and Switzerland forming a "knot" in the center from which other flags radiate. It is therefore easy to ascertain from this community motif that Austria and Switzerland see themselves as the two central Alpine countries, while other Alpine countries or signatories of the Alpine Convention, such as France, Italy, and Germany, are only included in the "flag wreath." Instead of the smaller Alpine states of Slovenia,[22] Liechtenstein, and Monaco, however, there are other European flags with no actual geographic relationship to the Alpine region, including even flags of three Scandinavian countries, Belgium, the Netherlands, Greece, and Turkey. Perhaps this alludes to the pan-European Alpine transit, but no "official" interpretation of the flag selection could be found.

In 2009, shortly before the UN Climate Conference in Copenhagen, the Austrian Postal Service issued a special stamp entitled "Conservation of the glaciers and polar regions" (Fig. 11b, Michel No. 2797 = ANK No. 2825). For the first time, the predominant environmental issue of global warming has been addressed. The image, based on a photograph, shows the Großvenediger mountain in the Hohe Tauern with an apparently already shrinking glacier.

---

21 For the Swiss special stamp issued at the same time, see Michel No. 1477 = ANK No. 1488.
22 At that time, Slovenia was a very young state, having declared its independence on 25 June 1991, but after that it was still in a state of war with the rest of Yugoslavia. The then-twelve-member states of the EC recognized the new state at the end of December 1991 and in January 1992, respectively. An inclusion of the Slovenian flag would have been a very strong political statement at the time.

Fig. 11: Environmental and climate protection as topics of Austrian special stamps: a) "Protect the Alps" (1992, Michel No. 2065 = ANK No. 2099); b) "Conservation of the glaciers and polar regions" (2009, Michel No. 2797 = ANK No. 2825). All images: © Österreichische Post AG.

From the period after 2000, there are finally some "experimental" stamps, which are based on Alpine themes, even propagating Alpine clichés. Several stamps are made of textiles. They represent an edelweiss (Fig. 12a, 2005, Michel No. 2538 = ANK No. 2572), a gentian (2008, Michel No. 2773 = ANK No. 2801), but also an Austrian dirndl dress in silhouette embroidery (2016, Michel No. 3285 = ANK No. 3314); additionally, a leather stamp was issued, in the form of leather trousers made of the microfiber fabric Alcantara, and it was decorated with Swarovski crystals (Fig. 12b, 2015, Michel No. 3231 = ANK No. 3260). Both the practicality and the nominal value show they are to be regarded as pure collectibles, which hardly came into non-philatelic circulation. Nonetheless, they are apt to position Austria more strongly as the "Land of the mountains."

Fig. 12: Alpine clichés propagated on "experimental" stamps made of textiles and leather: a) Edelweiss (2005, Michel No. 2538 = ANK No. 2572); b) Leather trousers decorated with Swarovski crystals (2015, Michel No. 3231 = ANK No. 3260). All images: © Österreichische Post AG.

Finally, two "Alpine icons" of Austrian post-war history will be discussed, which are found again and again on stamps. This includes the "myth of Kaprun," a high-Alpine storage power plant for electricity generation. Initial plans go back to the year 1928, but the groundbreaking finally took place on 16 May 1938, performed by Hermann Goering personally, shortly after the so-called "Anschluss," the annexation of Austria by Hitlerite Germany. The concrete construction work began in 1939 so that the huge dam was about half-completed by 1945, due to the work of, in particular, foreign forced laborers and prisoners of war. After the Second World War, the power plant project became the symbol for the reconstruction of Austria. The Nazi past of the project, however, was hidden as much as possible. In 1951, the first part was opened with the Limberg barrier; in 1955—the year of the State Treaty and the regaining of complete independence—the overall project was completed. School textbooks from the 1950s onward characterize the coverage by newsreels and numerous other publications between 1950 to 1955 as celebratory of this outstanding example of the reconstruction of Austria. More than a dozen Kaprun films provided for the anchoring of the rebuilding myth in the collective memory of the 1950s and 1960s. Indeed, the construction site of Kaprun even made it to an advertising poster of the Austrian cigarette brand "Elektra"; the power plant remains one of the most important tourist attractions in the Austrian Alps.[23]

---

23   Oliver Rathkolb et al., *Wasserkraft. Elektrizität. Gesellschaft. Kraftwerksprojekte ab 1880 im Spannungsfeld* (Vienna: Kremayr & Scheriau 2012), in particular 198–201 and also 195 with an image of the design for the cigarette brand mentioned.

Therefore, it is not surprising that several stamps also take up the motif of the Kaprun power plant. In 1955, immediately after completion, the impressive dam appeared on the highest value of the five-part special stamp set titled "Ten-year anniversary of the restoration of the Republic" (Fig. 13a, Michel No. 1016 = ANK No. 1025). Only a few years later, the motif was resumed, now within the scope of the special stamp set "Fifteen-year anniversary of nationalized electric industry" (Fig. 13b, 1962, Michel No. 1103 = ANK No. 1144). After that, the Alpine rebuilding myth obviously faded. The Austria that appeared on stamps defined itself more and more as a land of cities and artists outside the Alpine region.

Fig. 13: Kaprun storage power station in the Hohe Tauern: a) Motif of the special stamp set "Ten-year anniversary of the restoration of the Republic" (1955, Michel No. 1016 = ANK No. 1025); b) Motif of the special stamp set "Fifteen-year anniversary of nationalized electric industry" (1962, Michel No. 1103 = ANK No. 1144). All images: © Österreichische Post AG.

Only a few kilometers west of Kaprun, the road leads through the Fusch Valley up to the Hochtor, an old pass route to the south, which has been in use since Roman times, but only, for a long time, with mule animals. As part of a major governmental project to reduce unemployment during the global economic crisis in the early 1930s, a roadway was built across the Hochtor, which was completed in 1935. Due to the low degree of motorization in the 1930s, and the general political and economic crisis, tourism in this region initially had little economic importance. After World War II, however, it became by far the most important panoramic road in the Eastern Alps. A trip to the Pasterze, the glacier at the foot of the Großglockner, the highest mountain in Austria (3,797 meters above sea level), was part of every group or individual journey in the Hohe Tauern.[24]

Hardly any other motif is found more frequently on Austrian stamps than the Großglockner High Alpine Scenic Route and the Großglockner itself, with the Pasterze glacier. Over twenty-five years, stamps were used to commemorate the opening of this scenic road (Figs. 14a and 14b), as well as the 200th anniversary of the summit's first ascent (Fig. 14c). The top of the Großglockner has been used increasingly in recent years (Fig. 3h, Fig. 14d). Although the shape is not as distinctive as the Matterhorn in Switzerland, it is at least equivalent for the Austrians.

Fig. 14: Großglockner and Großglockner High Alpine Scenic Road: a) Twenty-fifth anniversary of the Großglockner High Alpine Scenic Road (1960, Michel No. 1080 = ANK No. 1122); b) Fiftieth anniversary of the Großglockner High Alpine Scenic Road (1985, Michel No. 1822 = ANK No. 1853); c) Bicentenary of the first ascent of the Großglockner (2000, Michel No. 2309 = ANK No. 2342); d) Peak of the Großglockner, definite stamp series "Impressions of Austria" (2015, Michel No. 3190 = ANK No. 3221). All images: © Österreichische Post AG.

---

24   On the history and identity-forming role of this scenic road, which has meanwhile gained candidate status on the UNESCO World Heritage list, see Bernd Paulowitz, and Johannes Hörl: "Die Großglockner Hochalpenstraße: Ein Gesamtkunstwerk auf dem Weg zum Welterbe" in *Alpenreisen: Erlebnis, Raumtransformationen, Imagination*, eds. Kurt Luger and Franz Rest (Innsbruck: Studien Verlag, 2017), 83–106.

Conclusion: Contextualizing the Results through a Short Comparison with Alpine Motifs on Swiss Stamps

At the end, we may ask how representative those results are for the reconstruction of an "official" perception of the Alps. In another study, I have tried to compare Alpine motifs on Austrian and Swiss stamps. The analysis has shown several parallels, but also some significant differences.[25]

The total corpus of Swiss stamps is about a quarter lower than the Austrian one and comprises, according to the ANK, 1,989 editions, which corresponds to an average of 28.0 stamps per year. However, even here the average value is deceiving. Until the year 2001, the average was 21.6 stamps per year (1,335 issues in total), whereas, for the period from 2002 to 2015, it jumped to 46.5 (652 stamps in total).

Around 279 Swiss stamps have a clear Alpine motif, which is about fourteen percent of the total number of stamps in the period 1945–2015. In contrast to Austria, however, the share in the definitive stamps is slightly lower (53 stamps of 230, about twenty-three percent). Regarding special stamps, Switzerland is different: until the 1960s, there were hardly any commemorative or other special editions with the exception of the annually published charity stamps of two influential foundations, the "Pro Juventute" (since 1913) and "Pro Patria" (since 1938). In the post-war period, the Swiss Postal Service published special stamp sets with usually four to five motifs on behalf of both foundations. In particular, the "Pro Patria" foundation chose numerous "patriotic" motifs with Alpine themes, specifically for sixty-one stamps, which accounted for around twenty percent of the total of 304 "Pro Patria" stamps in the investigation period. In the case of other special issues, the Alpine share is around 12.7 percent (147 stamps of 1,153 issues in total). Overall, the share amounts to 12.84 percent (1,759 special stamps in total) and is thus almost twice as high as similar special stamps in Austria.

Swiss definitive stamps with an Alpine reference were issued mostly in the late 1940s, and afterward only irregularly in single years. On the other hand, an accumulation of Alpine "Pro Patria" motifs are noticeable in the 1950s and again in the last ten years. The other special stamps with Alpine themes can be found to a large extent in the last fifteen years.

In the case of Swiss special stamps, the distribution by type of motif shows some remarkable differences with Austria (Fig. 15). Although the "Transport and Infrastructure" category is also the largest in Switzerland, but with only twenty-three percent (fifty-three stamps), relatively close

---

25   Forthcoming in Rohr, *Land der Berge*.

to "Landscape" (twenty-one percent, fifty stamps), "City or Village in the Mountains" (nineteen percent, forty-five stamps), and "Flora, Fauna, and Minerals" (nineteen percent, forty-four stamps), all of which come in a much higher proportion than in Austria. "Arts and Traditions" (seven percent, seventeen stamps) and "Sports and Leisure" (five percent, twelve stamps), however, are found more rarely than in Austria. The subject area "Environmental and Climate Protection," which is only marginal in Austria (four stamps), has at least to eleven stamps (five percent) in Switzerland.

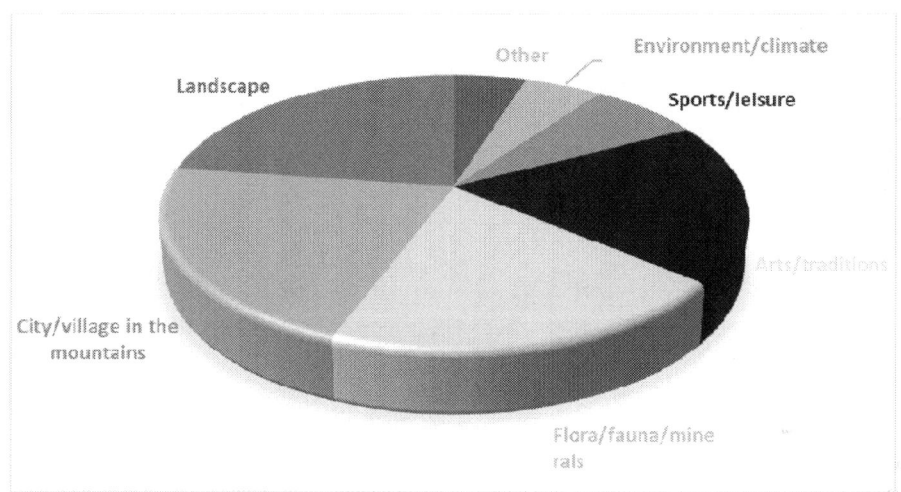

Fig. 15: Groups of Alpine motifs represented on Swiss special stamps, 1945–2015. Design by the author.

The "Pro Patria" charity stamps are a Swiss specialty and particularly relevant for the Alpine references examined here. The foundation "Pro Patria: Swiss *Bundesfeier* donation" was founded in 1909. On the day of the *Bundesfeier* (the national celebration day on 1 August), the population was encouraged to make a patriotic donation to preserve the cultural heritage.[26] This happened first through the sale of the "1st August badge," and since 1938 also via the "Pro Patria" charity stamps. These appeared individually in the beginning, and from 1944 onward, special stamp sets of four to five items per year, which carry patriotic motifs of all kinds, began to appear. Alpine landscape and culture play a central role in farmhouses in front of Alpine landscapes, Alpine rural equipment, or rural Alpine customs. The choice of explicitly Alpine motifs was, however, subject to fluctuations. They dominated until the late 1950s, but they were then found only

26 http://www.propatria.ch (last accessed 17 April 2018).

sporadically and increased again after the turn of the millennium. However, the more recent motifs were less rural-patriotic representations; rather, they had a tourist and conservation background, as in the propagation of the *Kulturwege* ("Cultural pathways") program of the Via Storia Foundation (2007–2009).

For the other special stamps, there are differences between Switzerland and Austria in their quantitative distribution according to motifs, but in terms of quality, the similarities prevail. In the area of transport and infrastructure, commemorative stamps referring to railway anniversaries are also common in Switzerland, although until the 1970s, the Alpine roads were also relatively often observed, as in a stamp released to celebrate the opening of the road tunnel on the Great St. Bernard in 1964.[27]

Portrayals of landscapes with the implicit goal of attracting tourists are at least as widespread in Switzerland as they are in Austria. In recent years, images are increasingly based on photos and appear like views from a tourist brochure, such as the block issues "Typical Swiss landscapes," with motifs from the Mattertal with the Matterhorn in the background[28] and the Emmental with the mountain backdrop of the Bernese Oberland in the background.[29]

Recreational and sporting activities, such as hiking and mountaineering, are also prominently featured in the stamp issues of recent years. When the Austrian Postal Service dedicated an individual stamp to the anniversaries of the "*Naturfreunde*" ("Friends of nature") and the Austrian Alpine Club, the Swiss Postal Service commemorated the anniversaries of the Swiss "*Naturfreunde*" (2005)[30] and the Swiss Alpine Club (2013)[31] with large-format block editions, each showing several forms of mountain sports.

In recent years, Alpine stereotypes are increasingly being used in Switzerland as well. An example of this is the block edition of the *Esposizione internazionale di filatelia trilaterale delle Alpi* ("International trilateral exhibition of Alpine philately"), which took place in 2003 in Locarno. The block shows a stylized mountain, out of which appears an oversized eagle head and as well as gentian blossoms.[32]

"Alpine icons" are also being recorded repeatedly in Switzerland. This is particularly true for the Matterhorn, which is probably the most well-known

---

27   Michel No. 791 = ANK No. 802.
28   Michel No. 2321 = ANK No. 2335.
29   Michel No. 2365 = ANK No. 2379.
30   Michel No. 1937–1940 = ANK No. 1945–1948.
31   Michel No. 2288–2291 = ANK No. 2302–2305.
32   Michel No. 1836–1837 = ANK No. 1847–1848.

mountain in the world, with its striking silhouette. It emerges as the main theme of stamps as well as in the background, for example, for the "Pro Aero" airmail stamp from 1988 showing a historical airplane in front of the Matterhorn.[33]However, in the case of one frequent topic related to the perception of the Alps, the two countries differ: the generation of electricity from hydropower in high Alpine terrain. Although this has a long tradition in both countries as a symbol of the autarchy of a small Alpine state, the issue has only found its way into stamps in Austria.

Overall, the quantitative and serial-iconographic examination of Austrian and Swiss stamps proves that the Alps serve as a constituent element of identity of both countries, albeit with certain changes over time, and subtle differences between Austria and Switzerland in detail.

For example, the topic of "alpine homeland" on Austrian stamps is expressed much more by costumes and traditional customs, from the late 1940s to the new millennium. In Switzerland in the 1940s and 1950s, however, this is rather pronounced by motifs such as alpine farmhouse styles. In recent times, stamps representing a healthy tourist mountain world or interpreting the Alps as an area of almost unlimited recreational opportunities have become dominant in Switzerland. Individual distinctive mountains such as the Grossglockner or the Matterhorn are present on stamps throughout and can therefore be interpreted as "alpine icons". Both countries have equally emphasized typical alpine plants and animals, above all alpine flowers such as gentian or edelweiss or alpine animals such as the golden eagle, the ibex or the marmot.

Considering the quantity and temporal distribution of Alpine issues on stamps, the tendency to define themselves as a "land of Alpine mountains" is evident in both countries, especially in the 1940s and 1950s. After that, the Austrian Postal Service turned away significantly from alpine motifs, only to return to it intensively in the mid-1980s. Overall, since the 1960s, however, the Austrian special stamps convey more of an Austrian identity defined by famous composers, painters and writers as well as touristically attractive cultural cities than by alpine cultures. In Switzerland, this course is similar, but not so distinctive. However, in contrast to Austria, it is noticeable that in the last 15 years the Alps have once again gained significantly more importance as a motif on special stamps. This fact might mirror the Swiss special path outside the European Union, with a noticeable emphasis of "Swissness" in politics and society.

---

33   Michel No. 1369 = ANK No. 1375.

Hydroelectric Power Generation in Austria:
A History of Archetypal Conflicts with Nature Conservation

Christina Pichler-Koban

Introduction

"Modern life is in many ways characterized by the ready availability of energy."[1]

The reliance of Western-style societies on technical power supply networks is increasing in virtually all areas of life. The investment of considerable resources is needed to make energy available, and this investment competes with the potential alternative use of these resources. This is the topic of this contribution.

The majority of people have, for centuries, lived on what nature provided readily or on what peasants gained from it through arduous work. This situation changed profoundly around the end of the nineteenth century, when Western society entered the age termed "High Modernism" by American political scientist James C. Scott.[2] This period was marked by a strong belief in technological progress and the concept of man being able to gain mastery over nature. Nature should be manageable and controllable; according to this technocratic notion of the world, nature was more or less the raw material for modern engineers, technicians, and planners to process and improve.[3]

Our concept of nature has changed as an anti-technocratic shift of paradigms developed along with a series of events—some of which will be explored in more detail below.

Rivers are multi-functional systems. They ensure the provision of water and have for centuries been used as transport routes. They have always been the reason for people to settle and establish businesses along their banks; they provide food, and they are used for a variety of recreational activities.

---

1   "Die moderne Existenz ist in vielfältiger Weise durch die leichte Verfügbarkeit von Energie geprägt:" Martin Schmid and Ortrun Veichtlbauer, *Vom Naturschutz zur Ökologiebewegung: Umweltgeschichte Österreichs in der Zweiten Republik* (Innsbruck: Studienverlag, 2006), 24.
2   James C. Scott, *Seeing like a State –How Certain Schemes to Improve the Human Conditions Have Failed* (New Haven-London: Yale University Press, 1998).
3   Schmid and Veichtlbauer, *Vom Naturschutz zur Ökologiebewegung*, 29.

Apart from the human needs they serve, rivers are of essential importance for the ecosystem.

Hydroelectric power generation is accompanied by massive interventions in the related aquatic ecosystem. Handling these interventions has always determined both scientific discourse and political debate, and it still does. The history of hydropower use is also the chronicle of an enduring confrontation between conflicting social value systems, needs, and images of nature.

The debate was, and even now continues to be, of great importance in many parts of the world, for example, in the mountainous regions of the Caucasus, the Himalayas, the Andes, and East Africa. This contribution traces this history of conflict based on the example of the alpine Republic of Austria. Here, topographic and climatic conditions favor the use of hydroelectric power to a special degree.

These topographic conditions have left their stamp on Austria's national identity and even found their way into the Austrian anthem "Land of mountains, Land by the stream" ("*Land der Berge, Land am Strome*"). In every survey about the assets of Austria, its beautiful landscape and intact natural wonders are regularly among the top mentions. Two iconic examples of such are the Hohe Tauern National Park in the Austrian Central Alps and the Donau-Auen National Park in the Danube floodplains. Plans to use hydropower played an important role in the history of both parks.

Nature conservation and the use of hydropower are two essential elements of the Second Republic, and the two interests collide in exemplary manner in the Hohe Tauern mountain range and the Danube floodplains. This article investigates the various concepts of nature conservation that became apparent in these confrontations.

The example of Austria highlights the conflicts, dilemmas, and ambiguities that exist in the dynamic relationship between nature conservation and hydropower use in archetypal discourses. It also illustrates the processes involved in the ongoing reassessment of a technology.

Hydroelectric Power Use in Austria

There is extensive documentation of the history of hydroelectric power use in Austria, with a particular focus on the years of National Socialism.[4] The brief historical overview below is intended to provide a better understanding of the events described in the following.

Established after the First World War in 1918, the Republic of Austria saw the development of an electricity supply industry based on hydropower as an opportunity to compensate for the loss of the monarchy's rich coal fields and to achieve energy self-sufficiency. Rivers have in fact been used extensively for the generation of energy in Austria since the Middle Ages, but as the energy produced had to be used on the site of generation, the number of small weirs and mill wheels was exceptionally high. With the development of new technologies, the location of energy production and the place of energy use finally became detached from each other. This made it possible to set up power stations in places where conditions were favorable and to transport the generated electricity long distances to the places where it was needed.[5]

Initially, the implementation of major power plant projects progressed slowly, mainly due to the failure to obtain financing. The annexation of Austria to the Third Reich brought with it the initiation of major power supply projects to serve the prestige of the National Socialist regime. Energy demand in Western Europe increased dramatically after the Second World War.[6] In the Second Republic, the use of hydropower constituted an important pillar in the reconstruction and the economic boom of the 1950s and 1960s.

---

4   Richard Hufschmied, "Wasserkraft, Elektrizität und Gesellschaft in Österreich von 1880 bis in die 1930er-Jahre" (PhD diss., University of Vienna, 2011); Richard Hufschmied, "'Weißes Gold' in (Deutsch-)Österreich – Kontinuität und Wandel mit dem Epochenjahr 1918," in *Wasserkraft. Elektrizität. Gesellschaft. Kraftwerksprojekte ab 1880 im Spannungsfeld*, ed. Oliver Rathkolb, Richard Hufschmied, Andreas Kuchler, and Hannes Leidinger (Vienna: Kremayr & Scheriau, 2012), 84–148; Oliver Rathkolb, Florian Freund, ed., *NS-Zwangsarbeit in der Elektrizitätswirtschaft der „Ostmark" 1938–1945* (Vienna: Böhlau, 2002); Georg Rigele, "Das Tauernkraftwerk Glockner-Kaprun – Neue Forschungsergebnisse und offene Fragen," *Blätter für Technikgeschichte* 59, (1997): 55–94; Marc D. Landry, "Europe's Battery: The Making of the Alpine Energy Landscape, 1870-1955," (PhD diss., Georgetown University, 2013); Schmid and Veichtlbauer, *Vom Naturschutz zur Ökologiebewegung*.
5   Gertrud Haidvogl, Sabine Preis, Severin Hohensinner, Susanne Muhar, and Michaela Poppe, "Flusslandschaften im Wandel," in *Flüsse in Österreich: Lebensadern für Mensch, Natur und Wirtschaft* ed. Gregory Egger, Klaus Michor, Susanne Muhar, and Betarice Bednar (Innsbruck: Studienverlag, 2009), 32–43.
6   Christian Pfister, "Das 1950er Syndrom: Die Epochenschwelle der Mensch-Umwelt-Beziehung zwischen Industriegesellschaft und Konsumgesellschaft," *GAIA* 3., no. 2 (1994): 71–90.

In the first decades of the twentieth century, criticism of hydropower projects was limited to isolated considerations from intellectual and academic circles. The construction of dams and storage reservoirs was even perceived as enriching and beautifying the landscape. In the 1950s, nature conservation activists began to oppose power plant projects for the first time. Some spectacular conflicts followed; a new way of thinking about the use of natural resources began. In the 1980s and 1990s, protest movements supported by large groups of the population brought power plant projects on the Danube (Hainburg) and in the Dorfertal in Tyrol to a standstill and in each case opened the way for the development of national parks. The conflicts eventually led to the emergence of new institutions, political parties, and nature conservation tools.[7]

The fifty most powerful storage power stations are currently located in the Alps of central and western Austria. Nearly all of them went into operation between 1950 and 1992. All of the ten most powerful run-of-river power plants are located on the river Danube and were completed before the Hainburg conflict, with the exception of the Freudenau power station (1998).[8]

An analysis of the historical sources shows that the changing debate surrounding hydropower is inextricably tied to the history and identity of the Austrian Republic.

Nature Conservation in Austria

The first statutory provisions with nature conservation in mind were issued in the second half of the nineteenth century; one of the earliest was the *Reichsforstgesetz* 1852. Alpine tourism that began in that era increased the pressure on Alpine flora, which led scientists to make the first proposals for the establishment of Alpine protected areas. Shortly before the collapse of the Austro-Hungarian Monarchy, plans to establish protected areas became more concrete.

During the First Republic, specialist departments for nature conservation were established in the federal provinces with the assistance of zoologist Günter Schlesinger, one of the leading figures of Austrian nature conservation. During the same period, the highly popular "Papers on Natural

---

7   Christina Pichler-Koban and Michael Jungmeier, *Naturschutz, Werte, Wandel: Die Geschichte ausgewählter Schutzgebiete in Deutschland, Österreich und der Schweiz*, Bristol-Schriftenreihe Band 46 (Bern: Haupt, 2015).
8   "Liste österreichischer Kraftwerke," *de.wikipedia.org*, accessed Jan. 31, 2018, https://de.wikipedia.org/wiki/Liste_%C3%B6sterreichischer_Kraftwerke.

History and Nature Conservation" (*Blätter für Naturkunde und Naturschutz*) were published. In these papers Schlesinger addressed, among other topics, the atmospheric value of landscape as well as the economic value of nature protection—thoughts that went beyond the pure conservation aspect of nature protection that had prevailed until then.

In the 1950s and 1960s, discussions on the construction of power stations and development projects dominated the Austrian nature conservation scene; the plans for the establishment of a national park remained unfulfilled.

The European Conservation Year proclaimed in 1970 by the Council of Europe was designed as an advertising campaign intended to create awareness for the concerns of nature conservation and environmental protection; one of its effects was that the Governors of the Austrian provinces of Carinthia, Salzburg, and Tyrol made a public commitment to establishing a joint Hohe Tauern National Park. The 1980s saw a number of conflicts about major projects—in many cases focusing on the conflict over the use of rivers and their importance for nature conservation. Many of the sites involved in these conflicts were later turned into national parks.[9]

A Brief History of Hohe Tauern National Park

Though always sparsely populated, human presence in the Hohe Tauern dates back to pre-Christian times, and traces of it are found along old trade routes across the Alps. Around 250 BC, people settled permanently in the valleys and took their domestic animals up to the mountain pastures to graze. An important source of income until the beginning of the nineteenth century besides agriculture was the mining of Tauern gold.[10] When mining was discontinued, the mountains and rivers remained the most promising assets of this region.

The boom of Alpine tourism began around 1900; the increasing mobility ensured by railways and automobiles instilled wealthy townspeople with a growing desire for travel. Ambitious road construction projects and fashionable hotels were planned in the area around the Grossglockner in particular.[11]

Regions that had so far been considered unreachable suddenly came within reach, and this also made the finite quality of unspoiled nature

9   Pichler-Koban and Jungmeier, *Naturschutz, Werte, Wandel.*
10   Fritz Gruber, "Der Edelmetallbergbau in Salzburg und Oberkärnten bis zum Beginn des 19. Jahrhunderts," in *Das Buch vom Tauerngold*, ed. Werner Paar, Wilhelm Günther, and Fritz Gruber (Salzburg: Verlag Anton Pustet, 2006), 193–295.
11   Markus Gesierich, *Hotels an der Großglockner Hochalpenstraße: Franz Wallack und das ideale Alpenhotel* (Vienna: Klein Publishing, 2016).

evident. Aware of this finite aspect, the nature conservation movement gained momentum, and soon the Hohe Tauern region was identified as a suitable place for a *Naturschutzpark* (nature conservation park) following the example of American national parks. The first steps were made by *Stuttgarter Verein Naturschutzpark*, which bought land in the Stubachtal and Felbertal valleys, but there were still many years to come before the Hohe Tauern National Park would actually be established. Carinthia started it in 1981; Salzburg (1983) and Tyrol (1993) followed. The intervening and subsequent history has been, and continues to be, eventful through the present day.[12]

Ultimately, a third option opened for the Hohe Tauern area in the early twentieth century: the Hohe Tauern mountains provided ideal conditions for the generation of energy from hydropower, with their abundance of water and favorable effective head. This potential was clearly seen, especially as the Austrian Government attached high priority to the development of "white coal" to reduce the young Republic's dependency on imported coal.

The three interest groups of tourism, energy industry, and nature conservation tried to assert their respective ideas in the Hohe Tauern area; there was no escaping conflict. The most prominent conflicts are listed below:

The struggle over the Kaprun Tauern power plant: *Allgemeine Elektrizitätsgesellschaft Berlin* (AEG) presented first drafts for a power plant project in 1928; the project was designed to combine the Tauern runoffs of Salzburg, East Tyrol, and Carinthia via sloping channels and tunnels in three large reservoirs in the Kaprun Valley and generate 6600 million kWh of electricity in several power plants. The economic crisis of the 1930s prevented the implementation of these plans. The National Socialists took up the plans again, but failed, despite the deployment of forced labor, because the treasury was empty due to the war. After the end of the Second World War, the Kaprun power plant was finally completed with funds from the Marshall Plan and went into operation in 1955.[13]

The dispute over Krimml: "Austrian League for Nature Conservation (Österreichischer Naturschutzbund, ÖNB) mobilized against Tyrolean Hydropower Corporation's (*Tiroler Wasserkraftwerke-AG*, TIWAG) plans to use the Krimmler Ache water for the production of energy and called

12   Anton Draxl, *Der Nationalpark Hohe Tauern: Eine österreichische Geschichte. Band 1. Von den Anfängen bis 1979* (Alpine Raumordnung 12) (Innsbruck: OeAV Fachabt. Raumplanung/Naturschutz, 1996); Patrick Kupper and Anna-Katharina Wöbse, ed., *Geschichte des Nationalparks Hohe Tauern* (Innsbruck: Tyrolia, 2013); Pichler-Koban, and Jungmeier, *Naturschutz, Werte, Wandel*.
13   Ute Hasenöhrl, "Naturschutz in der Zwischenkriegszeit (1918–1938)," in *Geschichte des Nationalparks Hohe Tauern*, ed. Patrick Kupper and Anna-Katharina Wöbse (Innsbruck: Tyrolia, 2013), 39–63.

for an Austria-wide petition in 1952. More than 120,000 people signed the petition and brought down the project. The Krimml Waterfalls were declared a natural monument in 1961 and awarded the European Diploma of Protected Areas by the Council of Europe in 1967.[14]

Protests against the Maltatal power station: In order to prevent the energy use of the runoff from the Carinthian Maltatal, the "Gößgraben-Maltatal" was declared a nature conservation area on the initiative of "German Alpine Association" (*Deutscher Alpenverein*, DAV) in 1943. In 1959, the storage power plant Maltatal was declared a preferred hydraulic engineering project, the nature conservation area was dissolved, and a dam was built in the 1970s despite the continued protest of nature conservation associations.[15]

Resistance in the Dorfertal, Tyrol: After many years of tough negotiations concerning a power station project of TIWAG in East Tyrol—with various nature conservation associations supporting both the opponents and the advocates of the power plant—the people of Kals took a clear position and brought about a decision. The majority decided against the project in a referendum and thus paved the way for the establishment of the Hohe Tauern Tirol National Park.[16]

A Brief History of Donau-Auen National Park

Reference is made here to various accounts of the history of the Danube and its riverscape[17] and the history of the National Park[18] for in-depth studies.

---

14   Georg Stöger, "Neuanläufe für einen Nationalpark (1949–1970)," in *Geschichte des Nationalparks Hohe Tauern*, ed. Patrick Kupper and Anna-Katharina Wöbse (Innsbruck: Tyrolia, 2013), 93–119.

15   Pichler-Koban and Jungmeier, *Naturschutz, Werte, Wandel.*

16   Roland Würflinger, "Die Etablierung des Nationalparks (1971–1992)," in *Geschichte des Nationalparks Hohe Tauern*, ed. Patrick Kupper, and Anna-Katharina Wöbse (Innsbruck: Tyrolia, 2013), 121–145.

17   Mathias Jungwirth, Gertrud Haidvogl, Severin Hohensinner, Herwig Waidbacher, and Gerald Zauner, *Österreichs Donau: Landschaft – Fisch – Geschichte* (Vienna: Institut für Hydrobiologie und Gewässermanagement, BOKU, 2014); Verena Winiwarther, Martin Schmid, and Gert Dressel, "Looking at half a millennium of co-existence: the Danube in Vienna as socio-natural site," *Water History* 5 (2013): 101-119.

18   Bund Naturschutz in Bayern e. V., Gregor Louisoder Umweltstiftung, and Claus Obermeier (eds.), *Der Kampf um die Donauauen: Erfolge und Niederlagen der Naturschutzbewegung* (Munich: oekom, 2015); Christina Pichler-Koban, Norbert Weixlbaumer, Franz Maier, and Michael Jungmeier „Die österreichische Naturschutzbewegung im Kontext gesellschaftlicher Entwicklungen," in *Geographischer Jahresbericht aus Österreich – Beiträge zur Humangeographie und Entwicklungsforschung*, vol. LXII and LXIII, ed. Helmut Wohlschlägl (Vienna: Institut für Geographie und Regionalforschung, 2007): 27–78; Pichler-Koban and Jungmeier, *Naturschutz, Werte, Wandel*; Schmid and Veichtlbauer, *Vom Naturschutz zur Ökologiebewegung.*

Until late into the nineteenth century, there were no man-made interventions in the riverbed of the Danube. There was regular flooding. The
river regulation of 1870 laid the basis for more intensive use of the landscape. The Lobau floodplain was first protected by law in 1959 when it
became included in the green belt of Vienna, the "Viennese Green belt"
(*Wiener Wald- und Wiesengürtel*). The Danube wetlands were imperial
hunting grounds until the Austro-Hungarian Monarchy collapsed in 1918;
from then on, they played an ever more important role for the people of
Vienna seeking recreation.

During the Second World War, *Obere* Lobau became an industrial
zone, and extensive infrastructure of strategic military importance was
developed. The Municipality of Vienna considered introducing a further
expansion of the oil terminal in Lobau in 1958, but these plans failed due
to the resistance of nature conservationists and the people of Vienna (for
further details on the Lobau oil terminal, please refer to the contribution by
Ortrun Veichtlbauer in this volume).

The fall of the river Danube along its free-flowing stretch in Austria is
significant, and the water volume is substantial, making it attractive for hydropower energy production. The 1950s saw the construction of a series of run-
of-the-river power stations and barrages called the "Golden Stairs"—(*Goldene
Treppe*), as the process was called—along the Austrian section of the Danube.
Eight barrages had been built to the north of Vienna by 1980; construction
of the Hainburg power plant was scheduled to begin in 1984. The resistance
to these plans—initially by a few nature conservationists—developed into a
conflict that would take hold of Austrian society and bring about a turning
point in the democratic policy of the Republic.[19] The Governors of Vienna
and Lower Austria celebrated the official opening of Donau-Auen National
Park in 1996 at the precise location of these disputes.[20]

Analysis

Any concept of nature conservation accordingly comprises intrinsic
conflicts. This paper draws on changes in conservationists' selected positions

---

19   Bund Naturschutz in Bayern, *Der Kampf um die Donauauen*; Bernhard Natter, "Die
'Bürger' versus die 'Mächtigen' – Populistischer Protest an den Beispielen Zwentendorf
und Hainburg," in *Populismus in Österreich*, ed. Anton Pelinka (Vienna: Edition Junius,
1987), 151–170; Günther Nenning, and Andreas Huber (ed.), *Die Schlacht der Bäume –
Hainburg 1984* (Vienna: hannibal, 1984); Schmid, and Veichtlbauer, *Vom Naturschutz zur
Ökologiebewegung.*
20   Pichler-Koban et al. "Die österreichische Naturschutzbewegung;" Pichler-Koban, and
Jungmeier, *Naturschutz, Werte, Wandel.*

during the development of two Austrian national parks. The analysis is intended to exemplify the complex conceptual roots of nature conservation and to reveal the conceptions, narratives, and discourses at work in this context. A large-scale study on the historical development of Alpine parks[21] identified different types of conceptual interaction between conservation and other interest groups that figured prominently. The interactions between nature conservation and tourism can, for example, be assigned six conceptions.[22] The following section elaborates on the question whether the same is also true for the interaction between nature conservation and the use of hydropower. The identified conceptions are:

Fundamental antagonism: The predominant narrative of this conception draws on the integrity and beauty of nature that gets disturbed and destroyed by any kind of human intervention. Hence, unspoiled nature must be protected against overwhelming human exploitation. Only a few (educated) visitors know how to behave; all others are a permanent and imminent threat to fauna and flora and must consequently be excluded.

Selective antagonism: This position claims that natural landscapes are remaining hideaways from everyday life. These landscapes are in danger of being spoiled by technical infrastructures, modern architecture, and noisy mass tourism. This conception was formulated and continues to be advocated by Alpine associations and mountaineering clubs, the early pioneers of Alpine tourism. These were primarily rooted in well-educated, economically well-situated circles of public and academic life, but have continuously broadened their member base throughout the twentieth century. Hence, these actors turned out to be the most influential drivers of a public discussion that opposed infrastructures such as skiing-resorts, cable-cars, hydroelectric plants, and grids in Alpine regions.

Opportunistic cooperation: There is no particular narrative in this regard, since the position refers to the concrete discourses and arguments that are used. However, a supposedly strong interest is used to support nature conservationists' positions. For example, it is argued that a project will lead to a loss of opportunities for tourism. This conception is used by different groups, but is mainly rooted in civil society actors. It is hard to distinguish between what is the "honest" conviction and what is already a compromise. Hence, the interpretation of this position is problematic. These opportunistic co-operations are generally limited in time. They are focused on a particular topic but remain fragile and are not bound to either

---

21 Pichler-Koban and Jungmeier, *Naturschutz, Werte, Wandel.*
22 Christina Pichler-Koban, and Michael Jungmeier, "Alpine parks between yesterday and tomorrow - a conceptual history of Alpine national parks via tourism in charismatic parks in Austria, Germany and Switzerland," *eco.mont* Vol. 9 (2017): 17–28.

side. The strategy clearly intends to influence public opinion and decision makers and is therefore an instrument of agitation.

Opportunistic appropriation: There is no general position in this respect, since the actors use conservationist arguments to support other private or institutional intentions. An example for this is the designation of "special nature reserves" (*Naturschutzgebiete spezieller Ordnung*) in the Third Reich. These were in fact designed to enable exclusive hunting activities for the leading officials of the regime.

Co-operative development: this conception is based on the idea that most conflicts between nature conservation and the energy industry can be solved by technical solutions and appropriate design of power stations, dams, and reservoirs. A partnership between the antagonistic groups is a course that enables good solutions to emerge, which satisfy the energy producers and at the same time fulfill conservationist requirements.

Integrative development: The representatives of this conception claim to see protected areas in an integrated/holistic manner. Good planning is intended to avoid conflict and take all interests into account.

Interdependence One: Nature Conservation – Technology

The first line of discourse explored here is dedicated to the relationship between nature conservation and technology as expressed in the positions of opponents and proponents of power plants.

Hohe Tauern National Park: the Discourse

In the interwar years, the energy sector clearly prevailed over nature and landscape conservation, a fact that was even accepted as an economic necessity by conservationists; they limited their demands to blending technical infrastructure in harmoniously with their surroundings. *Alpenverein* and *Verein Naturschutzpark* feared the failure of the *Naturschutzpark* in Hohen Tauern they yearned for. However, they did not oppose the construction of power plants in Stubachtal. Given the difficult economic situation, they had little chance of success.[23]

Some years later, in the 1930s, *Allgemeine Elektrizitätsgesellschaft* (AEG) considered using the runoffs from the Maltatal. To prevent this use, *Alpenverein* addressed a motion to the Governor of Reichsgau Carinthia to place the Maltatal under protection referring to its "utterly unspoiled

23   Hasenöhrl, "Naturschutz Zwischenkriegszeit," 54.

state."[24] *Alpenverein* was successful in this venture—at least for a time. In 1943, the establishment of a nature conservation area was ordered, and that was subsequently taken over by the Austrian Second Republic. Only in the 1970s was a new attempt by the hydropower industry successful.

In 1938, plans dating back to the interwar years were taken up again, and an overall energy utilization plan for the Hohe Tauern mountains was presented. An application of *Alpen-Elektrowerke* (AEW) for categorization of the infrastructure as "preferred hydro-engineering structure"[25] was quickly approved, with the procedure taking just a few days. The special representative for nature conservation group DAV, Paul Dinkelacker, opposed these plans, claiming they would compromise the national park and "rob it of all rushing and bubbling waters."[26] The head of the nature conservation department in the Reich Forestry Office, Lutz Heck, countered that, on the contrary, a "new plant worth seeing"[27] would be created. DAV, which was in charge of nature conservation in the Eastern Alps and the national parks to be established there, ultimately had to concede, and the ground-breaking ceremony for construction of the Kaprun power plant was held in 1938. The conservationists admitted that the power plant plans represented a "vital contribution to the entire energy management of the German people,"[28] and consequently advocates of nature conservation should work toward a compromise and intensive cooperation between nature conservation and engineering.

In the official publication on the opening of the upper barrage of the Kaprun Tauern power station in 1955, we read that "the landscape has been changed for the better; an idyllic Alpine lake has replaced the barren bottom of the valley and the destructive rivers."[29]

Twenty-five years later, Eduard Wallnöfer, Governor of Tyrol and as such a representative of the owners of TIWAG, commented along the same

24 "völligen Unberührtheit:" Hans Bach, "Das Maltatal – das Tal der stürzenden Wasser: Ein 25-jähriger Kampf," *Jahrbuch des Vereins zum Schutz der Alpenpflanzen und -Tiere* 34, (Munich: Selbstverlag, 1968), Sonderdruck, 8.
25 "bevorzugter Wasserbau:" Ortrun Veichtlbauer, "Großdeutscher Nationalpark im NS (1938–1948)," in *Geschichte des Nationalparks Hohe Tauern*, ed. Patrick Kupper and Anna-Katharina Wöbse (Innsbruck: Tyrolia, 2013), 65–91 (here 80).
26 "aller rauschenden und springenden Wasser:" Veichtlbauer, "Großdeutscher Nationalpark," 80.
27 "neue sehenswerte Anlagen:" Veichtlbauer, "Großdeutscher Nationalpark," 80.
28 "lebenswichtiges Werk für den gesamten Energiehaushalt des deutschen Volkes:" Veichtlbauer, "Großdeutscher Nationalpark," 82.
29 "Die Landschaft wurde gänzlich verändert. Das Bild des toten unfruchtbaren Talbodens mit seinen zerklüfteten Schluchten und zerstörend dahinstürzenden Bächen wurde abgelöst von dem Anblick einer ruhigen Gebirgslandschaft mit einem, die wilden Wasser bändigenden Alpensee, an dessen Ufern sich schüchtern wiedererwachte Vegetation bemerkbar macht:" Johann Götz and Robert Emanovsky, *Festschrift. Die Oberstufe des Tauernkraftwerkes Glockner-Kaprun*, (Zell am See: Tauernkraftwerke A.G., 1955), 54.

lines when he tried to convince the people in East Tyrol of the power plant project in the Dorfertal: "A power plant is an enrichment for any area."[30]

In the 1950s, the "Institute of Nature Conservation" (*Institut für Naturschutz*), which was related to ÖNB, was to provide the scientific basis for the establishment of a national park in the Hohe Tauern. It took every opportunity to provide technical justifications for the caveats of nature conservationists against various power plant projects.[31] And in the 1970s, it was the umbrella organization of Austrian nature and environmental protection organizations (Österreichische Gesellschaft für Natur- und Umweltschutz, ÖGNU, today known as *Umweltdachverband*) that demanded that the national park (by then promised by the governors) had to be taken into consideration whenever a new power plant project was planned. ÖGNU considered the realization of both plans to be incompatible.[32]

Hohe Tauern National Park: Identified Conceptions

Discourse surrounding the Hohe Tauern oscillated between the conservation of unspoiled nature (fundamental antagonism), similar to what *Alpenverein* had wished for the Maltatal, and the argument that the value of an area would be enhanced when nature was tamed and a "new landscape worth seeing" was created (opportunistic appropriation); this is the reasoning used by actors who must justify or push through the construction of a power plant. Many also believed that a compromise could be found and a balance between nature and technology created (co-operative development). This final perspective represents the dominant view at the time, which imagined a substantial alignment of interests between nature and society; this view was only renounced in the 1970s, with the turn toward the ecological paradigm.[33]

Donau-Auen National Park: the Discourse

In 1979, the Lower Austrian *Naturschutzbund* organization first proposed the establishment of a Donau-March-Thaya-Auen National Park.

---

30 "Ein Kraftwerk ist eine Bereicherung eines Gebietes:" Josef Klaus, "Eröffnungsrede des Herrn Landeshauptmann von Salzburg Dr. Josef Klaus," *Blätter für Naturkunde und Naturschutz* 37, no. 12 (1951): 193–194.

31 August Meisinger, "Nationalparke – nun auch in Österreich," *Natur und Land* 36, no. 11 (1950): 185.

32 Chronologie der Aktivitäten der Österreichischen Gesellschaft für Natur und Umweltschutz zum Nationalpark Hohe Tauern, Apr. 5, 1976, Archiv Umweltdachverband, Office Umweltdachverband, Vienna.

33 Schmid, and Veichtlbauer, *Vom Naturschutz zur Ökologiebewegung*, 33, 39.

Taking this into consideration, *Naturschutzbund* suggested building the planned Danube power stations Greifenstein, Regelsbrunn, and Hainburg in the wet instead of dry construction method in order to prevent further reduction of wetlands along the river Danube.[34]

The people planning the power stations along the river Danube urgently advised against leaving free-flowing stretches between the barrages. The bedload in the free-flowing sections of the Danube would accumulate at the upstream dams and then be lacking in the sections downstream of the dams. This would lead to further degradation of the riverbed and ultimately it would turn into a "canyon[,] and the wetlands would become steppe."[35] As eight barrages had already been built or were under construction north of Vienna by the year 1980, the intention behind this reasoning was to continue construction "to save the Danube."[36]

In line with this argument, energy industry representatives tried to obtain the approval of Nobel laureate Konrad Lorenz for the construction of a power station at Greifenstein. Lorenz ultimately believed their explanations that after the intervention the wetlands would be more beautiful, and that, due to the tendency of bed erosion, the ecological diversity of the landscape would be richer than it would be if no dams were built. When, after the completion of the structure, the riverscape, contrary to the predictions, had lost its original wetland character, Lorenz became one of the most ardent opponents of any further use of the river Danube for energy production.[37]

At the same time, the renowned zoologist Otto König was not a priori dismissive about the power stations planned along the river Danube. He demanded, of course, that the construction measures would have to account for the sufficient preservation of nature. König coined the term "second-hand habitat"[38] and said that it did not matter to organisms "how a habitat developed as long as it provides the conditions the organism needs to live."[39] To ensure that as little natural habitat as necessary would

34 "projektierten Donaukraftwerke Greifenstein, Regelsbrunn und Hainburg in Naßbau- und nicht in Trockenbauweise zu errichten, … um eine weitere Dezimierung der Augebiete entlang der Donau zu verhindern:" NÖ. Naturschutzbund, "Resolution," *Natur und Land* 66, no. 1/2 (1980): 59.
35 "zum Canyon und die Au zur Steppe werden:" Bernhard Lötsch, interview with author, July 24, 2012.
36 "die Donau zu retten:" Bernhard Lötsch, interview with author, July 24, 2012.
37 Bernhard Lötsch, interview with author, July 24, 2012.
38 "Lebensraum aus zweiter Hand:" "Otto Koenig (Verhaltensforscher)," Wikipedia, accessed Jan. 31, 2018, https://de.wikipedia.org/wiki/Otto_Koenig_(Verhaltensforscher).
39 "wie ein Lebensraum entstanden ist, solange er nur die Bedingungen erfülle, die der Organismus zum Leben brauche:" "Otto Koenig (Verhaltensforscher)," Wikipedia, accessed Jan. 31, 2018, https://de.wikipedia.org/wiki/Otto_Koenig_(Verhaltensforscher).

be destroyed, he argued, each construction project should be monitored by ecologists.

The start of construction works for the Hainburg project in 1984 was for many power plant opponents an example of the "notion that economy could do without attention to ecological aspects."[40] Nature would be "treated as an object of unscrupulous exploitation."[41] The power plant opponents (students, artists, intellectuals) understood the imminent destruction caused by the construction efforts as a "war against Nature, provoked by a State" that believes in the victory of technology over nature.[42]

Even after the end was certain for the Hainburg power project, ecologist Bernd Lötsch and artist Friedensreich Hundertwasser were not convinced that the threat of future power plant projects along the Danube would be contained. They wrote a manifesto calling on people to "free the enslaved nature of the Danube to give it back its beauty and dignity."[43] Together with the World Wide Fund for Nature (WWF) and with the support of the *Neue Kronen Zeitung* newspaper, they initiated the "Buy Nature's Freedom!" (*Natur frei kaufen!*) campaign in 1989. More than 120,000 donors followed their appeal and made possible the land purchase of what is now Donau-Auen National Park.

The Donau-Auen National Park was opened in 1996. The managers of the park and environmental protection organizations soon agreed that the erosion of the Danube due to the barrage in its headwaters was a real problem and that the wetlands—which were meant to be protected by establishing the national park—threatened to vanish. The counter measures to be taken are still dividing the factions. The national park managers are of the opinion that the "General Hydro-engineering Project" (*Flussbauliche Gesamtprojekt*, FGP) should make a win-win situation possible: the original state of the river should be restored to benefit both nature conservation and the role of the Danube as a waterway. The majority of the environmental protection organizations, however, are of the opinion that the FGP is a concession to the demands of shipping transport and reject it outright.

---

40 "Vorstellung, dass Ökonomie auf ökologische Rücksichtnahme verzichten könnte:" Friedensreich Hundertwasser, "Rede anläßlich der Rückgabe des Großen Österreichischen Staatspreises," in *Die Schlacht der Bäume – Hainburg 1984*, ed. Günther Nenning and Andreas Huber (Vienna: hannibal, 1984): 115–116.
41 "als Gegenstand bedenkenloser Ausbeutung behandelt:" Hundertwasser, "Rückgabe Staatspreis."
42 "Krieg gegen die Natur, angestiftet vom Staat, der noch immer an den Endsieg der Technik über die Natur glaubt:" Hundertwasser, "Rückgabe Staatspreis."
43 "die versklavte Natur der Donau freizukaufen, um ihr Schönheit und Würde zurück zu geben:" Bernhard Lötsch, interview with author, July 24, 2012.

Donau-Auen National Park: Identified Conceptions

In its first deliberations about the national park, *Naturschutzbund* admitted that it could be possible to design power plant structures in such a way that negative effects were minimized. Otto König assumed that, in the ideal case, an equal habitat could be created; both views are in line with the concept of co-operative development. König's proposal of supplementary ecological planning is state of the art today. Most nature conservationists of his time did not agree with him and accused him of leaning too far to the energy sector, a viewpoint that in turn took over the reasoning of the conservationists, who imagined saving the Danube by building dams (opportunistic appropriation). The power plant opponents—mainly young people of conservative backgrounds, students, scientists, and artists—saw the Danube wetlands at Hainburg as the expression of city dwellers' idea of wild rivers, manifesting the notion of fundamental antagonism. The people occupying the floodplains ignored the fact that the Danube had always been intensively used and that the Hainburg floodplains constitute appropriated nature and not the "last wilderness."[44] The commitment of the national park managers to the FGP added the concept of integrative development. Sound planning and targeted structuring of the river were intended to satisfy varying demands without putting the river system under an excessive burden. This would help establish the exact "technocratic natural management" that caused the opposition of the environmentalist occupiers. The current debate about the use of hydropower sees a similar phenomenon: power plant proponents defend their position by invoking the notion of environmentally friendly (being from renewable energy carriers), clean (compared to fossil raw materials), and safe (compared to nuclear power plants) production of energy. Most nature protection organizations, however, argue against it, following the principle of fundamental antagonism. This is true for both Hohe Tauern and the Danube floodplains.

Interdependence Two: Nature Conservation – Economy

The second line of the discourse investigates where nature conservation and economic interests meet and where they obstruct each other with regard to the use of hydropower. As the research material included only one example for Donau-Auen National Park, both national parks are covered in the same chapter.

---

44 Schmid and Veichtlbauer, *Vom Naturschutz zur Ökologiebewegung*, 41.

Hohe Tauern and Donau-Auen National Park: the Discourse

In 1904, a committee from the Carinthian Natural History Museum suggested sites that would be worthy of protection as natural monuments. Among those suggested were Möllfall and Jungfernsprung near Heiligenblut (both in the Hohe Tauern National Park area), because these waterfalls would contribute to "making the landscape rich,"[45] but if "their use for power generation purposes" was to be discussed[46] they could "generate more wealth" through this use[47] than by their conservation.

In 1950, official nature conservation organizations read in disbelief about the plans to use the Krimml Waterfalls for power generation: it was incomprehensible why sites of international reputation should be destroyed, and the effects this would have on tourism were incalculable.[48]

One year later, the Governor of Salzburg, Josef Klaus, in his opening speech on the occasion of the "First Austrian Nature Conservation Day" (*Erster* Österreichischer Naturschutztag*) commented on these plans: the destruction of the landscape would precipitate a decline in tourism, an important source of income in the province.[49] ÖNB in its journal "Nature and Land" (*Natur und Land)* reported that the construction of power plants at the Krimml Waterfalls would have significant consequences for tourism. The tourism industry would never approve of these plans.[50]

On the same issue "Union of Austrian Alpine Associations" (*Verband alpiner Vereine Österreichs,* VAVÖ), ÖNB, "Zoological-Botanical Association" (*Zoologisch-Botanische Gesellschaft)*, and the Austrian Academy of Sciences (Österreichische Akademie der Wissenschaften, ÖAW) warned against the perception of landscape purely in terms of utility, while ignoring the

---

45   "zur Belebung:" "Erhaltung der Naturdenkmale in Kärnten." *Carinthia II* 94, (1904): 55–56.
46   "die Verwendung derselben zu Kraftzwecken:" "Erhaltung der Naturdenkmale in Kärnten."
47   "mehr Wohlstand verbreiten:" "Erhaltung der Naturdenkmale in Kärnten."
48   "Niemand [würde] ... die Vernichtung zweier Sehenswürdigkeiten von internationaler Berühmtheit und ihre Rückwirkung auf den österreichischen Fremdenverkehr begreifen:" Gustav Wendelberger, "Rettet das Gesäuse! Rettet die Krimmler Fälle!," *Natur und Land. Blätter für Naturkunde und Naturschutz* 36, no. 9/10 (1950), 145–154.
49   "Eine Zerstörung unseres Landschaftsbildes würde auch eine Zerstörung unseres Fremdenverkehrs, einer wesentlichen Reichtumsquelle des Landes, bedeuten:" Klaus, "Eröffnungsrede Landeshauptmann von Salzburg."
50   "Errichtung von Kraftwerken an den Krimmler Wasserfällen ... von den Fremdenverkehr so schwer wiegenden Wirkungen begleitet wäre:" Gustav Wendelberger and Lothar Machura, "Resolution des Bundesarbeitsausschusses für Fremdenverkehr," *Natur und Land* 37, no. 4 (1951): 71.

moral and aesthetic effects and "sacrificing sublime beauty to economic utilitarianism."[51]

The "Friends of Nature" (*Naturfreunde*) nature association faced a difficult situation in the 1970s and 1980s. Because of its political affinity with the Austrian Socialist Party (SPÖ), it was also close to the energy sector. The energy industry expected *Naturfreunde* to also see the positive aspects of power plant projects, or at least to not oppose them publicly. While *Naturfreunde* demanded that any power plant plans should take the plans of a national park into account,[52] it also expected that the establishment of the national park "would be not incompatible" with the power plant in East Tyrol.[53]

In the Hainburg conflict, the *Naturfreunde* association was expected to represent nature conservation interests and to act in the name of the labor movement, which—with a view toward job creation—took the side of the power plant proponents. In its statements, *Naturfreunde* pointed out that the "unspoiled natural landscape was worthy of protection."[54] The organization criticized the lack of a reasonable dialogue on the complexity of linking nature conservation, environmental protection, clean energy production, and energy conservation in the Hainburg case.[55] In this context, it saw its calling in "promoting the concerns of nature conservation without conflicting with the interests of the working people."[56]

Hohe Tauern and Donau-Auen National Park: Identified Conceptions

As far as the development of the Hohe Tauern region is concerned, the use of hydropower seemed to be the better option than nature conservation

---

51 "die uns von der Natur verliehenen Gaben unseres Landes nur vom Nützlichkeitsstandpunkt aus zu betrachten und ihre ethischen und ästhetischen Wirkungen zu unterschätzen ... [und] ... die erhabene Schönheit unseres Landschaftsbildes ... Nutzzwecken zu opfern:" Wendelberger, "Rettet das Gesäuse."
52 "die Planungsarbeiten für das Kraftwerk Osttirol auf das Nationalparkvorhaben 'Hohe Tauern' Bedacht zu nehmen" hätten: Naturfreunde Österreich, "Resolution der Naturfreunde-Österreich zum Kraftwerksprojekt Osttirol," *Der Naturfreund* 72, no. 4 (1979): 24.
53 "nicht unvereinbar wäre:" Naturfreunde Österreich, "Resolution zur Schaffung des Nationalparks Hohe Tauern," *Der Naturfreund* 74, no. 4 (1981): 4.
54 "auf die Schutzwürdigkeit unberührter Naturlandschaft:" Manfred Pils, "Nach Hainburg," *Der Naturfreund* 78, no. 1 (1985): 8–9.
55 "Hainburg-Problem ... nicht ein vernünftiger Dialog über die Komplexhaftigkeit der Verknüpfung von Naturschutz, Umweltschutz, Landschaftsschutz, sauberer Energiegewinnung, Energiesparen geführt würde:" Pils, "Nach Hainburg."
56 "Naturschutzanliegen voranzutreiben ohne mit wohlverstandenen Interessen der arbeitenden Bevölkerung in Widerspruch zu kommen:" Pils, "Nach Hainburg."

in 1904. By declaring it a natural monument, especially attractive scenery was to be preserved for tourism. This is the first in a series of examples of the opportunistic cooperation concept that was particularly characterizing for the Hohe Tauern region. Nature conservation and tourism were the opposing sides in numerous conflicts (construction of cableways, development of skiing resorts). There was agreement, however, on one point: both interest groups were against power plant projects in the area of the designated national park and did not shy away from using the reasoning of the respective other side.

VAVÖ's reluctance to "sacrifice the sublime beauty of landscape to economic utilitarianism" is fully in line with selective antagonism, because the touristic use of the region by its members was in their view neither economic utilization nor impairment.

Naturfreunde which had to represent greatly differing, if not opposing, interests (nature conservation, energy industry, and labor) tried to find an acceptable way out of its dilemma by referring to co-operative development reasoning.

Other Interdependencies

Other lines of discourse playing a role in these two parks and in relation to the use of hydropower are the relationship between nature conservation and safety, the rule of law, and democracy—with this list being by no means exhaustive. These lines of discourse are, among other things, closely linked to the change of the political landscape and the development of the green movement in Austria.

Conclusion

This contribution aired the question of whether the interactions between nature conservation and hydropower display the same concepts identified in earlier contributions on the interaction between nature conservation and other interest groups. The analysis is based on the example of two Austrian national parks, the history of which is closely linked to the use of hydropower in Austria. Two lines of discourse are explored to shed light on the relationship between nature conservation and technology and between nature conservation and economy. The research material offers evidence for six of different concepts: fundamental antagonism, selective antagonism, opportunistic cooperation, opportunistic appropriation, co-operative development, integrative development. The order of these concepts corresponds to the order of their first appearance. While fundamental antagonism can certainly be rated as the oldest established notion and integrative development as the youngest, their use in the lines of discourse is not subject to chronology. The emergence of a new conception can be connected to particular societal developments and can thus be placed into a historical context. However, different conceptions co-exist simultaneously, and their use is not subject to an expiration date.

Practical nature conservation work is bound to valuations that are usually based on the concepts mentioned above. The generally unreflected coexistence of these concepts may lead to contradictions and ambiguities. Such contradictions also occur in Austria in other social spheres, for example when it comes to the working world or the health care system. In those fields however, the issues are discussed in a much more radical way as they directly affect people. Thus, the pressure of having confrontations and conflicts is much higher than in nature conversation which seemingly does not concern the everyday life.

The more recent concepts presented in this article (co-operative development and integrative development) are more in line with the requirements of a complex democratic society than the older ones. At the same time, they are challenged and put to a test by the older antagonistic concepts.

In Austria, many conservation questions that already have been raised in the past are being discussed and assessed again. An example is the question of either expanding energy production from renewable sources such as hydropower or conserving alpine river landscapes. The arguments reach as far as the current government program that features key words such as "elimination of gold-plating of EU-directives"[57], "refocusing location policy"[58] or "administrative simplification"[59]. The issue became a hot topic and makes continuing discussions appear sensible. The knowledge about its history can help to better understand and solve conflict situations.

---

57 "Gold-Plating gegenüber EU-Vorgaben beseitigen," Regierungsprogramm 2017–2022 der Neuen Volkspartei Freiheitlichen Partei Österreich, "Zusammen. Für unser Österreich," (Vienna: Bundeskanzleramt, 2018): 156.
58 "Neuausrichtung der Standortpolitik," Ibid. 175.
59 "Verwaltungsvereinfachung:" Ibid. 172.

Non-Topical Essay

Swarovski and the National Socialist Era: A Research Report[1]

Dieter Stiefel

The writing of history can be as fascinating as the history in question. In February 2011, Markus Langes-Swarovski commissioned a scholarly biography of his family and of the first hundred years of the Swarovski company's existence. Since then, the German-language Wikipedia entry on the company has stated: "The history of the company during the Nazi era, the proximity of the Swarovski family to National Socialism, their war profiteering, and especially their exploitation of forced labor are being examined by the economic historian Dieter Stiefel in a project that began in 2011." This project has been supported by Swarovski in every facet, including unlimited access to the company archive and with no influence of any kind having been exerted on the content of the work. Per prior agreement, the manuscript was submitted in May 2014. Markus was so enthusiastic that he immediately encouraged its publication in order to have 200 copies available for family and friends in time for Christmas. A 400-page copyedited, illustrated, and graphically designed manuscript was prepared entitled: *Daniel Swarovski 1862–1956*, and a contract was signed with the Böhlau publishing house. However, Swarovski is a family business with its own peculiarities. Essentially, the company is run by the families of the three sons of the founder: Wilhelm, Friedrich, and Alfred. Each of these families is represented in the business administration, and there is no company executive as such. In the context of this executive structure, the project got stuck. Objections were not formulated officially, but the most pertinent argument was presumably: "For what do we need this!" Swarovski should address the public with its products, and not through individual personalities. Other factors may also have been at play: for example, the fact that the three families did not all share an equal role or the fact that the history emerging from the archive sometimes differed from what was remembered.

Swarovski was one of the few large Austrian companies that had never spoken out about its history under National Socialism. To counter this, the relevant part of the manuscript was extracted and planned as a separate 159-page book with Böhlau publishing house entitled *Anpassung und Widerstand – Swarovski im Nationalsozialismus* ("Conforming and resisting:

---

1   Tim Corbett translated this essay from German into English.

Swarovski under National Socialism"). This gave the project a new impetus. In November 2016, the publication was presented in a podium discussion at the University of Vienna, the book was listed in the publisher's catalog, and 500 copies were printed. Its presentation to the media was planned for early July 2017 but was then surprisingly cancelled only a week in advance. Two members of the company board had objected; their reasons were not made public, so one can only speculate. Since then, 500 copies of a book on Swarovski under National Socialism lie locked away in the company basement in Wattens, Tyrol.

As this was an untenable situation, Markus Langes-Swarovski encouraged the publication of a scholarly contribution in a historical forum: "This contribution, intended as an objective scholarly presentation, is the independent and exclusive work of the author and requires no additional permission from Swarovski." This synopsis contains neither exaggerations nor omissions, yet some aspects naturally come up short. All the findings have been proven with archival sources, which can be viewed in the complete manuscript on the history of Swarovski, should it ever be made public.

The Actors

The roots of the company lie in the vicinity of Gablonz in Bohemia (today Jablonec in the Czech Republic), where glass production has a long history. Gablonz was home to the Swarovski and Weis families, who were not only related to each other professionally but by marriage as well: Daniel Swarovski and Franz Weis each married the other's sister. The brain behind further developments was Daniel, without a doubt one of the great entrepreneurs of the twentieth century. In 1891, he became one of the first to develop a machine for the cutting of glass jewelry and thus introduced this craft to industry and mass production. Armand Kosmann, a Jewish trader in Paris, realized the significance of this development and so began financing the undertaking. In 1895, Swarovski and Weis relocated to Wattens in Tyrol due to, among other things, the availability there of electrical sources of energy. In 1904, the glass-cutting company "Glasschleiferei Wattens, A. Kosmann, D. Swarovski & Co" was founded with its headquarters in Wattens. Daniel Swarovski and Armand Kosmann were personally liable unlimited partners, while Franz Weis was merely a limited partner.

The business administration was increasingly managed by Swarovski, with Daniel involving his sons in running the business: Wilhelm in the field of chemistry, Friedrich in technology, and Alfred in commerce. This was not actually Alfred's aspiration for life, but, as he was responsible for the commercial sphere, he also commanded the external networks. He therefore increasingly became the de facto head of the company from the 1920s onward, while his brothers took care of development and production. Armand Kosmann died in 1936 and, since he was unmarried and had no children, his portion went to Jean Crailsheimer, the son of his sister. After Jean's death in 1956, the inheritance passed over to various individuals and foundations, so that this portion of the company was liquidated and paid out following due process.

National Socialism

To date, every assessment of Swarovski under National Socialism has been impeded by the company's public relations activities. This is also true for engagements of the family members on behalf of National Socialism.[2] As a result, journalistic as well as scholarly representations have resorted to general accusations dating from the first years after the end of the war: "The Swarovski family one and all acted 'illegally' [meaning they were active Nazis during the period when the party was banned in Austria from 1 July 1933 to 13 March 1938] and rendered outstanding services to the Nazi Party in Tyrol." This claim references a report from *Reichskommissar* Josef Bürckel to the *Gauleiter* of Tyrol Franz Hofer, dated 19 December 1938, which states "that the Swarovski company in Wattens, Tyrol, had already in the years of struggle [meaning before the Anschluss in March 1938] been managed in an impeccable National Socialist manner, and that Swarovski's family had already been Nazi Party members before the party ban."[3]

The party membership of members of the Swarovski family can be checked anytime in the collections of the Tyrol State Archive.[4] These include the statistical survey of the party from 1939 and the registration papers following the *Verbotsgesetz* (Prohibition Act) of 1947.[5] Additionally, the registry of Nazi Party members can be viewed in the Federal Archive

---

2   Oliver Kühschelm, "Swarovski: Österreichischer 'Multi' und Tiroler 'Weltmarke'," in *Memoria Austriae 3: Unternehmer - Firmen - Produkte: Bd III*, ed. Emil Brix, Ernst Bruckmüller, Hannes Steckl (Vienna: Oldenbourg Wissenschaftsverlag, 2005), 137.
3   Horst Schreiber, *Wirtschafts- und Sozialgeschichte der Nazizeit in Tirol* (Innsbruck: Studien Verlag, 1994), 134.
4   Franz Weis bought a house in Liechtenstein in the 1920s and subsequently became a citizen of the principality, making membership in the Nazi Party unnecessary.
5   Registrierungsblatt zur Verzeichnung der Nationalsozialisten gemäß § 4 des Verbotsgesetzes 1947, BH Innsbruck, Meldestelle Wattens Nr. 385–383 and Parteistatistische Erhebungen 1939 des Reichsorganisationsleiter der NSDAP, Hauptorganisationsamt München, July 1, 1939, Tiroler Landesarchiv, NSDAP Mitglieder, Letter S, Box 28 and Swarovski Wattens, ATLR, Abt. Ic-NS, Box 24.

in Berlin;[6] however, the records do not always agree and are not always complete.

Both of Friedrich Swarovski's sons had already joined the party in 1932 and thus held correspondingly low membership numbers. There is no indication of illegal activity in the period when the Nazi party was banned in Austria. Such activities would have endangered the existence of the company and could have had grave consequences later on. The registry of the Nazi Party lists applications dated 16 May and membership granted retroactively from 1 May 1938. There may have been a family decision to join the party, a supposition supported by the fact that they received a block of membership numbers. The *Gauleiter* of Tyrol wanted to document that the industrialist family had already been on the side of the Nazi Party in the "time of struggle." The numbers they were assigned were low membership numbers reserved for the "illegals" in Austria. This led to the Swarovski family members generally being viewed as "illegal" party members after 1945. Wilhelm Swarovski was joined in party membership by his wife, while Friedrich was joined by his wife and their three sons. The wives of Daniel Sr. and Alfred did not join the party. At the time, only male members of the family could be active in the management of the company. The political entanglements thus relate exclusively to the male family members.

	Entry	Membership Number
Daniel Sr.	1938	6,181,200
Wilhelm	1933	1,621,960
Anna	1933	6,181,198
Friedrich	1933	6,181,201
Berta	1933	6,181,199
Manfred	1933	6,181,202
Fritz Jr.	1932	783,901
Daniel Jr.	1932	783,902
Alfred	1938	6,181,197

The Swarovski were not prominent in the party. Aside from Friedrich's son Fritz, who was a member of the SA from 1931 to 1932, none of them joined the "combat organizations" (SA, SS, etc.). They did not hold leading

---

6   Bundesarchiv Berlin, Bestand 31XX, Parteikartei NSDAP.

positions in the party organization and did not receive any decorations. Neither the activities of the company nor of their special interests in Tyrol amounted to party activity either in 1938/1939 or after 1945. The only accusation that could be leveled against them was that they had decisively joined the party and thus set an example reaching far beyond their workforce.

Daniel Swarovski Senior

Nazi Party membership number 6,181,200: born 24 October 1862, married, Old Catholic, independent entrepreneur. According to the 1939 party statistical survey, he had joined on 5 May 1938. According to the 1947 registry, he had been a candidate for membership from the summer or fall of 1938 to 1941 and then a party member until 1945. As of 1938, Daniel Swarovski had no longer been involved in the company management and, aged over seventy during the denazification process, he was excused from all punitive measures except for atonement charges. This charge consisted of forty percent of an individual's wealth and ten percent of their income. The company paid this for all affected partners, totaling 1.8 million Schilling.

Daniel Sr., like all the affected Swarovskis, requested that he be struck from the Nazi registry in early 1946. His request was accompanied by a rationale describing his professional history, then by the economic hardships of 1938, the necessity of political alignment with the Nazi Party, and finally by the significance of the company for Austria in the post-war period.[7] He justified himself by pointing to the fact he had never been a member of a political party before 1938. "The *Kreisleiter* repeatedly complained to the *Ortsgruppenleiter* about me joining the Nazi Party in 1938 following the occupation of Austria. Finally, I also saw no reason not to join the Nazi Party since some ninety-eight percent of the Austrian people had voted for the Anschluss. I was never involved in politics and, being seventy-six years old at the time, I wished all the less to expose myself or to put myself, given the position I was in, at the center of a public discussion through rejecting membership, thus also complicating the situation of the company. Joining the party under those circumstances was an act of pure reason. I never abused my position as a party member in any way. My achievements on behalf of Austria could never have been

---

7   Firma D. Swarovski, Meldeblatt zur Registrierung der Nationalsozialisten im Sinne des Verfassungsgesetzes vom 8. Mai 1945, Wattens April 17, 1946 (unless stated otherwise, all documents cited are from the Swarovski Archives in Wattens, Tyrol, from now on designated as SAW).

of a political nature, but always merely technical and inventive and thus purely economic."[8]

Wilhelm (Willi) Swarovski

Nazi Party membership number 1,621,960: born 28 March 1888, married, Protestant, independent entrepreneur. In the 1939 party statistical survey, which was signed by every member, he declared an entry date of 5 May 1933. The 1947 registry claimed he was a candidate for membership from 5 May 1938 and a member from the fall of 1938 to May 1945. Against his earlier declaration of having registered as a "candidate" on 14 July 1933, he successfully appealed that there had been no party membership in Austria from 1 July 1933 to 13 March 1938. However, his party membership before the Anschluss is incontrovertible: "Wilhelm Swarovski claimed in the party statistical survey, which he himself completed on 5 July 1939, that he joined the party on 15 July 1933 [note that the dates here do not exactly match those cited in the archive]. He was moreover recognized as an '*Alter Kämpfer*' ['old fighter'], which clearly refutes his claim not to have had anything to do with the Nazi Party during the period it was banned."[9]

Wilhelm also submitted a request on 2 December 1947 to be exempted from the prohibition on practicing business according to §27 (1) of the 1947 Prohibition Act. His request was granted by the Austrian president on 10 April 1948. The reasoning was that he may have been a party member since 1933 and thus an "*Alter Kämpfer*," but no abuse of his party membership could be ascertained, and he had since then completely broken with the Nazi Party.[10]

Wilhelm Swarovski was generally described as a quiet, artistic family man whose interests included field observation and optics. So how to explain his early commitment to National Socialism? "I was never a politician," he observed in a résumé, but still he had to explain why he then joined the *Heimwehr* (the armed paramilitary organization of Austria directed primarily against the left-wing workers' movement), the Fatherland Front (the unitary party of the Austrian Corporate State), and the Nazi Party.[11] "When we therefore joined the *Heimwehr* movement in 1927, we entertained

---

8   SAW, Grundsätzlich zur Registrierung bzw. Entregistrierung des Daniel Swarovski, Wattens Apr. 12. 1946 (unless stated otherwise, all documents cited are from the Swarovski Archives in Wattens, Tyrol, from now on designated as SAW).
9   Bezirkshauptmannschaft Innsbruck, Registrierungsbehörde, Innsbruck, Dec. 1, 1948.
10   Österreichisches Staatsarchiv Vienna, Archiv der Republik (hereafter AdR), Präsidentschaftskanzlei, 1948, 5474.
11   SAW, Wilhelm Swarovski, Lebenslauf, Wattens, Feb. 7, 1946.

no thoughts of Fascism or a dictatorial regime, but rather hoped for a final pacification of tempers, and it was not only us who hoped for this but millions of people along with us—otherwise this movement would never have achieved this proliferation....I was initially distrustful of the Hitler movement and only when Hindenburg decided to put the idea to the test did I begin to observe the movement more closely, but always only on the side—after all, I was very busy with my work." This all refers to the years 1936 and 1937. Then things calmed down, especially since he and his brother Alfred had pointedly joined the Fatherland Front. Following the Anschluss in 1938, Wilhelm "along with many others registered once more with the party." He describes the process: "A few weeks later, I received a green card (around Christmas time). In the maelstrom of the time, I remained totally neutral and was not subject to any further demands to adopt any kind of function. We in the company management had the impression that the workers regarded this as their revolution."[12]

Wilhelm had been an officer in World War I and therefore was ordered in 1944 to create a unit of 300 *Standschützen* (Tyrolean militia) and lead as *Kompanieführer*: "We conducted drills every Sunday for at least four hours as had been ordered. I only had them fall in, conducted a roll call, assigned them if needed, and then dismissed them. I managed to do this for three Sundays thanks to the disjointed orders from the *Standschützen*." Later, a stronger wind blew and he began to be supervised by the *Ortsgruppenleiter*. "Put briefly, things became increasingly uncomfortable: I was inspected even closer when we finally only had thirty men in the first squad. When the *Ortsgruppenleiter* began to hold a party-political speech at every exercise...I withdrew and declared myself ill and was discharged by Dr. Gamper (the community physician)."[13]

Friedrich (Fritz) Swarovski

Nazi party membership number 6,181,201: born 21 March 1890, married, deist, independent profession. According to the 1939 party statistical survey—signed not by him but by his wife Berta—he joined the party on 1 June 1933. Friedrich also requested a correction of the date of entry in the registry and on 2 December 1947 submitted a request according to §27 (1) of the 1947 Prohibition Act, which was granted by the Austrian president in 1948.

Friedrich Swarovski was the most involved in politics, having been a

---

12 SAW, Wilhelm Swarovski, Lebenslauf, Wattens, Feb. 7, 1946.
13 SAW, Wilhelm Swarovski, Lebenslauf, Wattens, Feb. 7, 1946.

local leader of the *Heimwehr* from 1927 to 1933.[14] When confronted about his membership in the *Heimwehr*, he retorted that it had been legal at the time: "The company did nothing that could be described in any way as illegal. Therefore, the company decisively rejects any construction of political incrimination against the company in the present based on this matter. At the time, we lived in a free, democratic republic, and every citizen had the right to freely express their convictions. The company did what was necessary for its development. Our understanding was that the *Heimwehr* movement, which was very popular at the time, was nothing more than an entirely natural reaction to a misguided construal of the democratic republic and the related confusions and complications in the state. Everything suffered under the conditions of the time, including companies and the workforces in the companies."[15]

Friedrich Swarovski described his membership in the Nazi Party as a business necessity: "The entry of the company owners into the party was necessary for economic reasons and today completely benefits the company and the Austrian national economy. The heads of the Swarovski company therefore did not act politically incorrectly, but correctly. It was not only important for the Swarovski company that a Mr. Swarovski was a 'special' National Socialist, but also for the Austrian and American national economies. Many difficulties and damages to the company could thereby be avoided."

Friedrich Swarovski was officially named *Betriebsführer* (factory leader, a title reflecting Nazi political hierarchies) of the company D. Swarovski in Wattens in the spring of 1938.[16] In this capacity, he also conducted the legally prescribed "*Appell*," a biannual roll call of the workforce including a political speech, held on 1 May and at the end of the year. "He was always fully aware of the importance of this position in the interest of preserving and developing the company. The company was more important to him than anything else. This is evinced among other things by the numerous pointed appearances he made before the party people, not only at the beginning of the Anschluss, but also during the war. Throughout the entire war, he took on a protective function over the company. The content of his biannual *Appell* primarily related in general terms to the first points of the Work Order Act, [*Gesetz zur Ordnung der nationalen Arbeit*], to working together in the factory, to comradery, and productivity with regard to quantity and

14   SAW, Alfred Swarovski an Dr. Anton Bauer, Innsbruck, Wattens, Apr. 14, 1946.
15   SAW, Firma D. Swarovski, Zum Problem der politischen Bereinigung und Entnazifizierung der Firma D. Swarovski in Wattens, Wattens, Feb. 12, 1946.
16   SAW, Firma D. Swarovski, Stellungnahme zur politischen Bereinigung, Wattens 1945/6.

quality. When the factory foreman requested that he be allowed to take over the political education aspects of the talk in his stead, Mr. Fritz Swarovski began over the years to take a stance towards the most salient points of the party program. These were in every respect lawful issues."[17]

On 6 May 1944, the Swarovski company was named a "model war factory" in the framework of the "performance struggle of German companies." The head of the employment agency in Innsbruck sent his congratulations: "You should be filled with proud satisfaction at this lofty recognition of your exemplary National Socialist work ethic now, in the fifth year of the existential struggle of our people."[18] The reply from the company management and the workforce revealed that they were very pleased with these congratulations: "Naturally, we will do everything in our power as before to cultivate the most exemplary National Socialist work ethic in our factory so that we may be in a position to meet the special challenge conferred upon us through this award."[19]

Friedrich Swarovski also opened his petition to be deregistered with an account of his professional résumé and his position in the company: "I dedicated my life to the technical development of this company." As head of the technical sphere, he had worked closely with the foremen and workers; thus, his workplace was not in the office but in the factory. Thereby, a close personal connection with the workers had emerged. "This special relationship of trust with the workforce led to me being appointed the official factory leader following the occupation in 1938. My entry into the Nazi Party was a necessary result of this appointment as factory leader." Otherwise, he argued, he would have been the object of political criticism that would have had a damaging effect on working relations.[20] The rapid conversion to arms production may have moved the high command of the Wehrmacht "to name the recently appointed technical leader of the company to an *honorary* leader of the military economy. This nomination is not to be understood as the adoption of an office in the German armaments industry, but merely as an award recognizing the *company as a whole*, of which Fritz Swarovski had been the factory leader since 1938 following the Work Order Act."[21]

17   SAW, Firma D. Swarovski, Zum Problem der politischen Bereinigung und Entnazifizierung der Firma D. Swarovski in Wattens, Wattens, Feb. 12, 1946.

18   SAW, Regierungsrat Helmer, Leiter des Arbeitsamtes Innsbruck an die Firma D. Swarovski, Wattens/Tirol, Innsbruck, May 9, 1944.

19   SAW, Firma D. Swarovski an den Leiter des Arbeitsamtes Innsbruck, Regierungsrat Helmer, Wattens, May 26, 1944.

20   SAW, Firma D. Swarovski, Grundsätzliches zur Registrierung bzw. Entregistrierung des Friedrich Swarovski, Wattens, April 13, 1946.

21   Emphases my own: SAW, Firma D. Swarovski, Grundsätzlich zur Registrierung bzw. Entregistrierung des Daniel Swarovski, Wattens Apr. 12, 1946.

It was clear, so the reasoning went, that he had to fully meet his obligations as factory leader in the interest of the preservation of the company. "In this position, I naturally had to deal with the social entrustment of the workforce and did whatever was possible under the circumstances for every individual, regardless of their political orientation. Ultimately, my decisions as factory leader were always guided by what was best for the company and thereby for the workforce, while political issues were recessive." He claimed in his position as a Nazi Party member to have "neither profited nor harmed anyone else. On the contrary, I always used this position to exercise absolute justice and to protect those of other political convictions in order to preserve the old potential of the factory. The entire workforce can attest to this, including the foreign laborers and the prisoners."[22]

Manfred Swarovski

Son of Friedrich Swarovski, born 15 July 1915, married, adherent of an alternative religious denomination, white-collar worker. The 1939 party statistical survey lists his membership number as 6,181,217 and the date of his entry into the party as 14 July 1933. The Nazi Party registry in Berlin lists his membership number as 6,181,202 and an entry date of 1 May 1938, which also corresponds to the information of the Tyrolean Security Directorate of 1949. There is no appertaining registration page for denazification present in the Tyrolean State Archive. Manfred claimed not to have cared for the party and that he had never paid his membership dues.

Fritz Swarovski

Nazi Party membership number 783,901: son of Friedrich Swarovski, born 16 July 1912, Old Catholic, white-collar worker. According to the 1939 party statistical survey—which was signed by his mother Berta—he joined the party on 13 January 1932. According to the 1947 registry, he was a member of the SA from 1932 to 1932, a party candidate from 28 February 1932 onward, and a member from August 1938 to 1945.

---

22 SAW, Fritz Swarovski, politisches Verhalten, April 1946.

Daniel Swarovski Junior

Son of Friedrich Swarovski, born 13 February 1914, white-collar worker. The 1939 party statistical survey lists neither his marital status nor his religious affiliation. He held membership number 783,902 and joined the party on 13 January 1932. He left the party on 31 March 1935 and was listed again from 1 May 1938 as "party candidate." He left the party again in 1944 and was thus excluded from the registry.[23] In 1937, he had volunteered for one year in the Austrian *Landschützenregiment* (a Tyrolean mountain infantry regiment) and was stationed in Solbad Hall. Following the Anschluss, he was integrated into the German Wehrmacht and served in the invasion of Poland. After that, he was declared "indispensable" to the company.

Daniel Junior claimed to be a politically minded person who tried to understand "the whole" above and beyond party politics. During his studies, he had been interested in National Socialism "in the hope that it could perhaps bring about a necessary novelty." He came to the conclusion, however, that Socialism could never be national, since it would then necessarily lead to hate and fanaticism;[24] so he wrote in 1946. He then had to explain his entry into the Nazi Party in 1938: The Nazi Party was the state party, so people in leading positions could experience serious animosity if they kept their distance from the party. "In my case, this would have been perceived as a downright demonstrative attitude, especially since all the male members of the family had already enlisted at this point";[25] he claimed only to have joined the party on the express wish of his parents and for the continued success of the company.

He was not a particularly good fit for the party. In April 1944, he wrote a four-page letter to the *Ortsgruppenleiter* explaining why he did not wear the party insignia, rarely visited obligatory functions, and too often greeted with a "good morning" or "*Grüß Gott*" instead of "Heil Hitler." He signed the letter "*Mit deutschem Gruß!*" (a Nazi greeting) and added: "I also want to request from my superiors to release me so that I may serve in the Wehrmacht. I want to serve my people in the coming weeks and months as a soldier."[26] "As uncomfortable as it makes me to potentially cause you

---

23 SAW, Bezirkshauptmannschaft Innsbruck, Registrierungsbehörde, Zl.Reg. 1423/2, Innsbruck, Aug. 20, 1947.
24 SAW, Daniel Swarovski junior an Herrn Landesrat Heinz (SPÖ), Innsbruck Landhaus, Wattens, Aug. 16, 1946.
25 SAW, Daniel Swarovski junior an Herrn Landesrat Heinz (SPÖ), Innsbruck Landhaus, Wattens, Aug. 14, 1946.
26 SAW, Daniel Swarovski junior, An den Herrn Ortsgruppenleiter, Betrifft bevorstehende Vereidigung, Wattens, Apr. 18, 1944.

further, seemingly unnecessary problems with this letter, it is precisely my National Socialist conviction—to which I am trying to remain faithful—that inspires me to act this way."[27]

Following a discussion with the *Ortsgruppenleiter*, Daniel Junior then announced in writing that he was leaving the party. He was subsequently ordered to appear before the *Kreisleiter* in Innsbruck, who could not believe that a young Swarovski would act in this manner when his entire family had fallen in line. To the question of what bothered him so much about National Socialism, Daniel Junior referred to the crimes committed by the SS in the occupied countries of Europe. The *Kreisleiter* admitted to these mistakes, which he said had happened without the knowledge of the Führer. He told Daniel Junior: "Actually, you deserve to be put in a concentration camp," but continued: "However, you are too young. I want to give you the opportunity to become a strident National Socialist by enlisting you in the Waffen-SS." Daniel Junior was first enlisted in the SS Panzergrenadier division, confirming his worst fears: "Luckily, during my six months of service I only came to the front in the last month and, through the assignment of my brigade as regular mountain troopers, I was never put into the position of having to act against my conscience."[28]

Alfred Swarovski

Nazi Party membership number 6,181,197: born 28 October 1891, married, Old Catholic. According to the 1939 party statistical survey, he joined the party on 15 May 1938. The 1947 registry lists him as a candidate from 1938 to 1941 and thereafter as a member until 1945. He belonged to neither any military organizations of the Nazi Party nor any of its attachments, he was not a supporting member, and did not hold any position of political leadership.[29] He objected to his inclusion in the registry, and on 27 October 1947 he submitted a request based on §27 (1) of the 1947 Prohibition Act, which was granted by the Austrian president on 31 January 1948.

Alfred Swarovski had been active in the Tyrolean Economic Chamber since 1919 and remained so until the Anschluss. Among other things, he was President of the Innsbruck Chamber of Commerce and of the Gau

---

27 SAW, Daniel Swarovski junior an den Ortsgruppenleiter Josef Gager, Wattens, am May 17, 1944.
28 SAW, Daniel Swarovski junior an Herrn Landesrat Heinz (SPÖ), Innsbruck Landhaus, Wattens, Aug. 14, 1946.
29 SAW, Daniel Swarovski, Eidesstattliche Erklärung vom September 1950.

Economic Chamber of Tyrol-Vorarlberg from 1943 to 1945. It is self-evident that the party did not place its enemies in such positions and that party membership was a prerequisite for these offices. Functions in economic interest groups, however, were not regarded as a party-political activity by either the Nazi Party or in the denazification process and were therefore not listed in the application forms of 1938, the 1939 party statistical survey, or in the denazification questionnaires of 1945/47.

Once Alfred held the commercial agendas, he became the actual head of the company and was consequently observed especially closely, politically speaking. He justified his party membership with the economic hardships following the Anschluss in 1938 and the war economy later, which made close cooperation with state agencies inevitable: "Under these circumstances, it necessarily became imperative for me to join the party in order to ensure the collaboration of the public and economic agencies. Every entrepreneur in Tyrol had to be a member of the Nazi Party if he did not wish his factory leadership, his work, and the peace at his factory and its production potential to be detrimentally affected by difficulties on behalf of the party, Gau, and Kreis leaderships. After all, there were various means through which one could cause all manner of trouble for entrepreneurs who kept their distance to the party. Joining the party was thus fundamentally in the interest of the company and its workforce, a necessity that no factory leader could evade."[30]

He claimed never to have abused his position as a member of the party, "and despite my exposed position as a businessman in wartime, I never harmed anyone nor gained any personal economic profit thereby." Alfred Swarovski pointed to the fact that he had lived through five political systems by this time: "Public, managing, fully liable partners could not afford, like private individuals, to adopt positions for or against the state leadership on the basis of their feelings. This company can only be preserved if it does not come into conflict with the prevailing state authority and if it always does its duty. Its origins reach back to the year 1890. It did its duty in the time of the Austro-Hungarian Monarchy, it did its duty in the Republic of Austria as well as in the time of the authoritarian regime, and it also had to do its duty in the most dangerous era, under the National Socialist state, at least insofar as this was in the interest of its entrusted employees and their families. It is thus equally self-evident that the company will do its duty in the new Austria and will commit itself to the state."[31]

---

30   SAW, Firma D. Swarovski, Stellungnahme des Unternehmens vom April 1946.
31   SAW, Firma D. Swarovski, Zur Begründung der Entregistrierung des offenen und geschäftsführenden Gesellschafters Alfred Swarovski, Wattens, Apr. 4, 1946.

Alfred Swarovski not only prevailed through the political attacks against him during denazification, but in fact emerged with an even better reputation. The numerous statements supporting his amnesty and removal from the registry emphasized his character and his economic and personal characteristics. His only opponent was the Socialist Party of Austria (SPÖ), whose branding of Swarovski as a Nazi company was aimed at potentially nationalizing the company.

Alfred Swarovski received support from a range of people, including the head of the State Police Department of the Federal Police Administration in Innsbruck, from the chairmanship of the Chamber of Trade and Industry in Tyrol, from the *Landeshauptmann* of Tyrol Dr. Alfons Weißgatter, from federal minister Erwin Altenburger, from state secretary Ferdinand Graf, from the federal party leadership of the Austrian People's Party (ÖVP), from the Austrian Economic Association, and from Ernst Löwenstein, who, due to his Jewish background had to emigrate to the United States in 1938. Finally, Alfred Swarovski submitted his appeal for clemency as an exception to the stipulations of the Prohibition Act.[32] He justified his appeal on the basis of

- the national economic significance of the company,
- his leading position,
- the fact that he only joined the Nazi Party in the interests of the company,
- the fact that he exerted no political influence on his employees,
- the fact that he had saved machinery for production in peacetime,
- the fact that he had prevented the "Aryanization" of Jean Crailsheimer's portion of the company,
- and his efforts on behalf of the resistance movement.

The Austrian president granted Alfred Swarovski's request on 31 January 1948. What remained unaffected by this clemency were both the one-off and recurring atonement charges that he was required to pay.[33]

On 27 September 1947, Alfred Swarovski submitted an appeal against his inclusion in the list of National Socialists as *"Minderbelasteter"* (less incriminated).[34] His justification was based among other things on the

---

32 SAW, Alfred Swarovski, Fabrikant in Wattens, an den Bundespräsidenten in Wien über die Bezirkshauptmannschaft in Innsbruck als Registrierungsbehörde I. Instanz, Wattens, Sept. 27, 1947.

33 SAW, Mitteilung des Bundesministeriums für Inneres, Generaldirektion für öffentliche Sicherheit, Zl.33755-/48, Feb. 18, 1948, signed Staatssekretär Graf.

34 SAW, Alfred Swarovski, Fabrikant in Wattens, an die Bezirkshauptmannschaft Innsbruck als Registrierungsbehörde I. Instanz über die Gemeinde Wattens, Sept. 27, 1947.

claim "that I engaged in the framework of the resistance movement with the full commitment of my person and my life." On the basis of an attestation by the Tyrolean resistance movement, Alfred Swarovski was struck from the register of the community of Wattens on 30 March 1948 following a decision by the Tyrolean state government.[35] He could have saved himself the trouble, for only a short while later an amnesty was decreed for all *Minderbelastete* and the *Wirtschaftssäuberungsgesetz* ("Law for the cleansing of the economy") was repealed.

His reference to the resistance movement calls for clarification. Alfred's political position corresponded to that of his father: "Politicization achieves nothings. We can only be helped through our own labor."[36] Everyone should privately have their political opinions, but these should be left at the factory gates. His company was his politics. Everyone who did their work properly and loyally belonged to the team, regardless of their orientation otherwise. In the interests of the company, Alfred adapted to the Nazi era, but this adaptation ended wherever it contradicted the interests of the company. Thus, he had been denounced multiple times for not scrapping the machines, instead having them hidden together with raw materials for future production in peacetime. His resolve in this respect was also testified to in an incident that took place at the end of the war.

On 1 May 1945, a farmer came to Alfred Swarovski and reported that the bridge over the river Inn in Wattens had been fixed with explosives and was under guard. He explained that he knew some spirited men who were ready to prevent by force the detonation of the bridge. First, however, he wanted to try and prevent the action by legal means through the Gauleiter. On the morning of 2 May, some employees announced that the bridges in Volders and Weer were also being prepared to be blown up. Alfred called the *Gauleiter* and demanded that this action be prevented. The *Gauleiter* promised to do everything in his power and, by that same evening, the explosives had been removed.

By the next day, however, there were demolition squads at the bridges again. This time, Alfred turned to the mayor and *Ortsgruppenführer* of Wattens, both of whom went to the gendarmerie, who agreed to intervene. The commander of the Wattens *Standschützen* also offered up a squad to prevent the detonations. The *Ortsgruppenleiter* sent the gendarmes to the bridges with an official letter, where they learned that the demolition squad was being housed in the Fiecht Abbey. Alfred drove there and found the division commander in an empty wing. Alfred demanded in the name of

---

35   SAW, Bescheid des Landeshauptmanns betreff Alfred Swarovski, Zahl Ic-NS-5578/1, Innsbruck, March 30, 1948.
36   SAW, Daniel Swarovski sen., Wattens, Oct. 7, 1949.

the Tyrolean population that the squad be withdrawn, which the commander rejected, as he had been ordered to make a stand. Alfred described the dissolution of troops that could be observed all over the place, with soldiers walking around in civilian clothes, having thrown their guns into the Inn. If the explosives were not removed, he warned, the civilian population would surely take the matter into their own hands. The soldiers were not impressed, and fully intended to blow up the bridges the moment the first enemy tank rolled over them. Alfred's only option, they said, was to turn to the commander-in-chief and Hitler's successor, Admiral Karl Dönitz. Finally, the squad let themselves be talked into bringing the matter up with the commanding general when they met for a briefing at three o'clock in the afternoon. Alfred then drove back to the bridges, but the attending officers were ready to detonate and would not be dissuaded. At four o'clock, Alfred was able to reach the *Gauleiter* once more, who told him: "Since my radio speech on Sunday, when I declared Innsbruck an open city and promised the preservation of the bridges, my position has become weaker by the hour." He promised to intervene nevertheless, though it is unknown whether he did. In any case, the bridges were preserved, and at 9:20 that same evening the first American tanks rolled into the lower Inn valley.[37]

This account was confirmed by the "head of the liberation movement of Wattens," who had been present in Fiecht Abbey: "We were aware of the potential consequences of this meeting. We had to expect—like so many who resisted the destructions undertaken by the Wehrmacht and Waffen-SS even before the end of the war—to be put against the wall." The men were allowed to leave unobstructed, but they had the feeling that the squads at the bridges were being reinforced in order to prevent the threatened action on behalf of the population. "I must emphasize emphatically that both of us were armed in order to be prepared for any eventualities. Mr. Alfred Swarovski was carrying a pistol in his bag, while I had armed myself with hand grenades." Back in Wattens, it was decided:

1. to prevent the destruction of the above-mentioned bridges through deployment of members of the resistance movement;

2. to recover weapons from a secret depot of the resistance movement, to which end Mr. Alfred Swarovski supplied a factory car and driver;

3. and to take up contact by telephone with the American vanguards as soon as possible.

---

37   SAW, Alfred Swarovski, Meine Intervention zur Vermeidung der Sprengung der Innbrücken bei Volders, Wattens und Weer, Mai 1946. This account was confirmed by Andrä Wieser and the "head of the liberation movement of Wattens," Wattens, May 1946.

"To this end, ongoing debates were conducted in Mr. Alfred Swarovski's residence, and he indeed managed both to obtain the acquired weapons in order to arm the members of the resistance movement and to take up contact with the American vanguards in order to provide them with orientation. In short, he managed to guide the resistance movement in such a manner that the aim of preventing the destruction of the bridges could in fact be achieved. I can confirm that Mr. Alfred Swarovski's actions were certainly perilous, as the Wehrmacht on the one hand and the Waffen-SS on the other were fighting on all sides at the time, and there was the steadfast intention of blowing up the bridge in Volders, as I deduced from a conversation with a lieutenant of the demolition squad, who told me that he could not see why Tyrol should be treated differently than the rest of the Reich, where all important objects were being blown sky high as had been ordered."[38]

This account was confirmed by the driver who was sent to collect the weapons: "I was the head of the transport ordered by Mr. Alfred Swarovski to take a factory car and drive to Walchen [Wattener Lizum, the head of the Wattental valley] to pick up weapons for the resistance movement. We did in fact succeed, though under enormous difficulties and with the aid of two corporals of the resistance movement. I am of the opinion that the bridge would in all likelihood have been blown up if Mr. Alfred Swarovski had not intervened in this manner."[39]

As a result of this action, Lieutenant Colonel E.S.M. Kee of the U.S. infantry made the following statement "to whom it may concern": "I hereby confirm that I have known Mr. Alfred Swarovski since 3 May 1945. I was one of the first American tactical officers to enter the state of Tyrol, Austria, on 1 May 1945. I then came into contact with Tyrolean partisans who were active underground fighters. The organization of which Mr. Swarovski was a member helped tactically in the conquest of the state of Tyrol. This unit and its occasional support helped the U.S. army and saved U.S. lives. Mr. Swarovski is to be commended for his role in a patriotic and efficient fighting organization."[40] On 23 January 1948, Alfred Swarovski

---

38 SAW, Rudolf Schwaiger, Leiter der Freiheitsbewegung von Wattens, May 1945; the same report appeared in Österreichische demokratische Freiheitsbewegung, Wattens, Aug. 2, 1945.

39 SAW, Bestätigung Giselher Langes, Friedrich Troppmaier und Friedrich Rost, Jan. 8, 1948.

40 K.S.M. Kee, March 20, 1948.

was inducted into the Tyrolean liberation movement, who wrote the following statement on his behalf: "Mr. Alfred Swarovski, industrialist, born 28 October 1891 in Johannesthal, resident in Wattens, Bundestraße Nr. 2, counts in the sense of the confirmation of the American headquarters of 20 March 1947 as a member of the Association of Tyrolean Liberation Fighters and as a fighter with weapon in hand in the ranks of the Allies. Protocol Number: 622, signed by the Chairman of the Association of Tyrolean Liberation Fighters Dr. Weißgatterer, Innsbruck, on 23 January 1948."[41]

The Employees and National Socialism

As soon as the war ended, Swarovski was already being vehemently attacked as a "Nazi company." It was claimed that the employees had been under pressure to join the party even before 1938. The company was accused of having funneled large sums of money to the illegal party and thereby made itself accountable for the strong party membership among the workers and white-collar employees. The foremen were claimed to have abused their positions to force their subordinates to join the party on punishment of dismissal. Friedrich Swarovski was accused of having strictly followed the orders of the government and the Gau administration until the very end of Nazi rule, and many former Nazis were allegedly still being employed after the collapse of the Third Reich.[42]

One of the means to "clarify the political situation" at the company was the appointment of an eleven-member industrial council, which consisted of representatives of the Socialist Party and the People's Party. This council concluded unanimously that great mistakes had been made. Even before the Anschluss, a large part of the workforce had been illegal Nazis, especially the white-collar employees. This had only been possible because the department heads and foremen, sanctioned and encouraged by the Swarovskis, had exerted pressure on the workers: "Wattens had a reputation as a stronghold of National Socialism, and not without reason."[43]

All eighty-seven of the "illegal Nazis" still employed at the company were questioned, revealing a consensus that denazification was basically acceptable, but not in one's own community or company, where one knew

---

41   SAW, Bestätigung des Bundes der Tiroler Freiheitskämpfer, Jan. 23, 1948.
42   SAW, Robert Tröbitsch, Anschuldigungen der Wiener und Tiroler Amtsstellen gegen die Herren Swarovski und gegen das Werk, Vienna, undated.
43   SAW, Abschrift! Stellungnahme des Betriebsrates der Fa. Swarovski zur Frage der Illegalen und besonders hervorgetretenen NSDAP-Mitglieder sowie zur Frage des Zusammenarbeitens mit der Firma in Zukunft, Wattens, Nov. 15, 1945.

people.[44] The basis for this interrogation was the 1939 statistical survey of the Nazi Party, which, alongside membership, also listed efforts made on behalf of the party before the Anschluss in 1938. The Wattens gendarmerie investigated whether any of the registered individuals had ever been the subject of enquiry. The comments on the list evince that the company wished to retain these employees. Practically all of them were described in the following terms: "performance: very good"; "operational management: very good"; and, "never reprimanded by the gendarmerie." The best assessments read: quiet, decent, modest, benign, harmless, reasonable, helpful, just, or comradely. When questioned, many workers argued that they had been subject to various pressures. For example: "I was unemployed at the time (the illegal time), I needed work desperately, and in order to get work again I had to join the party." People also claimed that they were afraid of being dismissed if they did not belong to the party.[45]

This interrogation was ultimately a strategy on behalf of the industrial council to stand protectively in front of their colleagues and to curb the impact of the denazification process. According to them, the blame lay with the company management and the leading employees, while the simple workers and other employees had merely been victims of political pressure. Characteristically, the council wrote to the company management in November 1945: "The strong participation of the workers and employees in the illegal doings of the Nazi Party is precisely now, at a time when denazification of private industry is to be carried out, a great burden to the company. Accusations are being levied against the company from various sides, indeed not only accusations; there are demands for a cleansing of all heavily incriminated National Socialists from the company. We are clear about the fact that a political cleansing of the company will be of great disadvantage to the company and not least of all to the workforce and the employees, especially if this cleansing is to be conducted rigorously. Since especially many employees in leading positions would be removed in such a cleansing, the danger arises that the company will thereby lose its best labor force and may even have to close some departments. In the interests of the company as well as of the workers and employees, this must be hindered at all costs."[46]

The council thus held the position that everything possible had to be done to avert a disturbance to the operation of the company. This corresponded

---

44   See Dieter Stiefel, *Entnazifizierung in Österreich* (Vienna: Europaverlag, 1981).
45   SAW, Aktennotiz über eine Besprechung mit Herrn Betriebsobmann Anton Wieser und unserem Herrn Alfred Swarovski am 1. Februar 1946, Wattens, March 16, 1946.
46   SAW, Stellungnahme des Betriebsrates der Fa. Swarovski zur Frage der Illegalen und besonders hervorgetretenen NSDAP-Mitglieder sowie zur Frage des Zusammenarbeitens mit der Firma in Zukunft, Wattens, Nov. 15, 1945.

with the position of management: "The experienced core workers and skilled professionals, some of whom have been employed at Swarovski for decades, are especially indispensable to the completion of the company's tasks that are so important to the future economy of Austria. A number of these are considered 'illegal.' From a national economic point of view, it is important that these people be left at the company in an appropriate form as the company is directly dependent on these workers for the completion of its tasks."[47]

The heavily incriminated employees were particularly problematic: "These forty-six men have been identified and should actually be arrested—all of them are most qualified employees in leading positions, thus representing the core capital of the company. We came up with the following idea to prevent these workers who are so important to us from being lost: we put a decommissioned peat-cutting site in the bogs around Kitzbühel back into operation, erected a hutment, and deployed these forty-six men to exploit peat that will in turn be used for our glass furnaces." The peat-cutting operation, conceived of as a kind of political penal camp, was managed directly by Swarovski and was supervised by the district authority of Kitzbühel. "We also ensured that our people were well cared for.... The general conditions, including in an internal political sense, improved rather rapidly, meaning that the conditions of detention could quickly be improved, the inmates were released to return home, and the camp was shut down again. The factory was already waiting urgently for the return of this large number of highly qualified workers. The exploited peat was returned to Wattens to dry but was never actually put to use as there was no longer any shortage of the usual fuel materials. This action was an interlude of extreme importance in order to retain our core workers who were so important to the resumption of production."[48]

Specific numbers were then raised in defense against the general accusation of being a "Nazi company": "At 1,100 and 1,200 respectively, the number of employees at the Swarovski company was the same at the time of the Anschluss as at the close of the war. In the final years of the war, this figure included about 110 foreigners, meaning that the number of local employees was between 990 and 1,090 at the end of the war."[49] In 1937/38, 115 employees (nine percent) had been members of the Nazi Party, rising to 296 (twenty-eight percent) in 1944/45. These numbers and percentages, so the argument went,

47   SAW, Firma Swarovski, Grundsätzlich zur Registrierung bzw. Entregistrierung des Daniel Swarovski, Wattens, Apr. 12, 1946.
48   Josef Schwaiger, *Im Dienste von vier Generationen der Firma D. Swarovski & Co, Wattens* (Wattens 1991).
49   SAW, Firma D. Swarovski, Zum Problem der politischen Bereinigung und Entnazifizierung der Firma D. Swarovski in Wattens, Wattens, Feb. 12, 1946.

were not characteristic of a "Nazi company," as according to the Chamber of Labor in Innsbruck this would have required a ratio of party members of eighty percent or higher. In December 1946, 116 employees remained in service who were included on the Nazi registry, six of whom were in leading positions. Twelve employees had been dismissed at this point for political reasons.[50]

The company management repeatedly emphasized that it had never exerted any party-political influence on its employees. During the Nazi period, the company had been reproached for not employing any Nazis in the upper management. Nine people had been hired in the management sector at the time, all of whom were known as opponents of the Nazis. Moreover, five permanent members of the company management hired earlier were also known as opponents of the Nazis. Among the entire management staff, with the exception of the heads, these gentlemen stood opposite only two party members. Then there were four employees who had been detained by the Gestapo and had been described as unacceptable, but who had not been fired from the company: "No employee who was ever employed by the company and was suitable for the work to which he had been assigned was ever dismissed for political reasons. Neither did the company dismiss detained workers upon their release." For example, five employees had been readmitted to the factory after their release from detention: "There was not a single case of someone arrested and later released who was dismissed by the company." Six individuals, office staff members and workers, were supposed to be removed from the factory for political reasons on the request of the *Ortsgruppenleiter*, but this was not carried out: "Moreover, the company always intervened with the Gestapo immediately asking for detained individuals to be released."[51]

Forced Laborers

In the fall of 1944, about one million forced laborers were being exploited in the present-day territory of Austria.[52] Following international pres-

---

50 SAW, Amtlicher Erhebungsbogen über die Entnazifizierung in der Privatwirtschaft einschließlich der freien Berufe für die Zeit vom 27. April 1945 bis 15. September 1946, D. Swarovski Glasfabrik und Tyrolit Schleifmittel Wattens-Tirol, Dec. 17, 1946.

51 D. Swarovski Glasfabrik und Tyrolit-Schleifmittel-Werke Wattens, Tirol, Zur Stellungnahme des Betriebsrates in Frage der Illegalen und besonders hervorgetretenen Mitgliedern der NSDAP, sowie der Frage der Zusammenarbeit mit der Firma in Zukunft auf Grund einer Besprechung innerhalb des Betriebsrates vom 15. November 1945, Wattens, March 25, 1946.

52 Florian Freund, Bertrand Perz eds., *Die Zahlenentwicklung der ausländischen Zwangsarbeiter und Zwangsarbeiterinnen auf dem Gebiet der Republik Österreich 1939–1945, Gutachten der Österreichischen Historikerkommission* (Vienna, 2000).

sure, a "Fund for reconciliation, peace, and cooperation" was established in Austria in 2000, which eventually raised some six billion Schilling (roughly 440 million Euros), about half of which was contributed by the state, the other half consisting of "voluntary contributions" from the business sector. These funds were paid out to about 132,000 people worldwide as financial compensation for their time as forced laborers. It was proposed that businesses contribute 0.2 percent of their turnover, and on 3 July 2000 the fund looked to Swarovski.[53] As with all companies, this was regarded as an "unusual business," and thus led to hefty discussions at Swarovski.[54] For too long, it was claimed, the media had trumpeted false figures, according to which up to 1,000 forced laborers had been employed at the company, a number almost equaling the entire employed workforce. Aside from this, discrimination in the market and damage to the name of Swarovski had made the financial participation of the company inevitable. Thus, the board, as the highest decision-making body in the Swarovski company, decided on 4 July 2000 to end the discussion by contributing ten million Schilling, far more than the prescribed 0.2 percent.[55]

In order to themselves gain an overview, the company commissioned internal research into the matter, based on the surviving personnel records, payrolls, the registration books of the community of Wattens, and documents from the regional insurance company. Figures could only be ascertained for the year 1944, however, even though there is evidence suggesting that the employment agency in Innsbruck had already been assigning foreign labor as early as 1941. In 1944, the company had on average 165 foreign workers, 124 of whom were classed as forced laborers. The proportion of foreigners over the months of 1944 ranged between thirteen and eighteen percent, while the length of employment ranged between one and twenty-five months, averaging nine. Based on the year of initial employment, 1941/42 witnessed first Belgians and Frenchmen being employed, and from 1943 Italians, but hardly any forced laborers from Eastern Europe, the group for whom the Reconciliation Fund was primarily intended.

The forced laborers were housed in barracks, although some also lived privately in Wattens and the surrounding area. It appeared that these workers were always treated decently, were paid, taxed, insured, and registered like local workers. All that remained unclear was whether they received

53 SAW, Regierungsbeauftragte Präsidentin i.R. Dr. Maria Schaumayer, Bundeskanzleramt an D. Swarovski & Co, Firmenleitung, Wattens, Vienna, July 3, 2000.
54 "Für die österreichische Versicherungswirtschaft beschrieben" in *"Unusual Business": Der Wiederaufbau der österreichischen Versicherungswirtschaft 1945 und ihr Beitrag zum Entschädigungsfondsgesetz 2001*, ed. Dieter Stiefel (Vienna: Böhlau, 2006).
55 SAW, Auszug aus Protokoll Beiratssitzung Nr. 8/2000, Feldmeilen, July 4, 2000.

a full wage or whether a part of their wage had to be surrendered to the employment agency. Some of the workers even remained in Wattens after the end of the war.

A special chapter in this history was the construction of an air raid shelter on the factory grounds in 1943 by the construction company Berger & Brunner. The aim of this shelter construction was the protection of the binocular production and of machines for future production in peacetime.[56] There are no documents pertaining to forced laborers in this endeavor, but only a very friendly retrospective comment: "We received a group of prison laborers from the camp at Prien am Chiemsee for construction of the shelter; an independently responsible camp leader was provided." These individuals were housed at plant number two, where they also received provisions. "We tried from the outset to treat these people well and care for them, all of whom were political prisoners and who of course had to conduct heavy labor. There were never any issues with dissatisfaction."[57] The shelter was never completed, and it would have taken several more weeks to move the most important machinery there.

The Company

The Anschluss of Austria to Nazi Germany on 12/13 March 1938 was met with the approval of many Austrians. This included several members of the Swarovski family, as documented in a report of the gendarmerie in Wattens: "On the evening of 21 February, 500 'nationalists' conducted a torch-lit procession from the sports hall of the German Gymnastic Club 'Friesen' in Wattens to what was then still called the Dollfußplatz, where the war memorial was located. The participants consisted of members of the gymnastic club and the 'Association of Germans of the Reich.' The majority were workers at the Swarovski company, who were accompanied by the industrialists Fritz and Willi Swarovski"; the Rattenberg band led the procession. "The march closed with shouts of 'Sieg Heil' and 'Heil Hitler' in front of the war memorial and with the singing of the first stanzas of the *Deutschlandlied*, with participants raising their arms for the Nazi salute."[58] The enthusiasm of Friedrich and Wilhelm Swarovski is astounding insofar as the Anschluss constituted an existential threat to the company. Nazi Germany was gearing up for war; there was no place in the armaments

---

56 Recherchen im Haus Swarovski, July 3, 2000.
57 Schwaiger, *Im Dienste von vier Generationen*. Prien was a satellite camp of the Bernau penitentiary.
58 Cited in Schreiber, *Wirtschafts- und Sozialgeschichte der Nazizeit*, 134–135.

economy for the products of this Tyrolean company; and currency and foreign trade conditions were extremely restrictive.

Additionally, Swarovski had been a part-Jewish company from its foundation, due to the partners Kosmann and Crailsheimer. These parts of the company should have been "Aryanized" under Nazi laws pertaining to Jewish property. However, Swarovski had this matter delayed through its attorney. Pressure increased even further with the outbreak of war as Crailsheimer, a French national, became an enemy alien. It was possible to delay "Aryanization" because the registration of Jewish property was to be undertaken at one's place of residence, which was hardly possible for Crailsheimer, who was a resident of Paris and Lausanne. This tactic of delay was effective in diverting the attention of the Nazi Party, and as a result the corporate relationship with Crailsheimer could be maintained. In order not to draw further attention to his participation, this was transformed into a silent partnership.[59] Jean Crailsheimer's participation internally, however, remained active and was properly recorded and billed. Alfred Swarovski met Jean Crailsheimer on numerous occasions during the Nazi period in Zurich. Money transfers to Crailsheimer must have continued after 1938; at least, his account continued to be updated. Jewish participation in the company was thus maintained throughout the entire Nazi period, which was surely a unique case.

The anti-Jewish laws also affected Ernst Löwenstein, a partner and close friend of Alfred Swarovski for many decades. He ran a trading company for glass jewelry in Gablonz, working exclusively for Swarovski from 1933 onward. In 1937, Swarovski entrusted him with the entire U.S. export operation with the exception of a few large customers. The Anschluss of Austria and the subsequent persecution of Jews was a warning to Ernst Löwenstein. He emigrated even before the Sudetenland, including his place of residence Gablonz, was annexed. In May 1938, he traveled to the U.S.A. with Alfred Swarovski to prepare his position there. Upon his return, he announced his move to the U.S.A. in Czechoslovakia, which was still independent at the time, and traveled on a one-way ticket to New York City in late August 1938. He changed his name to Ernest Lowenstein. He received American identity papers and became a naturalized U.S. citizen after five years. This was partly to ensure his safety, but also to protect Swarovski's position in the U.S., where Lowenstein was in charge of representation and sales on behalf of Swarovski. In order to stabilize his financial position, he was guaranteed a minimum income regardless of how business was going.[60]

---

59   SAW, Rechtsanwalt Dr. Arthur Lehndorff, Innsbruck, an die Firma D. Swarovski, Glasfabrik und Tyrolit-Schleifmittel-Werke, Wattens, Innsbruck, May 10, 1938.
60   SAW, Vertragsentwurf Firma D.Swarovski, Glasfabrik und Tyrolit-Schleifmittel-Werke, Wattens mit Ernst Löwenstein, May 1938.

Ernest Lowenstein was able to return the favor for the support he received in emigrating by playing a decisive role in the reconstruction of the company after the end of the war.

The Austrian Schilling also fell victim to the Anschluss.[61] The currency conversion was completed within only five days at a ratio of three Schilling to two Reichsmark, representing an appreciation of thirty-seven percent for the Schilling. This currency conversion was one of the largest problems altogether for the Swarovski company, raising serious questions about how its exports, which constituted over ninety percent of the turnover, were supposed to continue. Austria's external trading regulations were comparatively liberal in 1937, while Nazi Germany's external trade was strictly regulated. Moreover, duties on German imports to the U.S. were as much as twenty-seven percent higher than for imports from Austria, while the cessation of the most favored nation clause meant an additional ten percent tariff on imports to the U.S. These new conditions would have demanded a price increase of such proportions that they would have spelled the end of the company. Swarovski's chances now lay in the fact that Nazi Germany was deeply interested in foreign currency for the armaments industry and consequently provided significant export subsidies. Without this support from the state, Swarovski could not have maintained its exports. Therefore, the company entered into several rounds of negotiations with the Reich Ministry of the Economy in Berlin, which finally resulted in an export promotion of seventy-four percent for exports to the U.S., and a promotion of sixty-nine percent for exports elsewhere.

Additionally, the payment process had become more complicated. Prior to 1938, American customers had paid via the banks, and Swarovski had received the dollar assets according to the exchange rate in Schillings. Their customers were large jewelry makers on the east coast, which were predominantly Jewish-owned. After the Anschluss, these payments were directed via a German financial institution in New York that used these funds to buy copper from the world market. It is conspicuous that these payments were made via the copper account, as Swarovski was thereby co-financing the armament of Nazi Germany.[62] These were essentially barter deals.[63] The copper business only covered about forty percent, however, and Swarovski covertly received the rest from the Reich Ministry of the Economy. This was a dubious practice, since the entire import of the Swarovski company to

61   See Karl Bachinger, Felix Butschek, Herbert Matis, Dieter Stiefel, eds., *Abschied vom Schilling: Eine* österreichische Wirtschaftsgeschichte (Vienna: Syria, 2001), 135–139.
62   SAW, Alfred Swarovski, Lebenslauf als Unterlage für H. Paulin, Wattens, 1956.
63   SAW, Korrespondenz Swarovski Wattens mit Ernst Löwenstein, Hotel Wagram, Paris, Sept. 3 and 27, 1938.

the U.S. would have been shut down had the American authorities caught wind of this.

In the light of these difficulties, it is no wonder that their exports to the U.S. came under pressure. The outbreak of World War II on 1 September 1939 resulted in a blockade of the Atlantic. This impacted Swarovski directly: a week before, on 25 August, six boxes of jewelry stones had departed for the U.S. on the steamship *Hansa*, which then had to return to Hamburg. Swarovski tried next to transport its exports to the U.S. via the Pacific. As Russia had not yet been drawn into the war at this point, the cargo's "world trip" proceeded from Wattens to Königsberg, then following the Trans-Siberian Railway to Vladivostok, from where it was transported to the Japanese port of entry at Tsuruga and on to the port of export at Kobe, from where it was finally delivered to San Francisco and across the American continent to the east coast. The deliveries took months and often got stuck, especially in Japan. While Alfred Swarovski was still frantically trying to maintain peacetime production, his brothers had already began to reorganize the operation in line with the new circumstances.

Friedrich Swarovski had been named "factory leader" immediately following the Anschluss in 1938, with Wilhelm Swarovski as the deputy. The company was recognized as an armaments enterprise, ensuring its continued existence. However, this entailed extensive organizational measures, with the production focus, in particular, being subject to change. Peacetime production of jewelry stones was drastically reduced, while the production of abrasives was the first to be driven up, since this was an area where the company had much experience, having used these for the production of jewelry stones. Next, the company expanded its production of reflectors, which were used, among other things, for maritime signposts on buoys.

In 1939, the company solicited contracts for the construction of machines and instruments, and until 1940 attempted to produce detonator caps for munitions production. This was interrupted soon thereafter, however, as it was seen to hinder the future peacetime business after the end of the war. The company did go on, until 1945, to produce over three million mine detonators from pressed material.[64] Other items were also produced such as reflector sights for anti-tank cannons, and the company's workshops were well supplied with work through contracts with the Heinkel manufacturing plant in Jenbach. Nevertheless, turnover altogether decreased by twenty-nine percent from 1937 to 1940. This situation was untenable.

With preparations for war underway, it was made clear to Swarovski that the time for producing jewelry stones was at an end: "It was generally

---

64   SAW, Firma D. Swarovski, Monats-Betriebs-Übersicht Jahr 1945.

thought that our stone business was completely broken. We should just wave goodbye to it. It was said that this was a typical and purely Jewish business which had no place in the Third Reich. It was moreover thought that there were more important production programs than jewelry stones. We were also warned by the German Labor Front. I was personally told in Berlin: you know, Mr. Swarovski, you should finally come to terms with the fact that the global problem is the Jew. You should not feed the Jew. You have to follow a different line of business."[65]

From then on, Hugo Lindenberg also played an important role due to his good relations with the Nazi authorities. Aside from his family connections, he was also the company's advisor for questions relating to the defense economy and armaments production, remaining in constant contact with all the relevant offices of the Wehrmacht, the government, and the authorities. In the transition from peacetime to wartime production, he had led the negotiations with the high command of the military and with the Reich Ministry of Aviation. He was the one to suggest the production of optical instruments.

In simplified terms, Swarovski produced and processed glass. Optics therefore did not seem all too far-fetched. The company was in this regard able to rely on the prior work of Wilhelm Swarovski, who had begun experimenting with optical glass in 1933. The glass was produced in the factory, while Wilhelm personally cut the lenses and prisms at home. In 1935, he developed a prototype of binoculars that he registered under the trade name "*Habicht*" ("hawk") in 1938. Wilhelm Swarovski intended this item to make the company more crisis-proof: "I always imagined a 'people's binocular,' a good optical instrument that was also so cheap that just about anyone could afford it."[66]

Then the Anschluss occurred, followed by the armaments economy, and then the war. The military high command had commissioned seven companies in Germany to produce binoculars according to the Zeiss model 6x30, with blueprints provided for the production of these service binoculars.[67] The Swarovski products could be recognized by the debossed mark "cag." For this new product, Swarovski planned to use an empty factory building of a former soap manufacturer in Kematen, over twenty kilometers outside of Wattens. The military was a generous customer, taking care of the development costs and transacting large orders even before the company was

---

65   SAW, Alfred Swarovski, Lebenslauf als Unterlage für H. Paulin, Wattens 1956.
66   SAW, Wilhelm Swarovski, Lebenslauf, Wattens, Feb. 7, 1946. This employee was Dr. Max Zorzzi.
67   Auskunft Carl Zeiss Archiv, Jena, June 26, 2012. The Swarovski name does not appear in the Zeiss company history: Rolf Walter, *Zeiss 1905–1945* (Vienna: Böhlau, 2000).

able to deliver. But it also had very precise cost regulations and purchases were conducted on site through a military official.[68]

This mass production, for such a demanding client as the military, was an entirely new playing field. The company defaulted, and the first optical prisms produced were unusable. The delay in beginning production put the free employees at risk of being conscripted for military service. It took almost two years for the problem to be brought under control with the help of the Zeiss optical company in Jena. One of the Swarovski employees was even trained at Zeiss to this end. The factory in Kematen was abandoned, and the optical production was relocated to Wattens.

In December 1939, 380 staff members had to be laid off due to financial deficits, but by March 1941 these difficulties had been overcome: "It is significant for our operation that the production program has been secured for the foreseeable future and we do not need to accept any new contracts for the duration of the war. We are thereby in a position to prepare ourselves to continue optical production even later in peacetime."[69] Thus, the company was supposed to be on an even keel for the duration of the war: "Our labor demands will be covered by the assignment of foreign labor by the authorities."[70] Altogether, Swarovski produced 186,484 binoculars during World War II.

In 1941, Wilhelm Swarovski was called to the production ring of the optical industry in Jena, which had been commissioned to build the gunsights for the K43 gun for the infantry. No pressure was exerted within the company itself, since the ongoing binocular production alone was at the limit of capacity. There were no indications that the gunsights were, in fact, to be produced in Wattens; there were no orders on behalf of the high command of the Wehrmacht, and no delivery notes. However, some collectors—there are also collectors in this field—have located specimens with Swarovski's serial numbers, suggesting that a smaller quantity may indeed have been produced by them.

In order to free up capacity for the production of a new gunsight (the GwZF4), a relocation to Frastanz in Vorarlberg, 170 kilometers away, was planned in April 1944. In March 1945, however, it was found that, after almost half a year of production in Frastanz and "as a result of various circumstances," not even half of the planned quantity had been produced, and

---

68   Schwaiger, *Im Dienste von vier Generationen.*
69   SAW, D. Swarovski Glasfabrik und Tyrolit-Schleifmittel-Werke, Wattens, Tirol, Zur Lage der einzelnen Fabrikationszweige, Wattens, Nov. 23, 1940.
70   SAW, D. Swarovski Glasfabrik und Tyrolit-Schleifmittel-Werke, Wattens, Tirol, allgemeine Bemerkungen zur Übersicht über den Gesamtbetrieb zum 1.-3.1941.

assembly costs had been almost twice as high as in Wattens.[71] This problem resolved itself, however, as the war ended only a few weeks later.

The extent to which the bureaucracy of the military administration continued working unperturbed by the approaching end of the war is evinced by an order for 60,000 binoculars, an order that Swarovski applied for on 13 June 1944 and that was granted on 10 February 1945. The company would thereby have had its production accounted for until April 1946.[72] Production of abrasives was also continued as though there were no end in sight. In February 1945, Swarovski planned to install an electric tunnel kiln which would have increased the production of abrasives from 70 to 170 tons. This was supposed to go into operation in May 1945.[73]

Economic Balance

The general claim that Swarovski laid the foundations for its post-war success during World War II has also been made in scholarly publications. For example: "Thanks to intensive cooperation with the regime—and through the exploitation of forced labor—Swarovski laid the basis for its fruitful continued development after the end of the war."[74] The accusation of having profited economically from the war was already levied in the first years after the war's end. To counter this, Alfred Swarovski commissioned an expert assessment in 1947 about the damages and inopportune influences of the years 1938 to 1945.[75] Of lesser interest here was the fact that the capital ratios and financial figures had deteriorated in this same period. Of primary significance was the fact that no notable expansion of production had taken place, but rather a shift in production that was not maintainable after the war.

This was affirmed by the economic assessor in his report for the year 1945; by that time, jewelry stones accounted for only ten percent of revenues, demonstrating an "estrangement from the original production

71 SAW, D. Swarovski Glasfabrik und Tyrolit-Schleifmittel-Werke, Wattens, Tirol, Andreas Hofer, Reisebericht über meine Fahrt am 13. März 1945 nach Feldkirch und Frastanz, Wattens, March 14, 1945.
72 SAW, Firma D. Swarovski an das Oberkommando der Wehrmacht, Wünsdorf, Wattens, June 13, 1944 and Oberkommando des Heeres an Firma D. Swarovski Wattens, Berlin, Feb. 10, 1945.
73 SAW, D. Swarovski Glasfabrik und Tyrolit-Schleifmittel-Werke, Wattens, Tirol, Aktenvermerk Feb. 14, 1945.
74 Kühschelm, *Swarovski*, 134–135.
75 W.P. Hans Leyer an Dr. Anton Bauer, Rechtsanwalt, Innsbruck, Wattens, Oct. 21, 1947, Betrifft: Beeinflussung der Firma D. Swarovski 1938–1945. This report was compiled in the context of the cessation of the denazification process against Swarovski.

program."[76] The production of optical instruments, meanwhile, had innately been directed at a later reduction.[77]

Proportion of Total Revenue:

Year	Jewelry Stones	Abrasives	Optics	Other
1944	8%	34%	51%	7%
1949	88%	7%	4%	1%

Of course, Swarovski had been lucky. It was one of the few companies in Nazi Germany whose factories were spared aerial bombardment. The armaments production of abrasives and especially optics allowed for the attainment of high quality and quantity, and these two production fields had saved the company during the war. Wilhelm was the only one who envisioned optics as the future of the company, but he was warned from all sides. In the international optics field, Swarovski was a minor player with mighty competitors, while in the production of jewelry stones it remained a global market leader. The latter thus became once more the basis of the business, despite being precisely the area that had been largely neglected during wartime production, almost going under. It took almost two years for Swarovski to once more attain its "pre-war quality" in this field.

As Alfred Swarovski himself stated: "In this context, I would like to refer once more to the immeasurable damage caused by both world wars to the development and survival of the Swarovski company. Before World War I, we had just completed the construction of our glass factory, when, all of a sudden, mobilization led to the operation being interrupted for almost five years. We fared similarly during World War II. Then, too, our operation was almost completely shut down, in contrast to other industries, as far as I know. It did not matter whether it was a paper factory, a textile industry, or the Plansee factory [in Tyrol]. Far and wide, wherever one looked, industries were able to continue working through the war; all of them were, in fact, important to the war effort. Only the jewelry stones of the Swarovski company were not useful for the war. Our factories were on each occasion turned completely upside down. What could we do to save them and to save the most important staff members, whose experience was of such fundamental importance to us? On both occasions, we had to transition to an entirely different manufacturing basis, which constituted not only an

76   SAW, Jahresabschluss der Firma D. Swarovski, Glasfabrik und Tyrolitschleifmittelwerke, Wattens, Tirol, Dec. 31, 1945, Bericht W.-P. Hans Leyer, Graz, March 8, 1948, 8.
77   SAW, The establishment of Swarovski Optik GmbH on 4 January 1949 led to its spatial and legal separation.

immense mental effort but on each occasion also tore apart our operating capital. In every war, we were by far the worst off as a war industry."[78]

Conclusion

There were 536,000 registered National Socialists in Austria, each of whom had their own story. This is also true for the Swarovskis, and yet many questions remain unanswered. Individual attitudes toward National Socialism were highly variable, as evident alone from the variable dates of entry into Nazi Party membership. And yet a family decision was made in 1938 to fully and collectively join the party. This collective adaptation was conspicuous considering that in other areas the family offered "resistance," for example in preventing, among other things, the Aryanization of Jewish participation in the company, in failing to follow the order to scrap machines, and in hiding raw materials for later peacetime production.

Why was the operation not relocated to the U.S.A.? The production of glass jewelry was a hopeless endeavor in Nazi Germany, while large American jewelry producers were urging Swarovski to join them, insisting that there was plenty of capital and that financing was no problem. As an American company, Swarovski would have been able to continue its operation without being disturbed politically. The earlier relocation of the company from Bohemia to Tyrol had already evinced the flexibility of the operation. However, under the significantly more difficult conditions in 1938, the company shied away from another relocation.

In the denazification process after the war, it was beneficial to make one's own role appear as minimal as possible. The workers made comments to the effect that they had not foreseen the consequences of National Socialism and thus had later increasingly turned their back on this ideology. With the Swarovskis, however, there were no such indications of guilt or regrets. One had been forced by economic necessity, so the narrative went, to join the party in order to preserve the company through the war; with the company now in the post-war period, the company represented an important part of the Tyrolean economy: "The heads of the Swarovski company therefore did not act politically incorrectly, but correctly." However, another point of view also needs to be taken into consideration here: this was precisely the line of argument that was expected and accepted in Austria—in this sense, too, the heads of the company had acted politically correctly.

---

78   SAW, Alfred Swarovski, Lebenslauf als Unterlage für H. Paulin, Wattens 1956.

Naturally, this brief report cannot fully do justice to this topic. The Swarovskis' behavior can only be fairly and evenly assessed against the backdrop of the political and economic developments of the time. Whether the study offering this assessment will be published or not is now up to the Swarovskis themselves.

Forum: Austrians as Victims? Victimhood Discourses and Practices in the Age of World Wars

Introduction

Günter Bischof

The papers in this forum were first presented at the German Studies Association meeting in Atlanta, Georgia, in October 2017. They make a compelling case that recourse to "war victimhood" defines much of Austria's post-Habsburg history. In fact, Ke-Chin Hsia argues that "a palpable sense of victimhood" served as a "leitmotif of the post-Habsburg Austrian self-identity." While Hsia's and Philip J. Henry's papers deal with the victims of the World War I era in the 1920s and 1930s, Matthew Berg's and Nicole-Melanie Goll's essays cover Austrian perspectives on victimhood after World War II until today; Cathleen M. Giustino adds her powerful commentary to the papers.

Henry's intellectual history of Freudian psychoanalysis looks at the "unprecedented levels of victimization" of soldiers and children during the war, forcing Freud and his school to adjust their theories to deal with war trauma rather than the sex-induced neuroses of their traditional bourgeois subjects. Total war precipitated "a large-scale collapse of Vienna society," argues Henry, citing Freud's harsh judgement: "the Habsburgs have left behind nothing but a pile of crap." The governments of the newly established Austrian Republic had to deal with this mess of hundreds of thousands of *"Kriegsopfer"*—"invalid" soldiers and their families, the widows and orphans of those who "fell" on the frontlines of World War I left behind.

Hsia's essay also goes into the partisan politics of discourses in the veteran organizations and political parties around *"Kriegsopfer"*: while the conservative Christian Socials, who governed during most of the interwar years, pushed a narrative of "tragic heroism"—war invalids as "martyrs"—the Social Democrats argued that the invalids needed to be compensated since the "war-mongering ruling classes" had sent them to sacrifice on the war fronts for their "delusional" agenda; they instrumentalized victimhood to build a brighter democratic future. The war crimes committed by the Austria-Hungarian Army during World War I have only come to light more recently, and Austro-German perpetrators were never persecuted. Instead, the postwar governments from Renner to Dollfuß/Schuschnigg maintained to have been "innocent victims" of the Allied peacemakers at St. Germain.

Berg's paper deals with similar partisan debates over taking care of hundreds of thousands of returning soldiers and prisoners of war after World War II (1.3 million Austrians fought in the German armed forces and 480,000 ended up in POW camps during and after the war). Only the post-World War II "victims debate" operated in a different political environment. While the First Republic did not have a founding myth, the Second Republic operated with the founding myth of the "victim doctrine." With the Moscow Declaration of 1 November 1943, the Allies maintained Austria to have been "Hitler's first victim."[1] With such a favorable status handed to postwar Austria, practically on a silver platter, given the numerous Austrian perpetrators in Hitler's killing machine, the Provisional Renner Government logically jumped on the opportunity and incorporated much of the Moscow Declaration in its "Declaration of Independence" on 27 April 1945.[2] Austria fashioned itself as Hitler's "first victim," which served the country well to block Allied reparations and Jewish restitution demands. The many Austrian perpetrators of Hitlerite war crimes eagerly incorporated themselves in this vast postwar Austrian victims collective. Berg's fascinating case study of how subsistence and housing was provided to tens of thousands of Viennese victims, based on an analysis of social policies of the Social Democratic Viennese city government and their system of "*Opferfürsorgekarten*," offers unique insights into defining "victim status." The 1945 (revised in 1948) *Opferfürsorgegesetz* "placed political and so-called racial victims on an equal footing," argues Berg. His careful analysis of the "rank order system" of the "victims of Nazi terror in Austria" provides a clear hierarchy of Austrian "*Opfer*." Those who were in the active and passive resistance against the Nazis came first when it came to providing public welfare; those of "racial and national persecution" (i.e., surviving Jews) came last. This allowed the Social Democratic city government of Vienna to provide some modest "patronage" to their clientele.

Goll's paper looks at the "victims" of the "Allied bombing terror" during World War II and the long (post-)memory among Austrians about the hardships of surviving the Allied "bombing holocaust." While in Austria, some 35,000 civilians were killed by Allied bombs, Austrians

---

1   Stefan Karner, Alexander O. Tschubarjan, eds., *Die Moskauer Deklaration 1943: "Österreich wieder herstellen"* (Vienna: Böhlau, 2015).

2   Günter Bischof, "Die Instrumentalisierung der Moskauer Erklärung nach dem 2. Weltkrieg," *Zeitgeschichte* 10 (Nov.–Dec. 1993): 345–366; idem, "'Opfer' Österreich?: Zur moralischen Ökonomie des österreichischen historischen Gedächtnisses," in: Dieter Stiefel, ed., *Die politische Ökonomie des Holocaust: Zur wirtschaftlichen Logik von Verfolgung und "Wiedergutmachung"* (Vienna: Oldenbourg, 2001), 305–335; idem, "Die Moskauer Deklaration und die österreichischen Geschichtspolitik," in *Moskauer Deklaration 1943*, ed. Karner, Tschubarian, 249–259.

have conveniently forgotten that almost one hundred downed American pilots and bomber crews were "lynched" in the final months of the war on Austrian territory.[3] After the war Austrians saw themselves in the "dual role" of victims. According to the Moscow Declaration they were the "first victims of National Socialism"—as a result of Allied air raids, they also considered themselves "innocent victims of war." Looking at specific memory events of World War II, such as the dense 2005 commemorations, Goll makes a solid case that Austrians still saw themselves as victims of the bombing war (the "second" victim myth still prevailing today), after the official "first" victim myth of Austria as "first victim of Hitlerite Germany" collapsed in the 1980s during the intense debates over presidential candidate Kurt Waldheim's World War II past.

Giustino not only reflects over the double meaning of the German word "*Opfer*" as "victim" and "sacrifice," but, more importantly, she raises the issue of whether Austrians' notion of repeated "collective victimhood" is failing to consider its "moral and ethical implications." She puts it bluntly: "State actors who promoted the *Opfermythos* encouraged Austrians' disengagement from reflection on personal and national complicity in the Anschluss and the murder of the country's Jewish citizens." Such "disengagement from responsibility and accountability" is troubling. While she does not mention this, one could add that more recently state actors such as South Africa and Chile, which had to deal with murderous pasts, established "truth and reconciliation commissions" as tools of mastering their difficult histories.[4]

It is clear that traumatization of Austrians by the two World Wars did create widespread feelings of victimization, calling for state-directed welfare programs to take care of the many "*Kriegsopfer.*"[5] After two wars, hardly a family existed that had not lost loved ones. To this day every village cemetery in Austria has a *Kriegerdenkmal*—a monument to the soldiers lost in both wars. We also need to remember that both immediate postwar eras were also times of enormous economic hardship, when the two Austrian republican governments faced enormous challenges in providing for their veterans and citizens. Where it not for the support of the international community and especially American food aid after both wars ("Hoover aid"

3   Georg Hoffmann, *Fliegerjustiz: Gewalt gegen abgeschossenee alliierte Fluzeugbesatzungen 1943–1945*, Krieg und Geschichte (Paderborn: Ferdinand Schöningh, 2015).
4   Case studies of such "truth and reconciliation commissions" are included in Oliver Rathkolb.ed, Revisiting the National Socialist Legacy: Coming to terms with Forced Labor, Expropriation, Compensation and Restitution (Innsbruck: StudienVerlag, 2002).
5   Helga Embacher, Maria Ecker, "A Nation of Victims: How Austria dealt with the victims of the authoritarian Ständestaat and national socialism," in *The Politics of War Trauma: The Aftermath of World War II in Eleven European Countries*, ed. Jolande Withuis, Annet Mooij (Amsterdam: aksant, 2010), 15–47.

after World War I, and U.S. Army, CARE, UNRRA, and Marshall Plan aid after World War II), Austrians could hardly have survived.[6] Given the deep traumatization of the citizenship due to the war and Allied bombing—and what today we call the PTSD of the returning soldiers—and the economic dislocations after the war, it does not come as a surprise that the pragmatic postwar Austrian government seized the opportunity offered by the Allied Moscow Declaration. They latched on to the opportunity to claim "victim status" to postpone dealing with the crimes of Austrian perpetrators during the war and procrastinate on reparations and restitution payments.[7] But it is clear that in both postwar eras the survival of Austrians depended on "the kindness of strangers."

The question raised by these essays remains to be answered: whether Austrians' perennial claims of war victimhood in the post-Habsburg twentieth century (what Ernst Hanisch has called Austria's "self-infantilization"[8]) added an element of self-pity to their identity? While Austria's "German" identity was never settled during the First Republic, its anti-German post-World War II identity, based on new elements like its peaceful post-1955 neutral international status and its Marshall Plan-induced newfound economic prosperity, might need to be redefined.[9]

6   Hans Seidel, *Österreichs Wirtschaft und Wirtschaftspolitik nach dem Zweiten Weltkrieg* (Vienna: Manz, 2005); Günter Bischof, Hans Petschar, *The Marshal Plan since 1947: Saving Europe, Rebuilding Austria* (Vienna: Brandstätter, 2017).
7   Gerald Stourzh, *Um Einheit und Freiheit: Staatsvertrag, Neutralität und das Ende der Ost-West-Besetzung Österreichs 1945–1955* (4th ed. Vienna: Böhlau, 1998), 26–27.
8   Ernst Hanisch, "Gab es einen spezifischen österreichischen Widerstand?," *Zeitgeschichte* 12 (1984–85): 340.
9   Ernst Bruckmüller, *The Austrian Nation: Cultural Consciousness and Socio-Political Processes*, translated with an afterword by Lowell A. Bangerter (Riverside, CA: Ariadne, 2003).

"War Victims":
Concepts of Victimhood and the Austrian Identity
after the Habsburgs

Ke-chin Hsia

The importance of the concept of war victimhood to twentieth century Austrian history has been unduly underestimated. Before the more famous and complacent/optimistic concept of the "Island of the Blessed" (Pope Paul VI, 1971), a palpable sense of victimhood, sometimes implicit but more often explicitly felt and expressed, was one of the most important and probably the more fitting leitmotif of the post-Habsburg Austrian self-identity. It was already operational in 1918, not something emerging only in the 1930s or during World War II (both announced and "endorsed" by the Allies' Moscow Declaration of 1943), and continued to be vitally important well into the 1960s. In altered forms, it is still alive in some sectors of the Austrian population today. This essay aims to establish the starting point of the long arc of the twentieth century Austrian identity built on this leitmotif.[1] My colleagues on the forum will offer their respective empirical cases to exam its later iterations and development.

In 1918, the Austrian Republic emerged in the ruins of the Habsburg Monarchy. It is significant that the revolution, arguably, occurred by default: in terms of political legitimacy, there was nothing left from the old Habsburg structure; a revolution was the only option. As such, the republic had no explosive or heroic beginning with which to build a consensus-enabling foundational myth;[2] instead, the new political culture was threatened by crises on multiple fronts from the very beginning. One of the pressing issues was how to respond to the subsistence crisis embodied in a dramatic fashion by the so-called war victims.

1   For historical analysis of the Austrian identity in the twentieth century, Gerald Stourzh's *Vom Reich zur Republik. Studien zum Österreichbewusstsein im 20. Jahrhundert* (Vienna: Edition Atelier, 1990) and Ernst Bruckmüller's *Nation Österreich. Kuturelles Bewußtsein und gesellschaft-politische Prozesse*, 2nd ed. (Vienna: Böhlau, 1996) are still invaluable.
2   On the difficult or even reluctant attempts to find such solidarity myths and symbols, see Ernst Hanisch, "Politische Symbole und Gedächtnisorte," in Emmerich Tálos et al., eds., *Handbuch des Politischen Systems Österreichs: Erste Republik,1918–1933* (Vienna: Manz, 1995), 421–430. See also Erin Hochman, *Imagining a Greater Germany: Republican Nationalism and the Idea of Anschluss* (Ithaca: Cornell University Press, 2016), esp. 68–87 (the national/state anthem debate) and 107–130 (the meanings and representations of 12 November).

Who was a "war victim" in this context? Since the interwar period, the term "war victim (*Kriegsopfer*)" refers to people who were the most directly impacted by wars in which Austrians were direct participants. Soldiers disabled by war service, war widows and orphans, and other dependents of dead soldiers were called war victims; these people organized themselves in large and small war victim associations.

This usage was enshrined in the law that has been in force since the late 1940s: the War Victim Provision Law (*Kriegsopferversorgungsgesetz*, KOVG, BGBl. 152/1957 based on KOVG, 197/1949). But the term "war victim" was not the legal category used in the most important pieces of welfare legislation introduced at the beginning of the First Republic. In fact, the laws from 1919 and 1920 were written with the more technical, but also more graphic terms: war-damaged persons (*Kriegsbeschädigte*) and surviving dependents (*Kriegshinterbliebene*). Officials and the authorities often used the historical term "war invalids" (*Kriegsinvalide*) to refer to disabled veterans too. The term "war victim" was brought up occasionally in the early years of the First Republic, but it only gained prominence after the mid-1920s. This relatively late development can be seen in a 1925 list of major war victim organizations prepared by the Ministry of Social Administration. Out of the fourteen named organizations, only two used the term "victim" in their names, and neither of the two was singled out by the ministry as one of the four more important and larger organizations.[3]

The term "war victim" became more commonly used, and then the standard term of self-identification, after the late-1920s. Based on the names of identifiable war invalid organizations large and small, as well as the titles of their publications, the early adopters of the term "war victim" as the standard self-identification, and hence a form of social identity, were probably from the Catholic-conservative milieu. After years of being overshadowed by the Social Democrats in organizing war victims, the Christian Socials relaunched their effort in 1924. The revamped group was given a new name, *Reichsbund der Kriegsopfer Oesterreichs*, and its publication was called *Oesterreichs Kriegsopfer.*[4] After the February 1934 civil war, when Major Emil Fey's *Heimwehr* cadres took over the largest war victim

---

3   Österreichisches Staatsarchiv (ÖStA) Archiv der Republik (AdR) Bundesministerium für soziale Verwaltung (BMfsV) Kriegsbeschädigten-Fürsorge (KBF) Karton (K) 1437 50651/1925. For an overview and useful statistical picture of organized war victims during the First Republic, see Verena Pawlowsky and Harald Wendelin, *Die Wunde des Staates: Kriegsopfer und Sozialstaat in Österreich, 1914–1938* (Vienna: Böhlau, 2015), 475–519.

4   With a self-reported membership of approximately 23,000, it was still much smaller than the Social Democrats-friendly Zentralverband, whose federated organizations claimed to represent around 170,000 members. See AdR BMfsV KBF K1426 24063/1924 (Reichsbund)and K1428 73525/1924 (Zentralverband).

organization, *Zentralverband der Landesorganisationen der Kriegsinvaliden und Kriegshinterbliebenen Oesterreichs* and its provincial affiliates, and attempted to transform it into an all-encompassing, nationalist-fascist war victim organization, they renamed the former Social Democratic organization with the by then quite natural choice of Österreichischer Kriegsopferverband,[5] which published the now appropriately retitled *Österreichische Kriegsopfer-Zeitung*.

The replacement of the technical names—the war-damaged person—with a more emotionally and symbolically charged, even semi-religious concept of "victim" added the connotations of sacrifice, innocence, or being wronged by others' actions that led to loss or suffering beyond one's control. This change in terminology signaled an important development: the ongoing struggle over the Austrian identity in the First Republic, or even just a stable way to identify the collective self of the Alpine republic, had found victimhood as an integral part of its vocabulary by mid- to late-1920s.

However, the origin of victimhood self-identification can be traced to an even earlier point: the very beginning of the First Republic.[6] Before the term "war victim" became the common currency, there were already a multitude of identity discourses based on the losses and suffering of "war victims," or on a more general collective victimization by the war. These discourses were deployed to inspire activism and political mobilization, and to bestow the new republican government and its policies with the legitimacy they desperately needed in the earliest post-Habsburg days. They were also used to describe and express the contemporaries' views of post-Habsburg Austria. The April 1919 Austrian parliamentary debate about the proposed new war invalid and surviving dependent provision law gives us two revealing instances of such a development.

First, the parliamentary committee on social affairs proposed to add "female citizens (*Staatsbürgerinnen*)" to the draft law's First Article, which defines the law's intended beneficiaries. The committee explained that they wanted to include all those whose health suffered because of war service

5   ÖStA AdR Bundeskanzleramt (BKA)/allgem. Inneres 15/3 K2449 336069/1935, 335465/1935; Österreichische Kriegsopfer-Zeitung, 1 May 1934. The Christian Social *Reichsbund* called Major Fey's push for an all-inclusive *Einheitsverband* an unprecedented challenge in "*Urteilet selbst!*" *Oesterreichs Kriegsopfer. Organ des Reichsbundes der Kriegsopfer Oesterreichs*, March-April 1934, 1–2.

6   This line of suffering-based identity-making and community boundary-drawing can be seen as continuing the wartime development examined in Maureen Healy's path-breaking *Vienna and the Fall of the Habsburg Empire: Total War and Everyday Life in World War I* (Cambridge: Cambridge University Press, 2004), esp. 43–86, where she discusses the fleeting, unstable, but powerful community of hungry citizen-consumers that worried the authorities.

of all kinds, including nurses, female workers employed by the militarized industries, and other caregivers, and not merely "men who participated in war or their widows and orphans."[7] This change was later incorporated into the finalized Invalid Compensation Law (*Invalidenentschädigungsgesetz*, IEG, StGBl. 245/1919) of 25 April 1919. The all-inclusive approach of the new law had an immediate effect: organized war victims began to enthusiastically recruit women to join their ranks. The early, spontaneous organizing of invalids had always involved women's participation and active contribution. But the new law spurred the main organization at the time, the *Zentralverband*, to explicitly court women and even change its name, adding "*Kriegsbeschädigtenvereinigung der Invaliden, Witwen, und Waisen*" as the subtitle to the original male veteran-centered "*Zentralverband der deutschösterreichischen Kriegsbeschädigten.*"[8]

Furthermore, the catch-all approach of the new law marked a clear departure from the previous conceptual and legal separation of disabled veterans and surviving dependents. The categories of the war damaged/invalids (*Kriegsbeschädigten/Invaliden*) and surviving dependents (*Kriegshinterbliebene*) had always been clearly demarcated in the Austrian laws and administrative practices.[9] Although the broad category of "war victim" would not become popular for a few more years, and then it would be years more for it to become the standard terminology, the new parliament (the Constituent National Assembly in 1919) had consciously and purposefully imagined an all-inclusive community of beneficiaries. With many kinds of victims of war—man and woman, young and old, direct participants and dependents, soldiers, caregivers and workers, wounded in battles and on the home front—united under the same legal and administrative framework, a national community of sufferers of the war's most direct consequences—death and disabilities—was born.

Secondly, in debating the draft, the major political parties articulated their respective discourses on victimhood in justifying their positions. Though their war victimhood discourses were ostensibly about invalids and dependents, these were at the same time expressions of their views of the situation the new republic and its citizens were facing.

Speaking on behalf of the Christian Socials, Josef Aigner constructed a discourse of tragic heroism and demanded that due respect and thanks to

---

7   *Stenographische Protokolle der Konstituierenden Nationalversammlung für Deutschösterreich*, 10. Sitzung, 24 April 1919, 262.
8   ÖStA AdR BMfsV KBF K1377 21400/1919 (28 July 1919) in 29603/1920.
9   For example, the 1875 law (RGBl. 158/1875) only covered invalid veterans, and the 1880s laws (RGBl. 70/1880 and 41/1887) were specifically intended for widows, orphans, and other surviving dependents.

be given to war invalids. It was a grave mistake, argued Aigner, to see war invalids "not as heroes, but martyrs, and martyrs only," as Social Democrats and other pacifists allegedly did. Aigner claimed that he would leave the meaning of the war to "world history" and God, but he felt obligated to denounce the Social Democrats and others who portrayed the war and sacrifices as meaningless, in vain, or a mistake. The Austrian soldiers fought for their "home and hearth, wives and children, and their homeland"; these men were not merely martyrs, because they heroically fought for something precious and meaningful between 1914 to 1918; now their mothers and wives sacrificed in their wake. Aigner's tragic heroism discourse had its core in framing the war as principled sacrifice, but the defeat and physical losses were inseparable from it. Moreover, Aigner's tragic heroism discourse assumed that invalids' and widows' losses were the result of something beyond their control. The very fact that they were the victims—the blameless sacrificers—of external, overwhelming forces and insurmountable circumstances made them heroes. What the republic and the Austrians should do, then, was to let their moral obligations lead them and provide for these dutiful hero-sufferers.

Even more revealing was a vivid image Aigner painted of the new republican Austria: "The state itself is a war invalid. It no longer has straight and healthy limbs. Its internal and external organs are in disarray."[10] Just like its invalids and widows, the new Austria was a helpless and innocent victim, even if (or especially because) it was principled and sacrifice-ready. Aigner argued that the new provision law would be the republic's own principled sacrifice in a time of desperate shortages.

On the side of the Social Democrats, Anton Hölzl presented a more explicit victim discourse to talk about the origin and the necessary compensation for the invalids and surviving dependents. Countering Aigner, Hölzl argued that these people did not sacrifice for noble principles or lofty duties. They were the victims of the very tangible material interests of others, and they sacrificed for the "so-called glorious dynasty and insatiable imperialist power interests peddled by willing hacks."[11] It was "the governments' and the ruling classes' warmongering" that was responsible for "people's delusions, when they went to war as if going to play or dance." Many thus became the victims of "dynastic and imperialist interests" and should be characterized as such.[12] Hölzl actually used the term "war victims" in his

---

10 *Stenographische Protokolle der Konstituierenden Nationalversammlung für Deutschösterreich*, 10. Sitzung, 24. 4. 1919, 264–265.
11 *Stenographische Protokolle der Konstituierenden Nationalversammlung für Deutschösterreich*, 11. Sitzung, 25. 4. 1919, 275.
12 Ibid., 274.

parliamentary speech to underline his point that the masses' suffering and losses were not about heroism; it was a matter of victimhood at the hands of the oppressive classes and the old regimes.

In the Social Democratic victim discourse, building the republic to embody a new and different polity would repair the wrongs and redeem victimhood. The new law would usher in a new age of democratic decision-making through participatory mechanisms like the new invalid compensation commissions. Moreover, providing for war victims would become a "social obligation" in the new republic: "The entire nation has the duty to help and is willing to help." Unlike wartime care provision, the new system would no longer be a mix of private and semi-official charity work that turned war victims into objects of "vainglorious charity" and poor relief.[13] It was based on rights and duties of a socially-minded community of citizens. Hölzl's victimhood discourse turned suffering and losses into a stepping stone to a different, better, and democratic community—whether it was the small rump Austria or some kind of socialist Anschluss with Germany. Victimhood was lamentable, but it was also a key opportunity to usher in a better, brighter future.

It is worth noting that the main parliamentary parties had no major disagreement on the draft law itself, and all parties agreed that the law should be adopted as soon as possible. In fact, the Invalid Compensation Law was passed unanimously on 25 April. Dissenting views on the draft law's individual points, such as Christian Socials' hesitation about treating common law wives and formally married wives exactly the same in terms of benefits eligibility, were raised but no revisions were seriously considered. The strong consensus turned the debate on a quite technical piece of legislation into a forum where different political forces explored and expressed their views on the recent past as well as the future of the new Austria—even if they may not see a long-term future in an independent Austria (the draft law itself contains an article, §59, referring to the expected Anschluss). Importantly, despite quite different meanings attached to the war and to the creation of the rump Austrian Republic, victimhood—even if it was construed and defined differently—was a common theme embedded and indispensable in their respective discourses about the recent past, the present, and the future.[14]

---

13 Ibid.
14 For an insightful analysis of conflicting meanings of "wartime sacrifice" in interwar Austria, see Catherine Edgecombe and Maureen Healy, "Competing Interpretations of Sacrifice in the Postwar Austrian Republic," in Mark Cornwall and John Paul Newmanm, eds., *Sacrifice and Rebirth: The Legacy of the Last Hapsburg War* (New York: Berghahn, 2016), 15-34.

Whether it was explicitly used or not, the term "victim" and the victim discourses played a key role in producing social and political self-understandings for both those who were and those who were not disabled veterans, widows, or orphans in the First Republic. Aigner's Christian Social "invalid state" metaphor placed Austria and the post-Habsburg (German-) Austrians in the category of innocent tragic heroes. The Austro-Germans of the Alpine Republic did not have to worry about their responsibility or even guilt in the carnage of the First World War;[15] Austria's helplessness in the face of the victorious powers, exemplified by the Treaty of St. Germaine, only strengthened this sense of being the innocent victims of outside and superior forces. The Catholic-conservative milieu would later play up this self-image of Austria even within a revived militarism in both popular and political cultures, when the Habsburg military legacies were manipulated under Engelbert Dollfuß and Kurt Schuschnigg.[16] Dollfuß's own assassination, moreover, gave this dutiful-but-innocent victim self-understanding a concrete example and a precious reenactment; the Schuschnigg regime quickly promoted a state cult of the murdered chancellor, who was styled as the heroic victim of yet another superior outside force (Nazism).[17] The Social Democratic victim discourse worked differently. It wiped clean the slate and used the victimhood as the beginning of a liberated new future—a socialist future would raise the victims to the status of founding heroes for a new world. But this phoenix-like rebirth was still premised on first being the victim of a class system and aggressive capitalism.

This short reflection on the close connection between the twentieth century Austrian identity and war victimhood should end with the 1949/1957 war victim welfare law, which in a revised version is still in effect today. This law practically treated those who fought for the Habsburg Monarchy, the Austrian Republic, and the Third Reich (and against all sorts of opponents)

---

15   For examples of war atrocities committed by the Habsburg forces, Jonathan Gumz, *The Resurrection and Collapse of Empire in Habsburg Serbia, 1914–1918* (Cambridge: Cambridge University Press, 2009) and Hannes Leidinger et al., *Habsburgs schmutziger Krieg: Ermittlungen zur österreichisch-ungarischen Kriegsführung 1914–1918* (St. Pölten: Residenz Verlag, 2014) offer more recent studies. The postwar interest in investigating and prosecuting Habsburg army officers for wartime disasters and for abuses of their soldiers and/or civilians, under the rubric of "dereliction of duty (*Pflichtverletzungen*)," faded rather quickly, not to mention the always existing resistance to such efforts by various state agencies, career officials, and some party politicians. Wolfgang Doppelbauer, *Zum Elend noch die Schande: das altösterreichische Offizierskorps am Beginn der Republik* (Vienna: Österreichischer Bundesverlag, 1988), 228–232, 236–238, 282–283.

16   On the revival of militarism in interwar Austria see, for example, Ernst Hanisch, "Die Rückkehr des Kriegers," *Transit. Europäische Revue* 16 (1999), 108–124.

17   On the cult of Dollfuß, see Lucile Dreidemy, *Der Dollfuß-Mythos. Eine Biographie des Posthumen* (Vienna: Böhlau, 2014), 61–154.

in the same way in its provisions of services and compensation.[18] The Austrians who were ideologically irreconcilable foes or even deadly enemies in armed struggles may have been united, rather matter-of-factly and seemingly without much consternation, as beneficiaries of this ecumenical piece of welfare legislation. Was this development a coincidence? I would venture to say no. Austrians may not consciously engage in a "suffering Olympics" (Antony Polonsky's term, used in another context) with other Europeans. But war victimhood provided (and still provides) a ready common ground to weld together fragmented and often conflicting identities and memories. After the Anschluss and World War II, sweeping the inconvenient National Socialist associations under the all-encompassing war victimhood rug seemed to be more reasonable than ever as a way to move forward as a political community; a war victim identity as national identity was already in existence since the previous World War and needed only some expansion to serve the dominant national self-understanding. The ecumenical war victim welfare legislation, then, reflected and solidified this post-1945 development. After all, when it came to the twentieth century wars, Austrians of all political and ideological stripes could always claim to be victims.

---

18   Bundesgesetz vom 14. Juli 1949 über die Versorgung der Kriegsbeschädigten und Hinterbliebenen (Kriegsopferversorgungsgesetz-KOVG), BGBl 197/1949, §1.

Democracy's Children:
Psychoanalysis, the Great War,
and the Creatural Subject of the *Zwischenkriegszeit*

Phillip J. Henry

In the wake of the First World War, Vienna and its environs were the site of a wide range of experiments in the collective upbringing and group socialization of children and adolescents. The youth colonies, children's homes, and experimental schools that flourished in this context represented ambitious pedagogical, welfarist, and hygienic responses to the devastating effects of the conflict on the youngest and most vulnerable members of society. They also, however, sought to respond to a disruption of tradition-al modes of education and a disconcerting upsurge in youth delinquency over the course of the war, phenomena closely linked, in the eyes of many observers, to an undermining of patriarchal authority in both the family and the state.[1] In place of the hierarchical relationships that characterized traditional *Erziehung*, the organizers (and, in a qualified sense, leaders) of these experiments sought to fashion new forms of educational authority, ones suitable for a mass democratic age. Often housed in buildings taken over from the old regime and redolent of bygone imperial authority—army barracks, military hospitals, refugee camps, even the imperial palace at Schönbrunn—such experiments gave striking symbolic expression to the break with political, social, and cultural traditions brought about by the postwar revolutions. As representatives of the old order moved out, chil-dren and adolescents moved in, signifying by their presence the centrality of youth to the democratic order that emerged in the war's aftermath.[2]

---

1   On this subject, see especially Andrew Donson, *Youth in the Fatherless Land: War Pedagogy, Nationalism, and Authority in Germany, 1914–1918* (Cambridge: Harvard University Press, 2010), 137-53 and Maureen Healy, *Vienna and the Fall of the Habsburg Empire: Total War and Everyday Life in World War I* (New York: Cambridge University Press, 2007), 258–99.

2   Two such undertakings—Siegfried Bernfeld's socialist-Zionist children's home and August Aichhorn's *Fürsorgeerziehungsanstalten* (both discussed below)—would have enormous influence on interwar psychoanalysis, yet both were overshadowed in postwar Austria by a massive educational colony that emerged at Schönbrunn Palace. Organized by Social Democratic educators and run by the young socialist pedagogue Otto Felix Kanitz, the *"Das 'rote' Schönbrunn"* was the successor to a series of wartime relief actions organized by the educational associations of the party and to a Social Democratic *"Kinderrepublik"* established [Continued on following page]

In 1925, in a preface to a study of one such experiment, August Aichhorn's *Verwahrloste Jugend: Die Psychoanalyse in der Fürsorgeerziehung*, Sigmund Freud announced that the child had become "the main subject of psychoanalytic research," displacing "the neurotics on whom its studies began."[3] For Freud, Aichhorn's attempt to theorize youth delinquency with the help of psychoanalysis represented a welcome indication of the expanding scope and influence of his science.[4] Psychoanalysis, he wrote, "has shown how the child lives on, almost unchanged," in certain adult characters and has traced its fraught development to mature, encultured subjectivity. It was thus "no wonder," he wrote, "if an expectation has arisen that psycho-analytic concern with children will benefit the work of education, whose aim it is to guide and assist children on their forward path and to shield them from going astray." Indeed, "none of the applications of psycho-analysis has excited so much interest and aroused so many hopes, and none, consequently, has attracted so many capable workers, as its use in the theory and practice of education."[5]

Given that the child and its prolonged and difficult enculturation had long occupied a privileged place in psychoanalytic thought, the professional development that Freud described could be understood as part of a gradual and natural expansion of the disciplinary purview of his science. Yet the notion that the turn to the child and the ever-increasing application of

---

[Footnote 2, continued] in early 1919 at a refugee camp at Gmünd. Over the same period, a youth commune emerged at the former military barracks at Grinzing on the outskirts of Vienna—one that, in the volatile and often bewildering postwar political landscape, would play host for a time to György Lukács, Karl Popper, and Friedrich Hayek. At the heart of the radical ferment of the Grinzing colony was a group of youth, organized in the *sozialistische Mittelschüler* movement, who drew inspiration from Bernfeld's experiment and from a series of youth homes and colonies established by the pedagogue and philanthropist Eugenie Schwarzwald over the last years of the war. Their own educational undertakings would eventually, after a period of communist opposition, be integrated into the educational work of the Social Democratic party. On the *sozialistische Mittelschülerbewegung* see Friedrich Scheu, *Ein Band der Freundschaft. Schwarzwald-Kreis und Entstehung der Vereinigung sozialistischer Mittelschüler* (Vienna: Böhlau, 1985). See also Malachi Haim Hacohen's excellent biography, *Karl Popper, the Formative Years, 1902–1945: Politics and Philosophy in Interwar Vienna* (New York: Cambridge University Press, 2000); Georg Tidl, *Die sozialistischen Mittelschüler Österreichs von 1918 bis 1938* (Vienna: Österreichische Bundesverlag, 1977); Heinz Weiss, *Das rote Schönbrunn. Der Schönbrunner Kreis und die Reformpädagogik der Schönbrunner Schule* (Vienna: Echomedia, 2008).

3   Sigmund Freud, "Geleitwort zu *Verwahrloste Jugend*," (1925) in Freud, *Gesammelte Werke: Chronologisch Geordnet* (hereafter *GW*), 18 vols., ed. Anna Freud et al. (Frankfurt a. M., 1961–83), 12: 565. Unless otherwise noted, all translations of Freud's works are from *The Standard Edition of the Complete Works of Sigmund Freud*, 24 vols., ed. James Strachey et al. (London, 1953–74).

4   August Aichhorn, *Verwahrloste Jugend. Die Psychoanalyse in der Fürsorgeerziehung* (Leipzig, 1925).

5   Freud, "Geleitwort," 565.

psychoanalysis to education was part of a seamless arc in the evolution of Freudianism—a reading Freud himself sought to maintain—glosses over the profound upheavals that, in fact, precipitated this shift. Read against the backdrop of war and revolution—events that marked both traumatic ruptures and opened up new fields of experimentation—Freud's statement that the child had become the main subject of psychoanalysis speaks not to a smooth and continuous professional growth but rather to a profound shift in the way psychoanalysts thought about the selves they confronted. What I want to argue in what follows is that at the heart of psychoanalytic thought over these years was a far-reaching process of rethinking selfhood and sociality for a new era, one in which unprecedented levels of victimization went hand in hand with new possibilities for the remaking of social life and where both appeared to authorize the construction of new forms of educational and therapeutic authority. As a mass of children (and supposedly childlike masses) were set free of the traditional bonds of authority that constituted the old order, the disruptions of war and revolution prompted a fundamental revision of analytic thought and practice that would set the Freudian movement on a new course for the postwar era.

To begin to grasp the ramifications of this shift, it is worth considering the opening pages of the seminal text of the postwar revision of psychoanalytic theory, Freud's 1920 *Beyond the Pleasure Principle*. The point of departure for Freud's metapsychological speculations was a simple, if unsettling, question: why is the mind compelled to revisit and relive experiences of an unpleasurable kind? The question was an especially difficult one for a theory that had previously identified the pursuit of pleasure and avoidance of unpleasure (*Unlust*, the consequence of an unrelieved build-up of tension in the psyche) as the governing principle of mental functioning. While most sources of unpleasure posed no substantive challenge to the so-called pleasure principle, "the investigation of the mental reaction to external danger" raised new problems for the Freudian conception of the psychical apparatus. In particular, in the "traumatic neuroses" produced by the "terrible war that has just ended," Freud saw himself confronted with a category of neurotics whose fixation on traumatic experiences appeared to contravene the pleasure principle and undercut the theory of the neuroses it informed.[6] In attempting to make sense of these afflictions, Freud was led to consider what lay beyond, and indeed before, the pleasure principle: namely, the attempts of the primitive psychical apparatus to bind the invasive quantities of stimuli that threatened to overwhelm it.

To understand the compulsion of neurotic soldiers to return to the precipitating cause of their affliction and repeat this experience in their

---

6   Sigmund Freud, "Jenseits des Lustprinzips," *GW* 13(1920): 8–9.

dreams, Freud felt it necessary to "leave the dark and dismal subject of the traumatic neuroses and to pass on to examine" the operations of the mental apparatus in one of its "earliest *normal* activities": that of children's play.[7] Yet in turning from adult war neurotics to children, Freud was, in fact, recapitulating a move that his friend and follower Sándor Ferenczi had made in his contribution to the theorization of the war neuroses the previous year. In his essay, Ferenczi drew a connection between the symptoms of traumatized soldiers and the gestures of frightened infants; speculating further, he contended that both represented "atavistic reversions" to modes of reaction passed down from evolutionary prehistory.[8] By tracing an arc that led from adult neurotics to children and, in fact, *beyond*—in Ferenczi's case, to frightened infant primates and in Freud's to the most rudimentary form of organic life ("an undifferentiated vesicle of substance [...] susceptible to stimulation")[9]—psychoanalytic thought appeared to open onto the possibility of an almost limitless capacity for regression, one that resonated with fears of a potentially irrevocable collapse of civilization into infantilism and barbarity.[10] As soldiers became infants recapitulating adaptive behaviors from evolutionary prehistory, it seemed that the war had revealed a retrogressive tendency to organic life in which highly organized forms were in constant danger of sliding back into a pre-individual, pre-linguistic, creatural existence.

The perspective on neurotic suffering that Freud and Ferenczi developed in these writings was, in fact, anticipated by the contributions to the theorization of the war neuroses by Ernst Simmel, a psychiatrist who turned to Freudian thought during the war. In Simmel's writings, it was the vulnerability of an ego exposed to overwhelming violence from without and unmanageable affects from within that dominated the clinical picture, all but displacing the conflict between sexual desire and repression at the heart of the classical psychoanalytic etiology of the neuroses. "One must have experienced the war occurrences for one's self," Simmel wrote, or their recapitulation in analytic-cathartic hypnosis in order to understand what onslaughts the mental life of a man is exposed to: who, after receiving

---

7   Freud, "Jenseits des Lustprinzips," 11 (emphasis in original).
8   Sándor Ferenczi, "Die Psychoanalyse der Kriegsneurosen," in *Zur Psychoanalyse der Kriegsneurosen* (Leipzig, 1919), 30.
9   Freud, "Jenseits des Lustprinzips," 25.
10   For one striking illustration, see Ferenczi's letter to Freud from 7 November 1918 in which he alludes to the ominous possibility of the "collapse of the entire civilization of the world" and to the dawning of "an epoch of brutalization and infantilism" in the event that Bolshevism were to have its way in central Europe. In *Sigmund Freud-Sàndor Ferenczi: Briefwechsel*, vol 2, part 2, 1917–1919, ed. Eva Brabant, Ernst Falzeder, and Patrizia Giampieri-Deutsch (Vienna, 1996), 183.

multiple wounds, must return to the field; is separated from his own during
important family events for an unforeseeable time; finds himself exposed
irretrievably to that murderous monster, the tank or to an enemy gas attack
rolling toward him; who, after being buried and wounded in a direct hit by
a grenade, must lay, often for hours or days at a time, under the gory, muti-
lated bodies of his friends; and who, his self-respect badly injured by unjust
and cruel superiors, themselves dominated by complexes, must nonetheless
remain silent and allow himself to be overwhelmed by the fact that, as an
individual, he counts for nothing and is only an inconsequential component
of the mass.[11] Exposed to intrusive forces, humiliated by his superiors, and
forced to repress the violent affects within him, the rank-and-file soldier
experienced the war in the position of a vulnerable child, only now as a
child within a mass.[12]

Beyond the confrontation with the war neuroses and the problems such
disorders raised for Freudian thought, the war dramatically transformed the
social context in which analytic therapy operated. Well before the revolution that marked the war's end, when Freud announced bitterly that "the
Habsburgs have left behind nothing but a pile of crap," total war had precipitated a large-scale collapse of Viennese society, one that was especially
traumatic for the *Bildungsbürgertum* to which Freud belonged.[13] By eroding
the social barriers and undermining the forms of distinction that members
of this class had relied upon to preserve their distance from the masses, the
war displaced Freud and his fellow *Bildungsbürger* into a new, disconcerting
proximity to proletarian existence.[14] If "classical" psychoanalysis had reaf-
firmed the personal distinctiveness and independence of the ethically "valuable" and cultivated members of Freud's own class, the fear of sinking into the

11   Ernst Simmel, "Zweites Korreferat," *Zur Psychoanalyse der Kriegsneurosen*,
42–60 (here 45). Simmel's report built off his earlier monograph *Kriegsneurosen und
'Psychisches Trauma'. Ihre gegenseitige Beziehung, dargestellt auf Grund psychoanalytischer,
hypnotischer Studien* (Leipzig, 1918), a work that Freud eagerly recommended to his
closest followers.
12   The view that the traumatic experiences of war unleashed a process of regression that
reduced adult men to children was, of course, far from unique to Freudians. To quote merely
one contemporary, the British army diarist, Garfield Powell, writing during the Somme
offensive, "Shell shock! Do they know what it means? Men become like weak children,
crying and waving their arms madly, clinging to the nearest man and praying not to be left
alone." Quoted in Modris Eksteins, *Rites of Spring: The Great War and the Birth of the Modern
Age* (Boston: Houghton Mifflin, 1989), 173.
13   Freud to Ferenczi, 17 November 1918, in *Briefwechsel 2/2*, 186.
14   John W. Boyer, *Culture and Political Crisis in Vienna: Christian Socialism in Power, 1897–
1918* (Chicago: University of Chicago Press, 1995), 425. On the collapse of Viennese society, see
Healy's *Vienna and the Fall of the Habsburg Empire*. On the anxieties of the *Bildungsbürgertum*
amid total war and revolution, see also Martin Geyer, *Verkehrte Welt. Revolution, Inflation und
Moderne, München 1914–1924* (Göttingen: Vandenhoeck & Ruprecht, 1998).

proletariat unleashed in the *Bildungsbürgertum* by the rampant inflation and dire material shortages of the war ("all one's energy," Freud wrote, "is required to maintain one's economic level") effectively demanded a rethinking of the means and ends of analytic therapy.[15] Faced with a disintegrating social order and with subjects who resembled less the autonomous bourgeois individuals of "classical" analysis than vulnerable constituents of the masses, Freud was impelled to recast the liberal politics of psychoanalysis and to fashion new forms of analytic authority for the new era.

"One must proceed differently," Freud acknowledged in 1918.[16] While only the previous year, he had insisted that it was "only in the case of some very youthful or quite helpless or unstable individuals" that psychoanalysts were "unable to put the desired limitation of our role into effect" and compelled "to combine the function of a doctor and an educator," the situation had been radically reversed by war's end: "*Even with the majority* [italics mine]," Freud conceded, "occasions now and then arise in which the physician is bound to take up the position of teacher and mentor [*Erzieher und Ratgeber*]."[17] The exception had become the rule. As the childlike and vulnerable subjects at the margins of prewar psychoanalysis became a new norm, the limits that constrained the exercise of authority in "classical" psychoanalysis—limits that reflected a respect for the individuality and autonomy of the patient—came to appear impediments to the effective exercise of analytic therapy amid the disorder that marked the war's end. Reconstructing both damaged psyches and a collapsed social order required a new conception of psychoanalysis, one that Freud described as "active" and pedagogical in its exercise. In the post-classical vision he outlined in 1918, psychoanalysis would both mold observable behaviors, in order to restore social stability by facilitating re-adaptation to social demands and shore-up fragile egos tasked with resisting the overwhelming forces in their environment.[18]

---

15   Freud to Karl Abraham, 1 December 1919, in *Sigmund Freud – Karl Abraham. Briefe, 1907–1926*, ed. Hilda C. Abraham and Ernst L. Freud (Frankfurt am Main, 1965), 278. For the clearest articulation of the "classical" model of analytic therapy, see Freud, "Über Psychotherapie," *GW* 5 (1904/05): 13–26. See also Sarah Winter, *Freud and the Institution of Psychoanalytic Knowledge* (Stanford: Stanford University Press, 1999) and José Brunner, *Freud and the Politics of Psychoanalysis* (Cambridge, MA: Blackwell, 1995).

16   Freud, "Wege der psychoanalytischen Therapie," *GW* XII (1918): 181–194 (here 191). A more extensive discussion of this address can be found in Phillip J. Henry, "Recasting Bourgeois Psychoanalysis: Education, Authority, and the Politics of Analytic Therapy in the Freudian Revision of 1918," *Modern Intellectual History* (forthcoming), published online 18 October 2017.

17   Freud, "Vorlesungen zur Einführung in der Psychoanalyse," *GW* 11 (1916/17): 450 and Freud, "Wege der psychoanalytischen Therapie," 190 (emphasis added).

18   Freud, "Wege der psychoanalytischen Therapie," 185, 192–193.

In the wake of the war, Freud's rudimentary vision for a post-classical analytic therapy would be taken up by his followers—especially Sàndor Ferenczi and Wilhelm Reich—who sought to embrace ever-wider classes of sufferers by modifying analytic technique.[19] At the heart of these different procedures was a new conception of the sources of psychic suffering. If formerly pride of place in the Freudian etiology of the neuroses had gone to the excessive curtailment of sexuality in the course of upbringing and enculturation, now it appeared that the symptoms generated by strict upbringing were reflections merely of "good bourgeois'" neuroses, in Wilhelm Reich's words. Far more troubling than the neurotic symptoms generated by a bourgeois upbringing, Reich argued, were the profoundly disordered personality structures of the so-called "impulsive characters" he aimed to treat—patients whose disorders were transparent testimonies to the violence of their environment. Only an analytic therapy that made thorough use of educational procedures would be capable of reaching such patients, Reich averred.[20] As the pedagogical therapeutic techniques developed by Reich, Ferenczi, Anna Freud, and August Aichhorn illustrated, the war had altered the very status of education in psychoanalytic thought: previously a source of neurotic suffering ("nowhere else have civilization and education done so much harm" as in the sexual lives of neurotics, Sigmund Freud wrote in 1905), *Erziehung* now figured as a vital means of reconstructing a devastated social fabric and restoring a degree of equilibrium to profoundly disordered psyches.[21]

Social collapse, collective regression, and extreme vulnerability were entwined in postwar psychoanalytic thought in ways that demanded a rethinking of the fundamental principles of analytic therapy. At base, however, the refashioning of psychoanalysis that accompanied attempts to expand its social reach reflected a new conception of both selfhood and sociality in Freudian thought, one perhaps best captured in the emerging field of psychoanalytic social theory. In 1919, at the very moment that the

---

19 See especially, Sándor Ferenczi, "Weiterer Ausbau der 'aktiven Technik,'" in *Bausteine zur Psychoanalyse. Band 2. Praxis* (Bern 1984 [1921]), 62–86; Sàndor Ferenczi and Otto Rank, *Entwicklungsziele der Psychoanalyse. Zur Wechselbeziehung von Theorie und Praxis* (Leipzig, 1924); Wilhelm Reich, *Der triebhafte Charakter. Eine psychoanalytische Studie zur Pathologie des Ich* (Leipzig, 1925); and Wilhelm Reich, *Charakteranalyse. Technik und Grundlagen für Studierende und praktizierende Analytiker* (Vienna, 1933).

20 Reich, *Der triebhafte Charakter*, 16, 125.

21 Freud, "Über Psychotherapie," 25. In addition to the works by Ferenczi and Reich cited above, educational measures were central to the therapeutic technique developed by Anna Freud in her psychoanalytic work with children. See Anna Freud, *Einführung in der Technik der Kinderanalyse. Vier Vorträge am Lehrinstitut der Wiener Psychoanalytischen Vereinigung* (Vienna, 1927). Like Reich, Anna Freud was strongly influenced by the pedagogical therapy that Aichhorn first elaborated in his "Über die Erziehung in Besserungsanstalten," *Imago. Zeitschrift für Anwendung der Psychoanalyse* 9/2 (1923): 189–221.

Viennese analyst Paul Federn discerned the emergence of what he termed a "fatherless society" in an essay on the psychology of the revolution, the socialist-Zionist youth movement leader (and soon to be psychoanalyst) Siegfried Bernfeld was laying the foundations for an experiment in collective education that would encompass hundreds of orphaned Jewish refugees.[22] Like Aichhorn's undertaking, Bernfeld's *Kinderheim Baumgarten* implemented what might be termed a practical mass psychology in its attempt to fashion new forms of educational authority for the nascent democratic era. Suspended between the unruly masses of youth under their care and the now-vacant position of the patriarchal father, Aichhorn and Bernfeld sought to construct new, more legitimate and effective, modes of *Führertum*.

If the child had become the privileged subject of psychoanalysis over these years, as Freud declared in 1925, it was because all of the selves analysts confronted appeared to be vulnerable and dependent to a degree formerly deemed incompatible with "classical" analytic therapy. Where previously Freud had insisted that practicing analysts "should refuse patients who do not possess a certain level of education [*Bildungsgrad*] and a fairly reliable character," psychoanalytic thought between the wars would revolve around a subject that was almost the antithesis of the cultivated bourgeois individual—namely, a childlike creature of the masses.[23] Orphaned by the revolutionary upheaval and exposed to unprecedented levels of violence, this new subject required care and protection—more importantly, it required education.

The prominence of this new subject in psychoanalytic thought mirrored a number of cultural and intellectual developments that reached well beyond the Freudian movement. As Helmuth Lethen has shown, a new conception of human experience and subjectivity came to the fore over the 1920s in discourses ranging from animal behavior research to theology. The term *Kreatürlichkeit* ("creaturliness"), a neologism of the interwar years, captured a sense of the pitiless exposure of the human subject to overwhelming events. The opposite of the type that Lethen describes as the "cool persona," the creature felt itself "subject to a blind fate"—where the former was securely wrapped in an armored ego, the creature was bit of injurable organic matter that displayed all the credulity and irrationality of

22   Paul Federn, *Zur Psychologie der Revolution. Die vaterlose Gesellschaft* (Leipzig, 1919). Siegfried Bernfeld, *Kinderheim Baumgarten. Bericht über einen ernsthaften Versuch mit neuer Erziehung*, reprinted in *Sozialpädagogik*, ed. Daniel Barth and Ulrich Hermann, vol. 4 of *Siegfried Bernfeld: Werke*, ed. Urich Hermann (Giessen, 2012 [1921]), 9–155.
23   Freud, "Über Psychotherapie," 20–1.

the child in its tendency toward magical thought.[24] Drawing from the same discourse, but offering a somewhat different interpretation, Eric Santner has described the *Kreatur* of interwar thought as a subject exposed to the normative groundlessness of human sociality.[25] In the yawning state of exception that opened up after the war, this groundlessness was apparent as never before. While it would fuel existential anxiety, it would likewise inspire far-reaching attempts to overcome the vacuum of legitimate authority that emerged from the war's destruction.

Psychoanalytic thought exemplified the shift in thinking about selfhood and sociality over the interwar years as well as the turn to education it prompted. While prewar psychoanalysis had focused on subjects whose disorders had emerged within the hothouse confines of the Oedipal family, interwar psychoanalysis was haunted and unsettled by subjects who had been deprived of this sheltering matrix, subjects for whom it was not the constriction, confinement, and curtailment of traditional *Erziehung* but rather, in Reich's words, "the 'breadth' of communication between ego and external world"—the extent of the psyche's exposure to environmental forces—that accounted for the subject's disorders.[26] "Education," Anna Freud would write, "appears to us in a very different light when viewed not from the aspect of neurotic inhibition but, for example, from the aspect of delinquency." "No one had offered the love" (that is, the care and nurturing) necessary for education to really begin.[27] Left outside of culture and exposed to what Sigmund Freud increasingly described as "harsh reality" between the wars—to "the overwhelming and merciless forces of destruction" that "may rage against us" in the external world—such subjects were never able to

---

24   Helmuth Lethen, *Cool Conduct: The Culture of Distance in Weimar Germany* (Berkeley: University of California Press, 2001), 20, 196. Lethen's discussion recalls, of course, not only Freud's vesicle from *Beyond the Pleasure Principle*, but also Walter Benjamin's famous discussion of the destruction of *Erfahrung* in "The Storyteller": "A generation that had gone to school on a horse-drawn streetcar now stood under the open sky in a countryside in which nothing remained unchanged but the clouds, and beneath these clouds, in a field of force of destructive torrents and explosions, was the tiny, fragile human body." In *Illuminations: Essays and Reflections*, ed. Hannah Arendt, trans. Harry Zohn (New York: Schocken Books, 1968 [1936]), 84.

25   Eric Santner, *On Creaturely Life: Rilke, Benjamin, Sebald* (Chicago: University of Chicago Press, 2006), 22.

26   Reich, *Der triebhafte Charakter*, 77.

27   Anna Freud, *Einführung in die Psychoanalyse für Pädagogen. Vier Vorträge* (Bern, 1935 [1930]), 92. Years later, reflecting on her experiences observing patients in a psychiatric ward in the early 1920s, Anna Freud would write, in a similar vein, "you understand the neuroses entirely differently when you consider them against the background of the psychoses." Anna Freud to Eva Landauer, 15 March 1946, quoted in Elizabeth Young-Bruehl, *Anna Freud: A Biography* (New York: Summit Books, 1988), 122.

surmount the earliest stages of development.[28] Yet in the wake of a war that had profoundly unsettled bourgeois society, the question this perspective gave rise to was even broader and more troubling—as Anna Freud, put it, "Why are we all children who need to be held"?[29]

---

28   Sigmund Freud, "Das Unbehagen in der Kultur," *GW* 14 (1930): 434. See also Freud, "Die Frage der Laienanalyse: Unterredungen mit einem Unparteiischen," *GW* 14 (1926): 229: "Nicht wahr, das kleine Lebewesen ist ein recht armseliges, ohnmächtiges Ding gegen die übergewaltige Außenwelt, die voll ist von zerstörenden Einwirkungen."
29   Anna Freud to Eva Rosenfeld, 27 August 1931, in *Anna Freud's Letters to Eva Rosenfeld*, ed. Peter Heller, trans. Mary Weigand (Madison, CT, 1992), 169. It is worth noting that Anna Freud's question followed immediately on a discussion of August Aichhorn's "wonderful" institute.

Victims of Nazi Terror in Vienna: Legally Mandated Assistance and Social Democratic Patronage, 1945–48

Matthew Berg

Beginning in the 1980s and continuing into the 1990s, historians have examined how the *Opfermythos* (victim myth) served as a convenient foundation for postwar Austrian identity.[1] It was embraced by all three political parties and accepted by the victorious powers, despite occupation and denazification. For Austrians, caring for those affected by the war in its immediate aftermath was a non-partisan concern, although they weighed various categories of experience somewhat differently. For instance, officials at the local, provincial, and federal levels in the new Second Republic recognized the breadth and depth of the Austrian and international displaced populations' needs—housing, nourishment, medical care, economic recovery—and worked with the victorious powers and international donors to address them.[2] However, attending to the

---

1 On the Moscow Declaration and both official and informal Austrian references to it, as well as to Austrians as victims after 1945, see Robert H. Keyserlingk, *Austria in World War II: An Anglo-American Dilemma* (Kingston, Ontario: McGill-Queen's University Press, 1988); Günter Bischof, "Die Instrumentalisierung der Moskauer Erklärung nach dem zweiten Weltkrieg," *Zeitgeschichte* 20 (1993): 345–366. Meinrad Ziegler and Waltraud Kannonier-Finster eds., Österreichs Gedächtnis: Über Erinnern und Vergessen der NS-Vergangenheit, 2. Auflage (Vienna-Cologne-Weimar: Böhlau, 1997); Anton Pelinka and Erika Weinzierl eds., *Das große Tabu: Österreichs Umgang mit seiner Vergangenheit*, 2. Auflage (Vienna:Verlag Österreich, 1997); Gerhard Botz, "Geschichte und kollektives Gedächtnis in der Zweiten Republik: 'Opferthese,' 'Lebenslüge' und Geschichtstabu in der Zeitgeschichtsschreibung," and Brigitte Bailer, "Alle waren Opfer: der selektive Umgang mit den Folgen des Nationalsozialismus," in *Inventur 1945/55: Österreich im ersten Jahrzehnt der Zweiten Republik*, ed. Wolfgang Kos and Georg Rigele (Vienna; Sonderzahl, 1996), 51–85, and 181–200, respectively; Siegried Göllner, "'... die erbarmungslose Maschinerie ...': Die Diskreditierung der Entnazifizierungsgesetzgebung im Rahmen der Integration ehemaliger NationalsozialistInnen in das österreichische Opferkollektiv," in *Zeitgeschichte* 36, no. 5 (2009): 324–339.

2 The scholarship treating war-related refugee populations across Europe is a rich one. They include Sharif Gemie et al., *Outcast Europe: Refugees and Relief Workers in an Era of Total War, 1936–48* (London and New York: Continuum, 2012); Jessica Reinisch and Elizabeth White ed., *The Disentanglement of Populations: Migration, Expulsion and Displacement in Post-War Europe, 1944–1949* (Basingstoke, Hampshire, UK and New York: Palgrave Macmillan, 2011); Anna Holian, *Between National Socialism and Soviet Communism: Displaced Persons in Postwar Germany* (Ann Arbor: University of Michigan Press, 2011); G. Daniel Cohen, *In War's Wake: Europe's Displaced Persons in the Postwar Order* (Oxford and New York: Oxford University Press, 2011); idem, "Between Relief and Politics: Refugee Humanitarianism in Occupied Germany 1945-1946," in *Journal of* [Ccntinued on following page]

well-being of Austrian targets of Nazi terror (and, if deceased, their next-of-kin) and of ex-POWs was fraught with competing emotional, social, and political significance. Because these two groups, POWs and victims of Nazi terror, fell under the category of *Opfer* in popular understandings, affected individuals and their advocates engaged in competition for moral claims to welfare assistance—and thus actual benefits and official patronage. There can be no doubt that targets of Nazi persecution qualified as victims, whether they had been imprisoned or forced to lead underground existences. Yet, given the Moscow Declaration's wording, POWs—as long as they had not been Nazis—could also fall under this rubric without challenging the integrity of victim status, as it was legally understood, once the war ended.

Historians like Brigitte Bailer-Galanda and Ela Hornung established the foundations for contemporary work on victims' welfare in postwar Austria during the 1990s and early 2000s, respectively.[3] Their insightful studies, which focused on debates over federal law and the role of victims' organizations as advocacy and lobbying groups, have contributed significantly to my own work. This paper takes a different approach from theirs in several respects, however. First, my work is part of a broader inquiry that juxtaposes the reintegration of repatriated POWs with care for Viennese civilians who had either suffered incarceration under the Nazi regime, or had lived in hiding in the city to avoid capture. Second, this expanded focus on victims concerns itself with how municipal social democratic authorities

---

[Foonote 2, continued] *Contemporary History* 43, no. 3 (2008): 437–449; Pertti Ahonen, *People on the Move: Forced Population Movements in Europe in the Second World War and its Aftermath* (Oxford: Berg, 2008); Gernot Heiss and Oliver Rathkolb ed., *Asylland wider Willen: Flüchtlinge in Österreich im europäischen Kontext seit 1914* (Vienna: Jugend & Volk, 1995); Christoph Reinprecht, *Zurückgekehrt: Identität und Bruch in der Biographie österreichischer Juden* (Vienna: Braumüller, 1992); Mark Wyman, *DPs: Europe's Displaced Persons, 1945–1951* (Ithaca NY and London: Cornell University Press, 1989); and Thomas Albrich, *Exodus durch Österreich:die jüdischen Flüchtlinge 1945–1948* (Innsbruck: Haymon-Verlag, 1987). On prisoners of war, see, for example, Richard Lein, *Zurück aus dem Krieg: die Kriegsgefangenen- und Heimkehrerfürsorge der Republik Österreich nach dem 2. Weltkrieg* (Frankfurt/Main and Vienna: Peter Lang, 2006); Bob Moore and Barbara Hately-Broad ed., *Prisoners of War, Prisoners of Peace: Captivity, Homecoming and Memory in World War II* (Oxford and New York: Oxford University Press, 2005); and James M. Diehl, *The Thanks of the Fatherland: German Veterans After the Second World War* (Chapel Hill and London: University of North Carolina Press, 1993).

3 Brigitte Bailer, *Wiedergutmachung kein Thema: Österreich und die Opfer des Nationalsozialismus,* (Vienna: Löcker, 1993) and Ela Hornung, "Hierarchisierung der Opfer. Zur Sozialgesetzgebung für Kriegsopfer nach 1945," in *Konflikte und Kriege im 20. Jahrhundert: Aspekte ihrer Folgen*, ed. Harald Knoll, Peter Ruggenthaler and Barbara Stelzl-Marx (Graz-Vienna-Klagenfurt: Verein zur Förderung v. Folgen nach Konflikten und Krigen, 2002), 59–72.

sought to balance care for those who opposed the Third Reich, or had been targeted by the regime as opponents, with those who had served the regime in uniform – and how people who sought assistance represented their cases to social authorities. The focus here is not on POWs, but on civilians. Third, I rely on sources—*Opferfürsorgekarte*—to which neither Bailer-Galanda nor Hornung had access, and which serve as essential microhistorical narratives.

I take as my parameters the period between the introduction of the *Opferfürsorgegesetz*, in its restrictive and rather discriminatory form in the summer of 1945, and the law's 1948 revision that placed political and so-called racial victims on equal footing. Given my particular emphasis on rebuilding a social democratic milieu in the capital,[4] I argue that it is particularly important to explore the vigorous discussion of victimization and antifascism, to examine efforts to alleviate suffering in a polity whose leaders and their constituency publicly emphasized the rhetoric of social justice, and the realities of support services mandated by federal law but administered under social democratic auspices. As the country's largest population center, Vienna was the place of origin, or the final destination, for a significant number of civilians who had experienced life in hiding (so-called *U-Boote*) and others who had been liberated from concentration or labor camps, as well as for returning POWs. Moreover, Vienna had been home to the largest Jewish population in Austria, to especially strident anti-fascist sentiment, and to significant ambivalence toward, or outright embrace of, the National Socialist regime for reasons that ranged from opportunism to conviction.[5]

4   See Matthew Paul Berg, "Reinventing 'Red Vienna' after 1945: Habitus, Patronage, and the Foundations of Municipal Social Democratic Dominance," in *Journal of Modern History* 86, No. 3 (2014): 603–632.

5   The rich historiography on the themes of anti-semitism, Nazi sympathies, and antifascism in Austria includes: Ilana Fritz Offenberger, *The Jews of Nazi Vienna, 1938-1945: Rescue and Destruction* (New York: Palgrave Macmillan, 2017); Evan Burr Bukey, *Jews and Intermarriage in Nazi Austria* (Cambridge and New York: Cambridge University Press, 2011); idem, *Hitler's Austria: Popular Sentiment in the Nazi Era, 1938–1945* (Chapel Hill and London: University of North Carolina Press, 2000); Dirk Hänisch, *Die österreichischen NSDAP-Wähler. Eine empirische Analyse ihrer politischen Herkunft und ihres Sozialprofils* (Vienna-Cologne-Weimar: Böhlau, 1998); Bruce F. Pauley, *From Prejudice to Persecution: A History of Austrian Anti-Semitism* (Chapel Hill and London: University of North Carolina Press, 1992); Helmut Konrad, "Das Werben der NSDAP um die Sozialdemokraten 1933–1938" and Hans Schafranek, "NSDAP und Sozialisten nach dem Februar 1934" in *Arbeiterschaft und Nationalsozialismus in Österreich*, ed. Rudolf G. Ardelt and Hans Hautmann (Vienna and Zurich: Europaverlag, 1990), 73–90 and 91–128, respectively; Robert Schwarz, "Nazi Wooing of Austrian Social Democracy between *Anschluss* and War," in *Conquering the Past: Austrian Nazism Yesterday and Today*, ed. F. Parkinson (Detroit: Wayne State University Press, 1989), 125–136; Emmerich Tálos, Ernst Hanisch, and Wolfgang Neugebauer ed., *NS-Herrschaft in Österreich 1938–1945* (Vienna: Verlag für Gesellschaftskritik, 1988); Everhard Holtmann, *Zwischen Unterdrückung und Befreiung. Sozialistische Arbeiterbewegung und autoritäres Regime in Österreich 1933–1938* (Munich: R. Oldenbourg Verlag, 1978).

[U a Knight]

⟨ 266 ⟩   Berg: *Victims of Nazi Terror in Vienna:*
Legally Mandated Assistance and Social Democratic Patronage, 1945–1948

Categories of "Victims of Nazi Terror in Austria"

Within a few weeks of proclaiming independence in late April 1945, Austrian authorities at the provincial and local levels found themselves confronted with the necessity of providing assistance to "victims of Nazi terror" who resided in their communities, as well as to an influx of people who had been held in labor and concentration camps. Aid could take the form of cash payments and also assistance in obtaining clothing, furniture, household effects, or foodstuffs. The provisional federal government's *Staatsamt für soziale Verwaltung* offered assurances to regional authorities that the federal state would extend the lion's share of support.

Federal officials provided the following schema for relief allocation that provincial welfare offices and local welfare centers were to observe. Victims would be categorized according to a distinct rank order system that provided the basis for the *Opferfürsorgegesetz* introduced several weeks later.

Table 1: Federal Categories for Victims of Nazi Terror[6]

Group A: Active Resistance

1. Next-of-kin of:
    a. slain Austrian freedom fighters (partisans),
    b. Austrian political prisoners whose activities led to arrest and subsequent murder in Nazi custody,
    c. Austrian Wehrmacht soldiers or police killed during service [because of resistance to the NS regime (MB)].

2. Political prisoners involved in *organized* illegal political actions for Austria ("subject to rigorous verification") with:
    a. more than a three-year term in custody,
    b. between eighteen and thirty-six months in custody,
    c. between six and eighteen months in custody.

3. Austrian Freedom Fighters, namely:
    a. armed partisans,
    b. participants in illegal political activities for Austrian independence (recognized through central committee or party leadership of political parties),
    c. those who prevented destruction or removal of vital firms or infrastructure.

---

6   *Staatsgesetzblatt* (hereafter StGBl), Nr. 90/1945, "Gesetz vom 17. Juli 1945 über die Fürsorge für die Opfer des Kampfes um ein freies, demokratisches Österreich) Opfer-Fürsorgegesetz."

Group B: Passive Resistance

1. Political prisoners not involved in organized political activity with:
   a. more than a three-year term in custody,
   b. between eighteen and thirty-six months in custody,
   c. between six and eighteen months in custody.

2. Those taken into custody by the Gestapo or military police, including:
   a. deserters held for at least six months;
   b. those who had gone into hiding for at least one year;
   c. those who provided illegal shelter for those in hiding for at least one year.

3. Non-political concentration camp prisoners with:
   a. more than a three-year term in custody;
   b. between eighteen and thirty-six months in custody;
   c. between six and eighteen months in custody.

Group C: Racially or Nationally Persecuted

1. Jews or those who were considered Jews (required to wear the Star of David);

2. "Privileged" Jews (not required to wear Star of David);

3. "First Degree *Mischlinge*" married to Jews; also "Aryans" persecuted because of nationality [sic].[7]

It is clear that this schema favored those who had engaged in efforts to resist Nazism in the interests of Austrian independence over those the National Socialist regime had pursued as ostensibly biological enemies. Jews and others in Group C were eligible for higher priority consideration *only* if they had also been involved in activities consistent with Group A or B criteria. This discriminatory categorization—one informed, in significant measure, by the *Opfermythos*—would not be dropped until parliament approved a third revision of the *Opferfürsorgegesetz* in February 1949.[8]

---

7 WrStLA, MD A6/2, BA 577/45.

8 *Bundesgesetzblatt für die Republik Österreich* (hereafter BGBl), Stück 12, Nr. 58, 183/1949, 3.Opferfürsorgegesetz-Novelle, ausgegeben am 15. März 1949, Artikel I 2c), 276. See also Bailer, *Wiedergutmachung*.

Vienna's public welfare office communicated this schema to its district satellite branches in a circular dated 7 June 1945. The public welfare office noted, "as a rule, the outlay for apartment rent [...] and aid are to be granted as one-time assistance for a month's duration."[9] Such limited assistance was not an expression of indifference to applicants' circumstances. Rather, challenges in meeting needs reflected how postwar reconstruction sorely tested Austrian authorities' capacities to attend to pressing shortages of foodstuffs, clothes, medical care, lodging, and other necessities throughout much of the country—but particularly in the capital. Viennese applicants would be referred to a central registration office, the *Zentralregistrierung der Opfer des Naziterrors in Österreich* (also referred to as the *Zentralregistrierungsstelle*) within the public welfare office. Each applicant, or a surviving family member, was to complete a *Fürsorgekarte*. Once approved, this document would function as an identity card for victims of the Nazi regime with a recognized claim. Together with a valid photo ID, an approved *Fürsorgekarte* served as validation of victims' status for all "politically, racially, or nationally [i.e., *ethnically* – MB] oppressed Austrians" in their interactions with state and municipal authorities, and with functionaries of all political parties, trade unions, cooperatives, and professional boards.[10]

Between the end of April and the beginning of June 1945, some 8,000 individual cases had been registered, and approximately 1,000 of them thoroughly vetted by a staff of reliable antifascists.[11] These officials worked with great dedication but found themselves overwhelmed by the volume of applications. Although the staff expanded to more effectively address the influx of requests—into early 1946, the number of submissions would extend into the tens of thousands—applicants could find themselves waiting months for resolution, often under circumstances of great hardship. Even as aid brought modest alleviation of need, formal recognition of suffering was no less significant to many victims' sense of dignity, particularly once the most challenging period of postwar reconstruction had passed by the end of the 1940s.

My research into welfare assistance for those Viennese oppressed by the National Socialist regime draws on a random, representative sample of some

---

9   Wiener Stadt- und Landesarchiv (hereafter WrStLA), 1.3.208, Wohlfahrtsamt Allg. Registratur A2 (1945–1949). Magistrat der Stadt Wien, Verwaltungsgruppe X, Wohlfahrtswesen, Abteilung 1, an alle Fürsorgeämter, 7. Juni 1945.
10 WrStLA, MD A6/2, BA 577/45, Magistrat der Stadt Wien, Verwaltungsgruppe X, Wohlfahrtswesen, Zentralregistrierung der Opfer des Naziterrors in Österreich – Rundschreiben an alle Staatssekretariate, Parteivorstände der politischen Parteien, Bürgermeister, Stadträte, Fürsorgungsinstitute der Gemeinde Wien und Volkssolidaritätsausschüsse, [n.d.] Mai 1945.
11 WrStLA, MD A1 1945, 678/45, Box 627, 501-802. Hönigsfeld, eherenamtlicher Leiter, an die Magistratsdirektion, 5. Juni 1945.

3,000 submissions (women and men, categories A, B, and C) out of approximately 12,000 still held in the Wiener Stadt- und Landesarchiv for the period of June 1945 (when the *Zentralregistrierung der Opfer des Naziterrors* began its work) through March 1946 (in early April 1946, adjudication and administration of welfare cases became the domain of the municipal welfare office). The paper trail for the subsequent years ends there.[12] The *Fürsorgekarte* is a valuable source, for it provides us with a glimpse into the experience of the individual applicant—a microhistory, of sorts.

---

12 Latecomers will turn to the following welfare locations [in Vienna]: political prisoners with at least six months incarceration to the *Volkssolidarität* [...]; racially persecuted to the action committee representing those persecuted according to their respective ancestry [...]; those incarcerated in concentration camps to the *KZ-Verband* [...]; other Nazi victims to the welfare offices in their respective locations of registered residence." WrStLA, MD A1 1946, 758/46, Zentralreistrierungsstelle der Opfer des Naziterrors; Auflassung der Dienststelle. Aktenvermerk vom 2. April 1946.

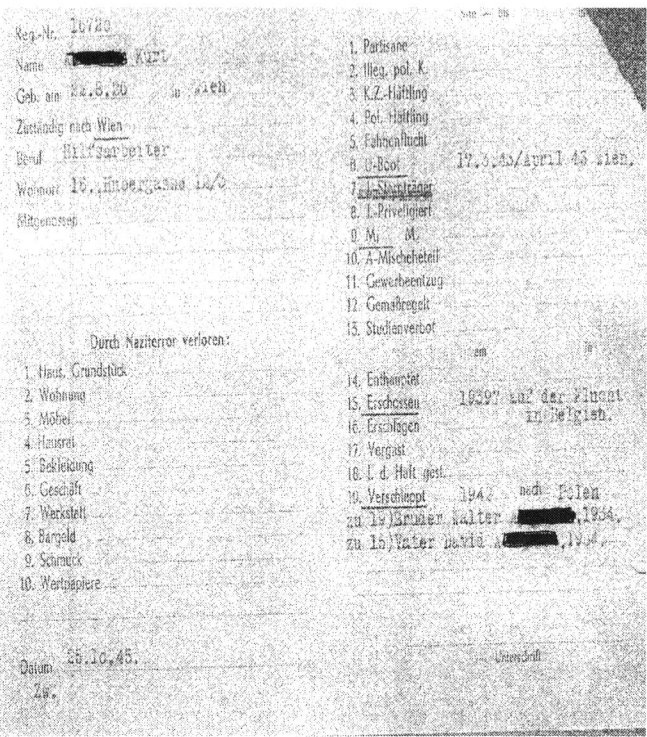

The great majority of applicants for *Opferfürsorge* in my large sample noted that they belonged to Group C, (racially or "nationally" persecuted), followed by a notably smaller number affiliated with the KPÖ. Social Democrats formed the third largest population, and Catholic conservatives the fourth. There is no compelling reason to doubt that my findings are representative of the sum total of applications, given the National Socialist regime's particular zeal in targeting Jews and Sinti/Roma, and the antipathy directed towards Communists.

A report to the city manager's office from 30 January 1946, reproduced in Table 2, reveals the total number of approved claims from the onset of *Zentralregistrierungsstelle* work in June 1945 to the end of January 1946.

A massive backlog of submissions processed by overworked reviewers explains only in part why the *Zentralregistrierungsstelle* approved such a relatively small proportion of cases out of the number submitted, which was undoubtedly several times larger. Corroborating evidence in the form of affidavits represented the touchstone for successful resolution of cases. Many applicants simply did not—or could not—provide them.

If the *Fürsorgekarten* provide us with rough sketches of how people communicated their experiences of victimization under the National Socialist

Table 2: Number of Claims Approved in Vienna June 1945 – late January 1946[13]

- Partisans (fallen Austrian freedom fighters; benefits to family members): 7
- Political prisoners (executed; benefits to family members): 869
- Members of German Wehrmacht (executed; benefits to family members): 227
- Political prisoners arrested for treasonous political activity
    more than three years: 634
    less than three years: 418
    less than eighteen months: 398
- Active (armed) resistance fighters: 273
- Illegal political activity for an independent Austria, acknowledged by a ranking political party official: 24
- Prevention of the destruction of essential infrastructure: 22
- Prisoners held for passive resistance
    more than three years: 651
    less than three years: 484
    six to eighteen months: 1,261
- Wehrmacht deserters, at least six months on the run: 48
- U-boot [person living in hiding] for at least one year: 329
- Providing illegal shelter for at least one year: 22
- Non-political concentration camp inmates
    more than three years: 622
    less than three years: 484
    six to eighteen months: 438
- Racially persecuted [Jews, "privileged Jews," "Mischlinge," Sinti/Roma, etc.]: 840
    non-political among the above: 66

Total number of approved cases: 8,177

---

13 Ibid., Magistrat der Stadt Wien, Verwaltungsgruppe X – Wohlfahrtswesen (Dr. Rieger) an die Magistratsdirektion, zu Handen Herrn Senatsrat Dr. Balacs, 30. Januar 1946. Later in 1946 Viennese municipal administrative units were reorganized, and Wohlfahrtswesen became Verwaltungsgruppe IV.

regime, supporting materials—above all affidavits, but, where present, also applicants' personal statements and other supporting materials—offer richer narratives crafted with great intentionality. The forms of evidence that had been considered essential for successful adjudication of an applicant's submission, identified by the director of the group responsible for issuing *Fürsorgekarten* in a memo to the city manager's office, are reproduced in Table 3.

Such materials are not only important sources for the study of everyday life between 1938 and 1945; they also offer insights into the ways applicants negotiated the bureaucratic process required to confirm victim status and receive emergency aid. Combined with personal narratives, particularly when applicants encountered the frustrating steps and halting pace often associated with the confirmation process, these documents illuminate the intersection of lived experience and policy that are the focus of my larger study. While welfare appeals continued after 1945/46, Viennese authorities found themselves particularly overwhelmed with cases during the initial postwar months.

Adjudicating Opferfürsorge between Legal Obligation and Party Patronage

The Social Democratic municipal officials walked a fine line between serving as executors of the party's political goals and as a responsible governing authority for all Viennese, regardless of party affiliation. In the former instance, the Viennese SP strived to reintegrate the Social Democratic *Lager* after a dozen years of illegality under the *Vaterländische Front* dictatorship (VF, also referred to here as the Austrofascist regime) and under Nazi hegemony, first by extending patronage to reliable loyalists with unimpeachable antifascist credentials, and secondarily to non-Social Democrats with requisite expertise and similar antifascist bona fides. Dedicated Social Democrats tended to assume that reconstitution of the party meant priority treatment – not only when it came to expectations of municipal civil service or Viennese party organization employment, but also with respect to claims and applications regulated by federal law.[14] Yet party members in the municipal civil service were obligated to function as neutral arbiters whenever party comrades submitted applications or requests to their bureaus. These officials could not legally justify demonstrating favoritism to Social Democrats unless the latter presented cases with merit equal to those presented by party outsiders. Patronage assistance could be extended only wherever it was legally

---

14 Berg, "Reinventing 'Red Vienna' after 1945," passim.

Table 3: Range of Evidence Expected for Adjudication of Opferfürsorge Claims[15]

For next-of-kin: death certificate or unimpeachable witness statement, confirmation of political nature of arrest and of sentence from the municipal district administration of one of the three parties [SPÖ, ÖVP, KPÖ].

For prisoners: protective custody order, confirmation from police prison, order for arrest or sentence, unimpeachable testimony from fellow prisoners, political party confirmation [SPÖ, ÖVP, KPÖ] or confirmation from the *Volkssolidarität* or *KZ-Verband*.[16]

For partisans: confirmation from state police, Hofburg section [...], military documents from Allied troops.

For deserters: sentence or communiqué from court or military authority, confirmation from the *Komitee der Wehrmachtshäftlingen*.

For *U-Boote*: affirmation from person who provided shelter and two witnesses, confirmation from ration card office [confirming that *U-Boote* was not registered to receive ration card – MB], personal documents.

For those who provided illegal shelter: affirmation from *U-Boote* and two witnesses confirmed by a notary.

For racially or nationally [sic] oppressed: Personal documents such as Jewish ID card, documentation from faith community, or, for gypsies [sic], confirmation from mayor's office.

---

15 WrStLA, MD A1 1946, 758/46, Verwaltungsgruppe X – Wohlfahrtswesen (Dr. Rieger) an die Magistratsdirektion, zu Handen Herrn Senatsrat Dr. Balacs, 30. Januar 1946.

16 The implementation decree issued by the Federal Ministry for Social Administration in connection with the *Opferfürsorgegesetz* noted that "the Gestapo issued no arrest confirmations whatsoever and collected protective custody orders and certificates of discharge from concentration camps when the prisoner was released. Thus, official documents related to arrest, release, or carrying out of sentence cannot be furnished in many cases." The supporting evidence referred to above represented suitable alternatives to those documents. See WrStLA 1.3.208, Wohlfahrtsamt, Allgemeine Registratur A2 (1945-49), "Sonderabdruck aus Heft 1/2 von 1946 der 'ämtliche Nachrichten des Bundesministeriums für soziale Verwaltung,' 1. Durchführungserlaß, Zl. IV-8840/16/46 zum Gesetz vom 17. Juni 1945, StGBl. Nr. 90, und zur Verordnung des Staatamtes für soziale Verwaltung im Einvernehmen mit dem Staatsamte für Finanzen vom 31. Oktober 1945, BGBl. Nr. 34/1946 (Opfer-Fürsorgeverordnung)," 1.

possible, discrete, or ostensibly required by extenuating circumstances. This practice held as true for *Opferfürsorge* as it did, for example, in the adjudication of housing claims under the federal *Wohnungsanforderungsgesetz*. This tension is revealed in the brief survey of representative examples offered below.

It should be noted that Social Democrats understood *Opferfürsorge* in two respects. On the one hand, it extended assistance to those who had suffered at the hands of the Nazis, as the three-tiered federal categorization required. Yet, on the other hand, Social Democrats saw *Opferfürsorge*—given the law's emphasis on resistance in the interest of an independent and democratic Austria—as an opportunity to gain formal recognition of sacrifices made and suffering incurred in resistance to the Austrofascist regime. This served several purposes. First, it would make a contribution to offsetting the material losses incurred by those who had been held in prison or in the notorious Wollersdorf concentration camp. Second, insofar as members of the Social Democratic paramilitary, party activists, and underground Revolutionary Socialists waged active resistance against the establishment of an anti-democratic regime, individual claims for suffering between 1934 and 1938 gave applicants the satisfaction of a poke in the eye to those former bitter adversaries. Although former Austrofascist officials were subsequently targeted by the Nazis, and could submit claims for victims' assistance, Social Democrats made it a point to remind *Volkspartei* officials and the broader public of the ÖVP's unresolved relationship to its authoritarian precursor whenever an opportunity presented itself. The efforts of *Volkssolidarität* to provide affidavits for applicants from experiences before the Anschluss also served as a reminder.

A few cases illustrate the kind of fate that Social Democrats experienced. The chauffeur Anton A. had been held in Wollersdorf for eight months during 1934 on charges of treason as an illegal Social Democratic activist; the SP district organization for Vienna-Schwechat vouched for his political reliability.[17] The clerk Robert H. was interned five months in Wollersdorf and several other Austrofascist detention facilities, and spent several weeks underground to evade arrest by the Gestapo in 1944. Viennese party authorities confirmed that H. had been active in the party since 1918 in several important capacities and had worked for democracy as a member of the Lower Austrian parliament.[18]

---

17 WrStLA 1.3.2.208 – Opferfürsorge: Fürsorgekartei (1945-46) A 13/1, Fürsorgekarte Nr. 10006.
18 WrStLA 1.3.2.208 – Opferfürsorge: Fürsorgekartei (1945-46) A 13/4, Fürsorgekarte Nr. 9869.

Those affiliated with Austrofascist regime could apply for victims' assistance as long as they met the qualifications for category A or B. For example, forestry official Franz U.'s were less clear. Franz had spent September 1938 through March 1939 in Buchenwald for illegal political activity in support of the since-outlawed Austrofascist regime. He noted that he had also been engaged in an illegal political struggle as a member of the *Heimwehr* in 1928—but at a point in the First Republic when these regional paramilitaries engaged in a struggle to institute authoritarian rule. He, too, qualified for victims' assistance under category A (active resistance). The law stipulated only that an applicant had engaged for an *independent*, but not specifically *democratic*, Austria.

A broader, if not legally mandated, understanding of who qualified as victim of Nazism offer us a glimpse into how the municipal Social Democratic patronage network functioned. Those concerned included returning prisoners of war or those who remained on the home front and sought assistance with political (re)affiliation, housing, employment, securing pensions, or other smaller forms of aid.[19] Indeed, once the SP's Ferdinand Freund took over municipal welfare administration from the Communists in January 1946, a consequence of the resounding social democratic success in the November elections, municipal welfare officials could extend the same sort patronage as colleagues in the *Wohnungsamt* and the *Magistratsdirektion* had begun to provide months earlier. Thus, welfare assistance in kind (shoes, clothing, etc.), when requested by Viennese SP officials and endorsed by party officials in civil administration positions, frequently found its way to needy Viennese who did not meet the legal definition of *Opfer*.

Patronage was not lavish; rather, it took the form of small, but meaningful, forms of assistance to these SP constituents—what we might call *discrete* forms of aid—as long as reputable comrades in the municipal civil service could vouch for them. Normally the needy were constituents and/ or civil servants working in SP controlled municipal agencies; in other instances, Social Democrats working in federal ministries contacted the welfare office on the behalf of friends or acquaintances. Although civil servants were expected to fulfill responsibilities with professionalism and within the framework of the law, assistance requests from welfare office

---

19 Matthew P. Berg, "Adjudicating Lodging: Denazification, Housing Requisition, and Identity in 'Red Vienna,' 1945–48," in *Narrating the City: Histories, Space, and the Everyday*, ed. Wladimir Fischer-Nebmaier, Matthew P. Berg, and Anastasia Christou ed. (New York and Oxford: Berghahn, 2015), 175–96; Berg, "Reinventing 'Red Vienna' after 1945; Berg, "Die SPÖ und die Praxis der Entnazifizierung," in *Entnazifizierung zwischen politischem Anspruch, Parteienkonkurrenz und Kaltem Krieg*, ed. Maria Mesner (Vienna and Munich: Oldenbourg Verlag, 2005), 145–85.

personnel, or other municipal or even federal officials, made on behalf of others, could serve to reinforce party loyalty and solidarity. Many of these requests involved needy employees; they almost always involved clothing and, especially, shoes.[20]

In such cases of discretionary aid—and there are hundreds upon hundreds of them—the distinction between humanitarian intervention and cultivating loyalty through patronage was negligible. Yet needy *non*-SPÖ members received these small distributions of clothing, foodstuffs, or even a very modest allocation of cash, too. Welfare office administrators understood that their work could never be distinctly partisan; a considerable minority of Vienna's residents were not Social Democrats, and such heavy-handedness would have been untenable in the wake of eleven years of consecutive single party dictatorships. Nonetheless, the SP were keen to look after their own to the greatest extent possible, given the parameters of the law and broader awareness of cases involving more pressing need among those outside the *Lager*. Responsible and compassionate government reinforced the habitus, and made possible the integration of others, including former Nazis who had been designated *minderbelastet* as per the 1948 amnesty. This shift came close to the same time that revisions to the *Opferfürsorgegesetz* abolished distinctions between "racial" and political victims—a bitter irony not lost on many of those who had experienced Nazi terror.

---

20 WrStLA 1.3.2.208 – A2 Allg. Reg. nach Registraturgruppe (1945-49), "Ämtliche Veranlassungen" 1946, Obermagsitratsrat Rieger an Herrn Referatsleiter Riedel, 3, 4, and 29 December 1946. See also WrStLA 1.3.2.208 – A2 Allg. Reg. nach Registraturgruppe (1945-49), "Ämtliche Veranlassungen" 1947, Obermagsitratsrat Rieger an Herrn Referatsleiter Riedel, 2 February 1947.

(handwritten notes in top margin: "(-)IIhP)", "(Niven)", "Bombenkrieg", "=) III")

"Terror Pilots" and "Bombing Holocaust":
Discourses on Victimization and Remembrance in Austria in the Context of the Allied Aerial Bombardment[1]

Nicole-Melanie Goll

In the memorial year 2005, sixty years after the end of war, as part of the "Twenty-five Peaces" campaign, an official part of the "Memorial Year" program, St. Stephen's Cathedral was bathed in alternating white and red light in remembrance of the air raid on central Vienna on 12 March 1945.[2] This initiative marked the start of a series of activities that were presented in public spaces between March 2005 and July 2006 and concentrated largely on Allied air raids on the National Socialist German Reich between 1943 and 1945. The same year, the FPÖ and EU parliamentarian Andreas Mölzer introduced a proposal in the EU Parliament calling for "a Europe-wide day of commemoration for the civilian victims of the bombing in Europe."[3] Mölzer went on to state "that the air raids in Europe caused incalculable suffering to the civilian populations of many European cities." He added numbers of victims: according to him, in "Austria around 35,000 and in Germany almost 600,000 civilians died, including 80,000 children."[4] Mölzer not only exaggerated the number of victims, he was also of the opinion that the victims of the air raids were deliberately not being mentioned.[5]

(handwritten margin note: "B. Niven")

---

1   This article brings together the first results of a project, "Gedächtnisort Bombenkrieg. Gesellschaftliche Erinnerungsdiskurse des alliierten Luftkrieges am Beispiel der Steiermark," carried out at the Karl-Franzens-University, Graz in collaboration with Georg Hoffmann and funded by the Land Steiermark and the Future Fund of the Republic of Austria. At this point I would like to thank Georg Hoffmann in particular for his support, help, and the lively exchange of ideas; and Ke-Chin Hsia, Günter Bischof, Cate Giustino, and Matthew Berg for stimulating discussions and additional information. Thanks also to Anne Kozeluh for the translation of the text.
2   "Rufzeichen in den Himmel," Die Presse, 14 March 2005, 10; Eberhard Schrempf, *Peace dokumentiert: [25 peaces]. Interventionen und Irritationen zur Erzeugung eigener Gedanken im Diesseits des öffentlichen Raumes und jenseits des offiziellen Gedankenjahres* (Vienna: 2006), 10–15. There was, however, no mention of the dual nature of this day of commemoration (on this day in 1938, the Anschluss took place).
3   Written declaration dated 21 February 2005 "zu einem europaweiten Gedenktag für die zivilen Opfer des Bombenkrieges in Europa, der vor 60 Jahren seinen Höhepunkt erreichte," accessed Sept. 20, 2017, www.europarl.europa.eu/sides/getDoc.do?pubRef=%2f%2fEP%2f%2fNONSGML%2bWDECL%2bP6-DCL-2005-0010%2b0%2bDOC%2bPDF%2bV0%2f%2fDE.
4   Ibid.
5   Ibid.

278   Goll: *"Terror Pilots"* and *"Bombing Holocaust"*:
Discourses on Victimization and Remembrance in Austria
in the Context of the Allied Aerial Bombardment

Ten years later, during the commemorative year 2015/16, seventy years after the end of the war, various parties called for the commemoration of the many civilian victims of the Second World War. The Allied air raids, the damage they caused, and the suffering of the civilian population increasingly became the focus of media interest and discussion.[6] For example, the *Uhrturm*, the party newspaper of the FPÖ in Styria's capital Graz, brought up the question of who was commemorating the civilian victims of the Allied air raids on Graz. The article that followed read:

Seventy years after the end of the Second World War, we mourn the millions of victims of the Third Reich. Never forget! This is a good thing. It is right and important that the city of Graz should dedicate a special council to this fateful date. But is it not rather one-sided mourning? Who is mourning the millions of innocent victims in the state territory of the German Reich, which had engulfed our Austria? Who is mourning those people? Millions were murdered, bombed out, robbed of their belongings, systematically displaced, abducted and raped. By whom? By those who were victorious and are thanked today as liberators.[7]

The examples mentioned clearly show that, over the past seven decades, but particularly in commemorative years, the air raids have increasingly gained attention on a regional, national, and supranational level, and are still a focus today. The air raids, attached to emotionally charged sites like Dresden and Hamburg, have become anchored in the collective memory as symbolic of society's victim perception.[8] While studies have already taken place for Germany, the same is not true of Austria; this article will venture to address this research desideratum. The subject of the article is this integration of the air raids into the individual recollections and collective

---

6   See for example: "Luftkrieg über Österreich," Wiener Zeitung, accessed March 6, 2015, http://www.wienerzeitung.at/themen_channel/wissen/geschichte/739045_Luftkrieg-ueber-Oesterreich.html; "Tödliche Fracht aus der Luft," www.kleinezeitung.at/steiermark/4703135/Serie_Steiermark-1945_Toedliche-Fracht-aus-der-Luft; "1943: Luftkrieg über Tirol," http://tirol.orf.at/news/stories/2701998/; "1945: Graz im schweren Bombenhagel," accessed Feb. 22, 2015, Kleine Zeitung online.

7   "70 Jahre Kriegsende," Der Uhrturm, 2/2015, 24.

8   See in particular: Malte Thießen, Eingebrannt ins Gedächtnis: Hamburgs Gedenken an Luftkrieg und Kriegsende 1943 bis 2005 (Munich: Dölling und Galitz, 2007). Jörg Arnold, The Allied air war and urban memory: the legacy of strategic bombing in Germany (Cambridge: Cambridge University Press 2011); Rolf-Dieter Müller, Nicole Schönherr, Thomas Widera, eds., Die Zerstörung Dresdens 13. bis 15. Februar 1945: Gutachten und Ergebnisse der Dresdner Historikerkommission zur Ermittlung der Opferzahlen (Göttingen: V&R unipress 2010). In 2005, a representative of the NPD in the Landtag of Saxony caused a stir by equaling Nazi crimes with allied bombing, using the term "Bombing Holocaust," see: "NPD-Mann spricht von Dresdner 'Bomben-Holocaust,'" der Spiegel, accessed Dec. 20, 2017, http://www.spiegel.de/politik/deutschland/skandal-im-saechsischen-landtag-npd-mann-spricht-von-dresdner-bomben-holocaust-a-337894.html.

memory of the Republic of Austria. The first phase will pursue the development of differing perceptions and notions regarding the air raids, as well as the possible interpretations offered by the National Socialist regime. This will form the foundation of the argument that the images and interpretations created in this context, and the resulting perceptions, not only became part of a (contemporary) social idea of victimization after 1945 but also an elementary, effective, and thus far hardly recognized building block of the Austrian victim myth, the core elements of which have persisted up to the present day. This approach refers to and expands on the theory of Heidemarie Uhl, who notes the existence of two victim myths in her examination of Austrian society in the post-war period: while the first victim myth can be seen as the well-known image of Austria as the "first victim" of National Socialism" in 1938, the second focuses more on the end of the war and thus on Austria's role as an "innocent victim of the war."[9] The role of air raids and their perception, despite their visibility in the final years of the war and the early post-war years—Echternkamp calls this the "key interface"[10]—have so far hardly been examined academically.

The expositions that follow trace the integration of various different memory elements into one Austrian memory, analyzing its transformation up to the present day—attached primarily to jubilee years and the corresponding memorial activities at a regional and national level.

While in Germany at the beginning of this century new research into the air raids developed based on social and cultural historical elements—as seen mainly in the debate around the works of Jörg Friedrich—thus opening up a new approach to the issues surrounding the air raids, with memory and remembrance as the central analytical fields, this is not the case in Austria.[11] This article provides an Austrian perspective (on different levels)

9   Heidemarie Uhl, "Das 'erste' Opfer: Der österreichische Opfermythos und seine Transformationen in der Zweiten Republik," Österreichische Zeitschrift für Politikwissenschaft 30, no. 1 (2001), 19–34.

10   Jörg Echternkamp, "Von der Gewalterfahrung zur Kriegserinnerung – über den Bombenkrieg als Thema einer Geschichte der deutschen Kriegsgesellschaft," in Deutschland im Luftkrieg: Geschichte und Erinnerung, ed. Dietmar Süß (Munich: Siedler Verlag 2007), 13–26 (here 13).

11   The two publications brought out by Jörg Friedrich in 2002 and 2003 led to heated discussions. See, among others, Lothar Kettenacker, ed., Ein Volk von Opfern? Die neue Debatte um den Bombenkrieg 1940–1945 (Berlin: Rowohl 2003); Bernd Greiner, "'Overbombed' Warum die Diskussion über die alliierten Luftangriffe nicht mit dem Hinweis auf die deutsche Schuld beendet werden darf. Review zu Jörg Friedrichs der Brand," Literaturen 03 (2003), 42–44; Klaus Naumann, "Bombenkrieg – Totaler Krieg – Massaker: Jörg Friedrichs Buch 'Der Brand' in der Diskussion," Mittelweg 36, 12 (2003) H. 4, 40–60. On new perspectives on aerial warfare research see, for example: Jörg Echternkamp, Gewalterfahrung.

280   Goll: *"Terror Pilots" and "Bombing Holocaust"*:
*Discourses on Victimization and Remembrance in Austria
in the Context of the Allied Aerial Bombardment*

that has so far been missing from this field of research and at the same time deals with the subject of reappraising Austria's past, which has as yet hardly been touched on.[12]

"Bomb Terror" and the "Terror Pilots": Construction of Memory

Hardly any other aspect of warfare during the Second World War had such far-reaching consequences as the strategic aerial warfare used by the Allies against the Third Reich from 1942 onward.[13] This resulted in a "blurring of boundaries in the war," which was now no longer waged at defined fronts on the ground, but penetrated deep into the heart of the Reich.[14] This meant that, for most of the German population, the increasingly intensive use of air raids was the predominant, often the only, aspect of the war they perceived, which had a lasting effect on their memories of the war.[15]

The humanitarian catastrophes, the unspeakable suffering, the destruction and an increasing feeling of helplessness and vulnerability—from the perspective of the air-raid shelters—grew into the dominant theme of the National Socialist state's domestic politics, and the regime began to fear internal collapse, brought about by the corrosion of "spirit and composure" and the loss of loyalty and trust.[16] The National Socialists' most important priority, provoked by air raids that they were no longer able to counter, was to secure and stabilize National Socialist rule, which was under threat from outside.[17] This is clear in the National Socialist regime's response with regard to the civilians affected. The party, and Reich Minister of Propaganda Joseph Goebbels, positioned themselves at the center of air-raid protection, the victims' welfare and "catastrophe management," giving themselves the power to determine the interpretation of the aerial bombardment and attempting to cushion the consequences of air raids. Their crucial strategy was to create and strengthen "communities" that would provide mutual

---

12   A first, significant contribution on this subject was made by Katrin Hammerstein in 2009: Katrin Hammerstein, "Weiße Flecken? Österreichische Erinnerungen an den Luftkrieg," in Luftkrieg. Erinnerungen in Deutschland und Europa, eds. Jörg Arnold, Dietmar Süß, Malte Thießen (Göttingen: Wallstein Verlag 2009), 114–128.

13   See also the standard work: Dietmar Süß, Tod aus der Luft: Kriegsgesellschaft und Luftkrieg in Deutschland und England (Munich: Siedler Verlag 2011).

14   Echternkamp, Gewalterfahrung, 13.

15   Ibid.

16   Dietmar Süß, "Nationalsozialistische Deutungen des Luftkrieges," in Deutschland im Luftkrieg: Geschichte und Erinnerung, ed. Süß Dietmar (Munich: Siedler Verlag 2007), 99–110 (here 100–101).

17   Georg Hoffmann, Fliegerlynchjustiz: Gewalt gegen abgeschossene alliierte Flugzeugbesatzungen 1943–1945 (Paderborn: Schöningh Verlag 2015), 84 and following.

assistance, which also allowed the regime to keep track of the people affected.[18] These "communities," woven into the National Socialist construct of the "national community" and heavily influenced by the concept of "mutual assistance," were clearly differentiated, but the form of assistance had to conform to behaviour defined by the regime, which meant that they became a central element of control for National Socialist air-raid policies[19] Propaganda stylised the Allied bombardment as a "crime"—as "air terror" that was not directed at the NS regime but was exclusively aimed at "wiping out the German people" and "German culture."[20] One example of how the National Socialist regime tried to deal with the air raids is a newspaper article published in the *Kleine Wiener Kriegszeitung* two days after the devastating air raid on Vienna on the 12 March 1945, which hit the city center, leaving the Albertina and the State Opera in flames and the Philipphof partially collapsed, burying 200 to 300 people beneath it. The article reads:

> Yesterday Anglo-American air terror tore a new and painful gash in the old city on the Danube. Rubble and debris litter the city's main streets, and smoke and flames are still rising from the ruins of precious, world-renowned monuments. The State Opera is burned to a skeleton, there is a gaping wound in the body of the Burgtheater and only by chance was Vienna's most striking landmark, St. Stephen's Cathedral with its tower, spared by the falling bombs. A bomb hit directly beside the cathedral, penetrating down into the vaults of the catacombs and spreading destruction all around on the square.[21]

As this passage shows, the implication was that the "enemy" was deliberately out to destroy the city center and important cultural monuments like St. Stephen's Cathedral.

Newspaper articles like this one, with corresponding illustrations, were intended as documentary proof of the planned destruction of European cultural assets.[22] They were designed to highlight the criminal nature of the

18 Dietmar Süß, "Der Kampf um die "Moral" im Bunker: Deutschland, Großbritannien und der Luftkrieg," Volksgemeinschaft. Neue Forschungen zur Gesellschaft des Nationalsozialismus, eds. Frank Bajohr, Michael Wildt (Frankfurt/Main: Fischer Taschenbuch Verlag 2009), 124–144 (here 143).
19 Hoffmann, Fliegerlynchjustiz, 81–84.
20 See for example: "Deutschlands sichere Chance," Marburger Zeitung, 13 February 1945, 1.
21 "Eine verfehlte Terrorspekulation," Kleine Wiener Kriegszeitung, 14 March 1945, 1.
22 "Baudenkmäler bildeten in Berlin das Ziel unserer Bomben," Völkischer Beobachter (Berlin edition), 27 November 1943, 1.

282   Goll: *"Terror Pilots"* and *"Bombing Holocaust"*:
*Discourses on Victimization and Remembrance in Austria
in the Context of the Allied Aerial Bombardment*

Allied aerial war. The enemy, according to the National Socialist Regime, was out to destroy German culture, but also to "completely annihilate" the German population.[23] By 1942, a ruling had already been passed on the language to be used, which would "reflect the criminal conduct of the enemy."[24] Consequently, neologisms such as "bomb-terror" and "air terror" or "child-murder" were assigned to the air raids, even replacing terms like "air raid" in official language, with long lasting effects.

The "assistance" following air raids was connected to a set of behaviors for the people affected, who were expected to "strike back" at these crimes. The National Socialist regime also saw this as an opportunity to mobilize German society. Alfred Rosenberg had noted very early on and with great cynicism that air raids would *"re-establish the age-old, organic relationship between the people and the war* [emphasis NMG]."[25] The struggle to cope with the consequences of air raids but also the internal pressure to conform were interpreted as a "fight," which gave the protagonists similar rights and duties to soldiers.[26] The people affected were placed on an invisible front. Their "fight" was against the air raids, which were now seen as a crime and therefore perpetrated by "criminals." This gave special significance to the shooting down or crash-landing of Allied planes and the capture of their crewmen, because the National Socialist regime could interpret it as a "victory over the air terror." The dimensions become clear when remembering that the U.S. Army Air Force and British Bomber Command alone lost 18,000 and 9,000 aircraft respectively and that around 60,000 British and American airmen were taken prisoner.[27] In line with the terminology used for air raids, National Socialist propaganda defined these crewmen as "terror pilots," "air gangsters," "air Huns," and "child murderers," at the same time stripping them of their status as soldiers.[28] This practice was clearly aimed at deflecting the people's rage toward a common and tangible enemy and ultimately at allowing violent reactions to take place. Violence would be the central instrument of power.

---

23   "Deutschlands sichere Chance," Marburger Zeitung, 13 February 1945, 1.
24   "Terrorangriff," Der Propagandist, 2nd year, issue 6, Graz, July 1942, 16.
25   Alfred Rosenberg, Der Mythus des 20. Jahrhunderts: Eine Wertung der seelisch-geistigen Gestaltenkämpfe unserer Zeit (Munich: Hoheneichen-Verlag 1936), 317.
26   Georg Hoffmann, Fliegerlynchjustiz, 121–126.
27   See: USAAF, Office of Statistical Control, Army Air Force Statistical Digest World War II, Washington DC 1945, Tables 34–37, 49–52; W. R. Chorley, Royal Air Force Bomber Command Losses of the Second World War, Vol. 1–9 (Hinckley: Midland Countries Publications 1992–2008) and Nicole-Melanie Goll, Georg Hoffmann, Missing in Acion – Failed to return: Ein Gedenkbuch (Vienna: BMLVS 2016).
28   Nicole-Melanie Goll, Georg Hoffmann, "'Terrorflieger:' Deutungen und Wahrnehmungen des Strategischen Luftkrieges in der nationalsozialistischen Propaganda am Beispiel der sogenannten 'Flieger-Lynchjustiz,'" JIPPS 1 (2011), 71–86; Hoffmann, Fliegerlynchjustiz, 149–154.

National Socialist propaganda also quickly found fitting terms for this specific form of violence, such as *"Fliegerlynchjustiz"* (lynch-law against airmen)
and *"Volksjustiz"* (the people's justice).[29] The impression was to be created that
these attacks on downed airmen were the independent actions of civilians, who
were *"taking the law into their own hands* [emphasis NMG]"[30] in dealing with
their "tormentors." But there was more to this lynch law against airmen, as
Georg Hoffmann recently proved: there was targeted control behind it, which
had a direct effect on the situation when aircrews were seized.[31] This lynch
law against airmen first started in the spring of 1944 but mainly took place
in June 1944, simultaneously all over Germany.[32] Figures are currently only
available for what are today Austria and Hungary, where a total of 600 crimes,
including 130 murders, have been discovered.[33] This *"Fliegerlynchjustiz"* was
assimilated into people's minds as the collective "act of revenge" of a "national
community" directly threatened by air raids, creating a lasting image that would
remain unchanged in the years that followed.[34] The important thing here is that,
regarding the victim-perceptions that were established, or rather were deliberately fostered, during the war, violence (characterized as counter-violence)
was argued and legitimized so that the victim-perpetrator positions in individual crime situations became reversed. This would have a lasting effect on
people's recollections. At the same time the *"Fliegerlynchjustiz"* was a building
block in a very specific interpretation of the aerial bombardment, which was
deliberately aimed at people's victim-perception and provided them with this
explanatory model, which would last for a very long time.

Difficult Memories of Air Raids in Austria

While in Germany in the years following the war the aerial bombardment
was the subject of discussions and attempts to process the facts, as well as

---

29   See: German Federal Archive Berlin (BA), NS 6/350, Volksjustiz gegen anglo-
amerikanische Mörder, 30 May 1944.
30   "Schluss mit den Kindermördern," Marburger Zeitung, 30 May 1944, 2.
31   Hoffmann, Fliegerlynchjustiz, 155–176.
32   There are no concrete figures for Germany. Barbara Grimm mentions 350 lynchings.
Barbara Grimm, "Lynchmorde an alliierten Fliegern im Zweiten Weltkrieg," in Deutschland
im Luftkrieg. Geschichte und Erinnerung, ed. Süß Dietmar (Munich: Oldenbourg 2007),
71–84 (here 75).
33   Hoffmann, Fliegerlynchjustiz, 233 and 383.
34   On the difficulties of dealing with this subject see: Georg Hoffmann, "Verdrängte
Erinnerung: Aufarbeitung und gesellschaftlicher Umgang mit dem Gewaltphänomen
'Fliegerlynchjustiz' im Kontext des alliierten Bombenkrieges," in *Luftkrieg und Heimatfront.
Ein vergessener Fliegerlynchmord in der "Stadt des KdF-Wagens"* ed. Günter Riederer
(Wolfsburg: Appelhans E. 2016), 76–87.

284   Goll: *"Terror Pilots"* and *"Bombing Holocaust"*:
*Discourses on Victimization and Remembrance in Austria
in the Context of the Allied Aerial Bombardment*

(locally confined) commemoration attempts, for example in Dresden and Hamburg, and the air raids were established as an element in the commemoration of the end of the war;[35] in Austria, despite the ever-present and visible consequences of the air raids, the subject was at first dealt with only superficially. In the anti-Fascist exhibition *Never Forget*, which opened on 14 September 1946 and in which Austria was also positioned as the first victim of National Socialism, there was a special art section of images, graphics, and sculptures that were to show the impact of war and fascism in Austria.[36] This included a series of different works, produced by Austrian artists such as Rudolf Schatz, Viktor Pipal, Emy Ferjanc, and Oskar Laske, and dealing with experiences during the Allied air raids.[37] A painting by Sergius Pauser called *Catastrophe 1945* was also shown, portraying, amidst all the images of concentration camps, the American air raid on Vienna's city center on 12 March 1945 in dramatic scenes as the "sacrifice" of the citizens of Vienna. The first time the air raids were "officially" dealt with was in the so-called *Austria Book* of 1948, which was published by Ernst Marboe under a commission from the federal news service.[38] Under the title *Das österreichische Nocturno*, the subject of the air raids on Vienna was broached: "Vienna's bitterest days had come. Above the city, which had been dragged into the machinery of armament, the bomber squadrons circled. The enemies from the front, destroying friends, in order to liberate."[39] Compared to 1946, by 1948 this portrayal was even more supportive of the image of Austria as a victim of National Socialism, which had been brought to Austria from the outside. This image had first started to develop

---

35 In both cities commemoration of the air raids started very early on—in Dresden, for example, on the first anniversary of the British air raids—but due to the differing political situations in the FRG and the GDR they took different forms. However, both took on, unbroken, the images and explanatory models established by Goebbels and his propaganda apparatus. Particularly in the case of Dresden, for example, and its remembrance of the air raids in February 1945, one finds conflicting interpretations, political instrumentalization by the SED (Socialist Unity Party of Germany) system and, after 1989, by various groups, mainly right-wing extremists. See: Thomas Fache, "Gegenwartsbewältigungen. Dresdens Gedenken an die alliierten Luftangriffe vor und nach 1989," in Luftkrieg. Erinnerungen in Deutschland und Europa, eds. Jörg Arnold, Dietmar Süß, Malte Thießen (Göttingen: Wallstein Verlag 2009), 221–238.

36 Oskar Helmer, "Österreich – das erste Opfer des Nazifaschismus," in "Niemals Vergessen:" Ein Buch der Anklage, Mahnung und Verpflichtung, ed. Gemeinde Wien (Vienna: Verlag für Jugend und Volk 1946), 28–30.

37 For example under the title "Die Fassung der Perle," pictures by Metzenbauer, Hafner, Schatz and Pipal illustrating the destruction of the city of Vienna by Allied air raids were shown. The area "Angst trieb uns unter die Erde" dealt with waiting in air raid shelters.

38 Ernst Marboe, ed., Das Österreich-Buch (Vienna: Verlag der Österreichischen Staatsdruckerei 1948).

39 Ibid., 535–540.

with the Moscow Declaration of 1943,[40] was only briefly interrupted by an
anti-Fascist phase in 1946, and was ultimately formalized as an important
and vital narrative connected with the negotiations for the State Treaty and,
until the 1980s, would determine the official self-image of the Republic.[41]
Although the air raids carried out by Allied forces starting in 1943 were the
central war experience of the civilian population, they were hardly included
in Austria's commemorative culture, if at all. This is surprising, in view of
the literary treatment of the air raids: while in Germany renowned authors
such as Heinrich Bröll, Gerd Ledig, and others dealt, more or less successfully, with (aerial) war experiences—usually their own—in Austria,[42] apart
from official interpretations, there was almost no discursive discussion of the
subject. As a foreign policy, this insistence on upholding the victim myth
continued after 1945, but domestically Austria was on a different course: the
dilemma of the Second Republic is illustrated by the political wooing of former Wehrmacht soldiers from the 1950s onward, their rehabilitation, and the
erection of monuments to fallen soldiers.[43] Local initiatives led to the names
of air-raid victims being added to monuments to the fallen, a fact that was
used as a shield during the debates, starting in the 1960s, on perpetration and
complicity. The air raids increasingly became an excuse for the unrestricted
perception of victimization, (Austria not only as the first victim of national
Socialism but as a victim of the war), linked with the symbol of St. Stephen's
Cathedral in flames, even though it had not been directly affected by air raids.
So, up until the 1980s, the air raids were not addressed but remained a central
element of Austria's victim-myth, increasingly perpetuated not by contemporary witnesses but by their descendants in the post-war period.

---

40 Günter Bischof, "Die Instrumentalisierung der Moskauer Deklaration nach dem 2.
Weltkrieg," Zeitgeschichte 20 (1993), issue 11/12, 345–366.
41 On the transformation of the Austrian victim myth see: Heidemarie Uhl, "Das 'erste'
Opfer."
42 Here, Hans Nossack's novel *Der Untergang*, which deals with the bombardment of
Hamburg, should be mentioned in particular. Gerd Ledig's novel Vergeltung, published in
1956, is a special case: the author gives an unembellished description of an American air raid
on an unidentified German city. He uses various perspectives to illustrate the experience:
that of the American bomber crew and those of various protagonists on the ground. Along
with the ill treatment of a crashed Allied airman, who ultimately dies of his injuries, Ledig
describes the rape of a woman in an air raid shelter. On its publication, Ledig's work was
met with shock and disgust, not least because his narrative contradicted the victim myth of
the Germans during the Allied aerial war. Gert Ledig, Vergeltung. Roman (Frankfurt/Main:
Fischer 1999); Hans Erich Nossack, Der Untergang (Frankfurt/Main: Suhrkamp 1976).
Summarised in: W.G Sebald, Luftkrieg und Literatur. With an essay on Alfred Andersch
(Frankfurt/Main: Fischer 2005).
43 Heidemarie Uhl, "Kriegerdenkmäler," in Memoria Austriae 1. Menschen – Mythen –
Zeiten, eds. Emil Brix, Ernst Bruckmüller (Vienna: Verl. für Geschichte u. Politik 2004)
545–559.

286   Goll: *"Terror Pilots" and "Bombing Holocaust":*
Discourses on Victimization and Remembrance in Austria
in the Context of the Allied Aerial Bombardment

The Victim-Myth Begins to Falter

The dispute over Kurt Waldheim's war past during his candidacy for Austrian President in 1986 decisively questioned the legitimacy of the victim myth, not only marking a turning point but also initiating a differentiated debate on National Socialist rule both in academia and the public arena. This was expressed in particular through increased public interest connected to research results, exhibitions, etc. in 1988, the so-called *"Bedenkjahr."*[44] According to Heidemarie Uhl, this clinging to the victim myth is "a largely marginalized and defensive argument stance,"[45] advocated primarily by the ÖVP. For example, *Bundesratsvorsitzende* Herbert Schambeck (ÖVP) remarked in his speech on the Anschluss at the memorial event of the national and federal council on 11 March 1988:

It should not go unspoken at this time that in Austria a total of 70,000 tonnes of explosive and incendiary bombs fell. Including soldiers, refugees, prisoners-of-war and foreigners, around 35,000 died and almost 57,000 were wounded as a result. Approximately 76,000 homes were totally destroyed and 101,000 partially. These figures are only the mathematical expression of everything that came upon our country as a result of 11 March 1938.[46]

The ÖVP politician thus called for a "double commemoration," a petition that came up again and again in 1988. Rudolf Kirchschläger, former *Bundespräsident* of the Republic, in turn emphasized that not only the political casualties of National Socialism should be remembered but also the fallen soldiers and air-raid victims, "only in this way could the fifty-year commemoration promote reconciliation."[47] Jewish victims and others, however, went unmentioned.

The memorial year 1988—just two years after the Waldheim Affair of 1986—served two purposes: on the one hand, particularly after the battering Austria's image took in 1986, the impression had to be created abroad that Austria was finally catching up and dealing with its past; on the other hand, the two major parties tried to come to a consensus and reach a harmonious agreement on the past. At the same time, as the statements quoted illustrate, the commemoration was increasingly linked with remembering air-raid victims. Austria's own victim status was to be reinforced by referring to the victims of air raids, and this created a victim rivalry. The commemoration of

---

44   See: Heidemarie Uhl, Zwischen Versöhnung und Verstörung: eine Kontroverse um Österreichs historische Identität 50 Jahre nach dem „Anschluss" (Vienna: Böhlau 1992).

45   Uhl, "Das 'erste' Opfer," 93.

46   Herbert Schambeck, speech, 11 march 1988, in Jahrbuch der österreichischen Außenpolitik/Außenpolitischer Bericht (Wien: Manz 1988), 465–469 (here 467–468).

47   Die Presse, February, 29 1988. Cited in: Uhl, Versöhnung, 137.

victims of Allied air raids became a contentious issue, illustrated particularly well by the conflict surrounding the "Memorial against war and fascism"
designed by Alfred Hrdlicka.[48] Approved by Vienna's council in 1983, the
monument, and even more the site where it was to be installed, were controversial.[49] Ultimately, the Albertinaplatz was chosen. This is where the
Philipphof once stood, before it was hit by the bomb dropped on 12 March
1945 and collapsed, burying 200-300 people who had sought refuge in the
air-raid shelter beneath it.[50] Objectors argued that the monument would
disturb the peace of the dead, although Hrdlicka's memorial included the
victims of air raids.[51] Despite opposition, the monument was realized in
1988. In the discussion that ensued, the ÖVP continually brought up the
proposal that a memorial site be created for Austrian air-raid victims, for
example, by putting the names of air-raid victims on the FLAK towers—
which ultimately did not play a decisive role as commemorative objects.[52] In
1988, the district administration office for the inner city set up next to the
memorial a commemorative plaque in remembrance of the 12 March 1945
and to "honor the memory of the dead and all the civilian victims of the air
raids during the Second World War on both sides."[53] In 2011, this plaque
was removed. Today, there is a cross at the edge of the square in memory of
the victims of the air raid.

"Destroyed" and "Annihilated": The Memorial Year 2005

The Memorial Year 2005 fell in the period of blue-and-black (FPÖ and
ÖVP) government, which put a lot of effort into the commemoration.[54] As

48   Holger Thünemann, Holocaust-Rezeption und Geschichtskultur: Zentrale Holocaust-
Denkmäler in der Kontroverse. Ein deutsch-österreichischer Vergleich (Idstein: Schulz-
Kirchner Verlag 2005).
49   "Älplerische Dumpfheit," Der Spiegel 30/1988, 118–120.
50   Dieter Klein, Martin Kupf, Robert Schediwy, Stadtbildverluste Wien: Ein Rückblick
auf fünf Jahrzehnte (Vienna: Lit 2005), 107–108.
51   Kronen-Zeitung, May 8, 1988; Hammerstein, "Weiße Flecken," 118.
52   "Flaktürme sollen Museen werden," Die Presse, February 26, 2005, 11.
53   Gedenken und Mahnen in Wien 1934–1945, Gedenkstätten zu Widerstand und
Verfolgung, Exil, Befreiung: Eine Dokumentation, ed. Dokumentationsarchiv des
Österreichischen Widerstandes (Vienna: Deuticke 1998), 32.
54   See: Günter Bischof, Michael S. Maier, "Reinventing Tradition and the Politics of
History: Schüssel's Restitution and Commemoration Policies," in The Schüssel Era in
Austria, Vol. 18, Contemporary Austrian Studies, eds. Günter Bischof, Fritz Plasser (New
Orleans: UNO Press/Innsbruck: Innsbruck University Press, 2010), 206–233 (here 217–
224). On the battle for hegemonial remembrance see: Matthew Berg, "Commemoration
versus Vergangenheitsbewältigung: Contextualizing Austria's Gedenkjahr 2005," German
History Vol. 26, No. 1 (2008), 47–71.

288   Goll: *"Terror Pilots" and "Bombing Holocaust":*
Discourses on Victimization and Remembrance in Austria
in the Context of the Allied Aerial Bombardment

2004 turned into 2005, *Bundeskanzler* Wolfgang Schüssel caused a stir with a speech in which he compared the destruction caused by the tsunami in Southeast Asia to Austria in the war's aftermath:

> Is it presumptuous to be reminded, when looking at images from the catastrophe regions, to be reminded of the sea of ruins sixty years ago in Austria, particularly in Vienna? I don't think so.[55]

He was not only comparing a natural disaster with events from the Second World War, but was also bringing to the fore the suffering of the civilian population.[56] This aspect, the suffering of the civilian population, was also included in all the activities of the commemorative year, which was peppered with a series of events "intended to make Austrian history palpable."[57] The memorial year 2005 in particular allows, according to Heidemarie Uhl, a "precise insight into the hierarchies of Austrian memories" of National Socialism after 1945.[58] In this context, the campaign "Twenty-five Peaces," organized by the planning office at the Federal Chancellery, must be emphasized.[59] Between March 2005 and July 2006, this campaign mounted several "interventions" and "happenings" in public spaces. The initiators declared that the aim was to speak to the public on an emotional level and "encourage them to think."[60] However, despite the Waldheim Affair and the memorial year 1988, the heart of this campaign was more focused on the unbroken narrative of Austria as a victim of the war and the occupation.

The first activity in the series of interventions, which began on 12 March 2005, was focused not on the Anschluss but on the heavy air raids

---

55   Wolfgang Schüssel in his speech on 14 Jan. 2005 opening the "Gedenkjahr," printed in: Program brochure 2005, ed. Bundeskanzleramt (Vienna 2005), 17–20 (here 17).
56   Robert Menasse referred to this speech in his essay published in 2005 in "Spectrum," writing: "The message was: even after the most drastic catastrophe, one should rise up from the wreckage through solidarity and the readiness to help—or was the message not in fact that Fascism was basically a natural disaster that had, like a flood tide, befallen an unprepared population that could not have wanted it, claimed innumerable victims, and reduced everything to ruins? Once it would have been considered a scandal even in Austria for Fascism to be compared to a natural disaster in parliament, but in 2005, there was not one report in the media, no commentary at all, finding fault with the tsunami-Fascism remark." Robert Menasse, "Österreich: Wende und Ende," Spectrum, Die Presse, 26 February 2005, I–V (here V).
57   Ibid.
58   Heidemarie Uhl, "'Österreich ist frei.' Die Re-Inszenierung der österreichischen Nachkriegsmythen im Jubiläumsjahr 2005," in Bedenkliches Gedenken: 1945–2005: Zwischen Mythos und Geschichte (=Schulheft 120), eds. Josef Seiler, Elke Renner, Grete Anzengruber (Studienverlag: Innsbruck 2005), 29–39 (here 30).
59   Schrempf, Peace dokumentiert.
60   Ibid., 3.

on Vienna in 1945: "peace *zerstört*" showed, "in memory of the victims of the most brutal bombardment, which Vienna suffered on 12 March 1945 at the hands of the Allies,"[61] several light and sound installations at various locations in the center of Vienna. The destructive effect of the air raids was clearly the focus. For example, in remembrance of the air raid and the burning city, St. Stephen's Cathedral was bathed alternately in white and red light—although the cathedral did not catch fire due to a bomb, but rather because of the looting that followed. Additionally, on the Neuer Markt, contemporary photographs of destroyed buildings and the names of casualties were projected on the walls of houses. The destroyed Philipphof was projected onto a wall of water, its outline traced by searchlights on the square in front of the Albertina. The final element of the installation was provided by spherical sounds. The intention of the organizers was to "remind people of what destructive power from the air was needed to defeat the terror on the ground"[62] and thus also to argue from the perspective of Austria as the victim. People experiencing the activity should "come so close to the horror of this time through sensory perception that they [could feel it]."[63] Two more activities dealt with the aerial bombardment: one was "peace *ausgelöscht*," where city maps, marked with white spaces to indicate buildings that had been damaged or destroyed by air raids, were handed out to those interested, in order to make people aware of "what unparalleled suffering war brought, not only to the wartime generation";[64] another was "peace *eingemauert*," which consisted of walling-in the two equestrian statues of Archduke Karl and Prince Eugene on the Heldenplatz.

"Twenty-five Peaces" triggered discussions in the media even before it opened.[65] For example, the light installations were deemed reminiscent of "the light columns by Albert Speer for the NSDP party conference"[66] or "a *son-et-lumière* spectacle with blackout,"[67] and the intervention series was seen as an "homage to the victim-myth."[68] The *Gedenkjahr* was dubbed the "*Gedankenlosjahr*"—the thoughtless year. The reason why Austria became the target of Allied air raids was never an issue, in fact the initiators were not interested in contextualizing, but far more in presenting, the destructive effects of the aerial bombardment and giving a biased view of a victimised

---

61 Ibid., 10.
62 Schrempf, Peace dokumentiert, 8.
63 Ibid., 12.
64 Ibid., 18; Menasse, Österreich: Wende und Ende, V.
65 See i.a. Bischof, Mayer, Reinventing Tradition. Also: "Gedenken im Geist der Opfertheorie," Der Standard, 7 February 2005.
66 Hans Rauscher, "Gedanken über den Bombenkrieg," Der Standard, 11 March 2005.
67 Robert Menasse, Österreich: Wende und Ende, V.
68 "Gedenken im Geist der Opfertheorie," Der Standard, 7 February 2005.

290   Goll: *"Terror Pilots"* and *"Bombing Holocaust"*:
Discourses on Victimization and Remembrance in Austria
in the Context of the Allied Aerial Bombardment

Austria, which was more fitting for the official programme of 2005's conservative government. While this central narrative of the Second Republic
focused on Austria as a victim of war and occupation, little attention was
paid to other groups of victims. What is particularly interesting about the
commemorative year 2005 is the handling of the double memorial day, 12
March. The heavy focus on 12 March 1945, connected with the tragedy of
the Philipphof, eclipsed the Anschluss to the German Reich in 1938.

The Regional Nature of Air-Raid Recollections

Regionally, memories of the Allied air raids took very different forms
after 1945. One particular example in this context is Wiener Neustadt, which,
due to the aircraft factories located there, was heavily hit by air raids and
suffered great damage. Victims here were already commemorated in 1946.
In September 1946, on the initiative of the mayor, a monument known as
the *"Bombensäule"* was erected as "a memorial of the 52,000 bombs that had
turned Wiener Neustadt into an expanse of rubble." Parts of the monument
were made of pieces of the town's destroyed buildings. This installation was
then set up in front of the Town Hall and was to have nails hammered
into it in the tradition of the charitable nailing of monuments during the
First World War. The proceeds would go to the rebuilding of the town.
Federal President Karl Renner ceremonially hammered in the first nail at a
commemorative event.[69] This example is an illustration of a very early and
unconventional form of local commemoration of the air raids, in which
the perception and visibility of the nation's role as a victim plays a crucial
part. Other forms of commemoration mainly appeared in the more recent
past. A series of memorial plaques were initiated, but the commemorative
events, held under the motto of "atonement" for the downed airmen, were
held not where the planes had come down but where they had dropped
their bombs.[70] In the community of Steyregg in Upper Austria, the only
"Aerial bombardment and peace monument" in Austria was erected in the
autumn of 2010, the central element being the remains of an aerial bomb.
The inscription on this monument reads: "From July 1944 to August 1945

---

69 "The commemoration in Wiener Neustadt," Österreichische Volksstimme, 1 October
1946, 3 and "The Bundespräsident in Wiener Neustadt," Neues Österreich, 1 October 1946,
3. On the function of the wartime nailing of wooden figures in Austria: Nicole-Melanie
Goll, "Kriegsfürsorge zwischen 'War Effort' und Herrschaftssicherung am Beispiel von
Graz (1914–1918)," in Historisches Jahrbuch der Stadt Graz 45–46 (Graz: Leykam 2016),
421–438.
70 E.g. in Fischbach, St. Jabob im Walde, Wenigzell and Ratten commemorative plaques
for downed American aircrews were installed.

during twenty-one air raids 8,400 bombs were dropped over Steyregg"; "154 houses were destroyed or seriously damaged"; "thirteen people died due to the bombs"; "The damage to nature is still visible today."[71] This monument, supported by the mayor and local political representatives, quickly came under fire. In particular, the Mauthausen Committee and other anti-fascist organizations in Upper Austria criticized the perspective of self-victimization. Two assessments classified the monument as "questionable" due to its lack context.[72] Sixty years after the end of the Second World War, the aerial bombardment was still being instrumentalized.

One particular element is the lack of commemoration of the victims of "*Fliegerlynchjustiz*" and of those shot-down Allied airmen who were actually murdered; they have been almost eradicated from memory. This finding is supported by the fact that despite there having been 130 documented murders, only one monument exists in remembrance of this National Socialist crime, and it is very controversial.[73] In Straßgang, a district of the city of Graz, early in March 1945 four airmen (possibly even six) were shot by the Waffen-SS and representatives of the National Socialist party apparatus in front of hundreds of spectators.[74] Shortly after the war ended, a stone memorial was erected on the site of the crime—which is, however, the subject of emotional debate to this day. There have been repeated calls for the replacement of this memorial stone with a monument to the victims of the air raid or to replace the inscription with the words "forgive us as we forgive them." It has not been possible to this day to have the names of the murdered victims listed on the monument.[75]

Conclusion

Today, the Allied aerial bombardment is still a controversial and much debated subject. This is illustrated by the German debates surrounding Jörg

---

71   Steyregger Nachrichten 6, October 2010.
72   "Academics criticise Steyregger 'Bombenkriegsdenkmal,'" Mauthausen Committee Austria (January 12, 2011), accessed November 30, 2017: www.mkoe.at/wissenschafter-kritisieren-steyregger-bombenkriegsdenkmal; "Kritik an Bomben-Mahnmal in Steyregg," Der Standard, (January, 12 2001), https://derstandard.at/1293370549648/Zumutung-Kritik-an-Bomben-Mahnmal-in-Steyregg;
73   Hoffmann, Verdrängte Erinnerung.
74   On the pilot murder in Straßgang see: Georg Hoffmann, "Der Fliegermord von Graz-Straßgang (4. März 1945)," in Historisches Jahrbuch der Stadt Graz, 45/46 (Graz: Leykam 2016), 439–458.
75   During the research project "Gedächtnisort Bombenkrieg" school children were involved in the renovation of the monument. See: Katharina Dick, Nicole-Melanie Goll, Georg Hoffmann, Bombenkrieg in Graz (Salzburg: self-publishing company 2017).

292   Goll: *"Terror Pilots" and "Bombing Holocaust"*:
Discourses on Victimization and Remembrance in Austria
in the Context of the Allied Aerial Bombardment

Friedrich, who in the early 2000s even compared the aerial bombardment to the Holocaust. Similar debates have not yet arisen in Austria, where a second victim-myth has developed around the question of whether Austria was "an innocent victim of the war." This replaced the first victim-myth (Austria as the first victim of National Socialism) when this construct collapsed as a result of the Waldheim Affair. The images and narratives built up around the aerial bombardment persist to this day, still leading to biased perceptions and the question of whether the aerial bombardment was a crime. Criminal aspects like the lynching of airmen, which do not fit the picture, are excluded from the debate. Another element that is not discussed is the fact that the National Socialist regime used the aerial bombardment to create a perception of victimization and shape perspectives, utilizing, to stabilize their own rule, perceptions of violence that in some cases are used to this day, unchanged and unfiltered. The aerial bombardment, its manipulation and perception, have not yet been completely processed. The image of St. Stephen's Cathedral in flames is still used as a symbol for the aerial bombardment of Austria. Past commemorations in 2005 and 2015 have shown how the unbroken victim myths continue to exist and are in some cases perpetuated. In the memorial year 2018, we will see how Austria will confront its past.

Behind the *Opfermythos*:
Fascism, Agency, and Accountability in Twentieth-Century Austria

Cathleen M. Giustino

Among the best-known photographs taken in twentieth-century Austria are those that recorded Jews being forced to scrub Viennese streets following the Anschluss in March 1938. For many viewing the pictures, the presence of ordinary citizens watching these humiliating scenes is evidence of Austrians' comfortable embrace of Nazi rule and complicity in the persecution and murder of the country's Jews, roughly 60,000 of whom perished in the Shoah. Those familiar with and critical of Austria's fascist pasts are sensitive to visible and invisible traces of Austrofascism and National Socialism in the black-and-white images of racism and discrimination being enacted in the country's capital.

These disturbing scenes of the persecution of an ethnic minority stand in contrast to, and rest uneasily with, the much more innocent vision of Austrians found in the *Opfermythos*. In this sanitized version of the past, Austrians living from the time of the Anschluss until the collapse of the Third Reich, regardless of any perpetration of violence that they committed, are universally presented as victims of Nazi power and injustice. It is a palliating storyline that hides the ugliness of Austria's fascist pasts. Since the war's end, the *Opfermythos* has been reproduced in party documents, government statements, historical scholarship, and children's textbooks. It has served as the official rendition of Austrian history for most of the Cold War with sizable critical assaults on it growing only as late as the 1980s, particularly once news of Kurt Waldheim's Nazi past became widely available to the public.[1]

The four articles under discussion here all speak to the *Opfermythos*. Taken together, they demonstrate that this representation of Austrian history during the Nazi era has been more than a therapeutic vision for helping a traumatized people to overcome difficult memories. It has also served as a resource with empowering potential, helping interest groups

---

1   For an informative survey of the history of the *Opfermythos*, also called the *Opfertheorie* and *Opferdoktrin*, see Heidmarie Uhl, "Das 'erste' Opfer: Der österreichische Opfermythos und seine Transformation in der Zweiten Republik," *Österreichische Zeitschrift für Politikwissenschaft*, 30 (2001): 19–34.

negotiate for political and economic resources in a society where the older, caste-like privileges of the estates system and *Honoratioren-Politik* stopped holding sway, and mass-democratic politicians became increasingly adept at reaching and bending the public's ear.

As Matthew Berg shows, since the collapse of the Third Reich, there have not been equal opportunities for all Austrians to enjoy the benefits of the *Opfermythos*. The postwar state created a complex set of hierarchical categories to classify victims of National Socialism and determine who was deserving of public assistance in the difficult early postwar years. Persons of non-Jewish descent who were able to prove they had fought in the resistance or spent time in Nazi prisons received the status of *Opfer* and associated funding sooner than did the small number of Jewish Shoah survivors. In this way, the *Opfermythos* was built, at least in part, on a continuation of the racism and discrimination seen in the photographs of Jews on their hands and knees, bowed over buckets and brushes, scrubbing Viennese streets.

Many scholars argue that the *Opfermythos* began with the Moscow Declaration in December 1943, in which Allied powers referred to Austria as the "first victim" of Nazi aggression. Ke-chin Hsia's article on interwar relief for veterans and their families, and Phillip J. Henry's study of shifts within Viennese psychoanalytic thought during the interwar period, suggest longer-term roots of the narrative and continuities across the Second World War. They urge recognition that May 1945 was no mere "zero hour" as well as consideration of how the trauma of the First World War and economic challenges during the interwar period prepared Austrian subjectivities for the *Opfermythos* and the concomitant avoidance of confrontation with ugly histories. Hsia's work suggests the need to reflect on how party-political competition for popular support in the First Austrian Republic contributed to the myth's development and establishment over time. Henry's piece encourages thought about the psychology behind the narrative and Freud's statement in *Civilization and Its Discontents* that, "life, as we find it, is too hard for us; it brings too many pains, disappointments and impossible tasks. In order to bear it we cannot dispense with palliative measures. 'We cannot do without auxiliary constructions,' as Theodor Fontane tells us."[2]

The word *Opfer* is generally translated as victim, a word that denotes a lack of agency, autonomy, and free will. Yet, the word does have another meaning. *Opfer* can also mean sacrifice, which implies having some possibility to be the master over one's own actions. Hsia's article suggests how this dual meaning gives the word a special empowering potential, one that

---

2   Sigmund Freud, *Civilization and Its Discontents*, trans. James Strachey (New York: W.W. Norton, 1961), 23.

allowed it to be used with different effects depending on circumstances and political goals. Each of the two meanings of the word *Opfer*, both of them emotionally charged, could be employed to appeal to a variety of audiences and for a variety of ends.

It is worthwhile to reflect on which contexts led to the word having the more common meaning of sacrifice, rather than victim. Also important are considerations about change over time, particularly beginning in the interwar period, going through the Nazi era, and moving across the postwar decades. Taken together, the four articles being discussed suggest a longer-term developmental trajectory in Austrian historical consciousness and national identity—one that transgresses the Second World War. They suggest that in this trajectory the word *Opfer* increasingly came to mean victim rather than sacrifice and that, as the scales tipped in the direction of victimhood, notions of agency, autonomy, and free will drained out of associations with the word and out of Austrian historical consciousness and identity.

The notion of collective victimhood is fraught with moral and ethical implications. It posits a situation in which independent thought and action are impossible due to intense contextual constraints and, as a result, individuals and groups are denied or think they are justified to deny accountability and responsibility. In this imagining of the human condition, everyone is stuck in a system that dictates human behaviors and in which even thinking people have no power to change the course of individual or national histories. This is to say that state actors who promoted the *Opfermythos* encouraged Austrians' disengagement from reflection on personal and national complicity in the Anschluss and the murder of the country's Jewish citizens. To borrow from the writings of the Austrian intellectuals Rudolf Burger and Ernst Hanisch, this suggests a "systematic self-infantalization" of Austrians.[3] Significantly—and here is a reason why the stakes of understanding the *Opfermythos* are so high—Austrian disengagement from responsibility and accountability for the Anschluss and the Shoah can extend to other contexts, including, for example, the plights of Turkish *Gastarbeiter* and Syrian refugees.

To fully appreciate the significance of the *Opfermythos* for Austrian agency and accountability, it is necessary to consider just how extensively this narrative has seeped into Austrian historical consciousness and self-understanding. After all, just because an official memory exists does not mean

---

3   Rudolf Burger, "Einleitung," *Faschismus in Österreich and International* (Vienna: Löcker Verlag, 1982), 12; and Ernst Hanisch, "Gab es einen spezifisch österreichischen Widerstand?," *Zeitgeschichte* 12 (1984-85): 340.

that it is internalized in the hearts and minds of all members of society. One way to evaluate the strength of the Austrian reception of the *Opfermythos* would be to situate the historical narrative within the wider landscape of memory politics in twentieth-century Austria. What other memory narratives or tropes were there in postwar Austria? Who are twentieth-century Austrian heroes, particularly the heroes who were not *Opfer* in any sense of the word?

Another way to explore the extent of the Austrian embrace of the victimhood myth is to move away from official memories of the Nazi years to private or personal memories.[4] In his article, Berg begins to do this with his analysis of *Opferfürsorgekarte* in postwar Vienna. By considering the documentation included with these applications for public assistance, Berg shows appreciation for how individuals aimed to negotiate between their personal experiences and state policies, sometimes taking on the identity of victim as a strategy for successfully achieving state support in difficult times. Nicole-Melanie Goll suggests another way to think about private memories and Austrians' embrace of the *Opfermythos*. Some Austrians personally experienced genuine fright and loss resulting from Allied bombings on their country during the Second World War. Recollections of those terrifying nights laid a basis for feelings of victimization—feelings that existed separately from, yet simultaneously could and did undergird, the official *Opfermythos*. One might wonder if personal memories of the bombings and private feelings of victimhood have been fading into oblivion as time passes and the generation that lived during the war passes away. In Goll's paper, this disappearance does not seem to be happening. Are memories of the bombings living on as post-memories, that is, as memories embraced by people who did not personally experience the event being remembered?[5]

Goll's article provides some evidence that Austrians did not universally embrace the *Opfermythos*, at least not during the 1980s, when revelations about Kurt Waldheim's wartime past led to much looking behind the cover of the official narrative, and a younger generation was asking hard questions about Austria's fascist pasts. She brings up debates about the placement of Alfred Hrdlička's *Monument Against War and Fascism* on Vienna's Albertinaplatz. The multipart work included a bronze statue of a Jew with

---

4   An older study of private memories of the Nazi years, based on oral-histories, is Meinrad Ziegler and Waltraund Kannonier-Finster, *Österreichisches Gedächtnis: Über Erinnern und Vergessen der NS-Vergangenheit* (Vienna: Böhlau, 1993).

5   On the concept of post-memory, see Marianne Hirsch, *Family Frames: Photography, Narrative and Postmemory* (Cambridge Mass.: Harvard University Press, 1997). See also the German Studies Association Presidential Address 2016: Irene Kacandes, "Die Ungnade der späten Geburt: Challenges in the Twenty-First Century for Central Europeans," *German Studies Review* 40, no. 2 (2017): 389–405.

a beard and a yarmulke lying prostrate on the pavement with a scrub-brush in his hand. Some Austrians had opposed situating the monument on this triangular space in the heart of Vienna, because for them it was associated with an alternate memory of victims and victimization. In March 1945, roughly 200 residents of Vienna died at this spot following an Allied air raid, and their bodies remain buried there, having never been unearthed. Despite the controversy over the monument's placement—controversy that Hrdlička and others inflamed with dramatic performances designed to provoke the public's confrontation with Waldheim's and other fascist pasts—it was unveiled on the Albertinaplatz in 1988.[6]

In 1990, Hrdlička affixed barbed wire to the back of his prostrate Jewish figure. While this alteration added further symbolism to the already rich monument, the intensification of meaning was not the primary impetus behind the change. The barbed wire was added to deter global tourists from using this evocative representation of Jewish suffering as a park bench— sometimes even eating ice-cream cones or posing for photographs while resting on it—as the Austrian filmmaker Robert Polak recorded.[7]

The fact that Hrdlička gave his scrubbing Jew the uncomfortable addition of sharp metal spikes so that visitors from around the world would be discouraged from sitting on it reminds us that Austrians are not the only people who have failed to confront, take accountability for, or even cared to know about ugly histories in the past. One can ponder German feelings of victimization during the Second World War found in Robert Moeller's book *War Stories* and ask if the *Opfermythos* is part of a common Central European political culture.[8] One can also reflect on current feelings of victimization in a former Cold War superpower known for "Coca-colonization" and the ease with which some politicians well beyond the borders of Austria and Central Europe encourage imaginings of innocence and helplessness—"systematic self-infantalization," some might say—in their quest for popular support and power.

---

6   A detailed discussion of Hrdlička's monument, which he dedicated "To the Viennese soul" as part of his criticism of Viennese indifference to the suffering of the Jews and Austrian complicity in that suffering, is in James E. Young, *The Texture of Memory: Holocaust Memorials and Meaning* (New Haven and London: Yale University Press, 1993), 104–112.
7   Michael Z. Wise, "Vienna Statue Altered," *Washington Post* (July 4, 1990), accessed January 31, 2018, https://www.washingtonpost.com/archive/lifestyle/1990/07/04/vienna-statue-altered/97ea7f2d-8d93-4b50-a0b0-4cec0edf0dfc/?utm_term=.3b69b3f89a8e
8   Robert G. Moeller, *War Stories: The Search for a Usable Past in the Federal Republic of Germany* (Berkeley and Los Angeles: University of California Press, 2003).

Review Essay

Gertrude Enderle-Burcel, Rudolf Jeřábek, Wolfgang Mueller eds., Die Protokolle des Ministerrates der Zweiten Republik der Republik Österreich: Kabinett Leopold Figl I., Vol. 7–10 (Vienna: Verlag der Österreichischen Akademie der Wissenschaften, 2016 –2017).

Günter Bischof

First, a personal story: when I began researching my dissertation in the mid-1980s, I was interviewed by a stern official in the Foreign Ministry to apply for access to do research in the "*Ministerratsprotokolle*" (the minutes of the "Ministerial Council" = Cabinet). I knew that the Cabinet met weekly and discussed the most important matters of state during the occupation decade, 1945 to 1955, the topic of my dissertation.[1] The Cabinet meetings represented the top of the decision making pyramid in Austrian politics. I was denied access. My dissertation adviser, Professor Ernest F. May, wrote a letter to Chancellor Franz Vranitzky, asking him to grant me access; it was denied again. In subsequent years, when I showed up in the Austrian State Archives on Nottendorfer Strasse, it is possible that I was sitting next to researchers who were working in the Cabinet minutes; in other words, select colleagues did receive access to study this important source. Therefore, steady progress in the publication of these minutes now being published jointly by the State Archives and the Austrian Academy of Sciences is much welcomed. Given the rate of publication—two months of minutes (approximately ten meetings) make up a published volume—nine more volumes or so should appear on the first term of Leopold Figl as Chancellor (Figl I). At the rate of two volumes a year, it will take another five years until the entire Figl I Cabinet minutes will have been published. Publication of Figl II and Raab I, II, and III will presumably happen in the more distant future.

The richness of the discussions in these four volumes under review confirms that these Cabinet minutes are a premier source for researching contemporary Austrian history. The most important subject matters cropping up almost every week in these meetings are: 1) The Austrian State Treaty

---

1   Günter Bischof, "Between Responsibility and Rehabilitation: Austria in International Politics, 1940–1950" (PhD Diss., Harvard University, 1989).

and domestic security; 2) the Austrian government's conflictual relations
with the occupation powers, especially the Soviets; 3) American aid programs, the beginnings of Marshall Plan aid and their role in both feeding
the hungry Austrians and postwar economic reconstruction; 4) the return
of Austrian prisoners of war (POWs); 5) the problem of refugees/displaced
persons (DPs) in postwar Austria.[2] These topics will be addressed in the
following pages.

Chancellor Figl and Foreign Minister Karl Gruber regularly reported
on the ups and downs of state treaty negotiations in almost every Cabinet
meeting. The state treaty, after all, was to end the four-power occupation of
Austria and give the country back its full sovereignty. In December 1947,
the Council of Foreign Ministers (CFM) met in London to negotiate the
German and Austrian treaties; German treaty talks were deadlocked and
overshadowed progress on the Austrian Treaty. But the Deputies of the
Foreign Ministers met again in London to negotiate the Austrian Treaty
and met regularly until May, when talks finally broke down over Yugoslav
territorial and reparations demands on Austria. Some progress was made
on the issue of "German assets"; the Vienna Treaty Commission had established precise lists of the contested "German assets" in Austria. An American
suggestion, presented to the public by French Deputy High Commissioner
Paul Cherièrre, for Austria to cede part of the Danube shipping and the
oil assets to the Soviets and redeem the rest of the German assets with a
"lump sum" payment to the Soviets was discussed in London. The Soviets
wanted $200 million for handing back these German assets to the Austrian
government after the conclusion of the treaty; after much bargaining, the
Deputies of the four powers agreed on $150 million.[3] Chancellor Figl
reported to the Cabinet, after the $200 million lump sum payment was
raised in the London Deputies meeting that "we need to do everything
in our might to receive these dollars from the Americans" (MRP 97 1 a,
1948-01-27, vol. 9, 6).[4]

Gruber reported on the London CFM on the eve of Christmas 1947
that the Soviets mainly used tactics of "sharp propaganda" to advance their
cause. The Western powers felt that "no progress could be made with Russia
at the moment." First Western Europe needed "to get healthy" with the
help of the Marshall Plan. The Western powers were not inclined "to close

---

2   These principal themes are concisely laid out and addressed in Stefan Semotan's
"historical introductions" to each of these volumes, MRP, Vol. 7, XI-XXXIX; vol. 8, XI-
XXXIV; vol. 9, XI-XXXIII; vol. 10, XI-XXXIII.
3   See also Günter Bischof, Austria in the First Cold War, 1945–55: The Leverage of the
Weak (Houndmills-New York: Macmillan/St. Martin's, 1999), 105–149.
4   All translations from the original German into English are my own.

the door" on Austrian Treaty talks. But they feared that signing a treaty and withdrawing their occupation forces at this point in time might lead to a collapse of the Austrian government, given the threat from Yugoslavia and a return of the Soviets to the country with their control of the Austrian oil industry (MRP 93 1 h, 1947-12-23, vol. 8, p. 203–204). After the resumption of the Deputies of the Foreign Ministers meetings in London in January, Gruber's regular reports to the Cabinet became even bleaker.

When the Czechoslovak Communists seized power in Prague in late February 1948, the tocsin of potential problems for Austria was sounded.[5] Already on 24 February, Figl reported to the Cabinet that "the situation in the CSR had repercussions in London." Austria's fight for freedom was getting more difficult with Czechoslovakia becoming a "people's democracy." No help could be expected from neighbors such as Italy and Switzerland; Italy was caught up in its forthcoming April elections, and the Swiss people "were even more nervous" than the Austrians living in the Soviet zone of occupation (MRP 101 1 a, 1948-02-24, vol. 9, p. 170–171). The Foreign Minister reported extensively in a special Cabinet session arranged for Karl Gruber, back from London in early March. The Communist coup in Prague made an "incredible impression" in London. These events "have taught the West a great lesson" and are unifying the West in "speeding up political and military preparations." The coup in Prague also increased the need for the Marshall Plan. The Western powers advised to maintain "the greatest caution" when it came to signing an Austrian treaty. As long as the occupation continued, Austria was secure. However, Austria needed to rearm to be prepared for the post-treaty era. Gruber advised that Austrians needed to find out from the Russians whether they could start building an army on the day the treaty was signed; this would only allow a three-month window for rearmament. Moreover, the "lump sum" the Russians demanded from Austria must not be so high that Austria's economic viability was threatened. The Americans wanted to make sure that Marshall Plan aid to Austria did not fall into Russian hands. Minister of Education Felix Hurdes noted that the Austrian public was following events in Czechoslovakia very closely and many have said: "We are very happy that the [Western] Allies are here" (MRP 102a 1, 1948-03-04, vol. 9, p. 245–248, p. 252).

In late March, while final passage of the Marshall Plan was being debated in the U.S. Congress, Gruber phoned Chancellor Figl from London,

---

5   The repercussions of the Prague Coup on Austria was already discussed in Günter Bischof, "'Prag liegt westlich von Wien': Internationale Krisen im Jahre 1948 und ihr Einfluss auf Österreich," idem/Josef Leidenfrost., eds., Die bevormundete Nation: Österreich und die Alliierten, 1945–1949 (Innsbruck: Haymon Verlag 1988), 315–345.

telling him that the Deputies' talks were "revolving around the issue of who will pay" the lump sum (MRP 105 1a, 1948-03-23, vol. 9, p. 352). In early April, Gruber was back in Vienna and reported that "there is a large movement afoot in Europe towards a security organization that could stop Soviet advances." The Marshall Plan was one approach; the Brussels Conference and the remilitarization of Western Europe was another. Gruber continued to state that some voices said the Russians wanted an Austrian treaty and a quick withdrawal of occupation forces to then return again. For this reason, Austria needed its own security forces—an army and the police—fully armed. Whether the Russians might be negotiated down to a lump sum payment of $100 million to be paid in three years was not clear yet; "*the result for Austria will always be that we cannot live without substantive help from the Americans*" (my emphasis) (MRP 106 4 & 4b, 1948-04-06, vol. 10, p. 13, p. 15–16). Figl reported in mid-April that treaty negotiations in London had been "hardening" (*versteift*). The Russians were not prepared to make any more concessions; the Western powers wanted to make sure that Austria could meet its financial obligations. The Americans did not want to pay for the lump sum, since it considered it a form of reparations: "*in this case America would pay reparations to Russia*" (my emphasis) (MRP 107 1d, 1948-04-13, vol. 10, p. 60). In May 1948, the American Deputy Samuel Reber walked out of the meetings in London over Soviet support of Yugoslav territorial and reparations demands, reported Figl. The conclusion of the Austrian Treaty was postponed once again (MRP 113 1 a, 1948-05-25, vol. 10, p. 285).

"Reparations" to the Soviets came in various forms of what could be called "occupation currency." As a "liberated country" Austria, of course, was not supposed to pay reparations. But the Soviets found many ways to extract payments (many in kind) from Austria. Austria paid hefty occupation costs for the armies of occupation.[6] The Americans stopped asking for occupation payments in 1947 (and returned those paid up until that point in time). The Soviets, British, and French continued to insist that their occupation troops (who also served as kind of security forces in their respective zones of occupation) be paid by the Austrian government (payments ceased in 1953); the Soviets always kept as many Red Army soldiers in their zone as the three Western powers combined did in their zones. On 20 May, 1948, the Austrian government sent a protest note to the Allied Council; it was

---

6   Austria paid approximately 3.2 billion Austrian Schillings in occupation costs between 1945 and 1947, 407 million in 1947 (minus 30 million for the U.S.); so, presumably, the Soviets, British, and French demanded some 377 million ATS for 1948, see Hans Seidel, Österreichs Wirtschaft und Wirtschaftspolitik nach dem Zweiten Weltkrieg (Vienna: Manz, 2005), 129–130.

published the next day in the official *Wiener Zeitung* to increase the public pressure on the powers that "three years of occupation" was enough (MRP 112 14 b, 1948-05-18, vol. 10, 268n85). Chancellor Figl reported to the Cabinet in the next meeting that the protest note "caused quite a stir," and he felt positive that it will lead to reduced payments (MRP 113 d, 1948-05-25, vol. 10, p. 285–286). In the beginning of June, Figl saw General Alesksej Zheltov, the Deputy Soviet High Commissioner, who "was upset" about the protest note, adding "he had to pay his soldiers." Zheltov felt Austria could easily afford the 600 million Schillings in occupation costs; as a gesture of good will, Figl noted that Austria only had "14 million available" (MRP 114 1 b, 1948-06-02, vol. 10, p. 326–327). Figl noted that the British were "checking" on the Austrian payments (MRP 115 d, 1948-06-08, vol. 10, 356).

Soviet demands on "German assets" were a premier challenge for the Austrian government in these years. They had seized hundreds of such assets in June 1946 from the Austrians and exploited them for "reparations out of current production." During a time when Austrians lacked coal and fuel to heat their homes and drive their economy forward, the Soviets shipped tens of thousands of tons of oil from the seized "Austrian" oil assets eastward, (after the Anschluss in 1938, the Nazis bought or seized American, British, and French assets in Austria), or sold them at high prices on the domestic market, without paying any taxes to the government. In the beginning of January 1948, the Russians threatened the Austrian government that "they had to increase mineral oil products by 100 percent," since they needed funds for new investments into the oil industry (MRP 95 1 c, 1948-01-13, vol. 8, p. 298–299). The Soviets also refused permission to ship flour from their zone to Vienna, thus threatening the bread supply for the Viennese (MRP 93 17 f, 1947-12-23, vol. 8, p. 222n125).

Food Minister Otto Sagmeister suggested that food (and coal) shortages were part of Moscow's plans to create "a supply crisis," presumably to help the Austrian Communists seize power (MRP 97 10, 1948-01-27, vol. 9, p. 24–25 and p. 25n94). The Soviets also had been seizing assets of the Austrian railroad corporation as "war booty": seventy-five locomotives ("German assets"), or hundreds of wagons (including wagons to transport the Austrian mail) – this at a time when all Austrian railroad assets were badly needed to transport American food aid from the Italian port of Trieste to Austria. Figl speculated whether "their constant demands were intended to create economic problems" for Austria (MRP 106 11, 1948-04-06, vol. 10, p. 24–26). In a typical meeting with Zheltov, Chancellor Figl raised the issue of railroad wagons and locomotives being seized, telephone lines to the West being cut, oil deliveries to the Austrian Railroads ÖBB being reduced, POWs not being returned, disappeared officials not being located, and the Soviets complaining that newspapers in the Tyrol were giving the Soviets "bad press" for apprehending Austrians off the streets (MRP 1051 c, 1948-03-23, vol. 9, p. 352–354).

Next to these constant economic depredations discussed in almost every Cabinet meeting, the most disconcerting policy of the Soviet occupation element was that during this time they regularly snatched people they suspected of spying or criticizing the Soviets in public. Ferdinand Riefler, a state representative from Lower Austria, had an altercation with a local Communist and was detained by the Soviets, put on trial and received six to eight years imprisonment "in Siberia." Interior Minister Helmer commented that such punishment reminded him of "medieval methods" (MRP 80 1 j, 1947-09-16, vol. 7, p. 49). The case of the official of the Austrian Federal Railroads Paul Katscher, who "disappeared" on his way home from work one day, was raised frequently in these meetings. The Soviets denied holding him in their prisons. Oskar Helmer, the outspoken Minister of the Interior, noted that "people disappear every day [...] all we can do is protest" (MRP 93 17 g, 1947-12-23, vol. 8, p. 223–326). It is assumed Katscher died in a transit camp in Lemberg in late June 1948 (see his short bio, vol. 8, p. 499). Hundreds of people disappeared in Russian jails in Austria and the Soviet Union—many did not return. When the Soviets tried to apprehend the high ministerial official Hans Wolf, he asked to be transferred to Linz. The Cabinet did not want to start transferring officials, like policemen, who were being intimidated in their jobs. Helmer reminded his Cabinet colleagues, "you have no idea how cowardly and intimidated officials are" (MRP 115 1 h, 1948-06-08, vol. 10, p. 157–158).

Maybe the most daunting challenge for the Austrian government—tying these four volumes of Cabinet minutes together—is the constant worry about how to feed the Austrian population. At the beginning of 1948, the goal of the Food Ministry was to feed the average Austrian 1,800 calories, increased to 1,900 daily calories with the onset of Marshall Plan deliveries. Of these, Austrian farmers only managed to supply 820 calories. The severe rationing of food supplies led the government to pressure Austria's farmers to deliver required amounts of grains, milk, meats, potatoes, etc. to make up this domestic Austrian portion toward achieving the daily calorie level needed for the population to survive. But many of the farmers did not listen to governmental mandates and preferred to sell on the black market, where they could fetch better prices. Alfred Migsch, the Socialist Minister for Energy and Electrification, questioned the low productivity of Austrian agriculture, growing only thirty-four percent of the 1937 production levels (when eighty percent of the daily 3,000 calories had come from domestic production). Despite agriculture receiving the lion's share of foreign aid, it was not increasing its productivity, Migsch complained. Josef Kraus, the conservative Minister of Agriculture, blamed the low productivity on a bad harvest in 1947 and lack of agriculture labor (WMK [*Wirtschaftliches Ministerkomitee* = Cabinet Subcommittee on Economic Issues] 49 3, 1948-02-18, vol. 9, p. 401).

One of the most bizarre discussions—plainly showing a high level of desperation in the Figl government—happened over acquiring 40,000 tons of Swiss potatoes; the Swiss would be compensated for 10,000 tons of potatoes with Austrian iron and wire. The Minister of Food asked Hans Rizzi, the President of the Austrian National bank, to guarantee 7.5 million in Swiss Francs to pay for the rest of the Swiss potatoes. Rizzi refused to issue such a guarantee, as the National Bank was out of foreign currency and close to bankruptcy. Helmer, the Socialist Minister of the Interior, warned his colleagues: "*If we have nothing to eat, we must be afraid of riots* [*Krawalle*]" (my emphasis). May 1948 will be the "critical month," Helmer cautioned, to secure sufficient food supplies. Chancellor Figl noted that the Swiss were afraid of a coup in Austria: "If they were so afraid and had sufficient potatoes, they might consider a deal [*sollen sie sich das etwas kosten lassen*]"; Figl suggested "to negotiate with the Swiss and to procrastinate" [*die Sache in die Länge ziehen*]. Peter Krauland, the conservative Minister of Property Control and Economic Planning, suggested that the National Bank take the risk and provide a guarantee for this transaction. He castigated the Swiss for "the flight of their capital to the U.S.," pronouncing that "the capitalists have always proven to be amongst the most idiotic people." In the end, the Cabinet approved of this deal, on the conditions that the Minister of Finance guaranteed the purchase and the National Bank provided the foreign currency. At the same time, the Foreign Ministry should, Krauland argued, negotiate with the Swiss to lower the price and ask the Americans whether they could pay for the Swiss potatoes (MRP 105 9 d, 1948-03-23, vol. 9, p. 363–367).

When the food situation got desperate in postwar Austria, the Cabinet expected the Americans to come to the rescue. After the U.S. Army and the United Nations Relief and Rehabilitation Administration (UNRRA, mostly financed by U.S. taxpayers) secured the survival of the Austrian population in 1945/46, the U.S. Congress passed two Interim Aid programs to feed the Austrians until the beginning of the Marshall Plan. Sale of American "excess products" provided interim help, as did Quaker aid, shipping 4,000 tons of food to Austria. The U.S. even provided 1,000 railroad cars to Austria to ship food financed by the Interim Aid program from Trieste to Austria. Chancellor Figl noted that "these wagons had to roll around the clock" (MRP, 94 1 n, 1948-01-06, vol. 8, p. 254). A whopping sixty percent of Austria's food supplies were financed by "American aid programs" like the Interim Aid Program (MRP 95 10 d, 1948-01-13, vol. 8, 317). The British provided a loan; the Canadians helped with food and medicine; Argentina offered some food.

Congress finally passed the "European Recovery Program" (ERP) in early April 1948, when the security situation in Western Europe worsened dramatically after the Prague Coup. The West was afraid that the Communists might win the election in Italy in April. Austria's food and security situation was so desperate that the West worried that the country might be next on the list of Communist takeovers.[7] Already, in January 1948, Figl asserted that the Marshall Plan needed to be seen "in conjunction with the building of the Eastern Bloc" (MRP 96 1 c, 1948-01-20, vol. 8, 333).

The crisis over Czechoslovakia provided the major impetus to pass the ERP in Washington. At the beginning of March, Gruber flew in from London for a special Cabinet session. He reported that events in Czechoslovakia had made "a tremendous impression" in the West. The crisis had been leading to "unity in domestic and foreign policies"; the events in Prague had provided the Marshall Plan with "new impetus [*Auftrieb*]". "Nothing will happen before the Italian election," Gruber warned, and the Western powers had become much more cautious when it came to conclude an Austrian treaty. They argued that "as long as the country is occupied, there will not be any incidents [*Vorfälle*]." Austria needed an army before the West would withdraw its occupation forces. While negotiations were beginning in Paris between the sixteen countries participating in the Marshall Plan, the Americans were worried about making sure that none of the Marshall aid would fall into Soviet hands (MRP 102 a 1, 1948-03-04, vol. 9, 246–257). In the weekly Cabinet meeting a few days later, Chancellor Figl warned his ministers that the "Communists were trying to create unrest with labor strikes," demanding better food rations and higher salaries, in the Soviet zone of occupation. Figl informed his colleagues that he wrote a letter to Secretary of State George C. Marshall, asking for at least eight weeks of food supplies. If only one week of rations were arriving, the entire Marshall Plan program was in jeopardy. He warned Marshall starkly: "*If Austria falls, all of Europe falls*" (my emphasis) (MRP 103 1 a, 1948-03-09, vol. 9, 276).

---

7   Bischof, *Austria in the First Cold War*, 111–116.

While the crucial nexus between American food aid through the Marshall Plan and the prevention of domestic unrest and Communist take-over was being established, the Cabinet also began to deliberate who would administer the Marshall Plan.[8] As always in important matters, a Cabinet subcommittee was set up to make suggestions to the full body; subcommittees also served as a means of procrastination. While Krauland's Ministry was responsible for the planning agenda, Gruber's Foreign Ministry would take charge of all negotiations with Washington and with the Marshall Plan bodies being set up in Paris (such as the Economic Cooperation Administration's (ECA) bureaus). The Federal Chancellery would take care of all financial and commercial transactions (the old UNRRA office called "Österreich-Hilfe" was located in the *Bundeskanzleramt*). It was also decided to send Rudolf Leopold, a food expert in the Foreign Ministry, and Hans Igler, a young planning expert from the Krauland Ministry, to Washington to provide additional expertise to the Austrian Embassy staff in their negotiations with the State Department (MRP 101 7 d, 1948-02-24; 103 8 d, 1948-03-09; 104 9 b, 1948-03-16, vol. 9, p. 191, p. 291, p. 333). In mid-March, Gruber attended the first big meeting of what would become the Organization of European Economic Cooperation (OEEC), where all the foreign ministers from the participating countries met. Gruber reported to Vienna that "the mood was good" as all non-communist countries were sitting together and worrying about the election outcome in Italy (MRP 104 1 b a and ad 1b, 1948-03-16, vol. 9, p. 314, p. 318). In preparation for the final passage of the Marshall Plan "country studies" had been prepared by experts in the State Department. According to the country study ("Brown Book"), Austria was scheduled to receive $151 million for 1948/49; Austria argued it required much more for its food and investments needs. In the end, Austria's first allotment for the first year of the Marshall Plan was $281 million (WMK 49 a, 1948-03-19, vol. 9, p. 409n3).

Stung by the Prague Coup, Congress passed the Marshall Plan at the beginning of April. Gruber reported back from London and Paris that the Marshall Plan served as the means "to stop Soviet advances" in Europe. At the same time military planning was going on in Brussels (what would become the "Western Union" and later NATO). Gruber predicted that 1948 would be "a year of insecurity" as long as the West was not organized militarily. The main goal of the Marshall Plan was "increased economic cooperation" in Europe. Treaties were also signed establishing the OEEC;

---

8   On the Marshall Plan and its administration, see Günter Bischof and Hans Petschar, *The Marshall Plan since 1947: Saving Europe, Reconstructing Austria* (Vienna: Brandstätter, 2017), 100–107.

Wilhelm Taucher, an economist, represented Austria in this body (MRP 106 4 and 4 b, 1948-04-06, vol. 10, p. 13, p. 15n52). Gruber reported to the Cabinet that Austria received $70 million per quarter in grants—the "highest amount" of Marshall aid of all sixteen participating countries. Taucher in the OEEC and the Austrian negotiators in Paris and Washington had done a fine job (MRP 112 ad 1 d, 1948-05-18, vol. 10, p. 258). At the beginning of June 1948, Chancellor Figl confirmed the positive outcome of the Marshall Plan negotiations in Paris, where Austria had received a "special position [*Sonderstellung*]" (MRP 115 b, 1948-06-08, vol. 10, p. 355).[9]

While the London Austrian treaty negotiations were slowing down and the Austrian food situation remained quite desperate until the arrival of Marshall aid, anxiety about a possible Communist coup continued. In a Cabinet meeting on 20 April, Chancellor Figl made fun of this constant "*Putsch Angst*" by noting "today a coup [*Staatsstreich*] was supposed to happen in Austria," and a French colonel called to wonder whether he should put the French Army in Austria "on alert [*in Alarmzustand setzen solle*]". Figl calmed him down, remarking that in spite of all the rumors floating around: "calm is prevailing in Austria [*in Österreich volle Ruhe herrsche*]" (MRP 108 1 d, 1948-04-20, vol. 10, p. 111–112).

The return of Austrian POWs from the Soviet Union was another topic coming up regularly in the Cabinet discussions in 1947/48. In the fall of 1947, Austrian POWs were beginning to be repatriated by the Soviet Union via a transit camp in Marmaros-Szigeth in Romania, where some 8,000 POWs were crowded into a camp waiting to come home. In mid-September, the second train, with 1,000 POWs, was arriving in Wiener Neustadt, and Interior Minister Helmer was there for the welcome. He asked his Cabinet colleagues to help him welcome 40 more trainloads of returning POWs, making sure that each train was welcomed by a member of the government (MRP 80 8 b, 1947-09-16, vol. 7, p. 61). During the next meeting, Helmer griped that conditions in Marmaros-Szigeth were bad and that the Austrian POWs were told "the [Austrian] government consisted only of fascists, who were pleased that the POWs were not returning home." Chancellor Figl confirmed that individual Cabinet ministers were to welcome back every train of returning POWs, for welcoming ministers "gave returnees [*Heimkehrer*] a feeling of security and took uncertainty away" (MRP 81 14 c, 1947-09-26, vol. 7, p. 101).

Helmer informed the Cabinet that returning POWs received fifty Austrian Schillings (ATS) from the federal government and eighty ATS

9   Was Austria a "special case" case in the Marshall Plan? See Bischof/Petschar, The Marshall Plan, 107–108.

from the City of Vienna—some local communities handed them as much as 500 to 1,000 ATS. Returning POWs from Western countries, however, received little attention and only ten ATS as welcome money. Helmer added: "In some communities the returnees were welcomed and handed around for kisses [*zum Kuss herumgereicht*]; the next day they are found out to have been Nazis" (MRP 82 11, 1947-10-07, vol. 7, p. 143–144). Half a year later, Helmer reported to the Cabinet a Soviet colonel had informed him that the return of some 55,000 Austrian POWs was completed. Yet some 8,000 to 10,000 thousand Austrian POWs were still in Soviet camps, Helmer protested, held back because they were Nazis, SS, or staff officers (MRP 102, 9 c, 1948-03-02, vol. 9, p. 229–230). Some 130,000 Austrian had been registered as POWs in Soviet camps. 1,124 Austrian POWs were convicted of war crimes and/or spying in 1949; many returned only by the mid-1950s. About a third of these were "rehabilitated" after 1996.[10]

Taking care of hundreds of thousands of Displaced Persons (DPs) in numerous camps in Western Austria was another highly contentious issue coming up regularly in these Cabinet discussions. The federal government had to take care of these refugees from all over Europe stranded in Austria at the end of the war (expelled *Volks-* and *Sudeten-* Germans from all over Eastern Europe, stateless people, Jews, etc.). In October 1947, 593,774 DPs (33,513 Jews) and refugees were still in Austria without any prospect for repatriation or new homes. The Americans refused to help pay for them; the International Refugee Organization (IRO) did not have sufficient funds to help pick up the slack (MRP 83 5, 1947-10-14, vol. 7 p. 196–197 [for the exact numbers, see p. 196n45]). Chancellor Figl told an American Congressional delegation that it was impossible for Austria to continue to feed half a million DPs. Helmer had reported earlier that on July 1, 1947, the U.S. transferred some 135,000 Jews—many of them in Upper Austrian camps—to the Austrian government, expecting Austria to take care of them. Helmer characterized them as being "unwilling to work" (MRP 81 1 1 & n, 1947-09-26, vol. 7, 81, 82–83). Socialist Vice Chancellor Adolf Schärf argued that Jewish DPs "ruined" entire areas such as the Gastein Valley, where they lived in hotels. Vinzenz Übeleis, the Socialist Minister of Transport, pronounced a general prejudice rampant at the time that "the DPs live better than the Austrian population" (MRP 104 5, 1948-03-16, vol. 9, 324–326).

---

10 The Ludwig-Boltzmann-Institute in Graz has researched the trial files of these 1,124 convicted Austrian POWs, see Harald Knoll, "Späte Heimkehr: Als Kriegsverbrecher verurteilte österreichische Kriegsgefangene in der Sowjetunion 1944 bis 1953," in: Günter Bischof, Stefan Karner, and Barbara Stelzl-Marx, eds., Kriegsgefangene des Zweiten Weltkrieges: Gefangennahme – Lagerleben – Rückkkehr (Vienna: R. Oldenbourg, 2005), 167–193.

One of the issues frequently discussed was the permanent relocation of DPs. Austria would have liked to keep the Germans from Southern Bohemia and Moravia, but they were supposed to be relocated to Bavaria. Germans from Yugoslavia (Batschka and Banat) were welcome to stay and receive citizenship (*Einbürgerung*). France and Great Britain wanted skilled workers. Helmer warned his colleagues that he did not want Austria to be stuck with the "refuse" of children and old people who would be a burden (*dass der Mist zurückbleibt*). The Cabinet decided to set up a fund to keep agricultural workers in Austria (*Sesshaftmachungsfonds*) (MRP 85 6, 1947-10-29, vol. 7, p. 271–275). When Argentina offered to take skilled workers, Helmer used the same language, stating that Austria did not want to be stuck with the "*Mist*" (MRP 1 e, 1948-03-16, vol. 9, p. 316–317). While Austria had half a million DPs in the land to support, the IRO only recognized 150,000 that it was willing to pay for—not accepting *Volks-* and *Sudeten-Germans* as being "DPs" (MRP 114 1 b, 1948-06-02, p. 330). As early as April 1946, the Austrian parliament had already called upon the Figl government to resolve the issue of DPs with the Allied Council, to spare the Austrian budget the high cost of feeding these people during these difficult times (MRP 114 1 b, 1948-06-02, p. 330n30).

These rank prejudices expressed by Cabinet members regarding Jewish DPs need to be seen against the larger backdrop of the extremely strained budgetary situation in postwar Austria and the major challenge of providing the Austrian population with sufficient food.[11] In the larger context, the Figl government struggled during these difficult months of 1947/48 with keeping both the Austrian population and democratic governance alive at a time when insufficient food supplies might lead to riots and a Communist takeover. The desperation of the government was also discernible in its struggles against Soviet depredations and keeping American aid flowing. Trying to get rid of the occupation powers and their many demands on the government, which would be brought about by the conclusion of an Austrian Treaty, was a top priority. There is many a *cri de coeur* in these

---

11　The British scholar Robert Knight received access to the Ministerratsprotokolle and published select bits and pieces of them dealing with "Jewish" issues, such as DPs and restitution, see Robert G. Knight, ed., 'Ich bin dafür die Sache in die Länge zu ziehen': Die Wortprotokolle der österreichischen Bundesregierung von 1945 bis 1952 über die Entschädigung der Juden (Frankfurt/Main: Athenäum, 1988). Interior Minister Helmer's suggestion "to procrastinate" on the issue of restitution of property to Jewish is not so remarkable when considering that procrastination—buying time—was a principle of Austrian governance at the time, as many issues that were hard to resolve were pushed back for a decision on a later day. Helmer, as it turns out when viewing the whole body of Cabinet meetings, consistently was the most outspoken member of the Cabinet, prone to using salty language.

Cabinet discussions that show the high level of desperation, and that might explain some of these highly prejudiced remarks. No question, the continuity of elite Austrian anti-semitism from the First to the Second Republic shows its ugly face here too.[12] The Figl government aimed at rebuilding a nation after World War II with much of its physical infrastructure in shambles. Any obstacle hindering this reconstruction process was quickly dismissed.

Many other issues come up in these discussions that cannot be treated in detail here. The currency reform of late 1947 is a prominent recurring subject, as are issues related to denazification and restitution and Allied censorship. Perhaps most bizarrely, every meeting had to approve lists of new citizens as well as promotions of government officials to coveted titles (without pay raises) such as "*Hofrat*" and "*Regierungsrat.*" Also, the appointment of every university professor in Austria had to be approved by the Cabinet.

The edition of these Cabinet meetings—the largest editing project on the history of the Second Austrian Republic—is a first-rate historical project. The editorial team needs to be congratulated on its clear and consistently high editorial standards and highly informative apparatus of additional information. The excellent lists of micro biographies of politicians and officials ("*Personenenregister*") at the end of each of these volumes alone are worth the price of admission.[13] No scholar of contemporary history can work without referencing this historical material. Now I regret even more never having been granted access to the Cabinet meetings when I wrote my dissertation. They add enormous richness and depth to the understanding of post-World War II Austria, not to speak of the drama of these difficult years of burdensome foreign occupation and the dynamics of the Austrian government's relations with the four powers.

---

12 Barbara Serloth, Von Opfern und Tätern und Jenen Dazwischen: Wie Antisemitismus die Zweite Repbublik mitbegründete (Vienna: Mandelbaum, 2016).

13 The basic editorial design is laid out at the beginning of each volume, e.g. see Gertrude Enderle-Burcel and Stefan Semotan, "Darstellung der Quelle, Grundsätzliches zur Edition," MRP, vol. 10, XXXV-XL. The transcripts of every Cabinet meeting contain numerous explanatory footnotes, which add a lot of value to the contextualization of the decision-making of the Figl I Cabinet. The principal German language secondary literature on these crucial postwar years is being mined by the editors; however, no publications in English or other languages are being cited.

Book Reviews

Andrew Denning, *Skiing into Modernity: A Cultural and Environmental History* (Sport in World History, 3) (Berkeley: University of California Press 2015).

Robert Groß

"Economic life in the Alps is attuned to the seasons" (1), Andrew Denning states in the introduction of his book. And indeed, former high alpine farming communities that transformed over the twentieth century into winter tourism centers were and are seasonal. Populated by farmers, remote villages experienced impoverishment and depopulation due to increasing industrialization in the valleys. However, Denning's focus on topographically exposed areas hides that some alpine valleys were among the earliest industrialized regions in, notably, the Austro-Hungarian Empire. Denning studies high alpine winter sport resorts visited by elitist tourists. He uses historical sources (paintings, graphics, media coverage, skiing manuals, and guidebooks) as produced and consumed by members of an educated and cosmopolitan middle and upper-class. Defining study area and research focus this way enables him to sharpen the central thesis of the book that modernity arrived in the Alps wearing a pair of skis (9). This central thesis is laid out over more than a century, well written and convincingly argued in three parts and eight chapters.

Part one gives fresh insights into the interplay of romantic alpinism and skiing. The author follows the import of skiing from Scandinavia to the Alps and shows how early skiing enthusiasts in the late nineteenth century praised skiing as romantic escape from an inhuman staccato in urban environments, but at the same time as a special type of modernity. Denning ventures into sport history when he discusses the conflict between the two skiing pioneers Mathias Zdarsky and Wilhelm Paulcke over inter-pretational hegemony of skiing technique, organization, and the diffusion of the sport among a growing middle class. In the very early phase, skiers and skiing practices resisted the intoxication of modernity; this changed after WWI. Core elements of modernity, such as bureaucratization, ratio-nalization, and domestication of nature diffused into the field of skiing. A novel liaison of skiers with speed characterized the interwar period, as did the fact that skiing became an element of popular culture (in film, for exam-ple). Drawing on ego documents, paintings, advertising posters, and films,

Denning argues that skiing practices were viewed as epitomes of modernity and its obsession with speed. For that, he interprets his sources against the backdrop of texts of contemporary thinkers (e.g., Freud, Simmel, Bloch, Spengler).

The environmental history aspects remain in the background until part two. John R. McNeill discerns a "cultural/intellectual wing"[1] in environmental history, which emphasizes "representations and images of nature in arts and letters, how these have changed, and what they reveal about the people and societies that produced them."[2] In part three, these themes are taken up. Denning traces how alpine skiing became part of mass consumer culture but also how a highly capitalized industry carried out massive interventions into alpine landscapes to provide ski slopes, uphill rides on ski lifts and artificial snow. Although the topic of technical interventions into alpine landscapes would be excellently suited to look at materiality rather than at its representation as text, image, or film, Denning offers solely a cultural history approach. By doing so, he forgoes the chance to extend his analysis into either political or material environmental history. Furthermore, by emphasizing cultural aspects when studying landscapes, dynamic snowfall patterns, and material infrastructure, Denning tends to generalize and simplify their function. This becomes obvious when he quotes John Bale and his term "sportscapes" as "monocultural sites given solely to sport, rather than multifunctional landscape." (56). Denning borrows this term to argue for the overriding of other landscape uses (e.g. hiking, hunting, nature appreciation, or preservation) by skiing, which is hardly ever the case. On the contrary, nearly all ski destinations in the Alps grew out of functioning alpine farming communities and retain some multifunctionality. The designed and artificially built ski slopes in particular would soon become dysfunctional if there were no alpine farmers mowing and fertilizing the land, cutting shrubs and young trees, or repairing damages in the turf in spring. These practices are not just subordinated to the winter tourism industry but are economically vital for ski lift manager and farmers alike. As in all history, the selection of sources proves decisive for the interpretation. Denning relies on material produced by elites; his view would be different if he had drawn on, for example, interviews with ski lift entrepreneurs or on administrative documents.

Denning's excellently written and very rich cultural study of skiing and ski tourism culture contributes little to an environmental history of the

---

1   John R. McNeill, "Observations on the Nature and Culture of Environmental History," *History and Theory. Studies in the Philosophy of History 42*, no. 4 (2003): 5–43 (here 6).
2   Ibid.

winter tourism industry in the Alps. The subtitle's program is only partially fulfilled. With all due appreciation of Denning's fine work, the hardly ever addressed environmental history of (winter) tourism remains a desideratum.

Tait Keller, *Apostles of the Alps: Mountaineering and Nation Building in Germany and Austria, 1860–1939* (Chapel Hill, NC: The University of North Carolina Press, 2016).

Carolin Firouzeh Roeder

In *Apostles of the Alps: Mountaineering and Nation Building in Germany and Austria, 1860–1939,* Tait Keller explores the role of the Eastern Alps as a contested physical and imaginary landscape in the framework of German and Austrian nation-building efforts. Turning the alpine borderlands into a national symbol was by no means a straightforward process, as Keller shows by weaving together narratives of environmental destruction and political conflict. Claims of undisturbed nature competed with attempts to technologically subjugate that nature, visions of idyllic peaks were disturbed by war, and narratives of human conquest of the landscape challenged alternative visions of national community. While mountaineers attempted to construct the Alps as a shared space of a *Grossdeutsch* community, the advent of mass tourism wrapped the Alps in different political ideologies, while infrastructure projects physically altered the landscape in order to "make the borderlands into the German heartland" (8).

In Part I, Keller examines the period from the establishment of the alpine clubs in the 1860s until the outbreak of World War I, focusing mainly on the role of the *Deutscher und Österreichischer Alpenverein* (German and Austrian Alpine Association, DOeAV) as a promoter of alpine tourism. Formed by a merger of two separate clubs in 1873, the association's local chapters disseminated alpine culture—or at least what urbanites thought of it—across the German Reich and financed an ever-expanding alpine infrastructure of huts and trails. As a transnational organization, the DOeAV utilized tourism to create a Greater German cultural identity in which the Alps as a shared space took center stage. Yet the environmental repercussions of mass tourism, including the quickly developing sport of skiing, complicated this project, forcing the DOeAV to mediate between those embracing new mountain sports and those loathing the demands for more comfortable huts, cable cars, and ski lifts. In this context, the DOeAV turned toward emphasizing a collective well-being based on the notion of a healthy *Volk* and efforts to educate the youths to preserve the alpine environment. The contradictions arising between mass tourism and claims of untouched nature were mitigated once war came over Europe. The warfare in the Alps, Keller argues, merged competing discourses into a single one in which views of mountaineering as a fight for the collective good substituted older narratives of mountaineering as an individual pursuit.

In the second part, Keller examines the transformation of discourses centered on the Alps and their physical changes in the interwar years, 1919–1939. After the dissolution of the Habsburg Empire, the loss of South Tyrol to Italy sharpened the nationalist discourse in the DOeAV, mostly due to the fact that all the Association's huts in the region were seized by the Italian government. While the sheer size of the Association—counting over two hundred thousand members by 1923—ensured its political heterogeneity, the liberal factions in the club eventually lost out to the ever-growing strength of the *völkisch* and anti-Semitic voices, culminating in the adoption of "Aryan paragraphs" and the expulsion of the mainly Jewish chapter, Donauland, in 1924.

As "mountain mania" continued to rise during the interwar period, debates over the construction of the cable car up the Zugspitze and the Grossglockner High Alpine Road confronted the *Alpenverein* with the inherent tensions between the longing for unspoiled nature and "modern machinery which brought mountain magic" to urbanites (Keller has a penchant for alliterations, as the reader will quickly notice). Critiquing the increasing accessibility of mountains and defending the purity of the sport, some alpinists linked environmental issues to gender debates, claiming that infrastructure led to a feminization of the Alps. Yet the "die-hard," "extreme" climbers who opposed mass tourism were not only "misogynist alpha males," as Keller calls them, "shamelessly egotistical" and full of "bigotry" (175–177), but also those who teamed up with populist anti-Semites in the club and turned to Adolf Hitler. Pointing out that not everyone followed the lead of these "hard-core" climbers, Keller remains ambiguous about whether there was strong support for the National-Socialist cause in the Association. He points out that many chapters eagerly took part in the process, while many others did not. While broader conclusions could have been drawn here about consent and opposition to the Nazi regime, Keller makes an important point about the uniqueness of the DOeAV: in regards to the central club (Dachverband), it was the transnational character of the Association that hindered its immediate *Gleichschaltung* and engulfed the club in a legal chaos during the tense years preceding the Anschluss.

Apostles of the Alps tells an engaging history of the *Alpenverein* and the historical processes that engulfed the Alps as a landscape of leisure. However, Keller's clamorous style, which often borders on the verge of colloquialism, too easily conceals analytical shortcomings and imprecisions. First and fore-most, the central themes of the book—mountaineering and nation-build-ing—often get lost in the narrative. Although the reader is presented with a rich story of alpine tourism, one learns very little about mountaineers; their names are hardly ever mentioned. Who were these "hard-core" climbers, and what made them earn this qualifier? Keller's awkward translation of the term *Hochtourismus*, which simply denoted classical mountaineering, with "ultimate tourism" suggests that the author lacks closer familiarity with the technical aspects of the sport. More importantly, Keller's portrayal of the Alps as a contested Greater German landscape is convincing, yet a more thorough conceptual engagement with nation-building would have allowed him to work out the argument in far greater complexity. Too often, the author merely glosses over the historiographical issues at stake and misses an opportunity to furnish his argument with greater analytical depth. This is evident in the brief mentioning of the *Sonderweg-Debatte* and in the shallow usage of the phrase "modernity" as in "modernized mountains," a frequently used term whose implications and theoretical underlining are not discussed in any depth. One would have also wished to see more engagement with recent works dealing with nation-building, mountains, and alpinism in other parts of the world. Keller is much stronger on the environmental dimensions of the story. Nonetheless, Keller's book demon-strates an impressive ability to weave in various approaches into a single story and offers a rich and accessible narrative based on impressive primary source research. *Apostles of the Alps* is a welcome contribution to German and Austrian studies, environmental history, and the history of tourism, filling a lacuna as the first English-language monograph on this topic.

Annemarie Steidl, Wladimir Fischer-Nebmaier, and James W. Oberly, eds., *From a Multiethnic Empire to a Nation of Nations: Austro-Hungarian Migrants in the US, 1870–1940* (Innsbruck: Studien Verlag, 2017).

Nicole M. Phelps

The study of migration between Austria-Hungary and the United States has long been stymied by two fundamental problems. First, and most importantly, accurate figures for Austro-Hungarian migration are nearly impossible to come by because of the way U.S. immigration and census officials recorded their data. They privileged a changing array of racial-ethnic categories over the political citizenship categories of "Austrian" and "Hungarian." That choice would not have been horrible for subsequent historians were it not for the fact that some of their categories did not align with the territorial boundaries of sovereign governments. Most notoriously, U.S. officials were willing to record people as "Poles," despite the fact that there was no sovereign Poland, and people who were linguistically and culturally Polish lived in Austria, Germany, and Russia. In addition, this approach to recording identity posited that each individual had a single identity, ignoring the fact that people spoke multiple languages, participated in different groups, and claimed identities strategically in different contexts. The second problem for studying Austro-Hungarian-to-U.S. migration is largely a function of the first: scholars have studied individual racial-ethnic groups that align with the U.S. statistics, rather than Austro-Hungarian migration as a whole. The available data shapes this choice, but such approaches also reinforce the narratives—"identity projects"—of Austria-Hungary's successor states (40).

In *From a Multiethnic Empire to a Nation of Nations*, the three members of the authorial team employ mixed methods and resources, concentrated at the University of Minnesota, to take on these problems. There is a heavy emphasis on synthesizing the fractured historiography, especially various quantitative social histories centered on particular racial-ethnic groups. The book also contains exploratory archival work, drawn primarily from the rich collections of Minnesota's Immigration History Research Center archives. Finally, there is original quantitative research using a dataset constructed from the Minnesota Population Center's Integrated Public Use Microdata

Series (IPUMS)—census data rendered compatible across the various iterations of the census, which did not use the same questions over time—and investigations of employment datasets created by other researchers.

The result does not really feel like a coherent monograph, particularly because the decision was apparently made not to adjust the writing so it read like the work of a single native speaker of English (42), but it does move the field forward and raises important questions for further research. And, despite my qualms about the prose, the two European members of the research team are to be commended for undertaking the writing of the project in English; composing academic prose in another language is no small feat.

The authors identify two cohorts of Austro-Hungarian migrants to the United States: those who arrived before 1890 and those who arrived after. The first cohort was dominated by both Czech- and German-speaking Bohemians, who largely engaged in agriculture and became settled landowners on farms, many of which were located in the Midwest. Compared with the second cohort, they sent little money back to Austria-Hungary and became U.S. citizens more quickly, as they had come to the United States with the intention of remaining there.

The second cohort was a more ethnically and linguistically diverse bunch, including people from throughout the Kingdom of Hungary, as well as Slovenes and Galician Poles from Imperial Austria. The authors label this cohort "transnational," as most were intending to work for a few years in the United States before returning to make their lives in Austria-Hungary; migration between the two countries was the core of their strategy. As a result, they were interested in maintaining ties, receiving news and sending remittances through the emerging system of post offices and related banks. They predominantly worked for wages in factories, mines, or domestic service, and they changed jobs frequently, which was normal in the United States at the time; they did, however, take positions that paid relatively higher wages than the national average. Roughly half returned, but World War I and related changes disrupted that process. Those that did end up staying in the United States took up U.S. citizenship after more years of residence than those in the first cohort.

The two cohorts did have some things in common, which are brought out in the book's two most important and original chapters, those on marriage and economics. The chapter on marriage—which is the most successful in combining the talents and contributions of all three authors—is based primarily on the dataset the authors constructed from the IPUMS data. The relevant IPUMS data is best interpreted by people who understand the demographic and political conditions in Austria-Hungary and are sensitive to issues of gender, age, religion, and processes of identification; the authors rise to this challenge admirably. The main finding is that both of the cohorts married amongst themselves in high numbers, signaling their lack of integration with the broader U.S. population. Their children also married amongst themselves, though the children of the second cohort did so at a greater rate than those of the first cohort—many of whom enhanced their marriage prospects by being able to speak German (and, often, English), lowering the barriers to marrying Reich Germans and their descendants. The authors' findings challenge the idea that migrants from small groups were obliged to marry outside their group and stress that a common language was important for fostering integration by marrying outside the group.

The other main thing the two groups had in common was high literacy rates. The authors include this information in the chapter on economics, as they argue that literacy was essential for keeping abreast of employment opportunities. Literacy also helped migrants take advantage of the "ethnic corridors" provided by the immigrant press, allowing them to better understand conditions in the United States (163–164). Austro-Hungarian migrants—especially those in the second cohort—were generally willing to change jobs often, take on dangerous but higher paid tasks, and move to new locations, making them a real asset to the U.S. economy; their labor was particularly flexible and could meet new demands quickly. Following the discussion of literacy, the economics chapter covers the sectors of employment Austro-Hungarian men and women engaged in, job turnover rates, and remittances. The authors make good use of existing datasets of employment records from the Pullman Palace Car Company, the Ford Motor Company, and the Pittsburgh-based iron company AM Byers. Their use of several early twentieth-century public policy studies is useful for fleshing out their other data, especially when it comes to the labor of married women, which was not captured in the U.S. census.

In addition to the chapters on marriage and economics, the book has quantitatively based chapters on migration within Austria-Hungary and Europe and the demographics of those who migrated to the United States, as well as qualitative chapters on the "management" of "identity projects" such as newspapers and fraternal organizations. The concluding chapter offers a brief look at data from the U.S. censuses since 1980 and the 2007–2009 American Community Study to see how people responded when asked about their "ancestry," finding that, despite the millions of immigrants from Austria-Hungary, more recent generations do not frequently identify their ancestry with groups that can be tied to the former empire. All of these chapters are more synthetic and/or exploratory than the chapters on marriage and economics.

Although it is helpful to have much of the fragmented literature pulled together in the book, there are some problems. The authors do a great service in drawing on journal articles and chapters, as well as many dissertations. Monographs are somewhat lacking, and this may be a function of bibliographic searching, rather than training in the field. To be clear, all three authors are professional historians with considerable experience and profound expertise. However, none of them appear to be trained as historians of U.S. immigration, which is a distinct field of inquiry, and that absence is felt in the book. Direct engagement with more of the recent literature in that field would raise the historiographical stakes of the book and increase awareness of Austria-Hungary as a whole in that scholarly community. It might also help to explain the changes between the end of the census data in 1940 and the "ancestry" data from 1980 and later. In that period, World War II, the GI Bill, and the Cold War helped to shift American discourse away from the more nuanced racial-ethnic categories of the previous decades toward a white/black binary and an emphasis on "Judeo-Christian religion" in opposition to Soviet godlessness, erasing or at least muting many of the distinctions that had previously shaped the lives of Austro-Hungarian migrants and their descendants.

Historiography aside, the most significant problem with the book is that it is fundamentally quantitative, and yet many of the graphs are virtually illegible. Several of the graphs rely on shades of grey and very small symbols, which—at least in my copy—did not reproduce well (see, among others, the graphs on pages 124, 126, 255, and 259). The main findings were, of course, discussed in the text, but better graphs would certainly add to the book's utility. Visualizing data is challenging, especially when trying to show change over time for multiple data series. The project may have been well-served by an online component or at least the use of other graph formats.

Despite these problems, the book raises questions for future research both explicitly and implicitly and provides an important starting point for pursuing them. We are clearly in need of a study of the portrayal of Austria-Hungary and its people in the mainstream U.S. press to help us better understand why perceptions of Austria-Hungary were so far off the mark, as well as to help us better contextualize the more often studied foreign language press. A study of vaudeville and other U.S. mass popular culture sources with an eye toward the representation of Austria-Hungary and its people would also be interesting and useful. Vaudeville was a key source of ethnic stereotypes in the United States, and, as the authors rightly point out, there seems to be a lack of enduring images and caricatures of certain Austro-Hungarians—especially Bohemians and South Slavs—in mainstream American popular culture. That absence must contribute in some way to people's subsequent lack of identification with Austro-Hungarian groups.

The field of U.S.-Austro-Hungarian relations—broadly conceived to include official and private interactions of all kinds—remains a wide open and fruitful place for historical inquiry. In grappling with the census problems, the authors have provided an important contribution that allows others to build on their work and pursue other questions.

Erin R. Hochman, *Imagining a Greater Germany: Republican Nationalism and the Idea of Anschluss* (Ithaca: Cornell University Press, 2016).

Janek Wasserman

Erin Hochman's deeply researched and trenchantly argued book revises our understanding of interwar German nationalism, providing a compelling reinterpretation of the histories of the Weimar Republic and the Austrian First Republic. Arguing that German and Austrian republicans counterposed a *großdeutsch* (greater German) nationalism to the *alldeutsch* (pan-German) nationalism of conservatives, Hochman demonstrates the existence of alternative German nationalisms. She challenges the common assumption that the political and ideological right possessed a monopoly on nationalist discourse. Using a series of flashpoints in interwar Central European culture wars—flag and anthem debates, national holiday commemorations, republican rallies for Anschluss—Hochman navigates this charged symbolic landscape to show how a transborder community fought "to realize a form of German unity even greater than Bismarck achieved" (8). She also manages to re-integrate Austria into twentieth-century German history, making this an outstanding exemplar of transnational Central European history.

Hochman differentiates between *großdeutsch* nationalism and conservative *Alldeutschtum* in her opening chapter. Rooted in the revolutionary ideals of 1848, *Großdeutschtum* was republican in spirit and peaceful in nature. It eschewed the militarism and imperialism associated with Prussian nationalism. The republican version evoked the inclusivity and tolerance against illiberal, *kleindeutsch* ideas. *Großdeutsch* republicans carved out space for "outsiders": Austrians, socialists, Jews, and minorities. They took the lead in shaping the early postwar republics, which they saw as the foundation of a future, democratic *Großdeutschland*. As Hochman puts it, "Republicans set out to nationalize democracy" (p. 37). The centrality of völkisch ideas to this story undercuts conventional arguments about the necessary connection between the right and the völkisch ideal.

Hochman then turns to cultural events to illustrate these nationalism debates. She begins with a fine-grained analysis of the controversies over the German flag and the Austrian national anthem. Hochman mines a trove of letters to show these battles over symbolic meaning. The contest between the 1848 "black-red-gold" and the German Reich's "black-white-red" reached around the globe, to *Auslandsdeutsche* everywhere. Meanwhile, in Austria, the anthem debate pitted those who wished to maintain ties to the past by using a version of the imperial hymn against those who wanted a clean break. Hochman elegantly outlines how the conflict between supporters of a *Nationalhymne* and exponents of a *Staatshymne* reflected the fraught interwar struggle over Austrian identity.

The chapter on national commemorations focuses on Constitution Day in Germany and 12 November in Austria, holidays that republicans attempted—with mixed success—to turn into celebrations of the state, the nation, and the *Volk*. The Weimar government and its republican backers, like the Reichsbanner, created programming to turn 11 August into a *Volk* festival for the best German values. For them, the new constitution meant a commitment to democracy, civic virtue, and national sentiment. Organizers turned the holiday into a popular one, even though resistance from the right remained strong. Resistance was even more pronounced in Austria, since 12 November represented the end of the Habsburg Empire to many. In contrast to Germany, the Austrian state did not take up the defense of the national holiday in earnest, which undermined the holiday—and perhaps the republic.

According to Hochman, cross-border rallies permitted republicans to show transnational, *großdeutsch* solidarity. While many more Austrians streamed into Germany, thousands of individuals participated in forging a *Großdeutsch* republican community. Germans invited Austrians to write in their journals, speak at their celebrations, and attend their symbolic events, and vice versa. Hochman looks at an array of associations and their members to illuminate the large network of like-minded German republicans. In this transborder community, Hochman identifies some fault lines, which centered on the connection between politics and Germanness. The lack of cross-party support of republicanism in Austria led German republicans from non-socialist backgrounds to question whether *großdeutsch* associations were truly nonpartisan. The fact that the political right felt the need to mobilize against republicans suggests the very strength of interwar republican nationalism, offering more credence to Hochman's claims.

In the final chapter, Hochman sets her sights on the Österreichisch-Deutscher Volksbund, the quintessential Anschluss organization. Delving into the association's archives, she elucidates the transversal appeal of *großdeutsch* nationalism—across borders, class lines, and political boundaries.

She also uses the group to show mounting tensions as the years went on. Offering a far-reaching description of the *Volksbund*'s members, activities, and beliefs, the chapter distills the book's arguments and presents them in rich and vivid detail. In highlighting the role of Austrians in the organization, she also drives home that *großdeutsch* nationalism was always a Central European affair. Moreover, by following the *Volksbund* from the beginning of the interwar era until its dissolution, the chapter offers a glimpse into the evolution of German nationalism across the entire period. The chapter is masterful.

Erin Hochman has produced a standout piece of historical scholarship and a signal contribution to interwar German, Austrian, and Central European historiography. Her able command of both German and Austrian scholarship is praiseworthy, allowing her book to speak to both communities with authority. Her discovery and use of remarkable archival sources and her sensitive readings of cultural phenomena are exemplary. The book loses momentum under the weight of those materials in the fourth and fifth chapters, which do not advance the argument much. Moreover, after such a riveting exploration, it comes as a slight disappointment to see how little attention the years after 1930 – especially after 1933 – receive. The Nazi period is only discussed in the last dozen pages; the Anschluss in a scant five. The lasting legacies of interwar republican nationalism also receive no mention. While these considerations would have pushed beyond the project's scope, they would have been welcome in ascertaining the significance of these ideas in later imaginings of German nationalism. None of these observations, however, detract from Hochman's accomplishments, which are substantial. *Imagining a Greater Germany* is a grand achievement from start to finish.

Anton Pelinka, *Die gescheiterte Republik: Kultur und Politik in Österreich 1918-1938* (Vienna: Böhlau, 2017);
Gudula Walterskirchen, *Die blinden Flecken der Geschichte: Österreich 1927-1938* (Vienna: Kremayr & Scheriau, 2017).

Timothy Kirk

While there have been any number of studies exploring all aspects of the history of Germany's Weimar Republic, from its "flawed" constitution to its "decadent" culture, furnishing reading material for a range of under-graduate courses in cultural and political history, there have been relatively few similar studies of Austria's First Republic, and even fewer published outside Austria itself. This is surprising, not least given the attention devoted to the preceding, fin-de-siècle period of Austrian history, which is meticulously documented and the subject of lively debate. Moreover, approaches to the history of the First Republic share some common ground with the historiography of Weimar Germany: both brave experiments in political democracy began with a social democratic revolution from below, and both met their demise at the hands of panicked conservatives with authoritarian instincts, who were prepared to use emergency legislation to subvert the constitution. Above all, both experiments have been considered failures, and the title of Pelinka's study reflects contemporary judgements on the First Republic of Austria, "the state that nobody wanted," which was perceived to be an "unviable" rump, left behind as the other national-ities constituted themselves on the basis of a "national self-determination" that was denied to the stranded Germans of the empire—and there was of course no "Austrian" nationality, a point that is repeatedly made in this study. More importantly, there was no consensus about what the founding constitutional concepts (democracy, republic) actually meant (p. 17). There was no meeting of minds, and Pelinka makes much of culture as an expla-nation of the Republic's "failure," in particular the irreconcilable political cultures of the tripartite system (described by Adam Wandruszka) after the war, a concept central to the founding mythology of the more successful Second Republic and the consensus politics on which it was based. This has proved an increasingly problematic model, not least since the post-war narrative started to unravel in the wake of the Waldheim affair and the takeover of the FPÖ by the extreme right.

The importance of culture is signalled in the book's subtitle, and indeed it starts with a discussion of the rather ambiguous, qualified positioning of a number of selected intellectuals, representative of an "unpolitical" culture, at least in the sense that politics was understood in a parliamentary democracy. It continues with an attempt to define the role of culture, and above all – and more confidently – political culture(s) in the conflicts of the period. The argument is framed in rather pessimistic propositions, above all in the two central chapters, dealing with the "flight" from the idea of the republic into various ideologies (Chapter 5), and the periodization of a republic that was by turn unloved, ignored, embattled as it faced the abyss, and finally forgotten (Chapter 6). Too many of Austria's leading politicians and intellectuals, it seems, were fixated either on the world of yesteryear or on a utopian future, a fixation posthumously legitimized by the notion that some of them might have been "too great for Austria" (a notion Pelinka finds absurd but nevertheless compelling). More importantly, amid the dogmatic confrontations of such attention-seeking politicians, much talent was lost to the Republic: despite their ostensible emancipation, women remained politically marginalized, and only a handful were elected to Parliament (a situation that remained more or less unchanged until the 1970s); Jewish citizens were confronted with a pervasive and increasingly strident anti-semitism; and liberals and intellectuals were arbitrarily associated with Jews in the increasingly debased political discourse of the period.

Pelinka's wide-ranging and thoughtful account covers the years between 1918 and its provisional end in 1934. It is followed by a brief discussion of the re-establishment of parliamentary democracy in 1945, when "to remember, was dangerous. To remember was painful. It was all about reconstruction." (p. 283). The past was suppressed, as it was almost everywhere across post-fascist Europe, ostensibly to enable confrontation to be replaced by consensus. The book concludes with an astute analysis of Austria's "second chance," and a useful reminder that the country's precarious internal truce was to some extent a result of the country's even more precarious international position.

With time, both the historical compromise and the comprised history have been eroded, giving way to a more sharply divergent view of Austria's recent past. If Pelinka's view of the First Republic is even-handed to a fault, with Walterskirchen's *Blinde Flecken der Geschichte*, we are firmly back on the terrain of Austria's recent culture wars. The book claims to "dispense with old myths" and "open up new perspectives," but in fact there is little here that is new in what is essentially a journalistic counterblast against the research findings of historians and political scientists who have finally, belatedly, turned their attention to the banal evils of the Dollfuss-Schuschnigg dictatorship. Its principal focus is the period between the Schattendorf murders of 1927 and the suppression of the labor movement by police and armed forces in 1934. The perspective is a familiar one, apart from the rather speculative claim that the "February rising" of 1934 was an attempted coup planned by the Social Democrats in cahoots with the Nazis. As intriguing a story as that might make, it would need far more substantial evidence to back it up than is presented here (contemporary press reports, a mixture of warmed-up memoir and hearsay from a police cell) to make it credible. This is a fast-paced book that makes its points very straightforwardly, but it remains essentially a political polemic—albeit a very readable one.

Philipp Rohrbach and Niko Wahl, eds.,
Austria – A Soldier's Guide. Österreich – Ein Leitfaden für Soldaten
(Vienna: Czernin Verlag, 2017).

Siegfried Beer

Historians of the Allied occupation in Austria from 1945–1955 – as the politics of control in the three western zones was effectively over by 1948/49 – have known for quite a while that it was the British who first started their preparations for a postwar role in Austria; the Americans came in a bit later. Both in London and in Washington, members of intelligence, research, and propaganda units of various types and origins were among the first to take up the question of what to do with and eventually in Austria. Thus, long before an Allied soldier set foot on Austrian soil, British organizations like Special Operations Executive (SOE), the MI6 Secret Intelligence Service, Political Warfare Executive (PWE), and later, of course, also army and air force intelligence were concerning themselves with Austrian matters. American counterparts in the Office of Strategic Services (OSS), the Office of War Information (OWI), and various units in the field were maybe a year or so behind. By 1943, they cooperated and attuned their policies with the British agencies.

The field guide, which the editors of this booklet claim to have "discovered" in 2016 while preparing for a Viennese exhibition entitled "*SchwarzÖsterreich:* The Children of Afro-American Allied Soldiers," has long since been known to specialists working on occupation issues of the early postwar years in Austria. For them, it was just another item among the tens of thousands of documents that became available at the National Archives in London-Kew and College Park, MD decades ago. However, this is not to say that this Soldier's Guide does not have a special appeal. It was printed in 1944 by what is identified as the "Information and Education Section" in the Mediterranean Theater of Operations, U.S. Army. This reviewer is not sure such an office ever existed; it may have just been a cover. The pamphlet certainly gives a somewhat hurried impression, which is why it could have been printed in Rome, soon after Anglo-American takeover in June 1944, when the Italian capital became headquarters of both Anglo-American Mediterranean contingents. This would explain why its exact origins are difficult to trace.

The editors of this quasi-reprint consider it probable that the anonymous author(s) of the booklet might have been Austrian exiles working for the Allied cause, but for this reviewer this guide reflects a collective effort. Its argumentation appears too wide-ranging for single authorship. Furthermore, the text is as British as it is American; there are actually more references to things British than American. Naturally, then, the message of the booklet for regular soldiers is topically influenced by British as well as American considerations and attitudes. The task at hand was pragmatic enough: to inform GIs as well as officers about a widely unknown country and its population, which they would encounter at the end of military fighting and potentially over a good period thereafter. This meant presenting facts and features, but also understandable interpretations thereof. A few examples must suffice: "You are going into Austria as a member of the Allied Armies both as victors and liberators"; "One of the Allied war aims is to restore a free and independent Austria"; "It was in part their own fault that their country was overrun by the Germans"; "The fact that we have beaten Hitler gives them another chance. They are lucky."

As indeed the Austrians were. These are facts. Then follow comparative and evaluative descriptions: "Austria is about as big as Scotland and South Carolina"; "Vienna is about four times the size of Cincinnati and Edinburgh"; "Though only a minority of Austrians had wanted the Anschluss, Hitler's invasion produced a wave of hysterical enthusiasm"; "The Austrians have 'charm'; they are friendly. [...] They have little respect for rules and regulations."

Similar selective facts and wordings were used by the British before their final entry into Styria, from Carinthia, in August 1945, about a year later:

> Most of us have now seen enough of Austria to have learned:
>   [that] the Austrians are fundamentally honest and can be trusted.
>   [That] they keep their houses spotlessly clean.
>   [That] most Austrians are well-educated and highly cultured.
>   [That] some, at any rate, of the Austrians were fairly lukewarm Nazis.

This last formulation hits the pinnacle of innocuousness quite elegantly. But the soldier's guide offered even more: a number of useful Do's and Don'ts, among them: "GO EASY on Schnaps"; "REMEMBER THAT VENEREAL disease is rampant"; "DON'T be sentimental. If things are tough for the Austrians, they themselves must share the blame"; "Don't believe Austrian accounts of the war [...]. They got most of their ideas on these subjects from lying propaganda."

There was method to this ambivalence. The British had a plan for Austria, which the Americans also chose to pursue: convince the Austrians that their culture is different from the Germans and help them accept their independent statehood by strengthening their distinct national identity. For this to happen, Austrians needed time and renewed interest in democracy; they also needed benevolence in the face of war guilt, to say nothing of economic and moral support from the victors. Austrian anti-communism made it easier for the Western Allies to provide the support necessary for their independence. In a fascinating way, this pamphlet portrays an attractive land, with problems, that should be manageable with time under Allied guidance. It turned out to have been a viable strategy, for about thirty years. Then history returned, fittingly represented by a national and international figure, Kurt Waldheim. Another thirty years later, Austrians and the world can have a more accurate picture of their involvement and responsibilities during the seven years of a previous "occupation" and six long years of war.

The presence of this benevolently minded thirty-four-page pamphlet as proof of early preparation and insight for a restorative task to be undertaken by the two leading democracies at the time deserves a much broader commentary, reflective of the existing national and international research on the first decade of the Second Republic. The English-language original should have been printed first and in facsimile style to convey the flavor of the effort. References to literature would not have harmed the publication. This guide, along with a balanced analysis of attitude and intent, would have been more educational than entertaining. In its published form, unfortunately, it also represents an opportunity lost.

Günter Bischof and Hans Petschar, *The Marshall Plan: Saving Europe, Rebuilding Austria. The European Recovery Program. The ERP Fund, The Austrian Marshall Plan Foundation* (Distributed in the U.S. by the University of New Orleans Press [UNO Press], published in English and German by the Christian Brandstätter Verlag, Vienna, 2017).

Charles S. Maier

Do not be misled by the lavish illustrations—photos, posters, maps, charts—in this large-format history of the Marshall Plan in Austria. Günter Bischof, director of the Austrian Marshall Plan Center for European Studies at the University of New Orleans, in collaboration with Hans Petschar, who has curated the striking visuals so integral to the text, has written a serious and encompassing volume. Bischof has devoted his scholarly career to the history of postwar Austria and the Marshall Plan. (Full disclosure: he did his graduate studies with the late Ernest May and myself years ago and was later my co-editor on a volume that examined the Marshall Plan's role in West Germany's postwar recovery.)

Do not be misled either by the openly commemorative and celebratory nature of the volume, corresponding with the seventieth anniversary of the 1947 origins of the European Recovery Program, the formal name for the Marshall Plan. The current volume was supported by the Austrian Marshall Plan Foundation (*Marshallplan-Jubiläumsstiftung*), the continuing endowment that originated with the counterpart funds (more on counterpart below) that the European Recovery Program mandated for recipient countries. But the text enters fully into the controversy that the Plan engendered and does not shirk from explaining the more intricate mechanisms of its financing and operation.

The Marshall Plan was designed as a European-wide recovery program and encouraged the partner countries to work together in assessing their respective needs, even as the American policy makers understood they faced individual countries with specific priorities. Austria (like Germany) had been divided into four zones of occupation with its capital, Vienna, inside the Russian zone. Even if the presence of the Western allies—France, Britain, and the U.S.—ensured that Austria as a whole was not likely to be forced into subservience to the Soviet Union, as happened with Hungary and Czechoslovakia on its borders, the country emerged from the war impoverished and vulnerable to political demoralization in the postwar years. Officially, the Allies declared Austria a victim of Nazi aggression, which, of course, belied the enthusiasm that so many Austrians had lent the enlarged German Reich after the Anschluss. Indeed, my major regret about this history derives from the fact that, as a commemorative history of success, it begins with the immiserated and prostrated provinces of 1945 and occludes the *Grossdeutsche* enthusiasms of the 1930s, which must underlie any discussion of reparations. It provides many economic comparisons with the interwar Republic but treats the politics as "*Stunde Null.*"

Admittedly, it is the postwar miracle as nurtured by the Marshall Plan that is the topic here. The stakes for the West and the United States in Austria were high—could this demoralized country be brought to a self-sustaining prosperity that it had never really attained in the interwar era, such that it might construct a stable democracy, albeit one that would have to be built on a major dose of amnesia? We owe this commemorative volume to the fact that the wager worked. Moreover, the Soviets allowed the Austrians, in contrast to the postwar Germans, to reunify in 1955 during the post-Stalinist "thaw," and they removed their troops. Of course, the geopolitical stakes were far higher in Germany. Austria did establish democratic rule, in part because the evenly-weighted Social Democratic and Catholic People's Parties (SPÖ and ÖVP) understood that they had to conduct politics with restraint, political coalitions, and a divvying up of offices (the famous *Proporz*), which neither side had been able to envisage in the decade from 1928 to 1938. Only in the moment, as this review is being written, does the cozy, shared domination of postwar politics by the Socialists and the *Volkspartei* seem to be eroding, as Greens on the left and the nationalist-populist Freedom Party on the right attract about half of today's voters in tense contests, with the Greens' Alexander Van der Bellen (running as an independent) narrowly winning the presidency in 2016 and the Freedom Party gaining an important cabinet role alongside the People's Party in the coalition government currently in power in Austria. This book, therefore, may end up serving as a monument to the creation of an era of centrist stability that is now ending after seven decades. It certainly points to one major conclusion about the long postwar period, namely that the United States played a critical role in nurturing this stability—and it should lead us to question the consequences of the retreat from foreign policy commitments that the current administration has so blithely signaled.

Bischof's text skillfully provides the narrative for an American-sponsored economic and political recovery, but it does not over-simplify the analytical story. Although Bischof notes the semi-starvation rations of 1945–1947, he also points out one of the usually unacknowledged assets that the fledgling Second Republic possessed: the legacy of what might mischievously be called Hitler's Marshall Plan. During the period of Anschluss, the Germans invested heavily in the industrial infrastructure around Hitler's hometown of Linz, the oil refineries near Vienna, in the hydroelectric potential of the Western Alpine area along with its steel and aluminum installations: "Without question, the Nazis modernized and industrialized the Austrian economy from 1938 to 1945 to achieve their war goals" (29). Austrian strategic assets remained initially out-of-reach of Allied bombers until the Allies had secured southern Italy, but they suffered heavy damage during 1944–1945.

By the end, the human and material tolls were heavy. Seventy-one percent of the air campaign's damage to manufacturing occurred in the northeast and the future Soviet zone of occupation. While the Germans added perhaps a third of the number of machine tools, by the end they had decreased by half, both from bombing and Soviet removals. A country with a prewar population of six million lost about 250,000 soldiers of the 1.3 million mobilized; hundreds of thousands were POWs, 120,000s died in concentration camps and prisons—not counting the 65,000 murdered Jews (and the 130,000 who fled). The country absorbed 1.5 million displaced persons over the next four years, eventually an asset, although initially a burden. The numbers deserve emphasis given the preoccupation with refugees today—to be sure, most were ethnically German or at least Central European.

As the authors stress, the UNRRA (United Nations Relief and Rehabilitation Administration) and GARIOA (Government Assistance and Relief in Occupied Areas) funds remained hugely important until the first year of the ERP aid, which was targeted at recovery of production and less at relief. Indeed, as is often forgotten, UNRRA and GARIOA amounted to more than Marshall Plan assistance. The graphs and charts, most reproduced from those created contemporaneously, render the information visible and dramatic. Traditional economic ties with Eastern and Southeastern Europe were ruptured. Food rations were down to 800 calories a day and significantly less in Vienna's first postwar winter. (The differing estimates provided in the text are not always consistent.) Bischof explains that the Potsdam agreement allowed the Soviets to seize "external," (i.e., German-owned) assets in their zone of occupation, a portion of which had

been confiscated from Jewish owners after 1938, and which they then organized into a massive holding company, the USIA. In effect, the economic
balance between reparations paid to the Soviets and the funds received
from American aid remained in rough equilibrium. Bischof calculates that
Austrian assets taken by the Soviets amounted to about $1.325 billion in
current dollars, while American assistance totaled $1.44 billion (97).

In response to the Soviet organization of "external assets," the Austrians
won the approval of the Western occupation authorities to nationalize
German assets in the western zones, yielding the largest nationalized sector
in Western Europe. Nevertheless, as the authors inform us (89), the Western
Allies and the Soviets both refrained from cutting off their respective zones
from economic intercourse, and unlike the German experience, zonal occupation did not lead to separate political units. Although peace negotiations and the reestablishment of sovereignty failed during 1948–49—not
surprisingly, as the German occupation zones consolidated their half-cen-
tury division of East and West in the same years—the confrontation in
Austria remained more muted than in divided Germany; the geopolitical
stakes were far lower. Once Marshall Tito broke with Stalin, moreover, the
Russians no longer sought to leverage Austrian concessions for Yugoslavia.
Still, the Austrians would have to wait for the post-Stalin "thaw" to secure
the bargain that Moscow and the West allowed: restoration of a sovereign
nation-state with a commitment to neutrality and independence.

A significant chapter is devoted to the genesis of the ERP itself, with
a focus on American policy-making, a relatively familiar part of the story,
but enlivened again with photographs and posters. A further chapter discusses the growing pains of the Austrian recovery program. United States
administrators sought to inculcate the values of productivity and mana-
gerial efficiency. Austrians lived in a system where political cliques, division of offices, and a large public economic sector, with its opportunities
for patronage, helped to overcome fundamentally conflicting ideological
orientations. Corruption was always a danger in such a close community;
Bischof cites the case where the Creditanstalt Bankverein—Austria's dominant bank with major connections to the *Volkspartei*—diverted Marshall
Plan funds for speculation in foreign currencies. Congressional Republicans
in Washington expressed outrage, but American ambassador Llewelyn
Thompson warned against handling the matter too rigorously lest it lead
to undesirable electoral results (173–76). In general, American officials in
the field, whether our ambassadors or the ERP representatives assigned
locally and coordinated by Averell Harriman's Paris-based Office of the
Special Representatives, consistently argued for moderating the hectoring

supervision demanded by officials of the ECA, based in Washington. After discreet investigations, designed in part to hold American politicians at bay, the new Austrian government agreed to a settlement without admitting guilt. More generally, Austria resisted pressures for a more open, competitive economy. Perhaps, as a result of the financial crisis of 2006–12, American banking-government relations seem to have regressed to the Austrian approach of one hand washing the other, which caused such indignation in the early 1950s.

Bischof does not make the comparison, but it is useful to think of the Italian situation alongside the Austrian one. American demands for efficiency and competitive markets similarly intruded in a society where collusion and accommodation allowed the red-black ideological distinctions to coexist within a more encompassing social equilibrium. It was not that each major political-party community—for the bipolar parties were far more than competitive electoral organizations—made concessions to the other. Rather, each came to recognize after the experiences of war and fascism that particular domains of faith, economic assets, the press, and cultural life, including recruitment of youth, must be tolerated. Some of the distinctions could be managed through corporatist networks and fiefs: municipal housing, the public industrial holding companies, and the Catholic church's institutions enjoyed protected relations. Some of the opposition was managed through territorial allocation: Vienna was dominated by the Socialists; the countryside and provinces abutting Slavic countries remained Catholic; Italy similarly had red provinces and black. And part of the overarching truce derived from the recognition that Europe itself was to be divided between Soviet Union and United States oversight.

The last chapters of this volume devote major attention to the publicity and propaganda campaigns that played so large a role in the Marshall Plan. Visuals play a crucial role in the book, as they did at the time; after all, the Marshall Plan was part of a struggle for the hearts and minds of European labor, agriculture, and intellectuals. The posters and charts exemplify the campaigns. They are what remains of the informational centers and the media campaigns, depicted in the Organization chart splayed across 188–89. The volume is filled with photos of blonde children at exhibits on the Marshall Plan, especially of the Train of Europe that traversed the country in 1952—the counterpart to the Freedom Train that crossed the United States in the same period with copies of our sacred founding texts, which this reviewer visited as a schoolboy. Bischof and Petschar, the co-author of this chapter, cite the pioneering work of David Ellwood, the authoritative historian of the "tens of documentary films, hundreds of radio programs…

millions of pamphlets." And they reproduce the children's art work that celebrated the Marshall Plan, including the "great painting and drawing contest about the Marshall Plan for children under sixteen years." They also highlight the energetic role of the American photographer, Yoichi Okamoto of the Vienna USIS Pictorial Services, who encouraged the emerging Austrian photographers of the postwar decade. Okamoto was a tireless impresario and a brilliant photographic dramatist, who dramatized the role of the ERP on the individual Austrian, worker or housewife; and Bischof and Petschar allow their words and pictures to play a major role.

It is tempting to react to this output with discomfort at the gender stereotyping or superciliousness at the crudeness of the appeals. One must recall that this aspect of the publicity campaigns formed just part of an overarching American effort to enlist not only children and housewives and trade-unionists, but also sophisticated intellectuals through subventions of sophisticated magazines such as *Encounter* or *Der Monat*. And the images remain inviting: they exemplify economic energy, in the form of muscular workers or hardworking peasants, or satisfied female homemakers examining washing machines in the 1953 Linz exhibit of "*Das Reich der Frau.*" The appeal of the latter may seem naïve, but it is hardly surprising. In no other aspect than the traditional family, by the early 1950s far more affluent than before the war, was postwar recovery so clearly an effort to reestablish the pillars of prewar hierarchies—to recover the gendered postulates that Christian Democratic parties stood for in continental Europe and that likewise attracted the working-class and middle-decision makers of Anglo-American society. The *Hausfrau* contemplating washing machines in 1953 was a world away from the potato scavengers and *Trümmerfrauen* of 1945. Moreover, the visual efforts testified to the capacity to mobilize public opinion, no longer around military imagery but the razzle-dazzle of mega-numbers—the triumph of the quantitative successes of growth—that both sides in the Cold War relied on. The Marshall Plan sacralized the project of statistical growth, and this book is a monument to its success in a small country then at the edge of the West.

Bischof closes with the aftermath of the Marshall Plan: the opening steps toward European integration, the conclusion of the Austrian State Treaty, and the role of the Marshall Plan Foundation resting on the Counterpart Funds turned over to Austrian uses in 1961. As the volume makes clear through its use of contemporary graphics, counterpart funds allowed the imports that American taxpayers paid for to be funneled into productive investments, such as the Kaprun dam, the rebuilding of factories, and even the reestablishment of tourism and ski resorts to attract foreign visitors. The Marshall Plan worked by overcoming Europe's dollar shortage in the early postwar years, but it required each recipient country to raise through taxes and the sale to domestic consumers a counterpart in local currency to the goods purchased by the ECA in the United States. In Germany and Austria, these funds were vested in specific agencies created to finance the local projects that met the approval of U.S. representatives, who usually acquiesced to local priorities. The agencies remained entrusted with the remaining funds as an endowment, which has, in the years since, paid for student and other exchanges. Austrians created a special Marshall Plan foundation in 1999 for this purpose. Bischof cites the memories of former American Marshall planners and current commentators at successive anniversaries over the past decades, including my own assessment in 1997 and his own 2005 exhibit at the Austrian Museum of Technology.

Both through the text and its generous imagery—much of which reproduces the exuberant images of the period—this volume testifies to the Marshall Plan as a major achievement. It was an achievement in skilled economic diplomacy that helped a demoralized Europe to carry on with recovery under a mixed economy, and it was further a skillful response to the Soviet military presence in Europe that compelled the Soviets own self-isolation in Western Europe. But it was also a monument to developments that remained implicit at the time and that we can only now put into a long-term perspective, namely the capacity to organize a public project to recast private relations and not simply to acquiesce in narrow self-interest; that is, to preserve and strengthen civil society even as civil society was being mobilized—in fact because it was being mobilized—around the ideas of growth and production, and market allocation. The Bischof-Petschar volume repays not merely reading and gazing, but sustained reflection, for it suggests historical currents that take us beyond the categories the authors themselves provide and that have traditionally characterized our accounts of Cold War history.

Social Ecology: Society-Nature Relations Across Time and Space
(Basel: Springer, 2016).

Reinhard Ferdinand Nießner

The Institute of Social Ecology in Vienna, founded in 1986, is well known for interdisciplinary research in the wide field of Social Ecology. The 2016 volume, *Human-Nature Relations Across Time and Space* "presents the current state of the art in Social Ecology" (xliii), as the editors point out in the introduction. The thirty-five authors combined research areas cover diverse disciplines, ranging from social science to the humanities to the natural sciences. This volume on social ecology is the latest impressive outcome of almost three decades of interdisciplinary research.

The 600-page volume is divided into five parts and consists of twenty-nine chapters. The first part, "The Conceptual Repertoire," presents the Vienna School of Social Ecology's theoretical frameworks. The seven chapters are of introductory character and provide an excellent basis for the understanding of the ensuing empirical studies. Social ecology is primarily located in a broad interdisciplinary research area (chapter one), and, according to the authors, the Vienna School represents just an island on this metaphorical archipelago. The other chapters provide the reader with an introduction to core concepts such as "Social Metabolism" (chapters two and three) and the colonization of nature, mainly dealing with land-use (chapter four). There are also reflections on the specific role of structures, systems and actors in the conception of social ecology (chapter five) and on historical long-term perspectives (chapter six), which is highly recommendable for environmental historians. A socioecological concept of human labor (chapter seven) finishes the first part. These introductory chapters reveal the School's conceptual mindset and shared interdisciplinary paradigm: social and natural systems coevolve and interact across time and space, and they are influenced by one another dynamically.

The remaining four parts deal with a wide range of empirical approaches and case studies. "Socioeconomic Metabolism" is stressed in the five chapters (chapters eight through twelve) of the second part, and material and energy use, both on a global and a national scale, are discussed. Another core concept, "Land Use and Colonization of Ecosystems," is empirically elaborated in the six chapters (thirteen through eighteen) of the third part. Part four deals with historical "Long-Term Socioecological Research" and consists of six chapters (19–24) on environmental history, which discuss a 250-year period and have a spatial focus on Austria, Bavaria, and the Philippines. In his contribution, Martin Schmid demonstrates how the colonization of nature in the Bavarian *"Donaumoos"* at the end of the eighteenth century led to a socioecological disaster forty years later. What can be explained with this long-term perspective is the ongoing challenge of the "risk spiral."[1] Every intervention—or, more precisely, every type of colonization of nature—provokes unintended side effects, which future generations will need to address.

The final part of the book is devoted to "Working with Stakeholders" and reveals some remarkable results, as in chapter twenty-nine on sustainability challenges in hospitals by Ulli Weisz and Willi Haas. Given that hospitals apply "materials- and energy-intensive 'repair' medicine" (563), the authors identify them as key contributors "to global problems of sustainability" (563). This exemplifies the broad theoretical and empirical horizon of the Vienna School. Weisz and Haas highlight the problematic character of hospitals in socioecological terms: they contribute to environmental problems, which cause health problems—and health care systems then have to cope with these self-made problems. An empirical study at the Otto Wagner Hospital in Vienna achieved three socioecological aims of sustainable development: (1) A reduction of cost and material (economic efficiency); (2) an enhanced intensive health care for long-term ventilated patients (social compatibility), resulting in the improvement of the third aim of sustainable development: environmental compatibility.

An innovative feature of the book are the so-called *Method Précis* lessons. These insertions provide in-depth studies of several empirical approaches and explain the applied methods in a comprehensive manner, making a twofold contribution. On the one hand, they guarantee a better understanding of the specific empirical approaches, and on the other hand, they enable the reader to gain insight into the complex methods established or used by the School. The *Method Précis* "Working with Historical Material" (411–415) examines the conditions of reconstructing the past and presents a useful introduction to some methodological problems of current historiographical research, for example the role of historians as "second-order observers" (412) and the construction of narratives by historians (414).

---

1   For the concept of the "risk spiral," see Rolf Peter Sieferle: "Die Risikospirale," in *Katastrophen in Natur und Umwelt*, ed. Verena Winiwarter (Vienna: Forum Österreichischer Wissenschaftler für Umweltschutz, 2006), 157–166.

Some other food for thought can be found while reading the conceptual repertoire: from a historiographical point of view, the reviewer gained the impression that a more far-reaching theoretical examination of Karl Marx's materialist conception of history could be of great value for environmental history. The earlier work of Rolf Peter Sieferle and some members of the Vienna School of Social Ecology can be regarded as an interesting example of utilization of Marxist thought for environmental studies.[2] Environment and nature play a key role in Marx's conception of history[3] and the base as the economic structure of society. In the dialectic process, changes in the base affect the superstructure and therefore have broad societal implications. Given that nature is considered a major factor of influence for the conditions and modes of production, research in environmental history can certainly profit from engaging with the base-superstructure-model. The potential of Marx's materialist conception of history is not yet fully exhausted and demands further theoretical consideration in environmental history.

In the introduction, the editors claim that their book differs from others because of "its high internal consistency" (xliv). This can only be confirmed. Many chapters are written by author collectives; this undoubtedly contributes to the "internal consistency." Yet it must be noted that the price they pay for this consistency is a recurring tendency to self-referential citing throughout the volume. Not only do the authors refer to other chapters of the book, which is common and allows for a higher level of comprehension, but they also quote a remarkable amount of publications associated with the Vienna School of Social Ecology. This critique by no means belittles the book's valuable contribution to a better understanding of society-nature relations and current research in social ecology. It is highly recommendable for both students and researchers in this interdisciplinary field. The School's core concepts, like the colonization of nature or social metabolism, are thought-provoking for environmental history. Environmental historians should at least reflect and also implement these useful theoretical concepts, especially for society-nature interactions. In an appendix, "Perspectives on Social Ecology" (583–588), some of the authors add a personal note to a

---

2   In chapter two, Marina Fischer-Kowalski and Karl-Heinz Erb point out that they developed their theoretical socioecological framework in "a long-standing intellectual exchange with the environmental historian Rolf Peter Sieferle" (30).
3   Karl Marx and Friedrich Engels, "Die deutsche Ideologie," in *Karl Marx/Friedrich Engels Werke*, ed. Institut für Marxismus-Leninismus beim ZK der SED, vol. 3, (Berlin, 1969), 5–530, here: 21. *"Alle Geschichtsschreibung muß von diesen natürlichen Grundlagen und ihrer Modifikation im Laufe der Geschichte durch die Aktion der Menschen ausgehen."* Translation: "The writing of history must always set out from these natural bases and their modification in the course of history through the action of men."

sustainable future. Asked what she would do with one million Euros at hand for future, socioecological sustainability, Marina Fischer-Kowalski would like to bridge the gap and "status fights" (586) between natural science and social and historical science. In comparison, Verena Winiwarter has a "social ecology of warfare and military spending" (586) in mind, because future sustainability can be realized exclusively in peacetime.

List of Authors

Siegfried Beer is professor emeritus for late modern and contemporary history at the University of Graz and Director of the Botstiber Institute for Austrian-American Studies at Media, PA.

Matthew Berg is Professor of Modern European History at John Carroll University.

Günter Bischof is the Marshall Plan Chair of History and the Director of Center Austria: Austrian Marshall Plan Center for European Studies at the University of New Orleans.

Michael Bürkner is affiliated with the Institute of Social Ecology Vienna (SEC) in the Department of Economics and Social Sciences at the University of Natural Resources & Life Sciences, Vienna (BOKU).

Simone Gingrich is a researcher and lecturer at the Institute of Social Ecology Vienna (SEC) in the Department of Economics and Social Sciences at the University of Natural Resources & Life Sciences, Vienna (BOKU).

Cathleen Giustino is the Mills Carter Professor of History at Auburn University.

Nicole-Melanie Goll is a research fellow at the House of Austrian History in Vienna.

Robert Groß is affiliated with the Institute for Social Ecology in Vienna and University Assistant for Social and Economic History in the Institute of History and European Ethnology, University of Innsbruck.

Gertrud Haidvogl is senior scientist at the Institute of Hydrobiology and Aquatic Ecosystem Management (IHG) in the Department of Water, Atmosphere and Environment at the University of Natural Resources & Life Sciences, Vienna (BOKU).

Phillip J. Henry (PhD 2018) is currently a lecturer in the Division of the Social Sciences at the University of Chicago.

Severin Hohensinner is senior scientist at the Institute of Hydrobiology and Aquatic Ecosystem Management (IHG) in the Department of Water, Atmosphere and Environment at the University of Natural Resources & Life Sciences, Vienna (BOKU).

Ke-chin Hsia is Lecturer in Modern European History at the Department of History, Indiana University, Bloomington.

Timothy Kirk is Professor of European History at Newcastle University, UK.

Martin Knoll is professor for European regional history at the University of Salzburg.

Fridolin Krausmann is professor of sustainable resource use at the Institute of Social Ecology at the University of Natural Resources and Life Sciences, Vienna.

Patrick Kupper is professor of economic and social history at the Institute of History and European Ethnology at the University of Innsbruck.

Marc Landry is an assistant professor of history and the Associate Director of Center Austria: Austrian Marshall Plan Center for European Studies at the University of New Orleans.

Charles S. Maier is the Leverett Saltonstall Professor of History and former Director of the Minda de Gunzburg Center for European Studies at Harvard University.

Sofie Mittas is currently working as a university assistant at the Department of Social and Economic History at the Johannes Kepler University, Linz. Her dissertation is supervised by professors Ernst Langthaler and Verena Winiwarter.

Reinhard Ferdinand Niessner is a doctoral student at the Institute of History and European Ethnology at the University of Innsbruck.

Irene Pallua is a doctoral student at the Institute of History and European Ethnology at the University of Innsbruck.

Nicole M. Phelps is an associate professor in the Department of History at the University of Vermont.

Christina Pichler-Koban is researcher at E.C.O. Institute of Ecology, Klagenfurt and member of the Environmental History Cluster Austria.

Carolin F. Roeder is currently a postdoctoral fellow at the Max Planck Institute for the History of Science, Berlin.

Christian Rohr is a Full Professor of Environmental and Climate History at the Institute of History, University of Berne.

Martin Schmid is associate professor for environmental history at the Department of Economics and Social Sciences (WiSo), University of Natural Resources & Life Sciences, Vienna (BOKU).

Gerhard Siegl, historian, is co-founder of Heidegger, Hilber und Siegl: Die HISTORIKERinnen (www.diehistoriker.at), currently working on the project "The Land Register of Francis I.: Silesia (Österreichisch-Schlesien) Editing, Digitization, Analyses" (Austrian Science Fund, Project No. P30396).

Dieter Stiefel is professor emeritus of social and economic History at the University of Vienna.

Ortrun Veichtlbauer works as a freelance scientific writer and publicist in Klosterneuburg, Austria.

Janek Wasserman is an associate professor in the Department of History at the University of Alabama.

Verena Winiwarter is professor for Environmental History at the Institute of Social Ecology, University of Natural Resources and Life Sciences, Vienna, Austria.

Contemporary Austrian Studies

Günter Bischof, Anton Pelinka/Fritz Plasser/Ferdinand Karlhofer,
Editors

Volume 1 (1992)
Austria in the New Europe

Volume 2 (1993)
The Kreisky Era in Austria
Oliver Rathkolb, Guest Editor

Volume 3 (1994)
Austria in the Nineteen Fifties
Rolf Steininger, Guest Editor

Volume 4 (1995)
Austro-Corporatism: Past—
Present—Future

Volume 5 (1996)
Austrian Historical Memory &
National Identity

Volume 6 (1997)
Women in Austria
Erika Thurner, Guest Editor

Volume 7 (1998)
The Vranitzky Era in Austria
Ferdinand Karlhofer, Guest Editor

Volume 8 (1999)
The Marshall Plan in Austria
Dieter Stiefel, Guest Editor

Volume 9 (2000)
Neutrality in Austria
Ruth Wodak, Guest Editor

Volume 10 (2001)
Austria and the EU
Michael Gehler, Guest Editor

Volume 11 (2002)
The Dollfuss/Schuschnigg Era in
Austria: A Reassessment
Alexander Lassner, Guest Editor

Volume 12 (2003)
The Americanization/Westernization
of Austria

Volume 13 (2004)
Religion in Austria
Hermann Denz, Guest Editor

Volume 14 (2005)
Austrian Foreign Policy in Historical
Perspective
Michael Gehler, Guest Editor

Volume 15 (2006)
Sexuality in Austria
Dagmar Herzog, Guest Editor